Plurality as the Core of Human Rights Universality

Gabriela García Escobar

Plurality as the Core of Human Rights Universality

Rediscovering the Spirit of the Universal Declaration of Human Rights of 1948 through the Right to Self-Determination

PETER LANG
New York - Berlin - Bruxelles - Chennai - Lausanne - Oxford

Library of Congress Cataloging-in-Publication Data

Names: García Escobar, Gabriela, author.
Title: Plurality as the core of human rights universality: rediscovering the spirit of the Universal Declaration of Human Rights of 1948 through the right to self-determination / Gabriela García Escobar.
Description: 1 edition. | New York: Peter Lang Publishing, Inc., 2024. | Includes bibliographical references and index.
Identifiers: LCCN 2023048426 (print) | LCCN 2023048427 (ebook) | ISBN 9781636673561 (paperback) | ISBN 9781636673547 (ebook) | ISBN 9781636673554 (epub)
Subjects: LCSH: International law and human rights. | Legal polycentricity. United Nations. General Assembly. Universal Declaration of Human Rights. | Self-determination, National.
Classification: LCC KZ1266. G37 2024 (print) | LCC KZ1266 (ebook) | DDC 341.4/8--dc23/eng/20231016
LC record available at https://lccn.loc.gov/2023048426
LC ebook record available at https://lccn.loc.gov/2023048427
DOI 10.3726/b21397

Bibliographic information published by the Deutsche Nationalbibliothek.
The German National Library lists this publication in the German National Bibliography; detailed bibliographic data is available on the Internet at http://dnb.d-nb.de.

Cover design by Peter Lang Group AG

ISBN 9781636673561 (paperback)
ISBN 9781636673547 (ebook)
ISBN 9781636673554 (epub)
DOI 10.3726/b21397

Published by Peter Lang Publishing Inc., New York, USA
info@peterlang.com - www.peterlang.com

This publication has been peer reviewed.

In dedication to my family and to the Cause of our joy.

Nothing is more difficult for the natural man than to understand a culture or social tradition different from his own, for it involves an almost superhuman detachment from inherited ways of thought and education and the unconscious influence of his social environment. Indeed the more highly educated he is in his own tradition the less will he be able to appreciate all that diverges from it.

Christopher Dawson[1]

1 Christopher Dawson, *The Dynamics of World History* (Sheed and Ward, 1956), 68.

TABLE OF CONTENTS

ACKNOWLEDGMENTS

This book is the result of several years of research and reflection upon the question of cultural diversity, pluralism, and human dignity. I must thank, first of all, to my husband Sébastien, who supported and accompanied me throughout the whole process as a family project.

I have a special debt of gratitude to professor Éric Wyler, who through his academic insights and personal virtues taught me that to be a professor is a vocation at the service of the holistic development of the human person. I am also deeply grateful to Pilar Zambrano, who helped me and encouraged me to publish this work.

I also want to express my gratitude to other legal experts who helped me with their comments and conversations: Pedro Pallares, Ignacio de Casas, Juan Pablo Andrade, Daniela Constantino, and Olivia Serrano. A special thanks to Manuel Enrique Tovar Hernández and Isabel Álvarez Peña, who have supported my academic and personal growth since my undergraduate years.

The contributions from other friends and colleagues were also an essential part of this journey. Thank you for providing me with a broader perspective on reality and the human condition through your friendship and conversations: Cristina García, Frouzan Moshaver, Meri Zargarova, and Carlos Ayxelá.

I also have a tremendous debt of gratitude to my family and friends, for we are never autonomous and self-made individuals. We owe who we are to our family and friends, and our most cherished attachments, which make human flourishing possible. Without the constant encouragement and love of my family throughout my life I would not be writing this page of acknowledgments.

Gabriela García Escobar
Universidad Panamericana
Facultad de Derecho
Álvaro del Portillo 49, Zapopan, Jalisco, 45010, México

LIST OF ABBREVIATIONS

ADRDM	American Declaration of the Rights and Duties of Man
Beijing Platform for Action	Beijing Declaration and Platform for Action
CAT	Committee against Torture
CDD	*Católicas por el derecho a decidir*
CEDAW	Committee on the Elimination of Discrimination against Women
CEDAW convention	Convention on the Elimination of All Forms of Discrimination against Women
CESCR	Committee on Economic, Social and Cultural Rights
CRC	Committee on the Rights of the Child
Declaration on Principles of International Law	Declaration on Principles of International law concerning Friendly Relations and Cooperation among States in accordance with the Charter of the United Nations
ECHR	European Convention on Human Rights

ECOSOC	Economic and Social Council
ECtHR	European Court of Human Rights
ESCR	Economic, social and cultural rights
EuCSR	European Committee of Social Rights
HRC	Human Rights Committee
HRW	Human Rights Watch
IACoHR	Inter-American Commission on Human Rights
IACtHR	Inter-American Court of Human Rights
ICCPR	International Covenant on Civil and Political Rights
ICESCR	International Covenant on Economic, Social and Cultural Rights
ICJ	International Court of Justice
ICPD	International Conference on Population and Development
ILC	International Law Commission
IPPF	International Planned Parenthood Federation
IUD	Intra-uterine device
NGO	Non-governmental organization
OAS	Organization of American States
OHCHR	Office of the High Commissioner on Human Rights
OSCE	Organization for Security and Co-operation in Europe
PCIJ	Permanent Court of International Justice
SCJ	Mexican Supreme Court of Justice
SRHR	Sexual and reproductive health and rights
UDHR	Universal Declaration of Human Rights of 1948
U.N. Charter	United Nations Charter
UNESCO	United Nations Education, Science and Cultural Organization
UNFPA	United Nations Fund for Population Activities
USAID	United States Agency for International Development

VCLT	Vienna Convention on the Law of Treaties
WHO	World Health Organization

INTRODUCTION

International institutions have suffered from an increasing backlash and contestation in recent years.[1] Nico Krisch states "international courts seem to be living in hard times".[2] In the field of human rights, this challenge is leading to a crisis of legitimacy. As Hurst Hannum remarks: "human rights are on the verge of becoming a victim of their own success".[3]

An increasing number of states have expressed criticism against the lack of democratic legitimacy and dismiss of the right to self-determination by human rights courts in their process of decision-making. Some judges and scholars have called for a more engaged judicial dialogue between national

1 See Stefanie Walter, "The Backlash Against Globalization," *Annual Review of Political Science* 24 (2021); David Bearce and Brandy J. Jolliff Scott, "Popular Non-Support for International Organizations: How Extensive and What Does This Represent?," *The Review of International Organizations* 14 (2019).

2 Nico Krisch, "The Backlash against International Courts," Verfassungsblog, 2014, https://verfassungsblog.de/backlash-international-courts-2/. Consulted on September 8, 2021.

3 Hurst Hannum, "Reinvigorating Human Rights for the Twenty-First Century," *Human Rights Law Review* 16, no. 3 (2016): 416.

and international judges, a broader margin of appreciation, and a more robust understanding of subsidiarity.[4]

Regarding the work of the European Court of Human Rights (ECtHR) Lord Hoffmann (a retired English judge who served as Lord of Appeal) gave a speech in 2009 highlighting that "human rights are universal in abstraction but national in application" and that "the fact that the 10 original Member States of the Council of Europe subscribed to a statement of human rights in the same terms did not mean that they had agreed to uniformity of the application of those abstract rights in each of their countries".[5]

A similar situation is taking place in the Inter-American system of human rights protection. Argentina, Brazil, Chile, Colombia and Paraguay issued in 2019 a joint declaration where they reaffirmed their commitment to human rights but requested that the Inter-American Court of Human Rights (IACtHR) recognize the doctrine of the margin of appreciation and respect internal democratic processes in the spirit of the system's subsidiarity.[6]

Connected to this backlash, the universality and neutrality of human rights norms have been constantly challenged in recent decades from different fronts, among them, the feminist and the cultural critics are the most salient.[7] The cultural critic insists that human rights have focused on the concerns of Western states, which demands a reexamination of the system to include the needs and ideas of the Global South.[8]

4 See Valery Zorkin, "The Extent of Flexibility," *Rossiskaya Gazeta*, 2010; Marc Bossuyt, "The Court of Strasbourg Acting as an Asylum Court," *European Constitutional Law Review* 8, no. 2 (2012); András Sajó, "Introduction," in *Human Rights with Modesty: The Problem of Universalism*, ed. András Sajó (Martinus Nijhoff, 2004).

5 Lord Hoffmann, "The Universality of Human Rights," Judicial Studies Board Annual Lecture, 2009, 11–12, https://www.judiciary.uk/wp-content/uploads/2014/12/Hoffmann_2009_JSB_Annual_Lecture_Universality_of_Human_Rights.pdf. Consulted on September 8, 2021.

6 Melina Girardi Fachin and Bruna Nowak, "The Joint Declaration to the Inter-American System of Human Rights: Backlash or Contestation?," Blog of the International Journal of Constitutional Law, 2019, http://www.iconnectblog.com/2019/12/the-joint-declaration-to-the-inter-american-system-of-human-rights-backlash-or-contestation/. Consulted on September 20, 2021.

7 For a summarized introduction to this topic see Eva Brems, "Enemies or Allies - Feminism and Cultural Relativism as Dissident Voices in Human Rights Discourse," *Human Rights Quarterly* 19, no. 1 (1997).

8 For instance, see Makau Wa Mutua, *Human Rights Standards: Hegemony, Law, and Politics* (State University of New York Press, 2016); Abdullahi Ahmed An-Na'im, *Human Rights in Cross-Cultural Perspectives: A Quest for Consensus*, ed. Abdullahi Ahmed An-Na'im

This criticism has grown since the Vienna Conference on Human Rights of 1993, where several non-Western voices have challenged the universality of human rights norms, which prompted the debate about human rights universality and cultural relativism.[9] They considered that Western historical dominion in the human rights sector seemed to be outdated in a post-Cold War multipolar context.[10] In this sense, the emergence of new states, together with the further individualization and secularization of Western societies, is leading to a deeper divide in the human rights project.

Discrepancies between Western and non-Western perspectives, and different viewpoints within Western societies themselves, have constituted a constant problem for the implementation of human rights norms and a challenge to their universality. For instance, in some European states the ideas of a majoritarian secularized population are in growing tensions with the views of minoritarian religious groups.

In Belgium, in protection of neutrality and secularism, a Muslim woman was fired from her job for refusing to remove her headscarf.[11] In Germany a ban on religious clothing and symbols for public servants, in the name of neutrality and secularism, has led some Muslim women to give up teaching.[12] The same situation can be appreciated regarding a ban on male circumcision affecting Jewish and Muslim communities.[13]

In France, two 12-years-old Muslim girls were expelled from school for refusing to remove their hijabs as part of a governmental ban on religious

(Pensylvannia University Press, 1995); Mashood A. Baderin, *International Human Rights and Islamic Law* (Oxford University Press, 2003); Onuma Yasuaki, "Toward an Intercivilizational Approach to Human Rights," in *The East Asian Challenge for Human Rights*, ed. Joanna Bauer and Daniel Bell (Cambridge University Press, 1999).

9 In this regard see Jack Donnelly, "Cultural Relativism and Universal Human Rights," *Human Rights Quarterly* 6 (1984): 400; Eva Brems, *Human Rights: Universality and Diversity* (Martinus Nijhoff, 2001); Shashi Tharoor, "The Universality of Human Rigths and Their Relevance to Developing Countries," *Nordic Journal of International Law* 59 (1990).

10 See Seth Kaplan, "Will Human Rights Survive in a Multipolar World?," *The Washington Quarterly* 42, no. 1 (2019).

11 Joseph H. H. Weiler, "Je Suis Achbita!," *EJIL: Talk!*, 2018, https://www.ejiltalk.org/je-suis-achbita/. Consulted on September 21, 2020.

12 "Germany: Headscarf Bans Violate Rights," *Human Rights Watch*, 2009, https://www.hrw.org/news/2009/02/26/germany-headscarf-bans-violate-rights. Consulted on September 21, 2020.

13 Joshua Hammer, "Anti-Semitism and Germany's Movement Against Circumcision," *The Atlantic*, 2013, https://www.theatlantic.com/health/archive/2013/01/anti-semitism-and-germanys-movement-against-circumcision/266794/. Consulted on September 9, 2021.

symbols in schools.[14] In the United Kingdom, religious minorities are holding nationwide protests against the school curricula on sexual education that they consider goes against their moral values.[15] Even in the United States, where the concept of freedom of speech and religious freedom is broader than in European states,[16] similar tensions exist regarding same-sex marriage, abortion, and sexual education.[17]

At the international level, this problem is perceived in the clashes between Southern cultural perspectives and the views of a Western-liberal oriented human rights sector.[18] An example is the reluctance of the transitional justice sector to recognize local forms of restorative justice and religious reconciliation in Rwanda and South Africa;[19] and tensions regarding the autonomy of indigenous peoples to decide their cultural and religious practices.[20]

Thus, the growing backlash against human rights seems to be based on two interrelated aspects. One has to do with the prioritization of global standards at the cost of local democratic determinations of how to interpret international norms. The second refers to a perceived lack of neutrality and universality with respect to human rights norms.

Looking at this situation, two attitudes have emerged. The first one (adopted by most human rights defenders) is to disregard these concerns, for

14 See ECtHR, *Dogru v. France* (Application no. 27058/05) Judgement of 4 March 2009; and ECtHR, *Kervanci v. France* (Application no. 31645/04) Judgement of 4 March 2009.

15 Donna Ferguson, "'We Can't Give in': The Birmingham School on the Frontline of Anti-LGBT Protests," *The Guardian*, 2019, https://www.theguardian.com/uk-news/2019/may/26/birmingham-anderton-park-primary-muslim-protests-lgbt-teaching-rights. Consulted on September 14, 2021.

16 See Peter Berger, Grace Davie, and Effie Fokas, *Religious America, Secular Europe? A Theme and Variation* (Ashgate, 2008).

17 An example is the case of the Christian baker that refused to make a wedding cake for a same-sex couple: U.S. Supreme Court, *Masterpiece Cakeshop, ltd., et al. v. Colorado Civil Rights Commission et al.* 584 U. S. (2018).

18 Some examples are Mutua, *Human Rights Standards: Hegemony, Law, and Politics*; An-Na'im, *Human Rights in Cross-Cultural Perspectives: A Quest for Consensus*; Sally Engle Merry, "Human Rights Law and the Demonization of Culture (And Anthropology Along the Way)," *Political and Legal Anthropology Review* 26, no. 1 (2003): 55–76.

19 See Daniel Philpott and Gerard Powers, *Strategies of Peace: Transforming Conflict in a Violent World* (Oxford University Press, 2010); Jennifer Llewellyn and Daniel Philpott, eds., *Restorative Justice, Reconciliation, and Peacebuilding* (Oxford University Press, 2014).

20 See Oswaldo Ruiz-Chiriboga, "Indigenous Corporal Punishment in Ecuador and the Prohibition of Torture and Il Treatment," *American University International law Review* 28 (2013): 975.

they are perceived as a minoritarian position held by narrow-minded people and authoritarian elites, who deny freedom and the universality of human rights.[21] It is true that some corrupt and self-serving governments want to avoid international scrutiny, like the cases of Venezuela and some Middle Eastern governments.[22]

However, this vision only responds to a small part of the problem, for the contestation of human rights does not only come from these actors. As explained above, national and international judges, democratic regimes,[23] and scholars committed to human rights norms have also expressed similar concerns.[24] Thus, the second possible attitude consists of engaging in a critical dialogue with this contestation and examining the current practice of human rights, so these norms can be better accepted and implemented in different contexts.

This book gambles for this second attitude because the basis of the authority of international human rights law (IHRL), and international law in general, does not rely on mechanisms of law enforcement (*potestas*), but on their persuasiveness and perception as legitimate standards (*auctoritas*). As research suggests, treaty ratification does not always correlate with human rights protection, rather the point of inflection has to do with the local appropriation of human rights norms to bring them into life through popular participation.[25]

21 See "Backlash against Women's Rights Progress Hurts Us All – Zeid," *OHCHR*, 7 March 2017, https://www.ohchr.org/EN/NewsEvents/Pages/DisplayNews.aspx?NewsID=21305; Olivier de Schutter, "Universalité Des Droits de l'homme et Mondialisation: La Question Des 'Valeurs Asiatiques,'" in *Droits Humains et Valeurs Asiatiques: Un Dialogue Possible?*, ed. Thierry Marrès and Paul Servais (Bruylant, 2002); Anne Bayefsky, "Cultural Sovereignty, Relativism, and International Human Rights: New Excuses for Old Strategies," *Ratio Juris* 9, no. 1 (1996).

22 Abdullahi Ahmed An-Na'im, "The Cultural Mediation of Human Rights: The Al-Arqam Case in Malaysia," in *The East Asian Challenge for Human Rights*, ed. Joanne Bauer and Daniel Bell (Cambridge University Press, 1999).

23 Leslie Vinjamuri, "Human Rights Backlash," in *Human Rights Futures*, ed. Stephen Hopgood, Jack Snyder, and Leslie Vinjamuri (Cambridge University Press, 2017).

24 See Mary Ann Glendon and Seth Kaplan, "Renewing Human Rights" [2019] *First Things* <https://www.firstthings.com/article/2019/02/renewing-human-rights>; Alfredo Vítolo, "El Valor de Las Opiniones Consultivas de La Corte Interamericana de Derechos Humanos a La Luz de Las OC-21/14 y 23/17," *Revista Jurídica Austral* 1 (2020); Phillip Alston, "Conjuring Up New Human Rights: A Proposal For Quality Control," *American Journal of International Law* 78 (1984) 78.

25 See the research of Emilie M. Hafner - Burton and Kiyoteru Tsutsui, "Human Rights in a Globalizing World: The Paradox of Empty Promises," *American Journal of Sociology* 110, no. 5 (2005).

For these reasons, the analysis of the prevailing paradigm of universality that is used by human rights mechanisms for the adoption of interpretations or standards is of utmost relevance because the definition of this concept will determine the breadth of pluralism or diversity and local democratic determination that is allowed in the implementation of international norms.

A more detailed analysis of these critical positions reveals that their concerns are not directed towards human rights norms as general and internationally recognized rights, as agreed in treaties. In fact, their arguments are based on human rights norms, although framed in different terms.[26] Their criticism is rather raised against what they perceive as a dominant *interpretative* paradigm that is used to establish the scope and content of human rights norms, which they do not recognize as neutral, universal, and legally founded.

In other words, the object of analysis of this research is not internationally recognized human rights norms themselves, but their *interpretations* or *standards* as adopted by human rights treaty body mechanisms and regional courts and then presented as universally agreed (and binding) norms. For there is a qualitative difference between the internationally recognized human rights norms in the main treaties and the human rights standards or interpretations adopted by different mechanisms of protection.

There are several works that have analyzed human rights universality in reference to the concept itself and the rights holder, but few works have studied universality in terms of interpretations or standards. Thus, few scholars have analyzed the universality of the interpretative framework used in the standard-setting process of human rights mechanisms.

This analysis has become more relevant in the last years because of the role that judgments and views of human rights mechanisms have acquired. Despite it being questionable whether this is legitimate or not,[27] today the functions of international courts are not restricted to dispute settlement; they are also involved in law-making, policy decisions, and they exercise a function of public authority.[28]

When analyzing the predominant framework of universality used by human rights mechanisms, it is notorious that the interpretation of norms has not been totally uniform. However, as several legal scholars have pointed

26 See in this regard Krisch, "The Backlash against International Courts."

27 See Bossuyt, "The Court of Strasbourg Acting as an Asylum Court."

28 As pointed out in the analysis of Armin von Bogdandy and Ingo Venzke, *In Whose Name? A Public Law Theory of International Adjudication* (Oxford University Press, 2014).

out,[29] a dominant analytical framework can be perceived in Western academic circles and human rights mechanisms alike, which will be called *liberal universality*. This paradigm refers to a very specific way of understanding the word "liberal", in terms of a "thick" or "comprehensive" form of liberalism in contrast to its "thin" or classical version.

A "comprehensive" or "perfectionist" liberalism works as a political morality, in contrast to its seventeenth century or classical form. The latter consists of a "thin" political proposal based on a limited government and an economic system based on private property for the sake of individual freedom, which was restricted to politics and did not require the adoption of a specific hierarchy of values in all spheres of life (e.g. the family, work, politics, sexuality, reproduction, and religion).

In contrast to this classical paradigm, a comprehensive liberalism assumes that all societies and all social institutions should prioritize personal autonomy over other values and should be based on an individualistic and secular worldview, which are the premises considered to be the building blocks of a free and equal society. Therefore, this vision as applied to the field of human rights means that the norms incorporated in all human rights treaties should be interpreted according to these parameters.

Consequently, interpretations which deviate from this (those that encourage communitarian or interdependent, or religiously based ideas) are framed as cultural relativism and in contradiction with human rights norms. Here, the appeal to cultural differences or to conceptions of the good life that do not prioritize autonomy are perceived as a denial of individual rights, and therefore, as inadmissible.

To illustrate the prevalence of this paradigm and its problems as a universal interpretative framework, two case studies regarding the implementation of sexual and reproductive health and rights (SRHR) in the developing world

29 For instance Mutua, *Human Rights Standards: Hegemony, Law, and Politics*; An-Na'im, *Human Rights in Cross-Cultural Perspectives: A Quest for Consensus*; Seth Daniel Kaplan, *Human Rights in Thick and Thin Societies: Universality without Uniformity* (Cambridge University Press, 2018); Stephen Hopgood, *The Endtimes of Human Rights* (Cornell University Press, 2015); David Kennedy, *The Dark Sides of Virtue: Reassessing International Humanitarianism* (Princeton: Princeton University Press, 2004); Ignacio de Casas, "¿Qué Son Los Estándares de Derechos Humanos?," *Revista Internacional de Derechos Humanos* 9, no. 2 (2019); Baderin, *International Human Rights and Islamic Law*; Costas Douzinas, *Human Rights and Empire: The Political Philosophy of Cosmopolitanism* (Routledge, 2007).

will be used. The first case refers to the implementation of the family planning program in India and the second one to the debate on abortion in Mexico.

In this regard, freedom and equality are values cherished by all different societies. Everybody can agree that freedom to decide on the number of children, access to safe and culturally appropriate family planning services, and the protection of pregnant women are objectives for the well-being of all societies.

While everybody agrees with these goals, the differences of opinion emerge at the level of how to better achieve these objectives, which is far from evident. There is widespread disagreement on whether contraception and abortion are the best means to respect the human dignity of women and men. While advocates of liberal universality argue that contraception and abortion are essential for women's empowerment and wanted by all women, other views maintain that these practices are not supported by many women and can be used for political purposes and as means of violence (see chapters two and three).

In the context of this discussion, non-governmental organizations (NGOs), Western states, several human rights mechanisms, U.N. agencies, and some ruling elites in the Global South have insisted on providing contraception and abortion as part of international human rights obligations. Legally speaking, this is problematic because there is no human rights treaty that establishes such an obligation, rather the term SRHR was adopted in non-binding documents in the context of U.N. sponsored population conferences, which emerged out of a concern with overpopulation.

Nevertheless, based on the anthropological assumptions of liberal universality, these actors insist that contraception and abortion are fundamental rights that should be provided through state policy. In this view, people who are opposed to them (or merely question them) are perceived as a fundamentalist and malevolent minority that deny women's freedom and equality.

In spite of these good intentions, liberal assumptions about the family, sexuality, and reproduction might not match what people want in all societies. Moreover, the uniform application of these criteria to all societies can actually diminish freedom to disagree with this paradigm and does not treat dissenting persons on an equal basis.

This is perceived in the case of India, where the family planning program created in the 1970s, without consulting the population for the design and implementation of the agenda, was largely opposed by the population and resulted in the catastrophe of 7 million forced sterilizations and millions of forced insertions of intra-uterine devices (IUDs).

In the case of Mexico, a similar disconnection can be seen regarding the debate on the legalization of abortion. Guided by the paradigm of liberal universality, several powerful actors have maintained that Mexico should provide access to abortion as part of its international human rights obligations. The U.N. deputy high commissioner for human rights, Kate Gilmore, has even labeled restrictions on abortion as "extremist hate" and "torture" at the Human Rights Council.[30] However, no treaty establishes so and the non-binding reports that have been adopted (in the context of population policies) indicate that this issue should be decided according to the domestic democratic process of each state.

In spite of widespread opposition from local congresses and public opinion (especially from vulnerable groups), Mexican authorities continuously and falsely insist that the need to legalize abortion is an urgent claim of society at large. This resulted in the 2021 judgment of the Mexican Supreme Court of Justice (SCJ) that constitutes the Mexican version of *Roe v. Wade*, which sets an important precedent that opens the door to the legalization of abortion in the whole territory.[31]

Thus, these cases suggest that when the implementation of SRHR ignores the ideas held by other cultures and traditions about the family, sexuality, and reproduction and instead liberal ideas are advanced, these good intentions might violate the right to self-determination and provoke unintended consequences of grave human rights violation. Although advocates of liberal universality look for a better society were everybody can decide on their own, in practice, the implementation of this paradigm can contradict the principles of freedom, equality, and viewpoint diversity.

Therefore, in order to address this problem, this book proposes to compare the development of the paradigm of liberal universality with another framework of universality that was adopted as early as 1948 and that was based on

30 Liz Ford, "US Abortion Policy Is 'extremist Hate' and 'Torture', Says UN Commissioner," *The Guardian*, 2019, https://www.theguardian.com/global-development/2019/jun/04/us-abortion-policy-extremist-hate-torture-un-commissioner-kate-gilmore. Consulted on April 20, 2020.

31 "Despenalización Del Aborto En Coahuila: Esto Es Lo Que Debes Saber Sobre La Resolución de La Corte," *El Financiero*, 2021, https://www.elfinanciero.com.mx/nacional/2021/09/08/despenalizacion-del-aborto-en-coahuila-esto-es-lo-que-debes-saber-sobre-la-resolucion-de-la-corte/. Consulted on April 26, 2021.

deep intercultural dialogue, but that has been forgotten in academic discussions. This paradigm of universality was also upheld in the two main human rights treaties of 1966, the International Covenant on Civil and Political Rights (ICCPR) and the International Covenant on Economic, Social and Cultural Rights (ICESCR) in its article one which establishes that "all peoples have the right of self-determination. By virtue of that right they freely determine their political status and freely pursue their economic, social and cultural development".[32]

Accordingly, this book proposes to rediscover the *pluralistic universality* of the Universal Declaration of Human Rights (UDHR) in light of the right to self-determination of peoples for the process of human rights standards setting or interpretations adopted by human rights treaty bodies. Such a framework can help to develop interpretations that are based on broad international support, intercultural dialogue, with robust democratic participation, and therefore will be more acceptable to different cultures and traditions.

This pluralistic universality of the UDHR establishes a model of unity in diversity instead of uniformity. It maintains that human rights were conceived as a *cross-cultural* or *transcultural* agreement, which means that it emerged out of commonly shared values among different philosophies, cultures, religions, and traditions, instead as in contradiction with them.

Thus, the notion of universality was understood as a set of values and principles shared by different cultures and traditions, but that would be interpreted and implemented in a diversity of legitimate ways depending on the notion of human flourishing cherished by each society. The process of human rights interpretations in this view is a bottom-up operation, not a top-down intervention, which requires ample popular participation and dialogue to grasp the different conceptions of the good that are upheld in diverse cultural settings.

In this regard, the UDHR did not envisage the concept of plurality in terms of liberal universality, for the declaration incorporates the notion of "human person" as a relational and situated being, the relevance of intermediary communities as essential places for the development of personality, and a notion of "freedom" both negative and positive. This means that the traditions that are welcomed to develop human rights interpretations are not

32 ICCPR (1966), <https://www.ohchr.org/EN/ProfessionalInterest/Pages/CCPR.aspx>; and ICESCR (1966) <https://www.ohchr.org/en/professionalinterest/pages/cescr.aspx>. Consulted on June 14, 2021.

restricted to secular and autonomy-oriented visions of society, rather more interdependent and religious views of the human condition were also accepted in this joint task.

As explained by a report of the United Nations Education, Scientific and Cultural Organization (UNESCO), this vision of human rights universality did not establish a specific hierarchy of values (like liberal universality proclaims with the triad of autonomy, secularism, and individualism), rather it provided ample space for each society to decide on how to balance and interpret different human goods.[33] As Seth Kaplan in his recent work on the UDHR stated:

> The framers would find alien the contemporary notion that the Declaration prescribes a single model of human rights (a model rooted in individualistic conceptions of selfhood and personal rather than communal empowerment) and that the only alternative is a relativistic approach that allows rights to be completely determined by circumstances. On the contrary, the framers were able to achieve broad consensus because they crafted a flexible legal document that everyone—from West, East, North, or South—could accept, and that everyone could believe was morally important.[34]

This position is corroborated by the inclusion of the right of peoples to self-determination as common article one both in the ICCPR and the ICESCR. This right has been mainly developed in the context of the decolonization process and regarding secessionist claims. However, the content of this right is broader than that and has a multidimensional nature. Self-determination, which was first enshrined as one of the purposes of the U.N. Charter, relies on the rationale that each society should be free to choose their own political, social, economic and cultural development.

Thus, self-determination presupposes the freedom of each society to determine their idea of human flourishing (as long as they incorporate all human rights) and the local ownership of human rights categories. Accordingly, self-determination is a human right that at the same time recognizes the right of each people to determine how to interpret and implement universally recognized human rights norms, based on different concepts of the good life, different hierarchies of values, and diverse ways of balancing the goods that are necessary for human flourishing.

33 See UNESCO, *Human Rights: Comments and Interpretations*, 1948.

34 Kaplan, "Will Human Rights Survive in a Multipolar World?," 115.

This right implies that the content of human rights norms cannot be decided in a unilateral manner by ruling elites, Western states, or even by human rights mechanisms alone. Therefore, according to this proposal, the standard-setting process of human rights norms should be close to the people affected by the decisions and owned by them. The determination of how to interpret and to give content to abstract/universal human right norms in different cultural contexts should be a bottom-up, democratic, dialogical, and participatory process. This implies a change in paradigm at both national and international levels.

As it is argued throughout this book, this paradigm seems to be more adequate for the promotion and acceptance of human rights norms in the Global South and in some segments of the Western world, than the prevailing framework. Some renowned scholars have been pointing out this situation for several years,[35] but as it is explained throughout the book there is a strong reluctance to recognize the problem. This situation has only worsened in the last years by intimidation and censorship, as experienced in first person by this author.

Thus, the continuous and global implementation of the paradigm of liberal universality will only prompt further resentment and backlash against human rights norms and a reasonable criticism against the system. Therefore, the legitimacy of the human rights system relies on its capacity for self-criticism and self-rectification when a certain idea has proven inadequate to promote human dignity.

The goal of this book is to contribute to the dynamic, democratic, and dialogical construction of human rights universality, which is an unfinished and imperfect task that cannot be restricted to elite circles in Geneva or New York. There is a crisis inherent to the paradigm of liberal universality, which could be redeemed through a return to the consensus reached in 1948.

Such a proposal can help to preserve the ideals of freedom, equality, and plurality that are core elements of human dignity. Paradoxically, the flourishing of this project requires reconfiguring the prevailing cultural and philosophical

35 See Michael J. Sandel, *Liberalism and the Limits of Justice* (New York: Cambridge University Press, 1982); Charles Taylor, "Conditions of an Unforced Consensus on Human Rights," in *The East Asian Challenge for Human Rights*, ed. Joanne Bauer and Daniel Bell (Cambridge University Press, 1999); Makau Wa Mutua, "The Complexity of Universalism in Human Rights," in *Human Rights with Modesty: The Problem of Universalism*, ed. András Sajó (Martinus Nijhoff, 2004); Yasuaki, "Toward an Intercivilizational Approach to Human Rights"; Mary Ann Glendon, "Knowing the Universal Declaration of Human Rights," *Notre Dame Law Review* 73, no. 5 (1998); Marta Cartabia, "The Age of 'New Rights,'" *Straus Institute Working Paper* 03/10 (2010).

assumptions, so that viewpoint diversity could stop being perceived as an obstacle to human rights and start being understood as the core of a pluralistic and dialogical universalism.

· 1 ·

THE UNIVERSALITY OF HUMAN RIGHTS STANDARDS: ANALYZING THE INTERPRETATIVE FRAMEWORK

Human rights norms as inscribed in international treaties are recognized by most states. However, the question of how to interpret those statements is not a settled one. How to determine the scope and content of each abstract and general right? How to discern whether a specific human right standard or interpretation is universal or not? Human rights treaties contain broad and general provisions, like "no one shall be subjected to arbitrary or unlawful interference with his privacy".[1] This ample sentence does not provide a specific answer, for it leaves open the subject of what constitutes "arbitrary" and what is within the scope of "privacy".

Internationally recognized human rights, just as other concepts of international law, are indeterminate to some extent.[2] This indeterminacy has provoked that human rights have been used to defend different and even contradictory claims that are based on different conceptions of the good life and of human flourishing.[3]

1 ICCPR, article 17.1.

2 See Martti Koskenniemi, *From Apology to Utopia: The Structure of International Legal Argument* (Cambridge University Press, 2006); Costas Douzinas, *The End of Human Rights: Critical Legal Thought at the Turn of the Century* (Portland: Hart Publishing, 2000).

3 See this argument in Mary Ann Glendon, "La Soportable Levedad de La Dignidad," *Persona y Derecho* 67, no. 2 (2012): 41–45; Martti Koskenniemi, "Whose Intolerance,

To respond to this situation, from a positivistic point of view it suffices to look at the jurisprudence of human rights treaty bodies and regional courts. Nevertheless, the process of interpretation is never settled. Legal interpretation of general provisions is not a neutral and strictly scientific process. It is unconsciously subjected to the interpreter's underlying theory about what human rights are, and what is their object and purpose.

At the same time, each interpreter's idea about what human rights are depends on a more fundamental question. At the core of each proposal there is a non-neutral decision that depends on the interpreter's idea of human flourishing. Every exercise of interpretation involves deep cultural and political assumptions about the concept of the good and about the human condition.[4] One of the main drafters of the UDHR, Charles Malik, famously said "when we disagree about what human rights mean, we disagree about what human nature is".[5]

As Martti Koskenniemi points out, the scope and limits of human rights are determined depending on "the choice of the relevant language" or the "frame of reference".[6] These are policy choices that will determine which interests and which visions of the good merit to be called "rights" and trump other objectives, and which are not afforded this legal protection.

Considering this, the most widely spread idea about the origins and concept of human rights relies on the narrative that views them as the product of the American and French revolutions, as the vehicles of moral and intellectual emancipation of the individual.[7] They are seen as the triumph of the Enlightenment's ideals of an instrumental-rationalistic way of thinking and a secular worldview, which is generally hostile towards religion and considers it as a private affair of preferences that has no place in a modern-liberal society.[8]

Which Democracy?," in *Democratic Governance and International Law*, ed. Gregory H. Fox and Brad Roth (Cambridge University Press, 2010).

4 See Martti Koskenniemi, "The Effects of Rights on Political Culture," in *The European Union and Human Rights*, ed. Phillip Alston (Oxford University Press, 1999), 108.

5 Quoted in Mary Ann Glendon, *A World Made New: Eleanor Roosevelt and the Universal Declaration of Human Rights* (New York: Random House Trade Paperbacks, 2002), 39.

6 Koskenniemi, "The Effects of Rights on Political Culture," 106.

7 As some examples of this position see Paul Gordon Lauren, *The Evolution of International Human Rights: Visions Seen* (University of Pennsylvania Press, 2003), 13–15; Ilias Bantekas and Lutz Oette, *International Human Rights: Law and Practice* (Cambridge University Press, 2013), 13–22; Walter Kälin and Jörg Künzli, *The Law of International Human Rights Protection* (Oxford University Press, 2009), 4–6.

8 See Aryeh Neier, *The International Human Rights Movement: A History* (Princeton University Press, 2012); Jack Donnelly, *Universal Human Rights in Theory and Practice*,

In this view, human rights' origins are traced back to the ideas of the seventeenth and eighteenth century thinkers like John Locke, Thomas Hobbes, and Immanuel Kant, based on contractarian theories and personal autonomy.

In this narrative, the content of human rights is restricted not just to a Western concept, but to a reduced vision even within Western traditions. It is usually traced to selective schools of thought (the Enlightenment, rationalism, and Marxism for economic and social rights), religious roots (Protestant Western Christianity), and periods of time (mainly the seventeenth and eighteenth centuries) of the United States, England, and France. Not even other philosophies, epochs or countries of Western origin are considered.[9]

Within the Western traditions, for instance, this partial and reductionist picture forgets that the roots of human dignity and the concept of human rights itself are also part of a wider legacy that involves Classical Antiquity, Medieval philosophy, and Catholic Christianity.[10] Moreover, it disregards that there are other contemporary Western traditions, besides the liberal ones, that have developed notions of human dignity and proposals for human rights interpretations.[11] Very few scholars provide a broader narrative of the modern human rights project that involves the participation of a richer set of ideas, cultures and periods of time.[12]

This reduced narrative is generally considered as neutral because it is fashioned according to the Enlightenment's premises of the rejection of all past

3rd ed (New York: Cornell University Press, 2013); Brems, *Human Rights: Universality and Diversity*, 17–20.

9 As remarked in Wolfgang Schmale, "Human Rights in the Intercultural Perspective and the Reorganization of the International Debate," in *Human Rights and Cultural Diversity: Europe, Arabic-Islam World, Africa, China*, ed. Wolfgang Schmale (Kelp Publishing, 1993), 20–25.

10 For instance: Jörn Rüsen, "Human Rights from the Perspective of a Universal History," in *Human Rights and Cultural Diversity: Europe, Arabic-Islam World, Africa, China*, ed. Wolfgang Schmale (Kelp Publishing, 1993), 34.

11 For example: Virginia Leary, "Postliberal Strands in Western Human Rights Theory: Personalist-Communitarian Perspectives," in *Human Rights in Cross-Cultural Perpestives: A Quest for Consensus*, ed. Abdullahi Ahmed An-Na'im, 1995.

12 Some examples are Schmale, "Human Rights in the Intercultural Perspective and the Reorganization of the International Debate"; Samuel Moyn, "Personalism, Community, and the Origins of Human Rights," in *Human Rights in the Twentieth Century*, ed. Stefan-Ludwig Hoffmann (Cambridge University Press, 2012); Wiktor Osiatynski, "On the Universality of the Universal Declaration of Human Rights," in *Human Rights with Modesty: The Problem of Universalism*, ed. András Sajó (Martinus Nijhoff, 2004).

traditions, context, and culture.[13] This idea comes from the liberal assumption that culture, religion, and traditions are oppressive. This has been the historical background that leads to the dominant vision in Western academic circles. It is based on the paradigm of *liberal universality*, which has been employed to determine what human rights are and therefore what is considered as universal and what constitutes cultural relativism.

The term "liberal" is an ambiguous notion that has acquired different meanings in recent decades.[14] The argument of this book does not refer to a "thin", classical or political liberalism, which is only concerned with some minimal procedural rules in the public sphere and the separation of power. Rather the focus is a very specific form of this philosophical doctrine as a "comprehensive" liberalism,[15] also called a "liberal monism"[16] or a social liberalism, which is a version of liberalism that has become influential since the 1960s in Western societies.[17]

Political or "thin" liberalism, according to John Rawls, is a procedural tool that sets minimal rules of cooperation among different worldviews in society.[18] As Rawls indicates, this "thin" conception of liberalism is reduced to aspects of political deliberation, it "does not deny there being other values that apply, say, to the personal, the familial, or the associational" domains.[19] In its origins, this "thin" liberalism emerged in Protestant Christian countries, where there was minimal and commonly shared metaphysical baggage and the concept of the good life was reserved for the church and family domains.[20]

Contrary to this procedural liberalism, as Rawls indicates, "comprehensive liberalism" involves a worldview or "conceptions of what is of value in

13 As criticized by Alasdair MacIntyre, *Whose Justice? Which Rationality?* (Notre Dame: University of Notre Dame Press, 1988), chap. 17.

14 See Stanford Encyclopedia of Philosophy, "Liberalism" <https://plato.stanford.edu/entries/liberalism/>. Consulted on January 5, 2019.

15 John Rawls, *Political Liberalism* (Columbia University Press, 1993), 60–61.

16 Kaplan, *Human Rights in Thick and Thin Societies: Universality without Uniformity*, 131.

17 See Michael J. Sandel, *Democracy's Discontent: America in Search of a Public Philosophy* (Harvard University Press, 1996); Mary Ann Glendon, *Rights Talk: The Impoverishment of Political Discourse* (New York: The Free Press, 1991).

18 Rawls, *Political Liberalism*, 29–35.

19 Rawls, 10.

20 Joseph Raz, "Facing Diversity: The Case of Epistemic Abstinence," *Philosophy and Public Affairs* 19, no. 1 (1990); Jürgen Habermas and Joseph Ratzinger, *Entre Razón y Religión: Dialéctica de La Secularización* (Fondo de Cultura Económica, 2008); Alexis de Tocqueville, *Democracy in America*, 2nd edn (Chicago University Press, 2002).

human life, and ideals of human character, as well as ideals of friendship and of familial and associational relationships, and much else that informs our conduct" that includes "nonpolitical conduct".[21]

This "thick" form of liberalism advances a progressive and secular worldview that permeates every aspect of human life. It proclaims that personal autonomy should be prioritized as the most important value in all societies and in all social institutions, disregarding other human goods and social, religious, cultural, or moral objectives.

In the words of Richard Shweder, an anthropologist of the University of Chicago, this vision considers that it is desirable to spread and enforce the "liberal conceptions and ideals for the good life in all corners of society and throughout the world".[22] In this sense, this comprehensive liberalism (or simply liberalism as will be used throughout the book) ceases to be purely procedural and becomes another philosophical comprehensive doctrine.[23]

Thus, this form of liberalism embraces a specific vision of human flourishing and only accepts those worldviews that subscribe to its premises, for only a life lived according to them is considered a dignified one. It establishes a specific hierarchy of values that determines the meaning of culturally charged and sensitive issues, like sexuality, child-rearing, family, marriage, or morality, according to the parameters of individualism, autonomy and secularism as moral imperatives, instead of as optional choices or values that can be ordered in a different manner.

Therefore, the object of analysis of this book refers to this predominant socio-cultural framework regarding acceptable ideas about the human condition, society, and human flourishing (or the good life), which can even be considered a deformation or a deviation from a classical or "thin" liberalism. This framework applied to the field of human rights results in the paradigm of *liberal universality*, considered mandatory for the interpretation and implementation of these norms.[24] Seth Kaplan calls this "Western universality" and he describes it in the following terms:

21 Rawls, *Political Liberalism*. Also see Nussbaum, "Perfectionist Liberalism and Political Liberalism."

22 Richard A. Shweder, "'What About Female Genital Mutilation?' And Why Understanding Culture Matters in the First Place," in *Engaging Cultural Differences: The Multicultural Challenge in Liberal Democracies*, ed. Martha Minow, Richard A Shweder, and Hazel Rose Markus (SAGE, 2020), 235.

23 Nussbaum, "Perfectionist Liberalism and Political Liberalism."

24 Some examples are Jack Donnelly, "Human Rights and Asian Values: A Defense of 'Western' Universalism," in *Human Rights in Asia and the Pacific*, ed. Ben Saul and

> Western universalists hold that international human rights treaties prescribe the adoption of values like autonomy, individualism, equality, choice, secularity, and rationality and that there is a particular ordering of these values vis-à-vis family, work, justice, politics, reproduction, and sexuality. When commentators describe human rights as universal, they are often implying that a certain way of life rooted in the Western, thin society concept of liberalism, individualism, and modernity ought to hold sway. States ought to uphold and enforce these values; all institutions (political, associational, and family) ought to be ruled by them; and international organizations such as the United Nations ought to promote them where they do not exist. Religious groups and Southern societies are urged give up or at least deemphasize traditional social institutions and values if they stand in the way. This is a dramatic change from an earlier era, when there was an "overlapping consensus" on human rights.[25]

According to this perspective, the ideal of human dignity lies in this capacity that is mainly focused on a negative form of freedom or the capacity to be detached from one's bonds. For this reason, a secularized notion of freedom (autonomy) ranks as the most important value to be protected by human rights norms.

Consequently, to determine which human rights interpretations enjoy the status of acceptable and universal, one has to ask whether they respond to these parameters or not. Here, the bar of what is universal is set by what fits this paradigm, while all other interpretations (based on interdependency, duties, and religiously grounded ideas) are considered cultural relativism and incompatible with the notion of human dignity.[26]

This is the worldview that has become dominant in Western Europe, the U.S., Canada and Australia, especially among a specific segment of the population: middle and upper social classes, with high educational attainment, and non-religious people.[27] However, this is not the dominant cultural

Catherine Renshaw (Routledge, 2014); James Griffin, *On Human Rights* (Oxford: Oxford University Press, 2008); Susan Moller Okin, "Is Multiculturalism Bad for Women?," in *Is Multiculturalism Bad for Women?*, ed. Susan Moller Okin (Princeton University Press, 1999).

25 Kaplan, *Human Rights in Thick and Thin Societies: Universality without Uniformity*, 3–4.

26 See Rhoda E Howard-hassmann and Rhoda E Howard, "Cultural Absolutism and the Nostalgia for Community Cultural Absolutism and the Nostalgia for Community," 1993; Fernando R Tesón, "International Human Rights and Cultural Relativism," *Virginia Journal of International Law* 25, no. 4 (n.d.); Susan Okin, Joshua Cohen, and Matthew Howard, eds., *Is Multiculturalism Bad for Women?* (Princeton University Press, 1999).

27 See Shinobu Kitayama and Ayse K Uskul, "Culture, Mind, and the Brain: Current Evidence and Future Directions," *Annual Review of Psychology* 62 (2011): 427, https://doi.org/10.1146/annurev-psych-120709-145357; Daphna Oyserman, Heather M Coon, and Markus Kemmelmeier, "Rethinking Individualism and Collectivism: Evaluation

framework in the rest of the world and among people in Western societies that are religious, belong to low socioeconomic classes, or have low educational attainment.[28] Their worldview is religiously grounded and based on an interdependent model of the self (in contrast to hyper-individualism), where duties and other human goods are cherished beyond autonomy.

Liberal Universality in International Law and Human Rights

The prevalence of this paradigm in international law is somehow evident, for most international lawyers belong to the middle-upper social classes and possess a postgraduate degree obtained from liberal-oriented institutions. Many scholars have criticized this homogeneity in the composition of the international legal community.[29] Oscar Schachter referred to this situation as the "invisible college of international lawyers".[30]

This concept has been further explored by several experts whose research indicate that "a small cluster of universities around the Paris-London axis and surroundings and the traditional U.S. East Coast legal educational establishment are the leading producers of international judges".[31] Martti Koskeniemi

of Theoretical Assumptions and Meta-Analyses," *Psychological Bulletin* 128, no. 1 (2002): 15, https://doi.org/10.1037//0033-2909.128.1.3; Gilda A Morelli et al., "Taking Culture Seriously: A Pluralistic Approach to Attachment," in *The Cultural Nature of Attachment: Contextualizing Relationships and Development*, ed. Heidi Keller and Kim Bard, vol. 22 (MIT Press, 2017), 145–146.

28 See Joseph Henrich, Steven J Heine, and Ara Norenzayan, "The Weirdest People in the World?," *Behavioral and Brain Sciences* 33, no. 2 (2010): 61–135; Richard Shweder, Nancy Much, Manamohan Mahapatra, et al., "The 'Big Three' of Morality (Autonomy, Community, Divinity) and the 'Big Three' Explanations of Suffering," in *Morality and Health*, ed. Paul Rozin and Allan Brandt (Routledge, 1997); Kaplan, *Human Rights in Thick and Thin Societies: Universality without Uniformity*, chap. 3.

29 See Leigh Swigart, "National Judge: Some Reflections on Diversity in International Courts and Tribunals," *McGeorge Law Review* 42, no. 1 (2017).

30 Oscar Schachter, "The Invisible College of International lawyers," *Northwestern University Law Review* 72 (1977).

31 See Mikael Rask Madsen, "Who Rules the World? The Educational Capital of the International Judiciary" [2018] *University of California Journal of International, Transnational, and Comparative Law* 21 to 22; Luiza Leão Soares Pereira and Niccolò Ridi, "Mapping the 'Invisible College of International lawyers' through Obituaries," *Leiden Journal of International Law* 34 (2021).

in the foreword to Anthea Robert's book, *Is International Law International?*, remarks the same observation:

> The culture of international law has grown around a limited number of academic centers. It is really hard to enter the profession without an LLM or a doctorate from one of a handful of law schools in the Anglophone world, or maybe Paris [...] access to the college is about being socialized into a professional vocabulary and a set of cultural mores conveyed through a well-known but narrow academic pathway.[32]

Other scholars also remark the disproportionate influence that Anglo-Saxon perspectives have played in the determination of what is "international",[33] and that this prevailing framework privileges liberal epistemologies, institutions, and scholarship, while interaction with other ways of thinking is marginalized.[34] This situation is problematic for international law if it wants to remain precisely *international*.

An article recently published by a Kyrgyz research fellow of the Max Planck Institute, Julia Emtseva, highlights this problem.[35] According to Emtseva, the structure of international law is basically made up of a very specific and homogeneous profile. She argues that

> What we see today in international law academia and practice is that only a few people from the Global South made it to be "big names" of international law. This inequality has been institutionalized already for a while: academic publishers and international organizations, like the UN, are running in vicious circles. They recruit or publish mostly the graduates of prestigious Western universities because only they can afford unpaid internships, and they are more likely to master English and obtain the necessary doctrinal legal education to produce the scholarship that fits the topical and writing style preferences of the Western publishers.[36]

32 Anthea Roberts, *Is International law International?* (Oxford University Press, 2017) xiv.

33 See Roberts, *Is International Law International?*

34 See Mohsen al Attar, "Subverting Racism in / through International law Scholarship" (*Opinio Juris*, 2021) <http://opiniojuris.org/2021/03/03/subverting-racism-in-international-law-scholarship/>. Consulted on April 15, 2019; Felix Lange, 'Hard Times for Voices from the Global South' (*Völkerrechtsblog*, 2019) <https://voelkerrechtsblog.org/de/hard-times-for-voices-from-the-global-south/>. Consulted on April 20, 2019.

35 Julia Emtseva, "Practicing Reflexivity in International law: Running a Never-Ending Race to Catch up with the Western International lawyers" (2021) No. 2021-11 <https://papers.ssrn.com/sol3/papers.cfm?abstract_id=3837283>. Consulted on April 20, 2021.

36 Emtseva, 3.

This structural inequality is of utmost importance for the international legal system, for these people are the ones that will arrive to top positions as judges, advisers, or state representatives, and then will be the ones that determine the content of international law. As Jan Kabblers indicates "international law is no longer what states do but, rather, about what academic international lawyers do".[37] According to Emtseva, this situation reduces viewpoint diversity in research and practice:

> Western scholarship and its academic system are almost independent of external influences and as a result, international law is predominantly interpreted and even designed by Western philosophical and epistemic traditions. Many issues relevant to the Global South like colonialism, poverty, development, racial injustice, and so forth remain marginal and if these topics are getting published, the arguments and analyses are largely presented and discusses by Western scholars from their Western perspectives.[38]

This problem of lack of pluralism and representation seems to be deeper, for it reflects the situation of many higher education institutions in the Western world, where diversity is reduced to external characteristics,[39] while viewpoint and religious diversity is not encouraged.[40] As explained by several studies, an overwhelming majority of American[41] and

37 Jan Klabbers, "On Epistemic Universalism and the Melancholy of International Law," *European Journal of International Law* 29 (2018): 1059.

38 Emtseva, "Practicing Reflexivity in International Law: Running a Never-Ending Race to Catch up with the Western International Lawyers," 7.

39 Nicholas Kristof, "A Confession of Liberal Intolerance," *The New York Times*, 2016, https://www.nytimes.com/2016/05/08/opinion/sunday/a-confession-of-liberal-intolerance.html.

40 See Neil Gross and Solon Simmons, eds., *Professors and Their Politics* (Johns Hopkins University Press, 2014); George Yancey, Sam Reimer, and Jake O'Connell, "How Academics View Conservative Protestants," *Sociology of Religion* 76, no. 3 (2015); Greg Lukianoff and Jonathan Haidt, *The Coddling of the American Mind: How Good Intentions and Bad Ideas Are Setting up a Generation for Failure* (Penguin Press, 2018); Seth Kaplan, "Religion: A Viewpoint Diversity Blind Spot?," *Heterodox Academy*, 2018, https://heterodoxacademy.org/blog/religion-a-viewpoint-diversity-blind-spot/.

41 Yoel Inbar and Joris Lammers, "Political Diversity in Social and Personality Psychology," *Perspectives on Psychological Science* 7, no. 5 (2012): 500, https://doi.org/10.1177/1745691612448792; Nathan Honeycutt and Laura Freberg, "The Liberal and Conservative Experience Across Academic Disciplines: An Extension of Inbar and Lammers," *Social Psychological and Personality Science* 8, no. 2 (2017): 115–123, https://doi.org/10.1177/1948550616667617.

British[42] professors share liberal views in social issues.

Research indicates that minority groups that are overrepresented share more liberal perspectives, while the same members of minorities who share more conservative views are underrepresented.[43] Columbia University sociologist Musa Al-Gharbi indicates that in American colleges, the groups that remain overrepresented among faculty members are: whites, liberals, lesbians and gays, non-Christian faiths, religiously unaffiliated persons, Asians, men and people coming from the upper social class.[44] The groups that remain underrepresented are: women, Christians, Afro-Americans, conservatives and Hispanics.

Moreover, a 2015 study indicates that American professors at universities generally hold negative perceptions against religious and conservative people, which influences the hiring process.[45] A recent study from the Pew Research Center of 2016 has revealed that political polarization is stronger among highly educated people than among less formally educated ones.[46] As Musa Al-Gharbi has expressed, many academics believe that discrimination based on ideological and viewpoint criteria is valid regarding those people who do not share socially liberal perspectives, which reduces the scope for research topics and questions that do not align with the prevailing views.[47]

In this regard, there is a growing concern among faculty members of American and British universities about the "no-platforming" of controversial speakers,[48] with some cases even involving death

42 Noah Carl, "Lackademia: Why Do Academics Lean Left?," *Briefing Paper*, March 2, 2017, 4–6, https://www.nas.org/academic-questions/31/2/homogenous_the_political_affiliations_of_elite_liberal_arts_college_faculty. Consulted on April 20, 2019.

43 Carl, 4.

44 Musa Al-Gharbi, "Data on How Ideological (under)Representation Compares to (under) Representation along the Lines of Race, Gender or Sexuality" (*Heterodox Academy*, 2018) <https://heterodoxacademy.org/ideological-underrepresentation-compared-to-race-gender-sexuality/>. Consulted on February 25, 2019.

45 Yancey, Reimer, and O'Connell, "How Academics View Conservative Protestants."

46 P. J. Henry and Jaime L. Napier, "Education Is Related to Greater Ideological Prejudice," *Public Opinion Quarterly* 81, no. 4 (2017): 931, https://doi.org/10.1093/poq/nfx038.

47 Al-Gharbi, "Data on How Ideological (under)Representation Compares to (under) Representation along the Lines of Race, Gender or Sexuality"; Musa Al-Gharbi, "A Lack of Ideological Diversity Is Killing Social Research," *Times Higher Education*, no. March (2017): 26–30.

48 See Rosemary Bennett, "Trans Rights Activists Halt Gender Debate at Essex University," *The Times*, 2019, https://www.thetimes.co.uk/article/trans-rights-activists-halt-gender-debate-at-essex-university-qf9sh5r3q; Sean Morrison, "Students at Boris Johnson's Former Oxford College Launch Petition to Have Him Banned from Campus," *Evening Standard*,

threats.[49] Also there have been several students that start initiatives to dismiss professors who do not share a liberal mindset.[50] This situation has led the University of Cambridge to change its freedom of thought and speech policy to emphasize the need to tolerate and respect different viewpoints, no matter how unpopular they might be in elite education.[51]

The dominance of liberal universality in human rights circles specifically has been recently studied by some scholars.[52] Their main concern is that such a paradigm leaves a narrow space for cultural, religious, and viewpoint pluralism. As argued throughout his book *Human Rights in Thick and Thin Societi* Seth Kaplan demonstrates that

> A certain segment of the Western population [...] sets the agenda for the whole human rights field. This group plays an outsized role in major human rights organizations [...]. The same group dominates Western universities, academic literature, the social sciences, and the media; has access to more resources to participate in debates and negotiations; and plays the leading role in funding NGOs in poor countries,

2019, https://www.standard.co.uk/news/politics/students-at-boris-johnsons-former-oxford-college-launch-petition-to-have-him-banned-from-campus-a4235566.html?utm_medium=Social&utm_source=Facebook&fbclid=IwAR05V9lEvAUlc2Chisg0L7H_ckMkGRGSO-RS8T5ATmRuuBQywhbnCNMQx; Olivier Bot, "Polémique Sur La Venue d'un Populiste à Genève," *Tribune de Genève*, 2016, https://www.tdg.ch/monde/polemique-venue-populiste-geneve/story/13374260.

49 See for instance "Oxford Professor given Protection Following Threats from Trans Activists," *BBC*, 2020, https://www.bbc.com/news/education-51248684. Consulted on February 25, 2020.

50 See Harriet Sherwood, "Oxford Students Call for Professor's Removal over Alleged Homophobia," *The Guardian*, 2019, https://www.theguardian.com/education/2019/jan/09/oxford-students-call-for-professors-removal-over-alleged-homophobia; David Rose, "'I Was Tossed out of the Tribe': Climate Scientist Judith Curry Interviewed," *The Spectator*, 2015, https://www.spectator.co.uk/article/-i-was-tossed-out-of-the-tribe-climate-scientist-judith-curry-interviewed.

51 Ben Quinn, "Cambridge University Urged to Re-Invite Rightwing Academic Jordan Peterson," *The Guardian*, 2020, https://www.theguardian.com/education/2020/dec/10/cambridge-university-urged-to-re-invite-rightwing-academic-jordan-peterson. Consulted on February 25, 2021.

52 See Kaplan, *Human Rights in Thick and Thin Societies: Universality without Uniformity*; Richard Shweder, "Moral Realism without the Ethnocentrism: Is It Just a List of Empty Truisms?," in *Human Rights with Modesty: The Problem of Universalism*, ed. András Sajó (Leiden: Martinus Nijhoff, 2004); Glendon, *Rights Talk: The Impoverishment of Political Discourse*; Daniel Philpott, *Just and Unjust Peace: An Ethic of Political Reconciliation* (Oxford University Press, 2012).

> there is a receptive ideological climate for its ideas, which are widely disseminated and rarely challenged.[53]

Kaplan is one of the first scholars to conduct detailed research on the dominion of liberal universality in the field of human rights, but he is not the only one that has raised these concerns. Makau W. Mutua stresses how human rights and a liberal morality have been transformed into synonyms:

> For human rights workers and thinkers in the West, liberalism –as expressed in the typology of political society they support- is a cultural, philosophical, and economic concern. It forms the type of society that they can imagine leading to the freedoms they expect [...] To INGOs [international non-governmental organizations] and leading Western academics, the purpose of the human rights movement is to bring about this type of society.[54]

The Nigerian human rights activist Chidi Anselm Odinkalu has raised a similar criticism, which explains why many African communities and groups are turning away from human rights discourses:

> Instead of being the currency of a social justice or conscience-driven movement, "human rights" has increasingly become the specialized language of a select professional cadre with its own rites of passage and methods of certification. Far from being a badge of honor, human rights activism is, in some of the places I have observed it, increasingly a certificate of privilege.[55]

Michael Freeman, professor of the University of Essex, also highlights this problem: "the apparent consensus on international human rights law is neither complete nor sincere [...] the partial consensus exists among state elites, who do not necessarily represent the people they rule".[56] He also indicates that many human rights NGOs have become the "elites of human-rights professionals",[57] who represent the interests of affluent segments of society, rather than the empowerment of local people.

53 Kaplan, *Human Rights in Thick and Thin Societies: Universality without Uniformity*, 7.

54 Mutua, *Human Rights Standards: Hegemony, Law, and Politics*, 89.

55 Chidi Anselm Odinkalu, "Why More Africans Don't Use Human Rights Language" in Human Rights Dialogue 2.1 (Winter 1999) "Human Rights for All?", Carnegie Council <https://www.carnegiecouncil.org/publications/archive/dialogue/2_01/articles/602>. Consulted on February 7, 2020.

56 Michael Freeman, *Human Rights: An Interdisciplinary Approach*, 2nd edn (Polity Press, 2011), 69.

57 Freeman, 171.

Samuel Moyn has pointed out that "the United Nations Human Rights Council, consisting largely of Western-trained academics (no matter what their passports say), is plausibly charged with reflecting Western values and perhaps Western interests".[58] Austral University of Argentina professor Ignacio de Casas, points out this monocultural approach that is rarely acknowledged by scholars and activists:

> *La ONU [Organización de las Naciones Unidas] también es una institución que [...] tiene su propia cultura [...] que depende de los funcionarios internacionales que la integran y que –por muy variada que sea su procedencia– suele estar influenciada por las culturas cosmopolitas de las ciudades donde se basan los organismos y las universidades de élite donde se forman.*[59]
>
> *[The U.N. [United Nations Organization] is also an institution that [...] has its own culture [...] which depends on the international civil servants who make it up and which—however varied their backgrounds—is often influenced by the cosmopolitan cultures of the cities where the agencies are based and the elite universities where they are formed].*[60]

Tom Zwart, professor of cross-cultural law at the University of Utrecht, has argued that "the human rights debate is currently being dominated by views which are popular in the North, while there is only limited attention for indigenous practices and perceptions in other parts of the world".[61] He further remarks that "the Northern view has almost become the exclusive perspective in academia, while pushing alternative approaches and critiques to the margins. As a result, the human rights discourse has been narrowed".[62]

Stephen Hopgood remarks the great discrepancy between the human rights concept shared by Western elites and middle-class people, and the vast majority of the world. He has stated that this situation provokes that "human rights remains a form of gift, a gift from 'us' to 'them' that can never be reciprocated and thereby establishes no ongoing set of mutual obligations. Human rights do not entail any structural redistribution of power away from the 1

58 Samuel Moyn, "Beyond the Human Rights Measurement Controversy," *Law and Contemporary Problems* 81 (2018): 125; Beth Simmons, *Mobilizing for Human Rights: International law in Domestic Politics* (Cambridge University Press 2012), 370.

59 de Casas, "¿Qué Son Los Estándares de Derechos Humanos?," 298.

60 All translations are my own unless otherwise noted.

61 Tom Zwart, "Balancing Yin and Yang in the International Human Rights Debate," Collected Papers of the Sixth Beijing Forum on Human Rights (Beijing, 2013), 16, http://www.chinahumanrights.org/html/2014/PAPERS_1102/1096.html. Consulted on February 25, 2019.

62 Zwart, 10.

percent".[63] Hopgood has further accused the human rights movement of being "a New York-Geneva-London-centered ideology".[64]

The scholarship development concerning theories of argumentation and interpretation also points towards this lack of intellectual diversity. Interpretative techniques that prioritize autonomy over all other human goods (like the ones proposed by Ronald Dworkin or Robert Alexy)[65] are widely used by apex courts.[66] In contrast, scholars that propose communitarian or relational perspectives (e.g. Francesco Viola, Carlos Massini, or Rodolfo Vigo) are barely used or even studied.[67]

Regarding the praxis of human rights, the prevalence of liberal universality can be seen in several examples, beginning with the composition of human rights treaty bodies, whose dominant profile is a Western European academic from elite universities.[68]

At the Inter-American system of human rights there have been recent controversies regarding the interpretations of the IACtHR on gender identity and abortion issued in 2017 in an advisory opinion, which are not contained in the American Convention on Human Rights.[69] In response, more than 670

63 Stephen Hopgood, "It Begins and Ends with Power," *Open Democracy*, 2013, https://www.opendemocracy.net/en/openglobalrights-openpage/it-begins-and-ends-with-power/. Consulted on February 25, 2019.

64 Stephen Hopgood, 'Human Rights: Past Their Sell-by Date' [2013] Open Democracy <https://www.opendemocracy.net/en/openglobalrights-openpage/human-rights-past-their-sell-by-date/>. Consulted on February 25, 2019.

65 Ronald Dworkin, *Taking Rights Seriously*, 5th edn (London: Duckworth, 2009); Ronald Dworkin, *Life's Dominion: An Argument about Abortion, Euthanasia, and Individual Freedom* (Harper Collins, 1993); Robert Alexy, *Teoría de Los Derechos Fundamentales*, 2nd edn (Centro de Estudios Políticos y Constitucionales, 2007).

66 Jud Mathews and Alec Stone Sweet, "Proportionality Balancing and Global Constitutionalism," *Columbia Journal of Transnational Law* 47, no. 72 (2008).

67 Francesco Viola, *Derecho e Interpretación: Elementos de Teoría Hermenéutica Del Derecho* (Dykinson, 2000); Carlos Ignacio Massini Correa, *La Ley y Su Interpretación Contemporánea* (EUNSA, 2006); Rodolfo L. Vigo, *El Iusnaturalismo Actual: De M. Villey a J. Finnis* (Mexico City: Fontanamara, 2007).

68 "The Independence of UN Human Rights Treaty Body Members," Geneva Academy of International Humanitarian Law and Human Rights Law, 2012, https://www.geneva-academy.ch/joomlatools-files/docman-files/The Independence of UN Human Rights Treaty Body MembersGenevaAcademGeneva (1).pdf. Consulted on February 25, 2019.

69 IACtHR, *Advisory Opinion OC-24/17 on gender identity, and equality, and non-discrimination of same-sex couples* (24 November 2017).

parliament members from 18 Latin America countries subscribed a letter to reject the IACtHR's interpretation.[70]

Another polemic issue emerged regarding some remarks of the president of the Inter-American Commission on Human Rights (IACoHR) Esmeralda Arosemena de Troitiño. She expressed that the greatest threat that Latin America is facing are morally conservative groups that she labeled as "*anti-derechos*" [anti-rights].[71] This provoked the outrage of several Latin American representatives and members of civil society, and also the hashtag in social media referring to this statement as *#EsmeraldaDiscrima* [EsmeraldaDiscriminates] became a trending topic in Twitter.[72] A member of the NGO *Autodeterminación de los Pueblos* [People's Self-Determination] expressed in this regard:

> *Así es señores, la gran amenaza contra los derechos humanos en el Continente no son las dictaduras, ni el hecho de tener la mayor tasa de homicidio en el mundo, ni 184 millones de personas en pobreza, sino quienes piensan distinto a la comisionada.*[73]
>
> [The great threat to human rights on the continent is not dictatorships, nor the fact that we have the highest homicide rate in the world, nor 184 million people living in poverty, but rather those who think differently from the commissioner].

The growing criticism against the ECtHR is another case at point. As Tom Zwart indicates, more and more European states are expressing their concern about ECtHR's judgments which do not comply with the legal rules and go beyond the international agreements.[74] Some state officials have considered that the Court has privileged some controversial views not shared by many countries.[75] Zwart warns that

70 Jacobo García, "Derrotada La Iniciativa Encabezada Por Colombia Para Reformar La Defensa de Derechos Humanos En La OEA," *El País*, 2019, https://elpais.com/internacional/2019/06/27/america/1561672485_548623.html. Consulted on February 25, 2019.

71 "Se Complica Reelección de Esmeralda Arosemena de Troitiño En La CIDH," *Press Reader*, 2019, https://www.pressreader.com/panama/critica/20190628/281560882336020. Consulted on February 25, 2020.

72 "Se Complica Reelección de Esmeralda Arosemena de Troitiño En La CIDH."

73 "Se Complica Reelección de Esmeralda Arosemena de Troitiño En La CIDH."

74 Tom Zwart, "More Human Rights than Court: Why the Legitimacy of the European Court of Human Rights Is in Need of Repair and How It Can Be Done," in *The European Court of Human Rights and Its Discontents*, ed. Spyridon Flogaitis, Tom Zwart, and Julie Fraser (Edward Elgar Publishing Limited, 2013).

75 Hoffmann, "The Universality of Human Rights"; James Slack and James Chapman, "I Will Defy Europe on Jail Votes, Says Cameron as He Sets on Collision Course with Judges in Strasbourg," *Daily Mail*, 2012, https://www.dailymail.co.uk/news/article-2149

> Although the Court's work may be still applauded by its inner circle, it seems to have lost at least some of its legitimacy among the wider public. This legitimacy deficit needs to be addressed quickly and decisively for the Court to survive as a bulwark for liberties and the Rule of Law.[76]

An example of this situation is the *Lautsi v. Italy* case.[77] In 2009 the Second Chamber of the ECtHR ruled that the display of crucifixes in Italian public schools violated the ECtHR, for it imposed an ideology upon students in a public setting.[78] Just as in the *Leyla Şahin v. Turkey* case,[79] the decision was taken considering that neutrality is synonym to the absence of religiously grounded views from the public sphere, while all non-religious worldviews are welcomed.[80] The former Spanish judge to the ECtHR Javier Borrego Borrego wrote in this regard:

> *La sentencia Lautsi es una decisión forzada, externa e internamente, que tiene mucho de previa opinión (no quiero hablar de previa ideología) y muy poco de sentencia adoptada por jueces en aplicación del Convenio y sus Protocolos a un caso concreto […] La confianza se pierde cuando un tribunal no hace Derecho, porque no aplica la ley al caso concreto, y confunde una sentencia con una lección profesoral.*[81]
>
> *[The Lautsi judgment is a forced decision, externally and internally, which has a lot of prior opinion (I do not want to speak of prior ideology) and very little of judgment adopted by judges in application of the Convention and its Protocols to a specific case […]. Trust is lost when a court does not make law, because it does not apply the law to the specific case, and confuses a judgment with a university lecture.]*

005/I-defy-Europe-jail-votes-says-Cameron-sets-collision-course-judges-Strasbourg.html; Zorkin, "The Extent of Flexibility."

76 Zwart, "More Human Rights than Court: Why the Legitimacy of the European Court of Human Rights Is in Need of Repair and How It Can Be Done," 78.

77 ECtHR, *Lautsi v. Italy* (Application no. 30814/06), Grand Chamber Judgement 18 March 2011.

78 ECtHR, *Lautsi v. Italy* (Application no. 30814/06), Second Section Judgement 3 November 2009, paras 48–58.

79 ECtHR, *Leyla Sahin v. Turkey* (Application no. 44774/98) Judgement 10 November 2005.

80 Joseph H. H. Weiler, "Lautsi: A Reply," *International Journal of Constitutional Law* 11, no. 1 (2013).

81 Javier Borrego Borrego, "Estrasburgo y El Crucifijo En Las Escuelas," *El Mundo*, 2009, https://www.elmundo.es/opinion/tribuna-libre/2009/12/21559042.html. Also see Silvia Borelli, "Of Veils, Crosses and Turbans: The European Court of Human Rights and Religious Practices as Manifestations of Cultural Diversity," in *Cultural Heritage, Cultural Rights, Cultural Diversity: New Developments in International Law*, ed. Silvia Borelli and Federico Lenzerini (Martinus Nijhoff, 2002).

In 2011, the judgment was reversed by the Grand Chamber, provoking outrage in Western academic circles where it seems that only one perspective in this regard is permitted.[82] The same approach has been followed by the IACtHR maintaining that human rights obligations require disregarding religiously grounded views on the question of marriage and sexuality,[83] and also in the debate on the beginning of life.[84]

Recent debates at the Human Rights Council provide another illustrative example. In 2009, during the follow-up on the implementation of the Vienna Declaration and Programme of Action, the Human Rights Council requested the United Nations High Commissioner for Human Rights (UNHCHR) to hold in 2010 "a workshop for an exchange of views on how a better understanding of traditional values of humankind underpinning international human rights norms and standards can contribute to the promotion and protection of human rights and fundamental freedoms".[85]

These values referred to dignity, freedom and responsibility and the role of the family, community, society and educational institutions in transmitting those values. The resolution further emphasized that "traditions shall not be invoked to justify harmful practices violating universal human rights norms and standards".[86] Not surprisingly, the resolution was adopted by the approval of 26 non-Western states, while the ones that voted against it were mainly Western European nations.

82 Lorenzo Zucca, "Lautsi: A Commentary on a Decision by the ECtHR Grand Chamber," *International Journal of Constitutional Law* 11, no. 1 (2013); Dominic Mcgoldrick, "Religion in the European Public Square and in European Public Life -Crucifixes in the Classroom ?," *Human Rights Law Review* 11, no. 3 (2011), https://doi.org/10.1093/hrlr/ngr024.

83 "The Court also notes that, at times, the opposition to the marriage of samesex couples is based on philosophical or religious convictions [...] these convictions cannot be used as a parameter of conventionality because the Court could not use them as an interpretative guide when determining the rights of human being. In that sense, it is the Court's opinion that such convictions cannot condition what the Convention establishes in relation to discrimination based on sexual orientation". IACtHR, *Advisory Opinion OC-24/17 on gender identity, and equality, and non-discrimination of same-sex couples* (24 November 2017), para 223.

84 IACtHR, *Artavia Murillo et al. ("in vitro fertilization") v. Costa Rica*, Judgement of 28 November 2012, paras 185 and 186.

85 Human Rights Council, Resolution 12/21 (12 October 2009) A/HRC/RES/12/21, para 1.

86 Human Rights Council, Resolution 16/3 (8 April 2011) A/HRC/RES/16/3, p. 2.

The results of the workshop were compiled in a report.[87] Several religious leaders and academics spoke about the importance of responsibilities, dignity, and traditions to uphold the values protected by human rights norms. During the event, Tom Zwart challenged "the misconception that international human rights norms required States to embrace Western values. Adherence to human rights did not necessarily require ascribing to a Western liberal conception of human rights or considering it to be superior to other conceptions".[88]

However, Western NGOs, like the International Commission of Jurists, the Youth Coalition for Sexual and Reproductive Rights, International Service for Human Rights, Human Rights Watch (HRW), and Western governments considered that traditional values were not compatible with human rights.[89] Their interventions focused on harmful practices and considered the family and religious spaces as inherently oppressive, instead of looking at a broader and more nuanced picture.

After the workshop, the Advisory Committee of the Human Rights Council prepared a report on this topic, which only highlights positive aspects of traditional values related to indigenous communities,[90] while all other cultural perspectives are considered harmful for human rights implementation.[91] The report specially focused on a one-sided negative vision of the family as a place for violence and transmission of harmful traditions. The document states with concern that "young children are particularly susceptible to absorbing values from their families, communities and educational institutions",[92] disregarding human rights treaties that demand protection to these places and the rights of parents. The report completely ignored the contributions made by dissenting voices in the workshop held in 2010.

Even among predominantly liberal societies, the discontent with this paradigm of universality is gaining force. In the U.S., in July of 2019, the Secretary of State Michael Pompeo announced the creation of the Commission on Unalienable Rights. The objective of this Commission was to "provide the

87 UNHCHR, Workshop on traditional values of humankind (13 December 2010) A/HRC/16/37.

88 UNHCHR, para 46.

89 UNHCHR, paras 35–40 and 59–60.

90 Human Rights Council, Study of the Human Rights Council Advisory Committee on promoting human rights and fundamental freedoms through a better understanding of traditional values of humankind (6 December 2012) A/HRC/22/71, paras 33–38.

91 Human rights council, paras 39–44.

92 Human Rights Council, para 60.

Secretary with advice on human rights grounded in our nation's founding principles and the principles of the 1948 Universal Declaration of Human Rights".[93]

It was composed by experts on human rights from different philosophical orientations and religious backgrounds, like Peter Berkowitz, Mary Ann Glendon, Hamza Yusuf Hanson, Paolo Carozza, Meir Soloveichik, and David Tse-Chien Pan. They argued from different positions for a more nuanced approach regarding the recognition of new rights that do not enjoy international support.[94] However, the work and creation of the Commission was deeply criticized by the executive director of HRW, Kenneth Roth, who considered that there was no need for clarifications of human rights interpretations.[95]

The latest corroboration of the prevalence of this paradigm and its intolerance towards viewpoint diversity occurred during the drafting process of my PhD's thesis at the University of Geneva. A professor (who currently holds a prominent position in the U.N. human rights system) threatened me with jail time for daring to write a research work that criticizes liberalism and the lack of a legal foundation for abortion as a human right. He made himself clear by yelling at me: "this is Geneva! Here it is prohibited to speak badly about abortion!". He also added: "you have to speak well about liberals if you want this thesis to be approved". When I tried to explain him that most people do not share this anthropological view, his reply only demonstrated the intrinsic problem of this doctrine: "it is scientifically proved that liberal Europeans are intellectually superior to all other peoples".

The Problem of Liberal Universality

In spite of this situation, the advocates of liberal universality defend this paradigm by considering it neutral, universal, and legally founded. Nevertheless, it is questionable whether liberal universality complies with these criteria. Regarding the aspect of neutrality, it has been largely disputed since the appearance of Rawls' book *A Theory of Justice* in 1971 by different philosophers

93 "Commission on Unalienable Rights," U.S. Department of State, 2019, https://www.state.gov/commission-on-unalienable-rights-member-bio. Consulted on February 25, 2020.

94 Report of the Commission on Unalienable Rights (2020) <https://www.state.gov/wp-content/uploads/2020/07/Draft-Report-of-the-Commission-on-Unalienable-Rights.pdf>. Consulted on February 25, 2021.

95 Kenneth Roth, "Prepared Testimony to Commission on 'Unalienable' Rights," Human Rights Watch, 2020, https://www.hrw.org/news/2020/01/10/prepared-testimony-commission-unalienable-rights. Consulted on February 25, 2021.

in the 1980s, like Charles Taylor,[96] Alasdair McIntyre,[97] and Michael Walzer.[98] Similar remarks about the lack of neutrality of liberal internationalism have been made by the professor of international law of the University of Helsinki Martti Koskeniemmi.[99]

Moreover, this has been acknowledged by world-renowned liberal philosophers. Rawls himself recognizes that the anthropological premises of a comprehensive liberalism are not neutral and universal, for they embrace very specific values as the most important ones above all other goods.[100] Jürgen Habermas has pointed out that liberalism requires an a priori and immanent acceptance of its own philosophical assumptions to participate in the political debate, which make it difficult to justify its neutrality towards comprehensive doctrines that have a different starting point.[101] Rawls' pupil Thomas Nagel has argued in the same line of ideas:

> It is a fundamental feature of Rawls' conception of the fairness of the original position that it should not permit the choice of principles of justice to depend on a particular conception of the good over which the parties may differ. The construction does not, I think, accomplish this, and there are reasons to believe that it cannot be successfully carried out. Any hypothetical choice situation which requires agreement among the parties will have to impose strong restrictions on the grounds of choice, and these restrictions can be justified only in terms of a conception of the good. It is one of those cases in which there is no neutrality to be had, because neutrality needs as much justification as any other position.[102]

Although it is necessary to set limits upon which conceptions of the good life are admissible and which ones undermine the well-being of people, the problem of liberal universality is about who determines which worldviews

96 Charles Taylor, *Philosophy and the Human Sciences: Philosophical Papers 2* (Cambridge, United Kingdom: Cambridge University Press, 1985), chap. 1.
97 MacIntyre, *Whose Justice? Which Rationality?*, chaps. 17–20.
98 Michael Walzer, *Spheres of Justice* (Blackwell Publishing, 1983), chap. 1.
99 Martti Koskenniemi, "The Politics of International law," *European Journal of International Law* 4 (1990): 58; Koskenniemi, "The Effects of Rights on Political Culture" (n 41); Koskenniemi, "Whose Intolerance, Which Democracy?" (n 40).
100 John Rawls, "Justice as Fairness: Political Not Metaphysical," *Philosophy & Public Affairs* 14, no. 3 (1985): 245–246.
101 Jürgen Habermas, "Reconciliation Through the Public Use of Reason: Remarks on John Rawls's Political Liberalism," *The Journal of Philosophy* 92, no. 3 (1995).
102 Thomas Nagel, "Rawls on Justice," in *Reading Rawls*, ed. Jonathan Daniels (Blackwell Publishing, 1989), 8–9.

are acceptable and according to which criteria. All societies can agree that the lifestyle of a murderer, a *genocider*, or a Nazi should be excluded from political debates, even if they have autonomously chosen these worldviews. Nevertheless, putting aside conceptions of the good that deny the intrinsic human dignity of every person, it is not evident which worldviews should be excluded from public deliberations. It is here where liberal universality finds a big obstacle as the global and universal doctrine for human rights interpretations.

In this regard, several scholars have criticized the scope of diversity provided by this paradigm. Michael Sandel has argued that sticking to the philosophical premises of this paradigm, there is no place left for the politics of the common good, where other values that are part of human flourishing can be considered as more important than autonomy (like solidarity, loyalty, family duties, and civic responsibility).[103]

As Martha Nussbaum indicates, diversity in a comprehensive liberalism encompasses lifestyles that prioritize autonomy and secularism, but considers as unreasonable worldviews the ones that rely on a different hierarchy of human goods.[104] This means that liberal universality is inhospitable to worldviews that rely on the promotion of virtue (e.g. Aristotelians or communitarians), that are less individualistic (e.g. personalism or Confucianism), and that rely on religiously grounded ideas (e.g. Judaism or Islam). Therefore, this interpretative paradigm leaves out of the political debate religious conceptions of the good life and interdependent lifestyles, cherished by many persons in developed and developing states.[105] Such a framework places these people outside of the human rights debate, which can hardly be perceived by them as a neutral and inclusive action.

Furthermore, the prioritization of autonomy, individualism, and secularism as the basis of political action implies that the government is sending the message that these values are more worthy of being upheld by public institutions than others. This problem can be seen in the human rights debate regarding abortion. Advocates of liberal universality consider that its legalization is neutral because it allows women to decide whether or not to abort, which according to them, respects both positions in favor and against this procedure. However, as noticed by Michael Sandel, neither the legalization

103 Michael J. Sandel, *Justice: What's the Right Thing to Do?* (New York: Farrar. Straus and Giroux, 2010), chaps. 9 and 10.

104 Nussbaum, "Perfectionist Liberalism and Political Liberalism."

105 Nussbaum, 14–20.

nor criminalization of abortion (or any other practice) are neutral decisions because both represent the official position of the state on this issue.[106]

Its legalization already resonates with a specific set of values as the most important ones for human flourishing: autonomy and secularism, but not with others like interdependency, responsibility, and solidarity. This implies already taking a position on at least four contested messages that are implicitly sent by the state. First, the government is sending a public message that abortion is morally good or at least morally tolerable, which excludes the contrary position that abortion is morally wrong. Second, the government is indicating that life does not begin at conception or that even if it begins it is legitimate to take it in this stage of development, excluding the contrary position that life begins at conception and that it should be protected in all stages of development. Third, the government is implying that autonomy is more worthy of respect than the right to life, which reduces the other argument to a private and unrealistic one. Finally, the legalization of this practice indicates that abortion empowers women, rejecting the argument that abortion might not be respectful of women's dignity.

In some Western states, where abortion has been legalized, pro-life groups have struggled to publicly express their views and participate in international debates because freedom of speech in this regard has been reduced.[107] They have also been censored by big technology companies, due to "public safety" concerns.[108] In other situations, like in Spain[109] and the

106 Sandel, *Justice: What's the Right Thing to Do?*, chap. 10.

107 Grace Melton, "UN Nairobi Summit on Population and Development Shuts Out the Pro-Life Message" *The Heritage Foundation* (2019) <https://www.heritage.org/life/commentary/un-nairobi-summit-population-and-development-shuts-out-the-pro-life-message>. Consulted on February 25, 2020; Fredrick Nzwili and Elaine Ruth Fletcher, 'US Rep At Nairobi Summit: No Support For Abortion In Family Planning.' *Health Policy Watch* (2019) <https://healthpolicy-watch.news/us-rep-at-nairobi-summit-will-not-support-abortion-in-family-planning/>. Consulted on February 25, 2020; 'Kenya Hosts Top Reproductive Health Summit amid Storm over Abortion' *The Nation* (2019) <https://nation.africa/kenya/news/kenya-hosts-top-reproductive-health-summit-amid-storm-over-abortion-222542>. Consulted on February 25, 2019.

108 Douglas Ernst, "Pinterest Blocks Pro-Life Group Live Action from Platform over 'public Safety' Guidelines," *The Washington Times*, 2019, https://www.washingtontimes.com/news/2019/jun/11/lila-roses-pro-life-live-action-content-banned-fro/.

109 "El PSOE Propone Penas de Cárcel Para Los Grupos Provida Que «obstaculicen El Derecho Al Aborto»," *ABC*, 2021, https://www.abc.es/sociedad/abci-psoe-propone-penas-carcel-para-grupos-provida-obstaculicen-derecho-aborto-202105301905_noticia.html. Consulted on February 20, 2021.

UK,[110] governments have banned pro-life discourses from public spaces. Just some months ago, in France, a deputy of the National Assembly requested to censor a movie that tells the personal story of a former abortionist who later joined the pro-life movement, which he perceived as a "crime".[111]

Next to this, medical personnel in Western societies are struggling to defend their right to work, not to be discriminated against, and their right to conscientious objection to not participate in abortion procedures, which have been dismissed by human rights mechanisms.[112]

Universality and Cultural Diversity Revisited

As explained in the introduction, in a post-Cold War multipolar scenario, the dominance of Western liberalism has been deeply scrutinized. Several non-Western[113] and Western dissenting voices[114] have criticized the universality of human rights as it is currently developed. Even within the Western liberal paradigm, feminist scholars have criticized this approach.[115]

The contestation of human rights universality and debates on cultural relativism have provoked heated discussions in academic circles.[116] The literature

110 "MP Seeks to Ban Demonstrations Outside Abortion Clinics," *BBC*, 2020, https://www.bbc.com/news/uk-politics-53150759. <https://www.bbc.com/news/uk-politics-53150759>. Consulted on February 25, 2021.

111 "Question Écrite N°40907 de Mme Bérengère Poletti," Assamblée Nationale, 2021, https://questions.assemblee-nationale.fr/q15/15-40907QE.htm. Consulted on July 25, 2021.

112 See: ECtHR, *Grimmark v. Sweden* (Third Section), 11 February 2020; and European Committee of Social Rights, *International Planned Parenthood Federation – European Network (IPPF EN) v. Italy (merits)*, 10 September 2013.

113 See Makau Wa Mutua, "What Is TWAIL?" (2000) 31 Proceedings of the Annual Meeting (American Society of International law); Luis Eslava and Sundhya Pahuja, "Between Resistance and Reform: TWAIL and the Universality of International law" (2011) 3 Trade, Law and Development; BS Chimni, "Third World Approaches to International law: A Manifesto," *International Community Law Review* 8 (2006).

114 See Rodrigo Guerra López, *Afirmar a La Persona Por Sí Misma: La Dignidad Como Fundamento de Los Derechos de La Persona* (Mexico City: Comisión Nacional de los Derechos Humanos, 2003); Leary, "Postliberal Strands in Western Human Rights Theory: Personalist-Communitarian Perspectives"; Moyn, "Personalism, Community, and the Origins of Human Rights."

115 See Hilary Charlesworth, Christine Chinkin and Shelley Wright, "Feminist Approaches to International law," *American Journal of International Law* 85 (2017).

116 See this debate in Donnelly, "Cultural Relativism and Universal Human Rights"; Brems, *Human Rights: Universality and Diversity*; Abdullahi Ahmed An-Na'im, "Problems of

on the subject traces the origin of this conflict to the Vienna Conference on Human Rights of 1993, where different regional perspectives challenged the prevailing paradigm.

Before the conference took place, each region of the globe held political meetings. The representatives of Asian states adopted the Bangkok Declaration. The polemic paragraph is the one that stresses:

> While human rights are universal in nature, they must be considered in the context of a dynamic and evolving process of international norm-setting, bearing in mind the significance of national and regional particularities and various historical, cultural and religious backgrounds.[117]

The regional meetings of African and Latin American representatives also resulted in the adoption of similar declarations.[118] The African group stressed that human rights are universal, but that "no ready-made model can be prescribed at the universal level since the historical and cultural realities of each nation and the traditions, standards and values of each people cannot be disregarded".[119]

In view of the controversies, the outcome document of the Vienna Conference on Human Rights adopted a paragraph that has provoked heated debates:

> While the significance of national and regional particularities and various historical, cultural and religious backgrounds must be borne in mind, it is the duty of States,

Universal Cultural Legitimacy for Human Rights," in *Human Rights in Africa: Cross-Cultural Perspectives*, ed. Abdullahi Ahmed An-Na'im and Francis Deng (The Brookings Institution, 1990); Yvonne Donders, "Human Rights and Cultural Diversity: Too Hot to Handle?," *Netherlands Quarterly of Human Rights* 30, no. 4 (2012).

117 Final Declaration of the Regional Meeting for Asia of the World Conference on Human Rights (1993). Available in <https://www.ohchr.org/en/aboutus/pages/viennawc.aspx>. Consulted on December 10, 2018.

118 Report of the Regional Meeting for Africa of the World Conference on Human Rights (Tunis, 24 November 1992), pp. 2–3 <https://undocs.org/A/CONF.157/AFRM/14>. Consulted on February 7, 2020; and Regional Meeting for Latin America and the Caribbean for the World Conference on Human Rights (San José, 11 February 1993), p. 4 <https://undocs.org/A/CONF.157/LACRM/15>. Consulted on February 7, 2020.

119 Report of the Regional Meeting for Africa of the World Conference on Human Rights (Tunis, 24 November 1992), p. 2 <https://undocs.org/A/CONF.157/AFRM/14>. Consulted on February 7, 2020.

regardless of their political, economic and cultural systems, to promote and protect all human rights and fundamental freedoms.[120]

Since then, there has been a growing debate on the part of Asian scholars and politicians that argue that human rights are not compatible with their values (giving place to the "Asian values debate").[121] Similar criticisms have been raised from African, Muslim, Arab, Latin American and other Western perspectives.[122]

These statements have been considered a rejection of universal human rights norms and a claim in favor of cultural relativism.[123] This entire debate has been labeled by liberal scholars as a backlash against human rights that emanates from the revival of traditions, ignorance, and authoritarian governments.[124] Others insist that the Asian values position is the opinion of oppressive politicians who are not representative of what people really think.[125] The same has been argued against other cultural perspectives, which are considered "non-Western particularist human rights discourses[s]".[126]

120 Vienna Declaration and Programme of Action, World Conference on Human Rights in Vienna (25 June 1993), para 5 <https://www.ohchr.org/en/professionalinterest/pages/vienna.aspx>. Consulted on February 7, 2020.

121 See Xiaorong Li, "'Asian Values' and the Universality of Human Rights," *Philosophical Dimensions of Public Policy*, 2019, 171–79, https://doi.org/10.4324/9781315126357-17; Amartya Sen, *Human Rights and Asian Values* (Carnegie Council on Ethics and International Affairs, 1997).

122 See José Antonio De la Torre Rangel, "Sobre El Origen de La Tradición Iberoamericana de Derechos Humanos," *Tradición Iberoamericana de derechos humanos* (Porrúa 2014); Leary (n 48); Ahmed El Demery, *The Arab Charter of Human Rights: A Voice for Sharia in the Modern World* (Council on International law and Politics 2015); Josiah AM Cobbah, "African Values and the Human Rights Debate: An African Perspective," 309.

123 See for instance de Schutter, "Universalité Des Droits de l'homme et Mondialisation: La Question Des 'Valeurs Asiatiques.'"

124 See de Schutter; Leena Avonius and Damien Kingsbury, "Introduction," in *Human Rights in Asia: Reassessment of the Asian Values Debate*, ed. Leena Avonius and Damien Kingsbury (Palgrave, 2008); Bayefsky, "Cultural Sovereignty, Relativism, and International Human Rights: New Excuses for Old Strategies"; Guy Haarscher, "Con Human Rights Be 'Contextualized'?," in *Human Rights with Modesty: The Problem of Universalism*, ed. András Sajó (Martinus Nijhoff, 2004).

125 See Ben Saul, Jacqueline Mowbray, and Irene Baghoomians, "Resistance to Regional Human Rights Cooperation in the Asia-Pacific: Demythologizing Regional Exceptionalism by Learning from the Americas, Europe and Africa," in *Human Rights in the Asia-Pacific Region: Towards Institution Building*, ed. Hitoshi Nasu and Ben Saul (Routledge, 2011).

126 Brems, *Human Rights: Universality and Diversity*, 363.

This debate has been understood on those terms because it has been framed according to the premises of liberal universality. Here, "universality" is perceived in terms of adopting uniform interpretations of human rights based on the idea of an abstract individual without social, religious or cultural background, as the parameters of this doctrine (individualism, secularism, and autonomy) demand.[127] In the absence of context of an atomistic individualism, autonomy is understood as the main goal for human dignity.

For these reasons, culture has been narrowly framed and mainly associated with negative connotations.[128] Western human rights scholars and activists automatically assume that any reference to culture is for the promotion of practices like honor killing, widow burning (*sati*), child marriage, or female genital mutilation,[129] rather than to conceive a broader picture that sees the positive elements of culture and religion. Accordingly, all the voices that do not agree with this individualistic and secular view of universality are perceived as based on an essentialization of culture, a monolithic view of society, and the representation of the interests of minoritarian elites.[130]

This doctrine structures the universality versus cultural relativism dichotomy by defining what is universal as equivalent to a liberal worldview, whereas "particularity" or "relativism" refers to all other perspectives. Then, liberal scholars consider that any criticism against the paradigm of liberal universality is an attack against human rights and human dignity and a claim in favor of cultural and ethical relativism.[131]

However, from another perspective, it can be perceived that the discussions held during the Vienna Conference on Human Rights of 1993 reveal a different narrative than the one proposed by liberal universalists. A deeper look to the cultural dissenting opinions indicates that the debate was not

127 See George Letsas, *A Theory of Interpretation of the European Convention on Human Rights* (Oxford University Press, 2007).

128 See for instance: Working Group on the issue of discrimination against women in law and in practice, Report of the Working Group on the issue of discrimination against women in law and in practice, A/HRC/29/40 (2 April 2015)

129 See for instance Brems, "Enemies or Allies—Feminism and Cultural Relativism as Dissident Voices in Human Rights Discourse," 150–153; Jessica Almqvist, *Human Rights, Culture, and the Rule of Law*, vol. 6 (Oxford: Hart Publishing, 2005), chaps. 2 and 4; Charlotte Bunch, "Women's Rights as Human Rights: Toward a Re-Vision of Human Rights," *Human Rights Quarterly* 12, no. 4 (1990).

130 See for instance: Special rapporteur on cultural rights (Karima Bennoune), "Universality, cultural diversity and cultural rights" (25 July 2018) A/73/227, paras 48–58.

131 See Tesón, "International Human Rights and Cultural Relativism."

about Asian, African, Muslim, or Latin American values as incompatible with human rights themselves. It is about the incompatibility between the prevailing values in these societies and liberal human rights *interpretations*.[132]

The different declarations of Asian politicians made in Vienna in 1993 support this argument. The Malaysian minister of foreign affairs, Datuk Abdullah Haji Ahmad Badawi, said that his country "takes a holistic view of human rights", because "excessive individual freedom leads to a decay in moral values and weakens the whole social fabric of nations".[133] He contended that "every opportunity should be given to the developing countries to shape their own political, social and economic institutions which reflect their own traditions and values".[134]

The Indonesian minister of foreign affairs, Ali Alatas, insisted that the West should be more sensitive towards other cultures: "a balanced relationship between individual human rights and the obligations of individuals towards their community" should be envisaged according to article 29 UDHR.[135] He claimed that "the way in which concerns on human rights are expressed at the international level has so far failed to reflect the immense political, economic, social and cultural diversity of the world we live in".[136] Myanmar's minister of foreign affairs, U Ohn Gyaw, argued that "our diversity in historical, cultural and religious backgrounds must never be minimized or forgotten" with a uniform implementation of standards, for "there is no unique model of human rights".[137]

As can be perceived, these other voices rely on a more interdependent vision of the human being, where duties towards the community and the family are cherished, and where religion and culture are part of human flourishing. As previously noted, most of the Asian, African, Muslim, Arab, Latin American and some Western perspectives share these premises about the human condition and the nature of society.

132 See for instance Theodore de Bary, *Asian Values and Human Rights: A Confucian Communitarian Perspective* (Harvard University Press, 1998), 8; Paul Cose and David Askew, *Asia Pacific and Human Rights: A Global Political Economy Perspective* (Ashgate, 2004), 134–140.
133 Quoted in Brems, *Human Rights: Universality and Diversity*, 61.
134 Quoted in Brems, 61.
135 Quoted in Brems, 63.
136 Quoted in Brems, 64.
137 Quoted in Brems, 65.

Thus, the criticism raised against liberal universality does not refer to the notion of universality itself, but rather to a specific way of understanding this concept: the way these universally agreed values have been developed. Accordingly, the object of analysis in this book is universality regarding the *interpretation* of human rights norms, as adopted through the standard-setting process of different human rights mechanisms that are then presented as universal and binding obligations.

The standard-setting process can be defined as the interpretations of human rights norms as adopted by human rights mechanisms through General Comments, statements, judgments, concluding observations, or any other tool that determines the scope and limitations of an internationally recognized human right for their concrete implementation.[138]

Thus, human rights norms and human rights standards or interpretations are two different concepts. Ignacio de Casas remarks that human rights *norms* refer to internationally agreed and general statements included in human rights treaties, which enjoy the status of universality.[139] In contrast, he highlights that human rights *standards* are interpretations regarding the scope and limits of these norms adopted by human rights mechanisms, which do not necessarily enjoy the same status of universality.[140]

Similar remarks have also been raised by the Chilean lawyer Tomás Henríquez, who recalls that there is a difference between the *concept* of human rights as envisaged by the UDHR, which was the product of a moral consensus, deep dialogue, and multicultural understanding, and the practice or *interpretations* that have been given to this list of rights.[141]

As Mashood Baderin highlights "state practice hardly supports any suggestion that in adopting or ratifying international human rights instruments, non-Western state parties were indicating an acceptance of a strict and exclusive Western perspective or interpretation of international human rights norms".[142] The Muslim scholar Ahmed El Demery also argues that "the expansion of the interpretations of some rights by some courts or scholars

138 de Casas, "¿Qué Son Los Estándares de Derechos Humanos?," 294–295.

139 de Casas, 294.

140 de Casas, 294–295.

141 Tomás Henríquez, "La Política y Politización de Los Derechos Humanos," in *Desarrollo Humano y Solidario: Nuevas Ideas Para Chile*, ed. Diego Schalper (Fundación IdeaPaís, 2017).

142 Baderin, *International Human Rights and Islamic Law*, 27.

should not be imposed on other states and regions as universal, unless there is widespread acceptance across the world of these new interpretations".[143]

Ideally, the standard-setting process involves recourse to the general rules of international law, like consultation of legal sources (treaties and custom), negotiations, and dialogue for the adoption of consensus-based interpretations on the meaning of human rights obligations. However, when interpreters assume the paradigm of liberal universality as the goal to be achieved, it curtails all this complex process by reducing it to a transformation of human rights norms to the parameters demanded by this paradigm. For in the mindset of the liberal interpreter, these standards are considered universally agreed and binding norms. They tend to make a leap of faith between the abstract norms agreed in human rights treaties and the standards set by treaty-monitoring bodies and human rights courts.[144] For this reason, they assume that a criticism against liberal human rights interpretations is a backlash against the whole human rights project.

The problem is precisely this gap between what was agreed in human rights instruments and how it has been developed through a liberal paradigm of interpretation, which has curtailed its universalistic spirit by adopting standards that do not enjoy broad international support. Most scholars do not perceive this subtle but significant distinction, for they presuppose that the concept of "universality" can only refer to liberal universality.[145] They assume that their idea of what is universal is universally accepted (or at least it should be). Then, they consider that this paradigm is truthful and superior, which leads them to the conclusion that any criticism against it or other worldviews can only be explained by ignorance or malevolence.

However, liberal scholars have missed that the core of the universalism vs cultural relativism debate is not about whether human rights are universal or not, but rather whether liberal universalism is truly universal, legally founded, and philosophically infallible. The core problem of liberal universality is that its supporters perceive universality as a neutral and already made top-down operation to implement their worldview, instead of as a collective dialogue

143 Demery, *The Arab Charter of Human Rights: A Voice for Sharia in the Modern World*, 75.

144 Dutch Advisory Council of International Affairs, 'Universality of Human Rights: Principles, Practice and Prospects', No. 63 (November 2008). Available in <https://www.advisorycouncilinternationalaffairs.nl/documents/publications/2008/11/05/universality-of-human-rights-principles-practices-and-prospects>. Consulted on May 23, 2019.

145 An example of this position is Donnelly, *Universal Human Rights in Theory and Practice*, 62–63.

and unfinished task.[146] The determination of what is universal is set according to liberal parameters, regardless of widespread disagreement and lack of legal basis, as seen in the case of SRHR (see chapters two and three).

In the liberal universalist paradigm, the kind of diversity or pluralism that is welcomed is restricted to the worldviews that subscribe to the prioritization of autonomy and secularism in all spheres of conduct. For this reason, its idea of inclusiveness accepts racial, religious, ethnic, and sexual diversity as long as these people understand their identities according to these standards, which nullifies the content of diversity in another sense: diversity of viewpoints and worldviews about the meaning of the human condition. Here, people might have different dress codes, food habits, and sexual preferences, but they should all agree with the premises of a comprehensive liberalism in order to be part of the human rights club.[147]

However, the liberal attitude when confronted with the world's diversity finds an unescapable reality. A considerable part of the global population shares a different view of the human condition that is not aligned with the premises of liberal universality. Therefore, the concept of "liberal diversity" is not inclusive of a huge part of the world's population, especially regarding sensitive issues (see chapter three).

These other perspectives do not deny the relevance of the human rights project, they are not based on cultural relativism but on a "different universalism".[148] However, the prevalence of liberal universality has impelled this dialogue, which has resulted in a very limited debate about universalism and relativism. Universality has been addressed in a limited manner, in terms of the rights holder (who is entitled to human rights?)[149]

146 See an analysis of this in Adamantia Pollis, "New Universalism," in *Human Rights: New Perspectives, New Realities*, ed. Adamantia Pollis and Peter Schwab (Lynne Rienner, 2000), 13.

147 See this argument in Kristof, "A Confession of Liberal Intolerance." Consulted on May 23, 2019.

148 Freeman, *Human Rights: An Interdisciplinary Approach*, 127.

149 Brems, *Human Rights: Universality and Diversity*; Donnelly, "Cultural Relativism and Universal Human Rights"; Peter van Dijk, "A Common Standard of Achievement: About Universal Validity and Uniform Interpretation of International Human Rights Norms," in *Human Rights: Chinese and Dutch Perspectives*, ed. Peter Baehr et al. (Martinus Nijhoff, 1996).

and the concept itself (does the concept of human rights exist in all cultures?).[150]

Nevertheless, the question of universality regarding human rights interpretations has been barely addressed in literature,[151] and mainly from the perspective of other disciplines different from legal studies.[152] Western scholars remain skeptical and suspicious of other frameworks in the human rights field. As Singapore's Minister of Foreign Affairs Bilahari Kausikan remarked at the American Society of International Law Annual Meeting: "Western overreaction to this simple description of reality –that moreover explicitly recognized the ideal of universality [...] continues to poison the atmosphere and fuels misunderstanding."[153]

This situation reveals the need for a thorough analysis on the concept of universality, especially in a highly divided world. For this reason, it is relevant to explore the ideas adopted by the drafters of the UDHR in a time of turbulence and deep disagreement. Such an analysis sheds some light to determine what kind of interpretative framework was recognized as universal and in which terms the word "universal" was framed in order to be as inclusive as possible of all different cultures and societies.

150 R. Panikkar, "Is the Notion of Human Rights a Western Concept?," *Diogenes* 30, no. 120 (1982): 75–102; Alison Dundes Renteln, *International Human Rights: Universalism versus Relativism* (SAGE, 1990).

151 See Glendon, "Knowing the Universal Declaration of Human Rights"; Henríquez, "La Política y Politización de Los Derechos Humanos"; Alfred Fernández, "De La Idea a La Cultura de Los Derechos Humanos: Los Derechos Humanos En El Siglo XXI," *Anuario de Derechos Humanos* 3 (2002); William Twining, *General Jurisprudence: Understanding Law from a Global Perspective* (Cambridge University Press, 2012).

152 See Dundes Renteln, *International Human Rights: Universalism versus Relativism*; Merry, "Human Rights Law and the Demonization of Culture (And Anthropology Along the Way)"; Almqvist, *Human Rights, Culture, and the Rule of Law*; Kaplan, *Human Rights in Thick and Thin Societies: Universality without Uniformity*; Federico Lenzerini, *The Culturalization of Human Rights Law* (Oxford University Press, 2014); An-Na'im, *Human Rights in Cross-Cultural Perspectives: A Quest for Consensus.*

153 Bilahari Kausikan, "An East Asian Approach to Human Rights," *Buffalo Journal of International Law* 2 (1996): 267–268.

· 2 ·

SRHR IN INTERNATIONAL LAW: CONSENSUS OR CONFLICT?

The dominance of the paradigm of liberal universality in the human rights sector has caused the displacement of all worldviews that propose a different idea about what is human flourishing. All doctrines that contradict, challenge, or disagree with this view are being ostracized from the human rights debate, which results in a poor dialogue that disconnects the project of universality from reality.

This provokes the interpretation of human rights norms to be decided by a very reduced set of actors and then implemented in a way that violates the principles of equality and freedom, and even causes gross human rights violations. The case study of the creation and implementation of SRHR is an illustrative example of this situation.

The Development of SRHR in International Conferences

It is pertinent to start this legal analysis highlighting that no human rights treaty contains the concept of SRHR. The only discussions in this regard that were held among the drafters of the UDHR were about the right to life in relation to abortion and the right to marriage. Regarding abortion, the drafters decided to exclude any consideration both in favor and against it, because there was no universal consensus on such a sensitive issue.[1] Regarding the right to marry and the protection of the family, the drafters did not establish a right to have children, a "right not to reproduce", nor to have less children.[2]

The idea to incorporate the term SRHR into the corpus of international law emerged from a blend of philosophies that gained momentum in the West in the late nineteenth century: Darwinism, neo-Malthusianism, eugenics, and some forms of feminism.[3] These doctrines promoted the creation of "population conferences", whose normative weight is very low, for they are non-binding texts adopted in an environment of strong disagreement among states.

Regarding eugenics, before World War I this was a pseudo-scientific idea that became "one of the most fashionable social reform movements in American history".[4] Eugenicists believed that "poverty 'handed down' over several generations was proof of genetic inferiority".[5] The goal was to encourage the reproduction of people with "correct" genes and to stop the "breeding" of the poor and "unfit" segments of society.

The first eugenic sterilization law was introduced in the state of Indiana in the U.S. in 1907. The Nazi sterilization laws were fashioned based on the American model.[6] In Europe, eugenics laws were introduced in the canton of Vaud in Switzerland in 1928, in Denmark the following year, in Germany in 1933, in Norway in 1934, in Sweden and Finland in 1935.[7] Between 1930 and 1949 "over eight and a half thousand Danes were sterilized for sexual and psychic abnormality".[8] In Norway around 43,000 citizens were sterilized for similar reasons.[9] The Scandinavian sterilization policy was "an accepted part

1 Åshild Samnøy, *Human Rights as International Consensus: Making the Universal Declaration of Human Rights 1945–1948* (Michelsen Institute, 1993), 95–97.

2 Alison Bashford, *Global Population: History, Geopolitics, and Life on Earth* (Columbia University Press, 2014), 346.

3 See Nancy Leys Stepan, *The Hour of Eugenics: Race, Gender, and Nation in Latin America* (Cornell University Press, 1991), 1.

4 Ian R. Dowbiggin, *The Sterilization Movement and Global Fertility in the Twentieth Century* (Oxford University Press, 2008), 18.

5 Ann Farmer, *By Their Fruits: Eugenics, Population Control, and the Abortion Campaign* (Catholic University of America Press, 2008), 4.

6 Farmer, 111.

7 Stepan, *The Hour of Eugenics: Race, Gender, and Nation in Latin America*, 30.

8 Stepan, 30; Gunnar Broberg and Nils Roll-Hansen, *Eugenics and the Welfare State: Norway, Sweden, Denmark, and Finland* (Michigan State University Press, 2005).

9 Dowbiggin, *The Sterilization Movement and Global Fertility in the Twentieth Century*, 84.

of a broad, state-run welfare system designed to improve the health and happiness of all citizens".[10]

In Sweden, the persons with mental disabilities were sterilized because care institutions were seen as too heavy a burden on society and the progressive Swedish elites considered these people as "unfit" to raise children and to propagate their genes.[11] Sterilization for eugenic reasons continued up to 1975 when the legislation was abolished. From 1935 to 1975 some 63,000 eugenic sterilizations were reported.[12] The legislation did not authorize coerced sterilization, but "persuasion" and pressure to apply for sterilization was possible, just as indirect compulsion.[13]

In the U.S., these laws were framed according to the same ideas. The legislation on eugenic sterilization was framed as part of a public welfare program that wanted to "alleviate" the suffering of poor and "unfit" people. This rationale can be seen in the infamous case *Buck v. Bell* of 1927 about the compulsory sterilization of a mentally ill woman. Justice Holmes stated that the rights of the "feeble-minded" and the interest of society are safeguarded through the "sterilization of mental defectives".[14] He also stressed that "it is better for all the world if, instead of waiting to execute degenerate offspring for crime or to let them starve for their imbecility, society can prevent those who are manifestly unfit from continuing their kind".[15]

These laws were viewed "as moderate, scientific, and progressive methods of implementing genetic hygiene".[16] The legislation was not removed until the mid-1970s, where awareness of the forced nature of sterilization began to rise.[17] By that time, around 63,000 people in America had passed through eugenic sterilization procedures.[18] As part of these eugenic policies, in the 1950s there were attempts to legalize abortion in order to prevent "the birth of children who were likely to perpetuate social problems and become public

10 Dowbiggin, 85.

11 Broberg Gunnar and Mattias Tydén, "Eugenics in Sweden: Efficient Care," in *Eugenics and the Welfare State: Norway, Sweden, Denmark and Finland*, ed. Gunnar Broberg and Nils Roll-Hansen (Michigan State University Press, 2005), 102.

12 Gunnar and Tydén, 109.

13 Gunnar and Tydén, 116–119.

14 *Buck v. Bell* 274 U.S. 2 (1927).

15 *Buck v. Bell* at 208.

16 Stepan, *The Hour of Eugenics: Race, Gender, and Nation in Latin America*, 30.

17 Johanna Schoen, *Choice and Coercion: Birth Control, Sterilization, and Abortion in Public Health and Welfare* (The University of North Carolina Press, 2005), 75.

18 Schoen, 82.

charges".[19] As recent cases regarding abortion of unborn children with Down Syndrome show, eugenics is not something of the past.[20]

Regarding neo-Malthusianism, this movement was stimulated by the so called "population problem".[21] This issue referred to "the unduly rapid rates of population growth in the developing world, resulting from the sharp decline in mortality after World War II and the continuation of high fertility".[22]

Population growth in non-Western nations was seen as a driver of poverty, migration, political unrest, and competition for natural resources that would affect the interests of Western states.[23] These fears prompted the creation of the population control movement, which was based on the premise that "fertility reduction ought to be the most important objective of global population policy".[24]

In the same line of ideas, in 1968 the physician Paul Ehrlich published his famous book *The Population Bomb*, which was an apocalyptic prediction of a future with overpopulation and food scarcity.[25] Although this book has been disqualified by several members of the scientific community for its lack of academic rigor,[26] it provoked worldwide fear regarding population growth.

In order to stop this alleged threat, the magnate John D. Rockefeller 3rd with his organization called the Population Council and together with

19 Schoen, 162.

20 Alexandra Topping, "Woman with Down's Syndrome Loses UK Abortion Law Case," *The Guardian*, 2021, https://www.theguardian.com/world/2021/sep/23/woman-with-downs-syndrome-loses-uk-abortion-law-case.

21 Kathleen Tobin, *Politics and Population Control: A Documentary History* (Greenwood, 2004), chap. 1.

22 Bernard Berelson and Jonathan Lieberson, "Government Efforts to Influence Fertility: The Ethical Issues," *Population and Development Review* 5, no. 4 (1979): 581.

23 See Matthew Connelly, *Fatal Misconception: The Struggle to Control World Population* (Harvard University Press 2008); Betsy Hartmann, *Reproductive Rights and Wrongs: The Global Politics of Population Control* (3rd ed, Haymarker Books 2016); Dennis Hodgson and SU.S.n Cotts Watkins, "Feminists and Neo-Malthusians: Past and Present Alliances" (1997) 23 Population and Development Review 469; Seamus Grimes, "From Population Control to 'Reproductive Rights': Ideological Influences in Population Policy," *Third World Quarterly* 19 (1998).

24 Paige Whaley Eager, "From Population Control to Reproductive Rights: Understanding Normative Change in Global Population Policy (1965–1994)," *Global Society* 18, no. 2 (2004): 161, https://doi.org/10.1080/1360082042000207483.

25 Paul Ehrlich, *The Population Bomb* (Ballantine Books, 1986).

26 See this criticism in: Ian Angus and Simon Butler, *Too Many People? Population, Migration, and the Environmental Crisis* (Haymarket Books, 2011).

the Ford Foundation, began to bring academics from elite American universities to develop family planning policies to address the "population problem".[27] In this regard, the professor of development studies Betsy Hartmann indicates that

> In the 1950s the Rockefeller and Ford Foundations became actively involved in promoting population control as an integral part of US foreign policy. Their most enduring legacy was the successful creation of an international academic and policy elite invested in fertility reduction as a national development strategy. One does not have to be a conspiracy theorist to recognise the way this network of experts was intentionally created. Foundation money spawned the establishment of population centres at major US universities [...] Foreign students were brought to the centres where they were persuaded of the urgent need to reduce birth rates.[28]

Other billionaires have also been continuously supporting the cause, like Bill Gates, George Soros (through the Open Society Foundation), Warren Buffett, Oprah Winfrey, David Rockefeller, and Ted Turner.[29]

Together with the eugenics and neo-Malthusian ideologies, a third idea was also introduced in Western politics: the birth control movement. This movement was an alliance between feminist, neo-Malthusian, and eugenics perspectives,[30] which were later joined by environmental concerns.[31] It was influenced by famous eugenic-feminists like Margaret Sanger from the U.S., Marie Stopes from the U.K., Elise Ottesen-Jensen from Sweden, and Rama Rau from India.[32]

A paradigmatic example of this mixture of ideas is Margaret Sanger, the founder of the American Birth Control League, which in 1942 became the

27 Hodgson and Watkins, "Feminists and Neo-Malthusians: Past and Present Alliances," 479.

28 Betsy Hartmann, "Liberal Ends, Illiberal Means: National Security, 'Environmental Conflict' and the Making of the Cairo Consensus," *Indian Journal of Gender Studies* 12, no. 2 (2006): 203, https://doi.org/10.1177/097152150601300204.

29 Paul Harris, "They're Called the Good Club - and They Want to Save the World," *The Guardian*, 2009, https://www.theguardian.com/world/2009/may/31/new-york-billionaire-philanthropists. Consulted on May 4, 2021.

30 See Hodgson and Watkins, "Feminists and Neo-Malthusians: Past and Present Alliances," 473–474; Bonnie Mass, *Population Target: The Political Economy of Population Control in Latin America* (Charters Publishing, 1976), chap. 1.

31 See Colin Hickey, Travis N Rieder, and Jake Earl, "Population Engineering and the Fight against Climate Change," *Social Theory and Practice* 42, no. 4 (2016); Hartmann, *Reproductive Rights and Wrongs: The Global Politics of Population Control*, 2016.

32 See Marc Frey, "Neo-Malthusianism and Development: Shifting Interpretations of a Contested Paradigm," *Journal of Global History* 6, no. 1 (2011): 78.

International Planned Parenthood Federation (IPPF), the world's largest contraception and abortion provider.[33] Its first board of directors was composed of the former presidents of the American Eugenics Society and the Race Betterment Conference.[34] In Sanger's most famous book, *The Pivot of Civilization*, she explained the objective of her organization, which is: "to enlighten and educate all sections of the American public in the various aspects of the dangers of uncontrolled procreation and the imperative necessity of a world program of Birth Control".[35]

It is also in this context that contraceptive technology was widely developed and investment in these products became popular. This is why some innovators had a preference for permanent methods or ones that did not require constant user control, even if they were unsafe and more harmful, than others that required the freedom and responsibility of the user.[36]

Based on these premises, the Population Council developed intrauterine devices (IUD), and the injectable Depo-Provera, because unlike the pill, they did not require continued consent from women to use it.[37] The Population Council considered the IUD was perfect for the developing world, because it was a permanent contraceptive and suited for poor "unmotivated" women,[38] despite the fact that around half of the patients stopped using the device less than two years after getting it, mostly due to infections, pain and bleeding.[39]

It is also for this reason that family planning agencies prioritized the use of IUDs, the injectable Depo-Provera and sterilization, instead of providing accurate and detailed information to women among a variety of family planning methods that are less harmful to women's health and more compatible with their cultural views.[40] Thus, it is no coincidence that the IUD and

33 See Donald Critchlow, "Birth Control, Population Control, and Family Planning: An Overview," *Journal of Policy History* 7, no. 1 (1995): 3.

34 Mass, *Population Target: The Political Economy of Population Control in Latin America*, 33.

35 Margaret Sanger, *The Pivot of Civilization*, 1922, http://www.gutenberg.org/files/1689/1689-h/1689-h.htm#link2HCH0004. Consulted on May 4, 2021.

36 See Betsy Hartmann, *Reproductive Rights and Wrongs: The Global Politics of Population Control* (South End Press, 1995), 38.

37 See Hodgson and Watkins, "Feminists and Neo-Malthusians: Past and Present Alliances," 485.

38 See Dowbiggin, *The Sterilization Movement and Global Fertility in the Twentieth Century*, 142.

39 See Donald T. Critchlow, *Intended Consequences: Birth Control, Abortion and the Federal Government in Modern America* (Oxford University Press, 1999), 29.

40 See Hartmann, *Reproductive Rights and Wrongs: The Global Politics of Population Control*, 2016, chap. 4.

sterilization are methods barely used in Western Europe and the U.S., while they are the most common ones in the developing world.[41] Together they constituted 56 percent of world contraceptive prevalence in 2015.[42]

With the aid of these technological innovations, in the 1960s USAID, the Population Council, the Ford Foundation, IPPF and the Swedish government were involved in family planning programs all around the developing countries.[43] As Columbia University professor of history Matthew Connelly indicates: "there can be no doubt that by the 1960s American foundations and corporations as well as government agencies were vital in developing and marketing new forms of birth control in poor countries".[44]

In this intellectual environment, the First International Population Conference was held in Geneva in 1927. In fact, it was the seventh International Neo-Malthusian Conference, but the organizers decided to change the name to avoid negative connotations.[45] This event was sponsored by Margaret Sanger and chaired by a prominent member of the British Eugenics Society.[46] Some decades afterwards, the UN hosted its first Population Conference in Rome in 1954, whose objective was the discussion of population reduction and food supply.[47]

The Declaration on Population Growth of 1966

The Second World Population Conference hosted by the UN was held in Belgrade in 1966. During the discussion days, not all participants viewed population growth as an economic and social crisis. Some considered that the socioeconomic problems in Africa were mainly related to under-population

41 UN "World Fertility and Family Planning 2020," 2020, 15, https://www.un.org/en/development/desa/population/publications/pdf/family/World_Fertility_and_Family_Planning_2020_Highlights.pdf. Consulted on May 4, 2021.

42 "World Fertility and Family Planning 2020."

43 See Frey, "Neo-Malthusianism and Development: Shifting Interpretations of a Contested Paradigm," 86.

44 Matthew Connelly, "Population Control Is History: New Perspectives on the International Campaign to Limit Population Growth," *Comparative Studies in Society and History* 45, no. 1 (2003): 127.

45 Bashford, *Global Population: History, Geopolitics, and Life on Earth.*

46 C. F. Close, "The World Population Conference of 1927," *The Geographical Journal* 70, no. 5 (1927): 471; Frank Lorimer et al., "The Role of the International Union for the Scientific Study of Population," *The Milbank Memorial Fund Quarterly* 49, no. 4 (1971): 86–87.

47 Peter Cox, "World Population Conference 1954," *The Eugenics Review* 46, no. 4 (1955).

in certain areas and land tenure rather than overpopulation.[48] Some commentators were concerned about the effect on the dependency ratios in the developing world with the introduction of population control methods.[49] The representative from the Soviet Union insisted that a better option was to improve social and economic conditions in the developing countries and a fair redistribution of goods.[50]

Despite these oppositions, the Declaration on Population Growth was adopted by members of 12 governments. The declaration was clear on the fact that "while population leaders and experts are by no means calling for a return to higher infant mortality rates, they explicitly desire fewer numbers of lives".[51]

A few years after the declaration, in 1969 the American President Richard Nixon created the Commission on Population Growth and appointed John Rockefeller III as its chairman.[52] This Commission recommended the legalization of abortion and giving minors access to contraception as a way to reduce fertility overseas, but the president disavowed the report.[53] The recommendations were too controversial for the prevailing moral environment and they would have raised suspicions of Western imperialism.

To avoid these accusations, the American government looked for an alliance with other governments and international organizations. For this purpose, in 1969 the United Nations Population Fund (UNFPA) was created with the objective of distributing contraception to address population growth in the developing world.[54] Matthew Connelly asserts that "Britain funded UNFPA with the idea that international agencies were ideal for pressuring these governments [developing nations]".[55]

48 Peter Cox, Peel John, and Thomas Clifford, "The World Population Conference Belgrade, 1965," *The Eugenics Review* 51, no. 1 (1966): 12.

49 idem.

50 Edith G. Adams, "World Population Conference, Belgrade August 30-September 10," *Population Index* 31, no. 4 (1965): 443.

51 Alisa Sánchez, "Population Discourse, Family Planning Policies, and Development in Colombia 1960–1969," in *Reproductive Justice and Sexual Rights: Transnational Perspectives*, ed. Tanya Saroj Bakhru (Routledge, 2019), 65.

52 James Reed, "The Birth Control Movement Before Roe v. Wade," *Journal of Policy History* 7, no. 1 (1995): 47.

53 Hodgson and Watkins, "Feminists and Neo-Malthusians: Past and Present Alliances," 486.

54 Eager, "From Population Control to Reproductive Rights: Understanding Normative Change in Global Population Policy (1965–1994)," 146; Connelly, *Fatal Misconception: The Struggle to Control World Population*, 285–287.

55 Connelly, *Fatal Misconception: The Struggle to Control World Population*, 291.

Since 1965, the U.S. government relied on the Population Council, IPPF, and the Ford Foundation to set an agenda of contraceptive services in the developing world.[56] At its peak, between 1969 and 1972, over four-fifths of all U.S. international assistance was dedicated to population programs and a decade later American public and private sources accounted for 85 percent of contraceptive research.[57] As Graduate Institute of Geneva history professor Nicole Bourbonnais indicates "by the early 1970s the study and control of population had become a multimillion-dollar, thoroughly transnational endeavor".[58]

By 1970, despite of the technocratic efforts of Western and local elites, the birth rates in the Third World were not reduced as expected. Therefore, the academic community and policy makers began to advocate for more intrusive measures.[59] Matthew Connelly indicates that "reform eugenicists believed that the whole future of family planning depended on their ability to manipulate a large segment of society they considered unfit for parenthood".[60] Within this intellectual environment, another population conference was organized.

The Third World Population Conference was held in Bucharest in 1974. The draft plan aimed at "the need to limit population growth through implementing population and social welfare policies with direct effects on fertility".[61] Neo-Malthusian supporters "promoted an individual's right to reproductive autonomy as a pragmatic way of furthering fertility control".[62]

The conference was conducted in a context of deep disagreement. Developing states were concerned that population control was privileged to meet the interest of some powerful states, at the expense of a person-centered

56 Critchlow, *Intended Consequences: Birth Control, Abortion and the Federal Government in Modern America*, 3–6.

57 Connelly, "Population Control Is History: New Perspectives on the International Campaign to Limit Population Growth," 127.

58 Nicole C Bourbonnais, "Population Control, Family Planning, and Maternal Health Networks in the 1960s/70s: Diary of an International Consultant," *Bulletin of the History of Medicine* 93, no. 3 (2019): 336.

59 Frey, "Neo-Malthusianism and Development: Shifting Interpretations of a Contested Paradigm," 89.

60 Connelly, *Fatal Misconception: The Struggle to Control World Population*, 107.

61 Jason L Finkle and Barbara B Crane, "The Politics of Bucharest: Population, Development, and the New International Economic Order," *Population and Development Review* 1, no. 1 (1975): 88.

62 Hodgson and Watkins, "Feminists and Neo-Malthusians: Past and Present Alliances," 490.

development.[63] Ali Oubouzar, the representative of Algeria, declared that "the underdeveloped countries want to restore the paramountcy of development over the matter of negatively influencing fertility rates".[64]

An opposition block emerged from Catholic, Socialist and African countries, who opposed a fertility control agenda.[65] A group of Latin American and African states argued that contraception was unnecessary if the efforts focused on improving living standards in their states.[66]

Despite these discussions, the outcome of the conference was the adoption of a World Population Plan of Action. This document for the first time included the right to decide on the number of children that one wants to have.[67] It highlighted that population policies should respect human rights and individual freedom.[68] However, the background driver of the conference seemed to be a concern regarding population growth:

> *En muchos países en desarrollo, y especialmente en los grandes países de Asia, se estima que el deseo de las parejas de tener familias grandes origina tasas excesivas de crecimiento de la población nacional, y los gobiernos tratan expresamente de reducir dichas tasas mediante la aplicación de medidas de política concretas.*[69]
>
> [In many developing countries, and especially in large Asian countries, the desire of couples to have large families is believed to lead to excessive rates of national population growth, and governments explicitly seek to reduce these rates through specific policy measures.]

For that reason, some months after the Bucharest conference, the National Security Council of the U.S. released a study entitled *National Security Study Memorandum 200: Implications of Worldwide Population Growth for US Security and Overseas Interests*, also known as the Kissinger Report.[70] It was

63 Burke Grant, "The World Population Conference: An Overview," *Journal of International Law and Economics* 9 (1974): 368; Eager (n 210) 152–154.

64 Critchlow, "Birth Control, Population Control, and Family Planning: An Overview," 15.

65 Finkle and Crane, "The Politics of Bucharest: Population, Development, and the New International Economic Order," 90; Hodgson and Watkins, "Feminists and Neo-Malthusians: Past and Present Alliances," 480.

66 Grant, "The World Population Conference: An Overview," 369.

67 "Informe de La Conferencia Mundial de Población," 1975, 13, https://repositorio.cepal.org/bitstream/handle/11362/21970/S7500346_es.pdf?sequence=2&isAllowed=y.

68 "Informe de La Conferencia Mundial de Población," 13.

69 UN "Informe de La Conferencia Mundial de Población," 10. Consulted on May 4, 2019.

70 U.S. National Security Council, *National Security Study Memorandum 200: Implications of Worldwide Population Growth for U.S. Security and Overseas Interests* (10 December

approved as the official American foreign policy in 1975 by President Gerald Ford.[71]

The U.S. government was concerned that a growing population would demand a greater share of wealth within developing nations and fewer cheap resources for developed countries.[72] Accordingly, the report makes several recommendations, like to continue with the promotion of contraceptive services in the Third World sponsored by the U.S., and the use of media to encourage the use of contraception and the desire for small families.[73]

The report is also cautious in warning that the strategy should be perceived as "local", for there is the problem that some counties "will see developed country pressures for family planning as a form of economic or racial imperialism; this could well create a serious backlash".[74] For that purpose, the report suggests to

> Minimize charges of an imperialist motivation behind its support of population activities by repeatedly asserting that such support derives from a concern with (a) the right of the individual couple to determine freely and responsibly their number and spacing of children [...] and (b) the fundamental social and economic development of poor countries in which rapid population growth is both a contributing cause and a consequence of widespread poverty.[75]

The report acknowledges that the desire to reduce fertility does not come from the citizens of the developing world, for it recognizes that many families in non-Western nations "consciously prefer to have numerous children".[76] For this reason, it indicates the relevance of "concentrating on the education and indoctrination of the rising generation of children regarding the desirability of smaller family size".[77] The report emphasizes the need "to convince the masses of the population that it is to their individual and national interest to have, on the average, only three and then only two children".[78] Additionally, the

1974), 66. Available at: <https://pdf.U.S.id.gov/pdf_docs/PCAAB500.pdf>. Consulted on February 22, 2021.

71 Marshall Green, "The Evolution of US International Population Policy, 1965-92: A Chronological Account," *Population and Development Review* 19, no. 2 (1993): 311.

72 Seamus Grimes, "The Ideology of Population Control in the UN Draft Plan for Cairo," *Population Research and Policy Review* 13 (1994): 213.

73 U.S. National Security Council, *National Security Study Memorandum* 200, 73–120.

74 U.S. National Security Council, *National Security Study Memorandum* 200, 77.

75 U.S. National Security Council, *National Security Study Memorandum* 200, 81.

76 U.S. National Security Council, *National Security Study Memorandum* 200, 92.

77 U.S. National Security Council, *National Security Study Memorandum* 200, 102.

78 U.S. National Security Council, *National Security Study Memorandum* 200, 102.

report remarks that "no country has reduced its population growth without resorting to abortion".[79]

The fourth World Population Conference was held in Mexico City in 1984. Again, a group of Third World states continued to oppose the prevailing narrative, while Western states advocated for the implementation of contraception through population policies.[80] The former president of the World Bank, Robert McNamara, declared: "family planning programs are less costly than conventional development projects".[81] He also supported a credit policy for developing countries conditioned on their commitment to reduce their population growth.[82] Consequently, the general opposition from developing states had greatly diminish, for indebtedness and dependence on aid were strong motivations not to damage the relationships with Western elites.[83]

The outcome of this conference urged states to adopt population policies and social and economic development policies to control demographic growth.[84] However, in accordance with the right to self-determination, the document recalls that these policies "should be responsive to local values and needs, and those directly affected should be involved in the decision-making process at all levels".[85] Also, they "should respect human rights, the religious beliefs, philosophical convictions, cultural values and fundamental rights of each individual and couple, to determine the size of its own family".[86] It stresses that "family planning information, education and means should include all medically approved and appropriate methods of family planning, including natural family planning, to ensure a voluntary and free choice in accordance with changing individual and cultural values".[87]

79 U.S. National Security Council, *National Security Study Memorandum 200*, 114.

80 See Davidson Gwatkin, "The State of the World's Population Movement: Implications of the 1984 Mexico City Conference," *World Development* 13, no. 4 (1985): 558.

81 Mohan Rao, *From Population Control to Reproductive Health: Malthusian Arithmetic* (SAGE, 2004), 112.

82 CONAPO, "Hacia Una Acción Internacional Para Frenar El Incremento de La Población," 1999, 70, https://www.gob.mx/cms/uploads/attachment/file/187565/Parte_III_-_Parte_VII.pdf. Consulted on May 4, 2021.

83 Lisa Richey, "Family Planning and the Politics of Population in Tanzania : International to Local Discourse," *The Journal of Modern African Studies* 37, no. 3 (1999): 461.

84 "Recommendations for Implementation of World Population Plan of Action," 1984, 24–26, https://www.unfpa.org/sites/default/files/event-pdf/Recommendations for implementation of World Population Plan of Action_1.pdf.

85 "Recommendations for Implementation of World Population Plan of Action," 26.

86 "Recommendations for Implementation of World Population Plan of Action," 27.

87 "Recommendations for Implementation of World Population Plan of Action," 37.

As for abortion, this was the first conference were American and Swedish representatives tried to frame this issue as a right, but the proposal was rejected.[88] The agreement reached finally calls "to take appropriate steps to help women avoid abortion, which in no case should be promoted as a method of family planning".[89]

The Cairo Conference and SRHR

The Fourth and most relevant World Population Conference was called the International Conference on Population and Development (ICPD) and it was held in Cairo in 1994. Its outcome document was the Programme of Action of the International Conference on Population Development, which like its predecessors is of a non-binding nature, full of reservations, and adopted with the strong opposition of several states, which drastically reduces its normative value.

The main concerns continued to be the growing population of the developing world, while the population of Europe decreased.[90] The opening statement of the Secretary General of the U.N. Boutros Boutros-Ghali highlights this concern: "States must be supported in their efforts to control population increase".[91]

An important contextual factor of this conference was the increasing momentum of human rights movements that had gained political attention since the 1970s.[92] Thus, the use of human rights language was popular, which provided an opportunity for civil society to be heard and actively participate in the decision-making processes. Also, there was a growing feminist movement that demanded increasing attention to women's rights and needs.

However, such a momentum also provided a political opportunity to frame population strategies in terms of human rights. This change of paradigm was attractive for some delegates because it framed sexuality in terms of

88 Grimes, "The Ideology of Population Control in the UN Draft Plan for Cairo," 215.
89 "Recommendations for Implementation of World Population Plan of Action," 31.
90 "Report of the International Conference on Population and Development" (Cairo, 1995), 32, https://documents-dds-ny.un.org/doc/UNDOC/GEN/N95/231/26/IMG/N9523126.pdf?OpenElement.
91 "Report of the International Conference on Population and Development," 158.
92 Bashford, *Global Population: History, Geopolitics, and Life on Earth*, 345.

women's autonomy over their reproduction, rather than as a form of population control.[93]

Based on these premises, the conference shifted from a population control paradigm to one of women's rights.[94] This allowed the population control lobby to be perceived as a pro-women's agenda and to gain the support of some feminist voices.[95] Accordingly, the Programme of Action of the ICPD shifted to highlight the relevance of contraception as an "unmet need" of the population in the developing world.[96]

It is in this troubling context where the new concept of "reproductive rights" first appeared in this document as a whole chapter.[97] Although the preamble of the ICPD is clear that it "does not create any new international human rights" rather "it affirms the application of universally recognized human rights standards to all aspects of population programmes".[98]

Like its predecessors, the ICDP Programme of Action remarks that it should be implemented "with full respect for the various religious and ethical values and cultural backgrounds of its people, and in conformity with universally recognized international human rights".[99] This principle is repeated several times throughout the document,[100] which indicates that internationally recognized human rights cannot be disregarded in the name of SRHR.

93 C. Alison McIntosh and Jason L. Finkle, "The Cairo Conference on Population and Development: A New Paradigm?," *Population and Development Review* 21, no. 2 (1995): 235–241.

94 Eager, "From Population Control to Reproductive Rights: Understanding Normative Change in Global Population Policy (1965–1994)," 146; Critchlow, *Intended Consequences: Birth Control, Abortion and the Federal Government in Modern America*, 178–181.

95 Jocelyn DeJong, "The Role and Limitations of the Cairo InternationalConference on Population and Developmen," *Social Science and Medicine* 51 (2000); Hartmann, "Liberal Ends, Illiberal Means: National Security, 'Environmental Conflict' and the Making of the Cairo Consensus"; Hodgson and Watkins, "Feminists and Neo-Malthusians: Past and Present Alliances"; Critchlow, "Birth Control, Population Control, and Family Planning: An Overview."

96 "Report of the International Conference on Population and Development"; Grimes, "The Ideology of Population Control in the UN Draft Plan for Cairo."

97 "Report of the International Conference on Population and Development," chap. VII.

98 "Report of the International Conference on Population and Development," 9.

99 "Report of the International Conference on Population and Development," 11.

100 "Report of the International Conference on Population and Development," paras. 1.15, 7.45, 7.47, 11.2, 11.11 and 15.13.

As for abortion, the document restated the agreement of 1984 in its paragraph 8.25: "governments should take appropriate steps to help women avoid abortion, which in no case should be promoted as a method of family planning".[101] It also established that the "prevention of unwanted pregnancies must always be given the highest priority and every attempt should be made to eliminate the need for abortion".[102] The program further states the following:

> Any measures or changes related to abortion within the health system can only be determined at the national or local level according to the national legislative process. In circumstances where abortion is not against the law, such abortion should be safe.[103]

Just as in other population conferences, the agreement of 1994 was not absent from controversies. Several states expressed reservations.[104] For instance, Afghanistan, Libya, the United Arab Emirates, Djibouti, Jordan, Syria, Yemen and Kuwait stated a general reservation regarding those parts that are not in conformity with Islamic Sharia and their ethical values. Brunei expressed a reservation on the definition of reproductive rights.

El Salvador, Honduras, Peru, Nicaragua, Paraguay, Guatemala, Ecuador, the Dominican Republic, and Argentina stated a reservation expressing that according to the American Convention of Human Rights of 1969 and their legislation life should be protected from conception. They also insisted that the concepts of "reproductive rights" and "family planning" should never include abortion. Libya, Malta, and the United Arab Emirates also indicated their opposition to the legalization of abortion as a means of family planning. Guatemala also expressed that "the General Assembly's mandate to the Conference does not extend to the creation or formulation of rights".[105]

The Peruvian representative stated that abortion should be tackled by education and responsible parenting, rather than through its legalization. Iran indicated that sexual education for adolescents should provide appropriate material, provided by the parents, and should be aimed at preventing moral and psychological diseases. The Holy See submitted a written statement expressing that the document "remains marked by an individualistic

101 "Report of the International Conference on Population and Development," 46.
102 "Report of the International Conference on Population and Development," 58–59.
103 "Report of the International Conference on Population and Development," para. 8.25.
104 All the reservations can be consulted in: "Report of the International Conference on Population and Development," 189–280.
105 "Report of the International Conference on Population and Development," 142.

understanding of sexuality which does not give due attention to the mutual love and decision-making that characterizes the conjugal relationship".[106]

The Follow-Up to the ICPD

There have been several conferences hosted as a follow-up to the ICPD. In all of them deep disagreement continues to be seen based on the same concerns regarding respect for different religious and cultural worldviews,[107] rejection to the category of SRHR as a new human right,[108] and objections to the imposition of measures such as the legalization of abortion.[109]

The most recent follow-up of the ICPD took place in 2019 in Nairobi (the Nairobi Summit or ICPD+25). It was organized by the government of Kenya, Denmark, and UNFPA. The summit was financed by Western European governments and private investment, like the Ford Foundation and Bayer.[110]

An interesting fact that indicates the level of disagreement is that for the first time, the follow-up was not an event organized by the U.N. General Assembly. On this topic, there have been several complains from pro-life groups alleging that they were excluded or banned from the meetings.[111] For this reason, protests were organized outside of the building that hosted the conference; this included Kenyan activists who requested the president cancel the summit.[112]

106 "Report of the International Conference on Population and Development," 145.

107 'Programme of Action of the International Conference on Population Development: 20th Anniversary Edition' (2014) <https://www.unfpa.org/sites/default/files/pub-pdf/programm e_of_action_Web ENGLISH.pdf> pp. 273–275. Consulted on January 8, 2020.

108 "Programme of Action of the International Conference on Population Development: 20th Anniversary Edition," 269.

109 "Programme of Action of the International Conference on Population Development: 20th Anniversary Edition," 267–81.

110 "Accelerating the Promise: The Report of the Nirobi Summit on ICPD25," 2019, 11, https://www.unfpa.org/sites/default/files/pub-pdf/Nairobi_Summit_Report_on_ICPD25.pdf. Consulted on January 8, 2020.

111 Melton, "UN Nairobi Summit on Population and Development Shuts Out the Pro-Life Message"; Nzwili and Fletcher, "US Rep At Nairobi Summit: No Support For Abortion In Family Planning"; "Kenya Hosts Top Reproductive Health Summit amid Storm over Abortion."

112 Nzwili and Fletcher, "US Rep At Nairobi Summit: No Support For Abortion In Family Planning"; "Kenya: Activists to Stage Protests in Nairobi Monday Against ICPD25+," *All Africa*, 2019, https://allafrica.com/stories/201911110079.html. Consulted on January 8, 2020.

Ignoring this situation, the UNFPA called the Nairobi Summit a "radically inclusive conference", which established "a shared agenda to complete the ICPD Programme of Action".[113] However, the outcome is a declaration adopted by some NGOs and drafted by the UNFPA, instead of a consensus-based document among state representatives.

In response, the U.S. government sponsored a statement that was joined by Brazil, Belarus, Egypt, Haiti, Hungary, Libya, Poland, Senegal, St. Lucia, and Uganda.[114] It criticized the preparation of the summit and its lack of consensus:

> We would have appreciated more transparency and inclusiveness in the preparation of the Conference, including regarding criteria for civil society participation. While the Cairo ICPD Program of Action was negotiated and implemented with and by the entire UN General Assembly membership, only a small handful of governments were consulted on the planning and modalities of the 2019 Nairobi Summit. Therefore, outcomes from this summit are not intergovernmentally negotiated, nor are they the result of a consensus process. As a result, they should not be considered normative, nor should they appear in future documents as intergovernmentally-agreed language.
>
> This Nairobi Summit is centered on only certain aspects of the ICPD Program of Action and does not fully reflect all views and positions of the Member States. In reality, the 2019 Nairobi Summit should have followed the spirit of the careful and delicate negotiations that led to the consensus-based 1994 ICPD Program of Action. Unless negotiated and adopted by consensus of all Member States, within the process and structure of an international body such as the UN General Assembly, no ICPD follow-on document has consensual weight or standing amongst governments.[115]

The statement also reaffirmed that the program should be implemented "with full respect for the various religious and ethical values and cultural backgrounds of its people, and in conformity with universally recognized international human rights".[116] The text also stresses that the original agreement regarding abortion has been ignored:

113 UNFPA, Nairobi Summit on ICPD25 ends with a clear path forward to transform the world for women and girls" (14 November 2019) <https://www.unfpa.org/press/nairobi-summit-icpd25-ends-clear-path-forward-transform-world-women-and-girls>. Consulted on May 20, 2020.

114 U.S. Department of Health and Human Services, "Joint Statement on the Nairobi Summit," 2019, https://srhrindex.srhrforall.org/uploads/2020/04/2019_Joint-Statement-on-the-Nairobi-Summit-on-the-ICPD25.pdf. Consulted on January 8, 2023.

115 "Joint Statement on the Nairobi Summit."

116 "Joint Statement on the Nairobi Summit."

> There is no international right to abortion; in fact, international law clearly states that "everyone has the right to life" [...] any measures or changes related to abortion within the health system can only be determined at the national or local level according to the national legislative process' [...]. This legislative process should reflect the democratic expression of the will of the people, through their freely elected representatives.[117]

Another important resolution was adopted in September of 2019, during the U.N. General Assembly high-level meeting on universal health coverage. A coalition between the U.S., Bahrain, Belarus, Brazil, Democratic Republic of the Congo, Egypt, Guatemala, Haiti, Hungary, Iraq, Libya, Mali, Nigeria, Poland, Russia, Saudi Arabia, Sudan, United Arab Emirates, and Yemen presented a joint statement, which declared that

> We do not support references to ambiguous terms and expressions, such as sexual and reproductive health and rights in U.N. documents, because they can undermine the critical role of the family and promote practices, like abortion, in circumstances that do not enjoy international consensus and which can be misinterpreted by U.N. agencies.
>
> Such terms do not adequately take into account the key role of the family in health and education, nor the sovereign right of nations to implement health policies according to their national context. There is no international right to an abortion and these terms should not be used to promote pro-abortion policies and measures [...].
>
> We therefore request that the U.N., including U.N. agencies, focus on concrete efforts that enjoy broad consensus among member states. To that end, only documents that have been adopted by all Member States should be cited in U.N. resolutions.[118]

In 2020, the U.S. presented to the U.N. General Assembly the Geneva Consensus Declaration on Promoting Women's Health and Strengthening the Family, signed by 34 countries.[119] This document reemphasizes that abortion is not a human right and that this decision should be taken at the national level

117 "Joint Statement on the Nairobi Summit."

118 HHS, Joint Statement on Universal Health Coverage, 74th Session of the UN General Assembly (23 September 2019) <https://www.hhs.gov/about/agencies/oga/global-health-diplomacy/protecting-life-global-health-policy/joint-statement-unga/index.html>. Consulted on February 11, 2022.

119 U.N. General Assembly, "Geneva Consensus Declaration on Promoting Women's Health and Strengthening the Family", A/75/626 (7 December 2020) <https://documents-dds-ny.un.org/doc/UNDOC/GEN/N20/344/30/PDF/N2034430.pdf?OpenElement>. Consulted on July 8, 2022.

through the regular legislative and democratic process, which provoked the outrage of Western media.[120]

World Conferences on Women

Parallel to the population conferences, the U.N. hosted four World Conferences on Women. The most relevant and controversial one was the event held in 1995 in Beijing. The outcome document was the Beijing Declaration and Platform for Action (Beijing Platform for Action).

Regarding abortion, this instrument restated the agreement reached in Cairo in 1994.[121] As in the population conferences, several states issued reservations and interpretative statements related to objections to abortion, respect to the right to self-determination, and concerns about the violation of other human rights through the implementation of SRHR.[122] The reservation of Malaysia reflects the general environment of the conference: "I wish to state that certain provisions within the Platform for Action remain unacceptable to us, but in the interest of achieving a consensus, we do not wish to stand in the way of its adoption".[123]

On the other hand, it is relevant to point out the topics that were left out of the debate regarding women's dignity due to an overemphasis of SRHR. The delegation of the Holy See, chaired by the Harvard law professor Mary Ann Glendon, regretted that no obligation "to provide care and assistance to motherhood" was incorporated in the final document, as required by article 25 of the UDHR.[124] Glendon stated that "this selectivity thus marks another step in the colonization of the broad and rich discourse of universal rights by an impoverished, libertarian rights dialect".[125] She argued during the conference:

> Surely we can do better than to address the health needs of girls and women by paying disproportionate attention to sexual and reproductive health [...] A document

120 Ariana Eunjung, "U.S. Joins 19 Nations, Including Saudi Arabia and Russia: 'There Is No International Right to an Abortion,'" *The Washington Post*, 2019, https://www.washingtonpost.com/health/2019/09/24/us-joins-nations-including-saudi-arabia-russia-there-is-no-international-right-an-abortion/.

121 "Beijing Declaration and Platform for Action" (Beijing, 1995), 40, https://www.un.org/womenwatch/daw/beijing/platform/index.html. Consulted on January 8, 2021.

122 ibid., 154–174.

123 "Report of the Fourth World Conference on Women," 166.

124 "Report of the Fourth World Conference on Women," 159.

125 idem.

> that respects women's dignity should address the health of the whole woman. A document that respects women's intelligence should devote at least as much attention to literacy as to fertility.[126]

Since the beginning, the preparatory document for Beijing was full of bracketed language, which indicated deep disagreement in key areas.[127] SRHR were deeply contested, not just from the point of view of states, but also of civil society. Western, educated, and middle-class feminists were the main representatives of a liberal position,[128] while women's groups from developing countries advocated for a more holistic vision of development focused on employment, basic health care, and the protection of children.[129]

Third World women have been highly concerned about coercive population policies, side effects of contraceptives, and the lack of choice for women when deciding over the methods to regulate their fertility.[130] However, non-Western women only appear in the media when they embrace liberal viewpoints; while their more conservative peers are overlooked and considered as an irrelevant "minority" or caricaturized as "as anti-woman, anti-sex, and in favor of unrestrained procreation".[131]

As in the case of population conferences, a deeper understanding of what happened in Beijing requires to see the broader context. In this regard, Mary Ann Glendon wrote an article about her experience during the event:

> At one point, when our negotiator attempted to intervene in support of a bracketed paragraph urging that women be informed of the health risks of promiscuity and certain contraceptive methods, the Chair ruled her out of order on grounds that the Holy See, as a Permanent Observer, did not even have the right to vote. By the time the Chair was forced to retract that mistake, the language in question had been eliminated. The tenor of discussion on the issue is captured by the remark of an Egyptian

126 "Report of the Fourth World Conference on Women," 160.

127 See Margaret E. Keck and Kathryn Sikkink, *Activists Beyond Borders: Advocacy Networks in International Politics* (Cornell University Press, 1998), 188.

128 See Jael Silliman, "Making the Connections: Women's Health and Environmental Justice," *Race, Gender & Class* 5, no. 1 (1997): 106.

129 See Keck and Sikkink, *Activists Beyond Borders: Advocacy Networks in International Politics*, 184–190.

130 See Keck and Sikkink, *Activists Beyond Borders: Advocacy Networks in International Politics*, 184–190.

131 See Mary Ann Glendon, "What Happened at Beijing," *First Things*, 2019, https://www.firstthings.com/article/1996/01/005-what-happened-at-beijing.

delegate: "If we start telling women about the harmful effects of contraceptives, they might not use them anymore".[132]

Also, a minority coalition led by fifteen member states of the European Union contested every effort to include the word "motherhood", except in a negative sense, and all references to religion or morals, except when presented in terms of intolerance or extremism.[133] This coalition also objected to an inclusion of freedom of conscience and religion in the context of education, although this is a right recognized by the UDHR, because the coalition was opposed to any inclusion of parental rights in the document.[134] These positions made no sense, for they were contrary to the prevailing provisions of most European constitutions, which reflected a more moderate view of sexuality at the time.

Several Western representatives that advocated for a liberal view were facing internal struggles. The sponsors of the conference themselves disregarded that there was no consensus on these topics even among their own citizens.[135] They acted on behalf of their governments, but not on behalf of their people.

In all these international conferences it is evident that the topics of reproduction and sexuality as part of IHRL are deeply contested issues. The outcomes of these events point more towards disagreement, rather than to consensus.

Framing Contraception as a Human Rights Obligation

As explained, the incorporation of SRHR as part of the international debate emerged out of non-binding instruments in the context of intergovernmental conferences about an increasing concern with population growth. Moreover, the adoption of these instruments was based on mixed intentions, rather than the protection of freedom, equality and human dignity.

However, as human rights mechanisms ignore this troubled background and adopt the parameters of liberal universality, they have developed

132 Glendon.
133 Glendon.
134 Glendon.
135 See R. Inglehart et al., "World Values Survey: Round Six—Country-Pooled Datafile Version," World Values Survey, 2014, http://www.worldvaluessurvey.org/WVSDocumentationWV6.jsp. Consulted on January 8, 2019.

interpretations that conceive contraception and abortion (as part of SRHR) as internationally recognized human rights obligations. This situation is problematic, for there is no legal basis in IHRL to support such a conclusion.

As will be developed in the following paragraphs, human rights mechanisms do not rely on the text of human rights treaties or customary law as sources for their interpretations, rather they develop their arguments based on philosophical and cultural premises that belong to the anthropological view of liberal universality.

A case in point is the Committee on Economic, Social and Cultural Rights (CESCR). In 2016 the CESCR adopted General Comment 22 on the right to sexual and reproductive health. This category is not enlisted in the ICESCR, but the CESCR argued that it was part of article 12 (the right to the enjoyment of the highest attainable standard of physical and mental health).

Regardless of that, the CESCR decided to hold a Day of General Discussion in November of 2010 on SRHR. The aim of this event was to gather ideas, opinions, and perspectives from different states and members of the civil society, so they can contribute to the interpretations developed by the CESCR for each right.[136]

All the invited panelists focused on a liberal interpretation of sexual and reproductive issues. Their main concerns were to provide more contraceptive methods, the legalization of abortion, and access to sexual and reproductive services for children and adolescents.[137] Some submissions from NGOs and academics also advocated for the same approach.

On the other hand, from the 23 submissions that the CESCR received from NGOs and academicians, at least 11 of them advocated for a different perspective on sexual and reproductive issues.[138] Some NGOs indicated that there was no provision on SRHR or abortion in the CESCR and that such an interpretation would be an ultra vires act on the part of the committee. They also contended that there was no right to abortion and that its promotion was excluded from the Cairo and the Beijing consensus. Other NGOs pointed out

136 Magdalena Sepúlveda, *The Nature of the Obligations under the International Covenant on Economic, Social and Cultural Rights* (Intersentia, 2003), 42.

137 All the interventions can be consulted in the web page of the CESCR: <https://www.ohchr.org/EN/HRBodies/CESCR/Pages/ContributionsDGD2010.aspx>. Consulted on September 2, 2020.

138 All the submissions can be consulted at: "Day of General Discussion on 'the Right to Sexual and Reproductive Health'", 15 November 2010, UNHCHR, https://www.ohchr.org/EN/HRBodies/CESCR/Pages/Discussion2010.aspx.

the need to respond to the economic needs of families and to help people to achieve their desired number of children, which in some socioeconomic contexts is difficult. Other submissions argued that the approach of the CESCR was very narrow and disregarded important aspects of sexual and reproductive health not related to contraception and abortion. Some NGOs that advocated for the rights of persons with disabilities remarked the need to protect people against forced sterilizations, forced abortions, and forced contraception, and insisted that these practices continue to be highly common.

Some academicians also argued that sexuality is understood in different ways in different societies and for that reason the CESCR could not adopt a liberal-uniform interpretation. Others noted the importance of highlighting the side effects of modern contraception and promoting non-harmful alternatives for the people that wish to regulate their fertility.

As can be appreciated, the General Discussion Day reflected the same diversity and controversies that took place in Cairo and Beijing, which pointed towards a lack of consensus on SRHR. However, the CESCR opted for liberal universality and disregarded the notorious lack of consensus on such a sensitive topic.

Although the General Comment states that the services and goods provided as SRHR "must be respectful of the culture of individuals, minorities, peoples and communities",[139] the problem is that this culturally sensitive approach is reduced to external aspects, like respecting different food habits and dress codes, but cultural diversity in its robust sense (different viewpoints and beliefs) is excluded. This is seen when "cultural acceptability" of sexual and reproductive issues is narrowly framed in terms of providing access to minorities and indigenous peoples, regardless of whether they agree or disagree with a liberal vision of sexuality.[140]

In other cases, a "culturally sensitive" approach is based on a strategy to understand local culture and religion, so it can be transformed from the inside to fit what liberal activists consider as appropriate. This is the approach followed by UNFPA. Its model of "cultural sensitivity" requires analyzing the political and cultural realities "to develop knowledge about the possibility of

139 CESCR, General Comment 22 (2016) on the right to sexual and reproductive health (article 12 of the International Covenant on Economic, Social and Cultural Rights), 2 May 2016, E/C.12/GC/22, para 20.

140 Special Rapporteur (Paul Hunt), The right of everyone to the enjoyment of the highest attainable standard of physical and mental health (16 February 2014) E/CN.4/2004/49, para 41.

change", in order to develop community acceptance of a liberal program of sexuality through "pressure groups".[141]

Following the same approach, the rest of the CESCR's General Comment framed sexual and reproductive health mainly as access to contraceptive methods and abortion, in terms of states' obligations to guarantee autonomy, privacy, and non-discrimination.[142] However, this idea of non-discrimination in practice discriminates against interdependent and religiously grounded worldviews without an objective and legally grounded reason, as required by human rights treaty bodies themselves.[143]

The CESCR's remarks regarding states' reports on the implementation of the ICESCR also reveal this problem. For instance, recently, the CESCR has insisted on the need to increase the use and provision of contraception, despite the high prevalence of people that are morally opposed to it. This is the case of the concluding observations of 2018 on Pakistan,[144] 2017 on Kenya,[145] 2017 on the Philippines,[146] and 2016 on Uganda.[147] The same approach is followed by the Human Rights Committee (HRC) regarding the provision of more

141 UNFPA, *Integrating Human Rights, Culture and Gender in Programming* (UNFPA 2009) 21-22.

142 CESCR, General Comment 22 (2016) on the right to sexual and reproductive health (article 12 of the International Covenant on Economic, Social and Cultural Rights), 2 May 2016, E/C.12/GC/22, para 34 and 36.

143 HRC, General Comment No. 18: Non-discrimination, Thirty-seven session (1989), para 13: "not every differentiation of treatment will constitute discrimination, if the criteria for such differentiation are reasonable and objective and if the aim is to achieve a purpose which is legitimate under the Covenant". The same parameters have been adopted by the CESCR, General Comment No. 20: Non-discrimination in economic, social and cultural rights (article 2, para. 2, of the International Covenant on Economic, Social and Cultural Rights) 2 July 2009, E/C.12/GC/20, para 9.

144 CESCR, Concluding observations on the initial report of Pakistan, 20 July 2017, E/C.12/PAK/CO/1, paras 77 and 78 The same approach in Pakistan is taken by the CEDAW: CEDAW, Concluding observations on the fifth periodic report of Pakistan (10 March 2020) CEDAW/C/PAK/CO/5, para 43.

145 CESCR, Concluding observations on the combined second to fifth periodic reports of Kenya, 6 April 2016, E/C.12/KEN/CO/2-5, paras 53 and 54.

146 CESCR, Concluding observations on the combined fifth and sixth periodic reports of the Philippines, 26 October 2016, E/C.12/PHL/CO/5-6, paras 51 and 52.

147 CESCR, Concluding observations on the initial report of Uganda, 8 July 2015, E/C.12/UGA/CO/1, para 35

contraception in Nigeria (2018),[148] Pakistan (2016),[149] and Ghana (2015),[150] among other states.

In the case of the HRC, this situation is even more controversial. The HRC argues that SRHR are part of its mandate based on the right to life (article 6 of the ICCPR), the principle of non-discrimination (article 3), the prohibition of torture and inhuman or degrading treatment (article 7) and the right to privacy (article 17). Such interpretation of these provisions is only evident within a liberal cultural view, but not from the ordinary meaning of the treaty or the prevailing international consensus on this subject.

Beyond this lack of legal basis, the CESCR and the HRC insisted on the need to provide more contraception, disregarding that these countries have high percentages of people who are morally opposed to artificial contraception. In Pakistan, for example, the percentage of people who are morally opposed to this practice is of 65 percent.[151] In Kenya the opposition is of 33 percent, in the Philippines of 29 percent, in Ghana of 52 percent, in Nigeria of 54 percent, and in Uganda of 38 percent.[152] There are other African countries that also show considerable percentages of disapproval for artificial contraception: Senegal 28 percent, South Africa 15 percent, and Tunisia 39 percent.[153]

This liberal approach implies that the limited resources of human rights treaty bodies are used only for the interests of some groups. While liberal concerns are overemphasized, other demands (expressly agreed in human rights treaties) are disregarded. For example, the protection of maternity and maternal health is only mentioned three times in the whole General Comment No. 22 of the CESCR, with a secondary phrase that states "special measures, both

148 HRC, Concluding observations on Nigeria in the absence of its second periodic report (29 August 2019), CCPR/C/NGA/CO/2, paras 22 and 23.

149 HRC, Concluding observations on the initial report of Pakistan (23 August 2017) CCPR/C/PAK/CO/1, paras 15–16.

150 HRC, Concluding observations on the initial reports of Ghana (9 August 2016) CCPR/C/GHA/CO/1, paras 23 and 24.

151 "Global Morality," Pew Research Center, 2014, https://www.pewresearch.org/global/interactives/global-morality/; Michael Lipka, "Africans among the Most Morally Opposed to Contraception," Pew Research Center, 2014, https://www.pewresearch.org/fact-tank/2014/04/16/africans-among-the-most-morally-opposed-to-contraception/.

152 Lipka, "Africans among the Most Morally Opposed to Contraception."

153 "Global Morality."

temporary and permanent, are necessary to accelerate the de facto equality of women and to protect maternity.[154]

This marginal consideration of maternity cannot be legally explained, for this is one of the human rights protected by the UDHR (article 25) and the Convention on the Elimination of All Forms of Discrimination against Women (CEDAW Convention) in articles 5.b and 11. This bias is also evident in that the CESCR has not developed a General Comment on article 10 of the CESCR, which establishes the rights of the family, the protection of maternity and children, and the rights of working mothers. It is puzzling that the CESCR has developed a General Comment on SRHR, which is a category not included in its mandate, while it has not developed explicitly included provisions.

Moreover, this overemphasis on abortion and contraception, disregards other concerns, like the Western family gap between achieved fertility and the desired number of kids.[155] As a report of the Organization for Economic Co-operation and Development (OECD) has pointed out: "in all countries the number of children women intend to have is far above the actual number they already have, which points to barriers in family formation".[156]

This oblivion of other demands is also prevalent in the report system of the CESCR. The majority of concluding observations do not mention any measures regarding the protection of the family and mothers. The most common mention of maternal health is only linked to encourage the legalization of abortion,[157] disregarding that there is no consensus in literature on whether

154 CESCR, General Comment 22 (2016) on the right to sexual and reproductive health (article 12 of the International Covenant on Economic, Social and Cultural Rights), 2 May 2016, E/C.12/GC/22, para 27. Also see paras 18 and 45.

155 Arnaud Régnier-Loilier and Daniele Vignoli, "Fertility Intentions and Obstacles to Their Realization in France and Italy," *Population* 66, no. 2 (2011); Dimiter Philipov, "Fertility Intentions and Outcomes: The Role of Policies to Close the Gap," *European Journal of Population* 25 (2009).

156 OECD, OECD Family Database "SF2.2: Ideal and actual number of children" (2016), 3 <http://www.oecd.org/els/family/database.htm>. Consulted on May 22, 2020.

157 See CESCR, Concluding observations on the initial report of Burundi, 16 October 2015, E/C.12/BDI/CO/1, paras 53 and 54; CESCR, Concluding observations on the third periodic report of Nepal, 12 December 2014, E/C.12/NPL/CO/3, para 26; CESCR, Concluding observations on the second to fourth periodic report of Rwanda, adopted by the Committee at its fiftieth session, 10 June 2013, E/C.12/RWA/CO/2-4, para 26; CESCR, Concluding observations of the Committee on Economic, Social and Cultural Rights on Sri Lanka, 9 December 2010, E/C.12/LKA/CO/2-4, para 34 ; and CESCR, Concluding observations of

or not this practice actually helps to reduce maternal mortality rates.[158] Moreover, the top global causes of maternal mortality do not enjoy the same privilege, such as hemorrhage, sepsis, pre-eclampsia and eclampsia, which amount to 67 percent of maternal deaths worldwide.[159]

Also, the concluding observations minimally address other pressing health related concerns, like infant mortality, the healthy development of children, improvement of the environment, and the prevention and treatment of epidemic, endemic, occupational and other diseases, which are expressly provided by the right to health as established in article 12 of the ICESCR.

The CESCR has also insisted that other "barriers" to sexual and reproductive rights include parental authorization for children's and adolescents' "access to sexual and reproductive health services and information, including for abortion and contraception".[160] The Committee on the Rights of the Child (CRC) has taken the same approach, arguing that "states should review and consider allowing children to consent to certain medical treatments and interventions without the permission of a parent, caregiver, or guardian", such as "contraception and safe abortion".[161]

Article 24 of the Convention on the Rights of the Child does not establish such an interpretation of the right to health. Rather the UDHR and the Convention on the Rights of the Child state the contrary. Article 26 of the UDHR provides for the right of parents to decide the education of their children, which evidently includes sexual and reproductive issues.[162] Articles 3, 5 and 29 of the Convention on the Rights of the Child expressly establish

the Committee on Economic, Social and Cultural Rights on Uruguay, 1 December 2010, E/C.12/URY/CO/3-4, para 24.

158 Elard Koch et al., "Abortion Legislation, Maternal Healthcare, Fertility, Female Literacy, Sanitation, Violence against Women and Maternal Deaths: A Natural Experiment in 32 Mexican States," *BMJ Open* 5, no. 2 (February 1, 2015), https://doi.org/10.1136/bmjopen-2014-006013. Consulted on October 12, 2020.

159 Special rapporteur on the right to health (Paul Hunt), The right of everyone to the enjoyment of the highest attainable standard of physical and mental health (13 September 2006) A/61/338, para 7.

160 CESCR, General Comment 22 (2016) on the right to sexual and reproductive health (article 12 of the International Covenant on Economic, Social and Cultural Rights), para 41.

161 CRC, General comment No. 15 (2013) on the right of the child to the enjoyment of the highest attainable standard of health (art. 24), CRC/C/GC/15, (17 April 2013), 5.

162 UDHR (1948) <https://www.un.org/en/universal-declaration-human-rights/>. Consulted on June 9, 2020.

the obligation of states to respect the rights and responsibilities of parents to provide care and guidance to their children and to educate them according to their values.[163]

Another consequence of the prevailing paradigm is that human rights mechanisms only consider harmful practices related to religion and culture in the family space, which is generally perceived as a dangerous place constituted for the oppression of women.[164] However, it disregards serious women's rights violations, which receive less attention and occur both in Western and non-Western settings, like human trafficking, pornography, and prostitution. Unlike contraception and abortion, these practices are expressly condemned by the CEDAW convention[165] and are widely considered as deplorable.

As a recent investigation published in *The New York Times* highlights, the major pornography companies distribute videos of "child rapes, revenge pornography, spy cam videos of women showering, racist and misogynist content, and footage of women being asphyxiated in plastic bags".[166] Nevertheless, this problem is rarely condemned by human rights mechanisms, for pornography has become an acceptable cultural practice in Western societies that fits the parameters of liberal universality.

Such biases have led the Committee on the Emination of Discrimination again Women (CEDAW) to expressed concern over the criminalization of prostitution in some states and has requested its legalization,[167] despite that its founding treaty,[168] and the Beijing's Conference of Women of

163 Convention on the Rights of the Child (1980) <https://www.ohchr.org/en/professionalinterest/pages/crc.aspx>. Consulted on June 9, 2020.

164 See UNFPA, *Against my will: Defying the practices that harm women and girls and undermine equality* (2020), 15 and 17; and Working group on discrimination against women in law and in practice, Report of the Working Group on the issue of discrimination against women in law and in practice, A/HRC/29/40 (2 April 2015).

165 Convention on the Elimination of all forms of Violence against Women (1979), art. 6 <https://www.ohchr.org/documents/professionalinterest/cedaw.pdf>. Consulted on September 20, 2020.

166 Nicholas Kristof, "The Children of Pornhub," *The New York Times*, 2020, https://www.nytimes.com/2020/12/04/opinion/sunday/pornhub-rape-trafficking.html?action=click&module=Opinion&pgtype=Homepage. Consulted on October 12, 2020.

167 See CEDAW, Summary record of the 884th meeting, forty-third session, CEDAW/C/SR.884, (27 May 2009), para 38.

168 CEDAW Convention (1979), art. 6 <https://www.ohchr.org/documents/professionalinterest/cedaw.pdf>. Consulted on September 20, 2020.

1995[169] condemn prostitution as a form of women's exploitation. This controversial approach to prostitution has also been adopted by some Western NGOs, like Amnesty International,[170] disregarding its harmful effects. These actors have ignored the evidence provided by the Special rapporteur on trafficking in persons based on her visits and expertise:

> For the most part, prostitution as actually practised in the world usually does satisfy the elements of trafficking. It is rare that one finds a case in which the path to prostitution and/or a person's experiences within prostitution do not involve, at the very least, an abuse of power and/or an abuse of vulnerability.[171]

As in the case of prostitution, this liberal perspective is blind towards the utilization of abortion and contraception as a form of exploitation of vulnerability.[172] The prevalence of these violations points out that many women that recur to the protection of their human rights are more concerned about the coercive effects of the legalization of abortion than its liberating promises.[173]

Many women around the globe undergo abortion forced by their male partners[174] or by socioeconomic circumstances,[175] rather than by their free and

169 "Report of the World Conference of the United Nations Decade for Women: Equality, Development and Peace" (Copenhagen, 1980), 55, https://www.un.org/womenwatch/daw/beijing/otherconferences/Copenhagen/Copenhagen Full Optimized.pdf.

170 "Q&A: Policy to Protect the Human Rights of Sex Workers," Amnesty International, https://www.amnesty.org/en/qa-policy-to-protect-the-human-rights-of-sex-workers/. Consulted on October 12, 2020.

171 Special rapporteur on trafficking in persons, especially women and children (Sigma Huda), Report of the Special Rapporteur on the human rights aspects of the victims of trafficking in persons, especially women and children, E/CN.4/2006/62 (20 February 2006), paras 42–43.

172 Special rapporteur on the right to health (Anand Grover), Right of everyone to the enjoyment of the highest attainable standard of physical and mental health (3 August 2011) A/66/254, para 12.

173 Several recent cases, where stories of forced abortion served to prove a situation of violence against women at different treaty bodies suggest this conclusion. See the following cases, all of them related to women who were forced to abort by their male partners: CRC, *Y and Z v. Finland* (15 May 2019) CRC/C/81/D/6/2016, para 2.1; CAT, *Mayantie Jasmina Soumahoro v. the Netherlands* (3 May 2019) CAT/C/66/D/757/2016, para 4.3; HRC, *Khairullo Saidov v. Tajikistan* (4 April 2018) CCPR/C/122/D/2680/2015, para 4.7; CEDAW, *J. I. v. Finland* (5 May 2018) CEDAW/C/69/D/103/2016, para 2.1; and CAT, *Y. H. G. v. Australia* (14 November 2013) CAT/C/51/D/434/2010, para 4.5.

174 Farmer, *By Their Fruits: Eugenics, Population Control, and the Abortion Campaign*, 51–52.

175 Sophia Chae and others, "Reasons Why Women Have Induced Abortions: A Synthesis of Findings from 14 Countries" (2017) 96 Contraception 233; Rachel K Jones, Lori

informed choice. The World Health Organization (WHO) and several studies have reported the close link between recurrence to and repeated abortions with intimate partner violence.[176]

Although the condemnation of these practices by human rights mechanisms is marginal, several recent cases at the ECtHR[177] and the CEDAW[178] demonstrate that forced sterilization and forced abortion continues to be a common practice. In 2019, the Special rapporteur on violence against women also recognized that forced abortions, forced sterilization, and forced contraception are widespread violations.[179] She indicated that a significant number of women have undergone these procedures either because of pure coercion, manipulation, or because they have been misled or misinformed.[180] General Comment No. 22 of the CESCR only dedicates three brief phrases to condemn these practices,[181] in contrast to all the attention paid to the legalization of abortion and the distribution of contraception.

Some other human rights actors have gone even further in their perspectives. They have labeled interdependent and religiously grounded sexual perspectives as dangerous, assuming that there is an international obligation to eradicate other visions. A case in point is the work of the Special Rapporteur in the field of cultural rights, Karima Bennoune. In 2017, she adopted two

Frohwirth and Ann M Moore, "More than Poverty: Disruptive Events among Women Having Abortions in the U.S.," *BMJ Sexual and Reproductive Health* 39 (2013).

176 "Global Status Report on Violence Prevention 2014," 2014, 16; Angela Citernesi et al., "Intimate Partner Violence and Repeat Induced Abortion in Italy: A Cross Sectional Study," *The European Journal of Contraception & Reproductive Health Care* 20, no. 5 (2015); Jay G. Silverman et al., "Male Perpetration of Intimate Partner Violence and Involvement in Abortions and Abortion-Related Conflict," *American Journal of Public Health* 100, no. 8 (2010).

177 ECtHR, *I. G. and others v. Slovakia* (Application no. 15966/04) 29 April 2013; ECtHR, *V. C. v. Slovakia* (Application no. 18968/07), 8 February 2012; ECtHR, *K.H. and others v. Slovakia* (Application no. 32881/04), 28 April 2009; and ECtHR, *L. H. v. Latvia* (Application no. 52019/07) 29 July 2014.

178 CEDAW, *J.D. et al. V. Czech Republic* (16 July 2019) CEDAW/C/73/D/102/2016; and CEDAW, *Andrea Szijjarto v. Hungary* (14 August 2006) CEDAW/C/36/D/4/2004.

179 Special rapporteur on violence against women (Dubravka Šimonović), A human rights-based approach to mistreatment and violence against women in reproductive health services with a focus on childbirth and obstetric violence, (11 July 2019) A/74/137, para 21.

180 Special rapporteur on violence against women (Dubravka Šimonović).

181 CESCR, General Comment 22 (2016) on the right to sexual and reproductive health (article 12 of the International Covenant on Economic, Social and Cultural Rights), 2 May 2016, E/C.12/GC/22, para 30 and 57–59.

reports that focused on the impact of fundamentalism and extremism on women's cultural rights. She contends that "anti-rights" trends and "fundamentalists and extremists" are attacking women's SRHR.[182]

With these labels she refers to all people that are opposed to a liberal interpretation of sexuality.[183] A similar approach has been followed by the U.N. deputy high commissioner for human rights, Kate Gilmore, who called opposition to abortion "extremist hate" and "torture" at the Human Rights Council.[184]

Ms. Bennoune argues that these people aim at the destruction of human rights, undermine universality, and "cannot be viewed as human rights defenders".[185] From the perspective of the dissenters, these affirmations are out of touch with reality. They imply that most of the world population are "extreme fundamentalists". This way of labelling dissenting opinions on sexual matters is in stark contrast with what the U.N. General Assembly and the Security Council actually consider extremism, which refers to serious violations of international law, such as genocide or sexual enslavement.[186] These kinds of statements demonize disagreement and reveal a deep ignorance regarding the true reasons to oppose a liberal vision of sexuality, which have nothing to do with oppression of women, especially if many women embrace it.

Framing Abortion as a Human Rights Obligation

Despite the lack of a legal basis and international consensus on abortion, as in the case of contraception, several human rights treaty bodies have insisted on the need to legalize it as an international obligation.

182 Special rapporteur on cultural rights (Karima Bennoune), Report of the Special Rapporteur in the field of cultural rights (16 January 2017) A/HRC/34/56, para 3; and Special rapporteur on cultural rights (Karima Bennoune), Report of the Special Rapporteur in the field of cultural rights (17 July 2017) A/72/155, para 40.

183 Special rapporteur on cultural rights (Karima Bennoune), Report of the Special Rapporteur in the field of cultural rights (17 July 2017) A/72/155, paras 70–72 and 88–94.

184 Ford, "US Abortion Policy Is 'extremist Hate' and 'Torture', Says UN Commissioner."

185 Special rapporteur on cultural rights (Karima Bennouna), Report of the Special Rapporteur in the field of cultural rights (16 January 2017) A/HRC/34/56, para 39.

186 U.N. General Assembly, Plan of Action to Prevent Violent Extremism: Report of the Secretary-General (24 December 2015) A/70/674, para 19. Also see: Security Council, Resolution 2250 (2015), S/RES/2250 (9 December 2015), paras 6–8.

A relevant example is the CEDAW, which has interpreted that the protection of women's rights involves the obligation to provide abortions,[187] and labeled its prohibition as a form of violence against women,[188] disregarding that there is no legal basis for such a statement in the CEDAW Convention.

Another example is the CESC, which has indicated that the denial of abortion can amount to a violation of the right to life and security and can constitute torture or cruel, inhuman, or degrading treatment,[189] although that no mention of such issues is found in its founding treaty. The CESCR has interpreted that restrictions on abortion are "not compatible with other fundamental rights, such as the woman's right to health and life, and it is not consistent with the dignity of women".[190]

In other cases, the CESCR has directly ordered decriminalizing abortion and providing access to it, as in the concluding observations of Ecuador of 2020,[191] Senegal of 2020,[192] Mauritius of

187 CEDAW, General Recommendation No. 30 on women in conflict prevention, conflict and post-conflict situations (1 November 2013) CEDAW/C/GC/30, para 52; and CEDAW, General Recommendation No. 35 on gender based violence against women, updating general recommendation No. 19 (26 July 2017) CEDAW/C/GC/35, paras 18 and 29; CEDAW, General Recommendation No. 34 (2016) on the rights of rural women (7 March 2016) CEDAW/C/GC/34, paras 37–39; CEDAW, General Recommendation No. 37 (2018) on the gender-related dimensions of disaster risk reduction in the context of climate change (13 March 2018) CEDAW/C/GC/37, para 68. Also see : CEDAW, Concluding observations on the sixth periodic report of Zimbabwe (10 March 2020) CEDAW/C/ZWE/CO/6, para 39; CEDAW, Concluding observations on the sixth periodic report of Eritrea (10 March 2020) CEDAW/C/ERI/CO/6, para 39; CEDAW, Concluding observations on the fifth periodic report of Pakistan (10 March 2020) CEDAW/C/PAK/CO/5, para 43; CEDAW, Concluding observations on the third periodic report of Afghanistan (10 March 2020) CEDAW/C/AFG/CO/3, para 47; CEDAW, Concluding observations on the fourth periodic report of Côte d'Ivoire (30 July 2019) CEDAW/C/CIV/CO/4, para 43.

188 CEDAW, General Recommendation No. 35 on gender based violence against women, updating general recommendation No. 19, (26 July 2017) CEDAW/C/GC/35, para 29.

189 CESCR, General Comment 22 (2016) on the right to sexual and reproductive health (article 12 of the International Covenant on Economic, Social and Cultural Rights), 2 May 2016, E/C.12/GC/22, para 10.

190 CESCR, Concluding observations on the sixth periodic report of Poland, 26 October 2016, E/C.12/POL/CO/6, para 47.

191 CESCR, Concluding observations on the fourth periodic report of Ecuador, 14 November 2019, E/C.12/ECU/CO/4, para 52.

192 CESCR, Concluding observations on the third periodic report of Senegal, 13 November 2019, E/C.12/SEN/CO/3, paras 36 and 37.

2020,[193] Cameroon 2020,[194] Argentina in 2019,[195] Pakistan 2018,[196] Dominican Republic in 2017,[197] Burkina Faso in 2017,[198] Honduras in 2017,[199] Kenya 2017,[200] Poland 2017,[201] the Philippines 2017,[202] Morocco in 2016,[203] Uganda in 2016,[204] Venezuela in 2016,[205] Chile in 2016,[206] Paraguay in 2016,[207] Uganda in 2016,[208] Guatemala 2015,[209] El Salvador 2015,[210] Sri Lanka

193 CESCR, Concluding observations on the fifth periodic report of Mauritius, 5 April 2019, E/C.12/MUS/CO/5, paras 51 and 52.

194 CESCR, Concluding observations on the fourth periodic report of Cameroon, 25 March 2019, E/C.12/CMR/CO/4, paras 58 and 59.

195 CESCR, Concluding observations on the fourth periodic report of Argentina, 1 November 2018, E/C.12/ARG/CO/4, para 56.

196 CESCR, Concluding observations on the initial report of Pakistan, 20 July 2017, E/C.12/PAK/CO/1, paras 77 and 78.

197 CESCR, Concluding observations on the fourth periodic report of the Dominican Republic, 21 October 2016, E/C.12/DOM/CO/4, paras 59 and 60.

198 CESCR, Concluding observations on the initial report of Burkina Faso, 12 July 2016, E/C.12/BFA/CO/1, paras 46 and 47.

199 CESCR, Concluding observations on the second periodic report of Honduras, 11 July 2016, E/C.12/HND/CO/2, paras 53 and 54.

200 CESCR, Concluding observations on the combined second to fifth periodic reports of Kenya, 6 April 2016, E/C.12/KEN/CO/2-5, paras 53 and 54.

201 CESCR, Concluding observations on the sixth periodic report of Poland, 26 October 2016, E/C.12/POL/CO/6, para 47.

202 CESCR, Concluding observations on the combined fifth and sixth periodic reports of the Philippines, 26 October 2016, E/C.12/PHL/CO/5-6, paras 51 and 52.

203 CESCR, Concluding observations on the fourth periodic report of Morocco, 22 October 2015, E/C.12/MAR/CO/4, paras 45 and 46.

204 CESCR, Concluding observations on the initial report of Uganda, 8 July 2015, E/C.12/UGA/CO/1, para 35.

205 CESCR, Concluding observations on the third periodic report of the Bolivarian Republic of Venezuela, 7 July 2015, E/C.12/VEN/CO/3, para 28.

206 CESCR, Concluding observations on the fourth periodic report of Chile, 7 July 2015, E/C.12/CHL/CO/4, para 29.

207 CESCR, Concluding observations on the fourth periodic report of Paraguay, 20 March 2015, E/C.12/PRY/CO/4, para 29.

208 CESCR, Concluding observations on the initial report of Uganda, 8 July 2015, E/C.12/UGA/CO/1, para 35.

209 CESCR, Concluding observations on the third periodic report of Guatemala, 9 December 2014, E/C.12/GTM/CO/3, para 23.

210 CESCR, Concluding observations on the combined third, fourth and fifth periodic reports of El Salvador, 19 June 2014, E/C.12/SLV/CO/3-5, para 22.

2011,[211] and Uruguay 2011.[212]

The CESCR has adopted this approach regardless of the high percentages of women and men that are opposed to this practice in most of these countries. For instance, in El Salvador in 2015 the percentage of opposition to abortion was as high as 85 percent; in the Philippines it is of 93 percent; and Pakistan it is of 85 percent.[213]

In the concluding observations of 2019 on Argentina, the CESCR expressed that it "regrets that the bill to decriminalize abortion was not adopted".[214] In other situations, as in the concluding observations of Poland of 2017, the CESCR has expressed concerns about new restrictions to abortion that were being discussed in the parliament and the ruling of the Constitutional Court of 2015 that protects conscientious objection.[215]

The HRC has also requested the legalization of abortion as a human rights obligation in the concluding observations of the Central African Republic (2019),[216] Senegal (2018),[217] Nigeria (2018),[218] El Salvador (2017)[219], and Ghana (2015),[220] among others.

The CRC has also insisted on access to abortion for children and adolescents "without the need for the consent of and to be accompanied by a parent or legal guardian",[221] which puts children at risk of being sexually abused

211 CESCR, Concluding observations of the Committee on Economic, Social and Cultural Rights on Sri Lanka, 9 December 2010, E/C.12/LKA/CO/2-4, para 34.

212 CESCR, Concluding observations of the Committee on Economic, Social and Cultural Rights on Uruguay, 1 December 2010, E/C.12/URY/CO/3-4, para 24.

213 "Global Morality."

214 CESCR, Concluding observations on the fourth periodic report of Argentina, 1 November 2018, E/C.12/ARG/CO/4, para 55.

215 CESCR, Concluding observations on the sixth periodic report of Poland, 26 October 2016, E/C.12/POL/CO/6, paras. 46 and 47.

216 HRC, Concluding observations on the third periodic report of the Central African Republic (30 April 2020) CCPR/C/CAF/CO/3, paras 15 and 16.

217 HRC, Concluding observations on the fifth periodic report of Senegal (11 December 2019) CCPR/C/SEN/CO/5, paras 22–23.

218 HRC, Concluding observations on Nigeria in the absence of its second periodic report (29 August 2019) CCPR/C/NGA/CO/2, paras 22–23.

219 HRC, Concluding observations on the seventh periodic report of El Salvador (9 May 2018) CCPR/C/SLV/CO/7, paras 15 and 16.

220 HRC, Concluding observations on the initial reports of Ghana (9 August 2016) CCPR/C/GHA/CO/1, paras, 23 and 24.

221 CRC, Concluding observations on the combined fifth and sixth periodic reports of Rwanda (28 February 2020) CRC/C/RWA/CO/5-6, para 36. Also see: CRC, Concluding

without the consequence of pregnancy and without sanctions for the aggressor.[222] Even the Committee against Torture (CAT), whose mandate seems to be totally removed from this debate, has recommended the need to legalize abortion.[223]

The same approach has also been followed by some mandate holders of the special procedures of the Human Rights Council. The Special rapporteur on the right to health has insisted on abortion[224] and sterilization[225] as part of sexual and reproductive health. The Special rapporteur on the rights of persons with disabilities has also recommended the legalization of abortion and the need to provide contraception to persons with disabilities.[226] At the same time, she recognizes that currently these persons suffer from forced contraception, forced abortion, and forced sterilization based on eugenic ideas,[227] which prompts the question of whether access to these procedures is for their best interest or for someone else's benefit.

The Special rapporteur on violence against women has determined that the prohibition of abortion is discrimination against women, violates their

observations on the combined third to fifth periodic reports of Kenya (21 March 2016) CRC/C/KEN/CO/3-5, paras 49 and 50.

222 The CRPD has demonstrated concern for this situation in a similar case: "Forced contraception and sterilization can also result in sexual violence without the consequence of pregnancy, especially for women with psychosocial or intellectual disabilities". CRPD, General comment No. 3 (2016) on women and girls with disabilities (25 November 2016) CRPD/C/GC/3, para 45.

223 CAT, Concluding observations on the seventh periodic report of Peru (18 December 2018) CAT/C/PER/CO/7, paras 40 and 41; and CAT, Concluding observations on the seventh periodic report of Poland (29 August 2019) CAT/C/POL/CO/7, paras 33 and 34.

224 Special Rapporteur (Paul Hunt), The right of everyone to the enjoyment of the highest attainable standard of physical and mental health (16 February 2014) E/CN.4/2004/49, para 30; and Special rapporteur on the right to health (Paul Hunt), The right of everyone to the enjoyment of the highest attainable standard of physical and mental health (13 September 2006) A/61/338.

225 Special rapporteur on the right to health (Anand Grover), Right of everyone to the enjoyment of the highest attainable standard of physical and mental health (3 August 2011) A/66/254, para 52.

226 Special rapporteur on the rights of persons with disabilities (Catalina Devandas), Sexual and reproductive health and rights of girls and young women with disabilities (14 July 2017) A/72/133, paras 3 and 11.

227 Special rapporteur on the rights of persons with disabilities (Catalina Devandas), Sexual and reproductive health and rights of girls and young women with disabilities (14 July 2017) A/72/133, paras 3, 11, 31, 40, 49 and 60.

right to health, and constitutes violence against women.[228] Even the Special rapporteur on religious freedom, whose mandate is to protect freedom to manifest diverse beliefs, has determined that the denial of abortion and opposition to contraception are "religious practices" that treat women as inferior to men.[229]

It seems that the only different and marginalized perspective on abortion is the one of the Special rapporteur on the right to privacy, Joseph Cannataci, who has acknowledged that framing abortion as part of the right to privacy is a cultural perspective not shared by everybody.[230]

Another relevant example of this bias towards liberal universality is the adoption by the HRC of the General Comment No. 36 on the right to life in 2018. This General Comment was controversial because part of the debate was the inclusion of abortion. HRC held a General Discussion Day where they received 23 submissions from states, seven from U.N. agencies, 33 from academicians, and 117 from NGOs.[231]

Regarding states' submissions, Austria, Japan and Malta, insisted that there is no international obligation to legalize it. Poland criticized that the General Comment only referred to the right to life of pregnant women in relation to abortion. Russia criticized the inclusion of abortion and argued that the CEDAW should discourage it instead of promoting it. The U.S. insisted that abortion was not part of the mandate of the ICCPR and that this issue was expressly excluded from its provisions, according to its drafting history. The only states' submissions that supported abortion were Denmark, Sweden, and the Netherlands.

From the academic submissions, at least 19 out of 33 opposed the inclusion of abortion in the General Comment. Several academicians insisted that

228 Special rapporteur on violence against women (Dubravka Šimonović), A human rights-based approach to mistreatment and violence against women in reproductive health services with a focus on childbirth and obstetric violence, (11 July 2019) A/74/137, paras 9, 76 and 81.

229 Special rapporteur on religious freedom (Abdelfattah Amor), Study on freedom of religion or belief and the status of women in the light of religion and traditions (24 April 2009) E/CN.4/2002/73/Add.2, paras 113, 131–133, and 198.

230 Special rapporteur on the right to privacy (Joseph Cannataci), Report of the Special Rapporteur on the right to privacy (24 November 2016) A/HRC/31/64, para 23.

231 All submissions can be consulted at: which is the following "General Comment No. 36 on Article 6 of the International Covenant on Civil and Political Rights—Right to Life.," OHCHR, n.d., https://www.ohchr.org/EN/HRBodies/CCPR/Pages/GC36-Article6Righttolife.aspx.

there was no right to abortion, that it contravened the right to life, and that this constituted an ultra vires act on the part of the HRC. Some highlighted that abortion is not a therapeutic procedure for the protection of health because pregnancy is not an illness. Others insisted that this was a consensus document, so that controversial and sensitive issues had no place in it. A submission insisted that abortion was contrary to the recognition of unborn life as stated in the ICCPR, regarding the prohibition of death penalty for pregnant women in article 6(5).

Concerning the NGOs submissions, at least 55 out of 117 opposed abortion. Some African NGOs alleged that abortion was an ideological imposition from Western donors. An NGO of women who regret their abortions insisted that abortion was not an informed and harmless choice, for they had testimonies from different victims that now regret the procedure. Even medical associations considered that abortion provides only one option for women and one which does not respect their dignity. They highlighted that it is not evident that unborn human beings deserve no legal protection.

Nevertheless, the HRC ignored all those dissenting voices and decided to include abortion as part of the right to life of women.[232] The lack of consensus on this controversial issue was seen even within the HRC's members themselves. During the adoption of this General Comment the chairman of the meeting, the Egyptian diplomat Ahmed Amin Fathalla, accused the treaty body of "permitting abortion with no criteria or restrictions or conditions, and leaving such a decision to the free will of a woman and a girl under the cover of respecting their free choice and privacy", which he argued would deny the right to life of the unborn child and contradict the supremacy of this right as recognized by the HRC itself.[233] Mr. Fathalla further indicated that the HRC should not prioritize the right to privacy over the right to life and

232 HRC, General Comment No. 36: Article 6 the right to life (3 September 2019) CCPR/C/GC/36, para 8: "restrictions on the ability of women or girls to seek abortion must not, inter alia, jeopardize their lives, subject them to physical or mental pain or suffering that violates article 7 of the Covenant, discriminate against them or arbitrarily interfere with their privacy […] States parties should remove existing barriers to effective access by women and girls to safe and legal abortion."

233 U.N. Web TV, "(Part Four) General Comment—3561st Meeting 124th Session of Human Rights Committee", 124th session (30 October 2018), starting in 46:25 <http://webtv.un.org/meetings-events/human-rights-treaty-bodies/human-rights-committee/watch/part-four-general-comment-3561st-meeting-124th-session-of-human-rights-committee/5855729620001/?term=>. Consulted on June 14, 2021.

the scientific evidence that demonstrates the life of the unborn child.[234] Mr. Fathalla's comments where furiously criticized by the French, Tunisian, and American members of the HRC.[235]

Regarding the provisions invoked to justify the alleged right to abortion, it is relevant to notice that the process followed by human rights mechanism to arrive to this conclusion is not based on a legally grounded reasoning. They do not stick to the rules of treaty interpretation, the normative weight of the texts used is highly questionable, and they do not look for state practice to see how these norms have been developed. Rather the rationale of their views is based on self-referential statements and their own philosophical assumptions about the meaning of each human right provision.

For instance, in the case of the CRC, the Convention on the Rights of the Child in its article 24, which is used to frame a right to abortion, refers to access to health care, to diminish infant mortality, to combat disease and malnutrition, and to ensure pre- and post-natal care for mothers. It is difficult to assume through a literal reading of this article that it includes access to abortion, especially if most states of the world see this procedure as a crime (see chapter three).

On the contrary, a systematic reading of other articles can be interpreted as excluding abortion as something beneficial for children. Article 27 declares "the right of every child to a standard of living adequate for the child's physical, mental, spiritual, moral and social development",[236] which according to the legislation of most states and the opinion of many societies do not include a right to abortion.

As for the Convention against Torture and Other Cruel, Inhuman or Degrading Treatment or Punishment, the CAT justifies its insistence on abortion based on articles 2 and 16 that set the obligation to prevent acts of torture, which is defined by article 1 of the convention as

> Any act by which severe pain or suffering, whether physical or mental, is intentionally inflicted on a person for such purposes as obtaining from him or a third person information or a confession, punishing him for an act he or a third person has committed or is suspected of having committed, or intimidating or coercing him or a

234 U.N. Web TV, "(Part Four) General Comment - 3561st Meeting 124th Session of Human Rights Committee".

235 U.N. Web TV, "(Part Four) General Comment - 3561st Meeting 124th Session of Human Rights Committee".

236 Convention on the Rights of the Child (1989), art. 27 <https://www.ohchr.org/en/professionalinterest/pages/crc.aspx>. Consulted on June 7, 2020.

> third person, or for any reason based on discrimination of any kind, when such pain or suffering is inflicted by or at the instigation of or with the consent or acquiescence of a public official or other person acting in an official capacity.[237]

The prohibition of abortion can hardly amount to this crime. There is no intentionally inflicted severe pain or suffering by a public official or a person acting in an official capacity, for the purpose of a confession, punishment for someone else's actions, intimidation, or discrimination. As recognized in the American case *Roe v. Wade*, the prohibition of abortion responds mainly to the protection of two goods: unborn life and the protection of women from being forced to undergo an abortion.[238]

As for article 16, it establishes the obligation to prevent other cruel, inhuman or degrading treatment or punishment. In this regard, the HRC in its General Comment has recognized that there is no definition of this category, "nor does the Committee consider it necessary to draw up a list of prohibited acts [...] the distinctions depend on the nature, purpose and severity of the treatment applied".[239]

The *travaux préparatoires* of the ICCPR indicate that the drafters understood this concept in terms of severe crimes, like slavery, compulsory labor or forced servitude.[240] In this context, it is hard to maintain that the denial of abortion fits this category. Moreover, no legislation considers the prohibition of abortion on those terms. On the contrary, abortion is a crime for most state parties to the Convention against Torture and Other Cruel, Inhuman or Degrading Treatment or Punishment and the ICCPR.

On the part of the HRC, this committee has invoked several provisions: the principle non-discrimination (article 3), the right not to be subjected to torture or to cruel, inhuman or degrading treatment or punishment (article 6), and the right to privacy (article 17) of the ICCPR.

In the case *Mellet v. Ireland* of 2016 the HRC decided that Ireland's balance between the protection of the unborn and access to abortion was not justified,

237 Convention against Torture and Other Cruel, Inhuman or Degrading Treatment or Punishment (1984), art. 1 <https://www.ohchr.org/en/instruments-mechanisms/instruments/convention-against-torture-and-other-cruel-inhuman-or-degrading>. Consulted on June 7, 2020

238 U.S. Supreme Court of Justice, *Roe v. Wade* 410 U.S. 113 (1973).

239 HRC, General comment No. 20: Article 7 (Prohibition of torture, or other cruel, inhuman or degrading treatment or punishment), forty-fourth session (1992), para 4.

240 See Marc Bossuyt, *Guide to the "Travaux Préparatoires" of the International Covenant on Civil and Political Rights* (Martinus Nijhoff, 1987), 161–176.

for Mrs. Mellet experienced "intense physical and mental suffering", which per se amounted to cruel, inhuman or degrading treatment.[241] To experience "intense physical and mental suffering", because of life circumstances merits compassion and help, but the category of cruel, inhuman or degrading treatment or punishment is a legal one that requires a reasoning that fulfills certain parameters to justify it. In order to claim such a violation the HRC required to analyze whether this suffering was a treatment or a punishment, and then whether its nature, purpose and severity amounted to such a classification.[242]

Regarding the right to privacy, in the case *Whelan v. Ireland* of 2017 the HRC stated that according to its own jurisprudence "the scope of article 17 encompasses a woman's decision to request termination of pregnancy".[243] It constituted a self-referential statement, without looking to any other legal sources, not even the ICCPR itself. As a member of the Norwegian Center for Human Rights remarks:

> Treaty bodies use their own jurisprudence and General Comments to interpret their covenant's provisions even further, or to confirm their own interpretations. Ultimately, this method may alienate human rights interpretations from national state practice and implementation. When referring mainly to General Comments and their own jurisprudence, human rights interpretation is only concerned with the treaty body's own perception of the rights enshrined in "its" convention.[244]

Considering that most legislations in the world see abortion as a crime, it is probable that this action is not contemplated within the scope of protection of the right to privacy. Moreover, the *travaux préparatoires* of the ICCPR indicate that the state representatives understood privacy as linked to the family space and the reputation of individuals against unlawful governmental attacks,[245] something far removed from issues like abortion.

241 HRC, *Mellet v. Ireland* (17 November 2016) CCPR/C/116/D/2324/2013, para 7.4–7.6.

242 HRC, General comment No. 20: Article 7 (Prohibition of torture, or other cruel, inhuman or degrading treatment or punishment), forty-fourth session (1992), para 4.

243 HRC, *Whelan v. Ireland* (17 March 2017) CCPR/C/119/D/2425/2014, para 7.8.

244 Birgit Schlütter, "Aspects of Human Rights Interpretation by the UN Treaty Bodies," in *UN Human Rights Treaty Bodies: Law and Legitimacy*, ed. Helen Keller and Geir Ulfstein (Cambridge University Press, 2012), 292.
Birgit Schlütter, "Aspects of Human Rights Interpretation by the UN Treaty Bodies," in *UN Human Rights Treaty Bodies: Law and Legitimacy*, ed. Helen Keller and Geir Ulfstein (Cambridge University Press, 2012), 292.

245 See Bossuyt, *Guide to the "Travaux Préparatoires" of the International Covenant on Civil and Political Rights*, 341–347.

Ignoring this, the HRC argued that the balance made by Ireland between the interests of the woman and the protection of the unborn was "unreasonable and that it thus constitutes an arbitrary interference in the author's right to privacy".[246] The rationale for this conclusion is that the prohibition of abortion caused "mental anguish".[247] Nevertheless, to determine whether an interference is "arbitrary or unlawful", the HRC needed to prove that it was not envisaged by the law or, even if lawful, it was not "in accordance with the provisions, aims and objectives of the Covenant" or was not "reasonable in the particular circumstances".[248]

There is no reason to a priori exclude that the protection of unborn life and protection against forced abortions as a form of violence against women are manifestly unreasonable aims. Moreover, it is difficult to maintain that these reasons are contrary to the purpose and object of the ICCPR. Only an interpreter based on the paradigm of liberal universality would conclude that access to abortion is within the ICCPR's aims and objectives.

As for article 3 of the ICCPR, the HRC has also claimed that the prohibition of abortion is a violation of the right to non-discrimination. In *Mellet v. Ireland* the HRC stated that the criminalization of abortion subjected Mrs. Mellet "to a gender-based stereotype of the reproductive role of women primarily as mothers".[249] This is not a legal analysis, nor even a fact, rather it is a culturally conditioned prejudice that has become common wisdom in Western societies, but that requires to be justified.

From another perspective, it is at least questionable whether motherhood is a negative stereotype (a statement that would be offensive and degrading to any mother) and whether the criminalization of abortion encourages this idea, especially when the UDHR itself contains a provision to protect maternity in article 25. As indicated by the individual opinion of the HRC member Anja Seibert-Fohr, the true rationale behind the prohibition of abortion is "grounded on moral views on the nature of life which are held by the Irish population".[250]

On its part, the CEDAW has invoked the right not to be discriminated against (article 12) and the obligation to modify social and cultural patterns

246 HRC, *Whelan v. Ireland*, para 7.9.
247 HRC, *Whelan v. Ireland*, para 7.9.
248 HRC, General comment No. 16: Article 17 (Right to privacy), thirty-second session (1988), para 3-4.
249 HRC, *Mellet v. Ireland*, para 7.11.
250 HRC, *Mellet v. Ireland*, 29.

harmful to women (article 5) of the CEDAW Convention to justify a right to abortion. In the case *L.C. v. Peru* of 2011, the CEDAW assumed that access to abortion is part of the right to health,[251] although there is no international agreement on that. Furthermore, the CEDAW considered that the denial of access to abortion was "influenced by the stereotype that protection of the foetus should prevail over the health of the mother".[252] However, no evidence is provided to support this affirmation, for this is also a widespread cultural prejudice, not a legal or scientific reasoning.

At the regional level, the IACtHR and the IACoHR have also relied on the same approach. The IACoHR in its report on violence and discrimination against women declares that women should have access to abortion, regardless of the obligations assumed according to the American Convention on Human Rights (which protects the right to life from conception).[253] This commission has determined that abortion is part of women's SRHR only based on the self-referential statement that this has been affirmed by human rights treaty bodies.[254]

The IACoHR has gone even further ordering El Salvador,[255] Honduras,[256] Dominican Republic[257] and Nicaragua[258] to decriminalize abortion as a human

251 CEDAW, *L.C. v. Peru* (17 October 2011) CEDAW/C/50/D/22/2009, paras. 8.10–8.16.

252 CEDAW, *L.C. v. Peru*, para 8.15.

253 IACoHR, Violencia y discriminación contra mujeres, niñas y adolescentes: Buenas prácticas y desafíos en América Latina y en el Caribe, OEA/Ser.L/V/II (14 November 2019), para 205.

254 IACoHR, Violencia y discriminación contra mujeres, niñas y adolescentes, paras 205–210.

255 IACoHR, Anexo al Comunicado No. 011/18. Conclusiones y observaciones sobre la visita de trabajo de la Comisión Interamericana de Derechos Humanos a El Salvador (29 January 2018) <http://www.oas.org/es/cidh/prensa/comunicados/2018/011.asp>. Consulted on October 4, 2019.

256 IACoHR, Comunicado de Prensa No. 171/18. CIDH concluye su visita a Honduras y presenta sus Observaciones Preliminares (3 August 2018) <https://www.oas.org/es/cidh/prensa/comunicados/2018/171.asp>. Consulted on October 4, 2019.

257 IACoHR, Informe Anual 2018 - Capítulo IV.B República Dominicana (2018), paras 91–106 <https://www.oas.org/es/cidh/docs/anual/2018/docs/IA2018cap.5RD-es.pdf>. Consulted on October 4, 2019.

258 IACoHR, Informe Anual 2018 – Capitulo IV.B Nicaragua (2018), paras 219 <http://www.oas.org/es/cidh/docs/anual/2018/docs/IA2018cap.4B.NI-es.pdf>. IACoHR. Anexo al Comunicado No. 011/18. Conclusiones y observaciones sobre la visita de trabajo de la Comisión Interamericana de Derechos Humanos a El Salvador (29 January 2018) <http://www.oas.org/es/cidh/prensa/comunicados/2018/011.asp>. Consulted on October 4, 2019.

rights obligation. Regarding El Salvador, the IACoHR has requested provisional measures in the case "B" in order to allow a woman to abort, despite the legislation and popular opinion in the country.[259]

In June of 2022, the IACoHR congratulated Mexico via *Twitter* for the legalization of abortion in the state of Guerrero,[260] which prompted a reaction from the Colombian commissioner Carlos Bernal Pulido. Mr. Bernal Pulido expressed his disagreement with the position of the IACoHR insisting that there is no internationally recognized human right to access abortion and reminding the IACoHR to protect life from conception as stated in article 4 of the American Convention on Human Rights.[261]

At the IACtHR a similar situation arose. The case *Manuela v. El Salvador* of 2021 was about an infanticide,[262] but the topic of abortion was brought up several times as a contextual element. In his partially dissenting opinion, Judge Eduardo Vio Grossi expressed his concern about the IACtHR's conclusions:

> It is also necessary to indicate that the Court's jurisdiction is exercised within the framework of international law, based on the objective nature of the State's international responsibility for an internationally wrongful act; that is, the State incurs in this if an action is attributable to it under international law, and if this constitutes a breach of one of its international obligations. In this regard, it is undeniable that, as indicated in one of my separate opinions, there is no inter-American or international legal provision, either in a convention or by international custom or general principle of law, that recognizes abortion as a right. There are only resolutions of international

IACoHR, Comunicado de Prensa No. 171/18. CIDH concluye su visita a Honduras y presenta sus Observaciones Preliminares (3 August 2018) <https://www.oas.org/es/cidh/prensa/comunicados/2018/171.asp>. Consulted on October 4, 2019.
IACoHR, Informe Anual 2018 - Capítulo IV.B República Dominicana (2018), paras 91–106 <https://www.oas.org/es/cidh/docs/anual/2018/docs/IA2018cap.5RD-es.pdf>. Consulted on October 4, 2019.

259 IACtHR, Medidas cautelares respecto de El Salvador Asunto B (29 May 2013).

260 The tweet is available at: <https://twitter.com/CIDH/status/1532853712653324290>. Consulted on January 30, 2023.

261 The tweet is available at: <https://twitter.com/carloslbernal/status/1532857383793397763?s=20&t=-NNLANkaE58ayU_K4AMMqw>. Consulted on February 26, 2023.

262 As stated in the autopsy report: "The corpse was at a stage of accelerated putrefaction owing to the fecal material, the heat of the tank, and the humidity. Internally, it was found that excreta obstructed the upper airway, the optic dosimasia revealed total expansion of both lungs in the thoracic cavity; the hydrostatic docimasia was positive for air, which shows that the infant was born alive and breathed. The cause of its death was mechanical asphyxiadue to obstruction ofthe upper airway with excreta, and severe umbilical hemorrhage." IACtHR, *Manuela v. El Salvador* (Judgment of 2 November 2021), at footnote 128.

> bodies –most of them composed of international officials and not of representatives of States—resolutions that, moreover, are not binding and do not interpret valid international law, but rather reflect aspirations that the latter be amended in the sense they suggest.[263]

Moreover, the topic of abortion in the Inter-American system is intensifying due to the case *Beatriz v. El Salvador* that will be addressed by the IACtHR in the following months as this book is being written. In its merits report, the IACoHR is requesting this regional court to declare that the legalization of abortion is an international human rights obligation for the states party to the American Convention on Human Rights.[264] The sources invoked by the IACoHR are treaty body pronouncements, reports of special rapporteurs, and the ICPD,[265] but it ignores article 4 of the American Convention on Human Rights on the protection of life from conception and paragraph 8.25 of the Beijing Pogramme and Platform of Action regarding abortion.

Furthermore, the IACoHR uses isolated quotations of three cases of the ECtHR (*Tysiąc v. Poland*, *A, B, C v. Ireland*, and *R.R. v. Poland*) that are totally out of context to justify the existence of a right to abortion. A careful reading of these cases demonstrates a different situation in the European human rights system than the one presented by these commissioners.

The ECtHR has also embraced a liberal vision of sexuality, but it has not considered that access to abortion is a human right.[266] This court has been more rigorous in its legal analysis by recognizing that there are several human rights and interests at stake.[267] It has also determined, contrary to the HRC, that the prohibition of abortion, even if it can cause inconvenience and suffering to the petitioner, cannot be considered as cruel, inhuman, or degrading treatment.[268] The ECtHR has also refrained from making cultural claims about gender-stereotypes, as the CEDAW has done.

Regarding the Polish cases (*Tysiąc v. Poland* and *R.R. v. Poland*) neither is about a right to abortion or the legalization of this practice in Poland. Both

263 IACtHR, *Manuela v. El Salvador* (Judgment of 2 November 2021) Partially dissenting opinion of Judge Eduardo Vio Grossi, para 13.

264 IACoHR, *Beatriz v. El Salvador*, Informer 9/20, Caso 13.378 (3 March 2020).

265 IACoHR, *Beatriz v. El Salvador*, paras 86, 97, 103–114.

266 ECtHR, *P. and S. v Poland* (Application no. 57375/08) 30 January 2013, para 96.

267 Grégor Puppinck, "Abortion on Demand and the European Convention on Human Rights" in EJIL: Talk! (23 February 2013) https://www.ejiltalk.org/abortion-on-demand-and-the-european-convention-on-human-rights/>. Consulted on May 10, 2021.

268 ECtHR, *A, B, C v. Ireland* (Grand Chamber), 16 December 2010, para 239.

cases are about the circumstances to access a lawful abortion according to the exceptions already established in Polish law.[269]

The first case concerns whether or not the denial to access a lawful abortion based on therapeutic reasons violated the right to privacy of a pregnant woman. The ECtHR's assessment was about the available mechanisms to implement Polish law regarding lawful abortion due to a risk to the woman's life or health.[270]

The case of *R.R. v. Poland* was about timely and adequate access to prenatal genetic tests to determine whether the applicant was a candidate to a lawfully available abortion according to the exceptions recognized by Polish law.[271]

These judgments can be criticized because the ECtHR acted as a fourth instance judge by scrutinizing the correct or incorrect implementation of a national law.[272] However, it is relevant to highlight that both cases contain dissenting opinions that emphasize that the disputes were not about the existence of a right to abortion.[273]

In the case A, B, C *v. Ireland* of 2010 the ECtHR has assessed access to abortion within the scope of the right to privacy (article 8) of the ECHR. Although, the ECtHR recognized that "article 8 cannot be interpreted as meaning that pregnancy and its termination pertain uniquely to the woman's private life as, whenever a woman is pregnant, her private life becomes closely connected with the developing foetus".[274] The ECtHR recognized that the issues at stake refer to: "on the one hand, the first and second applicants' right to respect for their private lives under Article 8 and, on the other, profound moral values of the Irish people as to the nature of life and consequently as to the need to protect the life of the unborn".[275]

The ECtHR recognized that the protection of health and morals, through the protection of the life of the unborn, was a legitimate aim.[276] Contrary to treaty bodies, this court remarked that the prohibition is not based on

269 ECtHR, *Tysiąc v. Poland* (Application no. 5410/03) 24 September 2007, para 114.
270 ECtHR, *Tysiąc v. Poland*, para 124.
271 ECtHR, *R.R. v. Poland*, (Application no. 27617/04) 28 November 2011, para 196.
272 As explained in the separate opinion of judge Borrego in *Tysiąc*.
273 See the separate opinion of judge Bonello and the dissenting opinion of judge Borrego in *Tysiąc*; and the partially dissenting opinion of judges Bratza and Gaetano in *R.R.*
274 ECtHR, A, B, C *v. Ireland*, para 213.
275 ECtHR, A, B, C *v. Ireland*, para 230.
276 ECtHR, A, B, C *v. Ireland*, para 222.

discrimination, rather it relies on a moral and scientific view about the beginning of life and the need to protect it.

The ECtHR acknowledged that "the question of when the right to life begins came within the States' margin of appreciation because there was no European consensus on the scientific and legal definition of the beginning of life".[277] Thus, the ECtHR did not find a violation to article 8 regarding Ireland's general ban on abortion.

The ECtHR is more cautious, but still it framed abortion within the scope of application of the right to privacy, which only makes sense within the paradigm of liberal universality. Moreover, the ECtHR has recently declared the inadmissibility of cases related to conscientious objectors to abortifacients and abortion procedures, based on the premises of this framework.[278] Thus, although the ECtHR generally follows the paradigm of liberal universality, this court has been more moderate in its approach to abortion than treaty bodies or the IACoHR.

277 ECtHR, *A, B, C v. Ireland*, para 237.

278 ECtHR, *Bruno Pichon and Marie-Line Sajous v. France*, (Application n° 49853/99) 2 October 2001; and ECtHR, *Grimmark v. Sweden* (Third Section), 11 February 2020.

· 3 ·

THE IMPACT OF LIBERAL UNIVERSALITY ON PEOPLE'S LIVES

After analyzing the situation of SRHR in human rights mechanisms of protection, it is relevant to conduct a deeper scrutiny of the disconnection between what has been agreed in international settings and the views of the people that have been affected. For the purpose of human rights is not to satisfy the interests of states or ruling elites, but to protect the human dignity of concrete human beings.

Global Opinions on Sexual Morality

Two world-renowned institutions, the World Values Survey and the Pew Research Center, have conducted surveys all around the world to understand people's opinion on several moral issues. According to the results, the former director of the World Values Survey and professor at the University of Michigan, Ronald Inglehart, concluded that today's Western societies show a tendency towards greater support for abortion, legal prostitution, same-sex relations, pre-marital sexual intercourse, and divorce.[1] Although this

1 See Ronald Inglehart and Pippa Norris, *Rising Tide: Gender Equality and Cultural Change Around the World* (Cambridge University Press, 2003), 61–62.

paradigm of sexuality is new in Western societies, just before the 1960s they used to have a less liberal vision of sexuality.[2] However, it is interesting to note that most non-Western societies and religious groups within the West have more traditional views of sexual behavior.[3]

A 2014 study conducted by the Pew Research Center in 40 countries and with 40,117 people surveyed revealed that Western countries (especially Western European ones) are world outliers in their liberal conceptualization of sexual behavior.[4] Around 65 percent of the Europeans interviewed considered that extramarital affairs are morally wrong, compared to 76 percent of Latin Americans, 81 percent of Asians, 79 percent of Africans, 93 percent of people in the Middle East, and 84 percent of Americans.[5] France is the country that tolerates the most marital infidelity, where only 47 percent of people consider this issue as morally wrong and 40 percent think that this is not a moral issue.[6]

Regarding the permissibility of abortion, only 26 percent of the Europeans interviewed (and 26 percent of Canadians and Australians)[7] consider that it

2 See Critchlow, *Intended Consequences: Birth Control, Abortion and the Federal Government in Modern America*, 57–60.

3 See the research of Horst Helle, *China: Promise or Threat?* (Brill, 2017), https://doi.org/10.1163/9789004330603; Lene Arnett Jensen, "Coming of Age in a Multicultural World: Globalization and Adolescent Cultural Identity Formation," *Applied Developmental Science* 7, no. 3 (2003), https://doi.org/10.1207/S1532480XADS0703; Kaye Wellings et al., "Sexual Behaviour in Context: A Global Perspective," *Lancet*, 2006, https://doi.org/10.1016/S0140-6736(06)69479-8; Inglehart and Norris, *Rising Tide: Gender Equality and Cultural Change Around the World*; Sunday E Adaji et al., "The Attitudes of Kenyan In-School Adolescents Toward Sexual Autonomy," *African Journal of Reproductive Health* 14, no. 1 (2010); Cynthia Patel and Trisha Kooverjee, "Abortion and Contraception: Attitudes of South African University Students," *Health Care for Women International* 30, no. 6 (2009); Sharon Ghuman et al., "Continuity and Change in Premarital Sex in Vietnam," *International Perspectives on Sexual and Reproductive Health* 32, no. 4 (2006); Joseph Chan, "The Asian Challenge to Universal Human Rights: A Philosophical Appraisal," in *Human Rights in Asia and the Pacific*, ed. Ben Saul and Catherine Renshaw (Routledge, 2014); Ronald Inglehart and Pippa Norris, "The True Clash of Civilizations," *Foreign Policy*, no. 135 (2003): 63–70, https://doi.org/10.2307/3183594.

4 See Pew Research Center "Global Morality."

5 See Richard Wike, "Europeans Hold More Liberal Views on Moral Issues," Pew Research Center, 2014, https://www.pewresearch.org/fact-tank/2014/04/16/europeans-hold-more-liberal-views-on-moral-issues/.

6 Pew Research Center "Global Morality."

7 Pew Research Center "Global Morality".

is morally wrong in all situations, compared to 77 percent of people in Latin America, 58 percent in Asia, 81 percent in Africa, 54 percent in the Middle East, and 49 percent in the United States.[8] Regarding European perspectives, even among the different countries of this region there are different perspectives. While in France and Germany only between 14 and 18 percent of the people consider abortion as morally wrong in all cases, in other countries the percentage is substantially higher (for instance, in Italy 41 percent, Poland 47 percent, and Russia 44 percent of the people).[9]

On the legalization of abortion, seven Eastern European countries (Greece, Belarus, Poland, Russia, Ukraine, Moldova and Georgia) present percentages of opposition that go from 52 percent to 85 percent.[10] Another survey from 2008 of the Atlas of European Values also reveals low levels of approval for abortion in non-Western societies, while in Western states and some Eastern European ones, it is considerably higher.[11]

As for the reasons to permit an abortion, the most contestable and rejected one is abortion on demand, even in European societies. The 2017–2020 survey of the World Values Survey conducted on 80 countries indicates most people are either totally opposed to the legalization of abortion or only consider it permissible in restricted cases.[12] Support for abortion on demand is approved by less than 20 percent of the population in non-Western countries.[13] Contrary to this, in Western states, the approval for abortion on demand is higher, but still involves a small percentage of the population in some states: in Australia is 24 percent, Germany 19 percent, Netherlands 25 percent, New Zealand 22 percent, Spain 19 percent, and the U.S. 10 percent.[14] Only in Norway (39 percent) and in Sweden (50 percent) there are higher percentages of approval

8 Wike, "Europeans Hold More Liberal Views on Moral Issues."

9 Pew Research Center "Global Morality."

10 "Eastern and Western Europeans Differ on Importance of Religion, Views of Minorities, and Key Social Issues," Pew Research Center, 2018, https://www.pewforum.org/2018/10/29/eastern-and-western-europeans-differ-on-importance-of-religion-views-of-minorities-and-key-social-issues/. Consulted on January 8, 2020.

11 "Society," Atlas of European Values, 2008, http://www.atlasofeuropeanvalues.eu/new/ziewereld.php?year=2008. Consulted on January 8, 2020.

12 Ronald Inglehart, C. Haerpfer, and Alejandro Moreno, "World Values Survey: Round Seven—Country-Pooled Datafile Version," World Values Survey, 2020, http://www.worldvaluessurvey.org/WVSOnline.jsp.

13 Inglehart, Haerpfer, and Moreno.

14 Inglehart, Haerpfer, and Moreno.

for abortion on demand.[15] It seems that although Westerners are more permissive on abortion, most of them have a middle ground position on this subject, which contrasts with the prevailing permissive legislation of their states.[16]

On the question of contraception, as is explained in the next section of this chapter, due to public campaigns and pressure perceptions in this regard have drastically changed in recent years. Nevertheless, there are still considerable percentages of people who do not consider contraception as acceptable for them. The African continent shows the greatest percentages of opposition in the world, with 54 percent in Nigeria, 52 percent in Ghana, 39 percent in Tunisia, 38 percent in Uganda, 33 percent in Kenya, and 28 percent in Senegal.[17] Countries in other regions also indicate relevant percentages of opposition, like 65 percent in Pakistan, 40 percent in Malaysia, 29 percent in the Philippines, 19 percent in Bolivia, 13 percent in China, 23 percent in El Salvador, 14 percent in Greece and Mexico, 17 percent in Poland, and 15 percent in South Africa.[18]

Regarding perceptions on pre-marital sexual relations, an important percentage of the world population considers them as morally wrong.[19] Contrary to this tendency, only 11 percent of Europeans (15 percent of Australians, 15 percent of Canadians and 21 percent of Japanese people)[20] agree with this, compared to 67 percent of Asians, 77 percent of Africans, and 90 percent of Middle Eastern people.[21] Although in this topic there is variability in Eastern European countries, where 22 percent of Poles and 30 percent of Russian consider it as morally wrong.[22] The situation of disapproval in these two countries is similar to Latin American ones (35 percent) and to the United States (30 percent).[23]

15 Inglehart, Haerpfer, and Moreno.

16 Angelina Theodorou and Aleksandra Sandstrom, "How Abortion Is Regulated around the World," 2015, https://www.pewresearch.org/fact-tank/2015/10/06/how-abortion-is-regulated-around-the-world/.

17 Lipka, "Africans among the Most Morally Opposed to Contraception." Consulted on January 8, 2020.

18 Pew Research Center "Global Morality."

19 "Global Views on Premarital Sex 2013," Statista, 2013, https://www.statista.com/statistics/297288/global-views-on-premarital-sex/. Consulted on January 8, 2020.

20 Pew Research Center "Global Morality."

21 Wike, "Europeans Hold More Liberal Views on Moral Issues."

22 Pew Research Center "Global Morality."

23 Wike, "Europeans Hold More Liberal Views on Moral Issues."

Also, within the Latin American region there is great diversity. There are some countries that present low percentages of people who consider pre-marital sex as morally wrong, like Chile (13 percent), Argentina (22 percent), and Venezuela (21 percent); while some others have higher percentages, like Mexico (44 percent), El Salvador (56 percent), and Bolivia (53 percent).[24] The 2008 Atlas of European Values also shows that approval of casual sex in European nations is not as high as usually considered. The highest percentages of approval are found in Finland, Iceland and Norway and they do not surpass 40 percent.[25]

In the World Values Survey of 2017–2020, the acceptance of pre-marital sex also seems to be very low in many parts of the world. The highest percentages of people who consider pre-marital sex as always justifiable are found in Western Europe.[26] In other Western nations, like the United States, the percentage is lower: 24 percent, for it seems that most Americans share a middle ground position.[27] In contrast to this, in Africa, the Middle East and Asia many people consider pre-marital sex as never justifiable (for instance, in Jordan 89 percent, Pakistan 79 percent, Turkey 61 percent, Bangladesh 75 percent, Nigeria 53 percent, and China 40 percent).[28]

In other regions, there are unneglectable percentages of people that do not share a liberal view on this aspect (43 percent in Nicaragua, 31 percent in Bolivia, 26 percent in Mexico, and 30 percent in Romania among others).[29] Even if there seems to be an international increase in pre-marital sex, most of the non-Western regions (with some exceptions in parts of Latin America and the Caribbean) seem to report little or no change in their sexual behavior.[30]

24 Pew Research Center "Global Morality."

25 Atlas of European Values "Society."

26 Inglehart, Haerpfer, and Moreno, "World Values Survey: Round Seven - Country-Pooled Datafile Version."

27 Inglehart, Haerpfer, and Moreno.

28 Inglehart, Haerpfer, and Moreno.

29 Inglehart, Haerpfer, and Moreno.

30 See Aisha NZ Dasgupta, Philipp Ueffing and Vladimíra Kantorová, 'Sexual Activity by Marital Status and Age: A Comparative Perspective' (2018) 2017/11 <https://www.un.org/en/development/desa/population/publications/pdf/technical/TP2017-11.pdf>. Consulted on January 8, 2020; Cynthia Lloyd, ed., *Growing Up Global: The Changing Transitions to Adulthood in Developing Countries* (National Research Council, 2005); Eric D Widmer, Judith Treas and Robert Newcomb, 'Attitudes Toward Nonmarital Sex in 24 Countries' (1998) 35 The Journal of Sex Research; Green (n 193).

These surveys also demonstrate internal diversity in each state. The data collected by the World Values Survey presents differences of views on sexuality according to socio-economic status and sex.[31] In some states the upper and middle social classes are the ones most opposed to premarital sex (e.g. Algeria). In other countries, both the people in the lowest and the highest income scale are the groups most opposed to abortion (e.g. Mexico, Brazil, Jordan, Poland, Rwanda, Singapore, and Zimbabwe). In other cases, women and the lowest social classes are the groups most opposed to abortion (e.g. Malaysia, Netherlands, Peru, South Korea, Argentina, Japan, Colombia, Turkey, Brazil, China, Jordan), to premarital sex (e.g. Ghana, Colombia, South Korea, Malaysia, Netherlands, Japan, Turkey, Mexico, Jordan) to consider same-sex relations as acceptable (e.g. Malaysia, Peru, South Korea, Turkey, Jordan) and to legalized prostitution (e.g. Peru, Colombia, China, Netherlands).

In some countries the difference between women and men on their opposition to abortion is contrasted by an unneglectable difference: in Brazil 73 percent of women are opposed to abortion in all cases compared to 65 percent of men; in Mexico the numbers are 63 percent of women compared to 59 percent of men, in Poland 48 percent of women compared to 39 percent of men, in South Korea 39 percent of women compared to 33 percent of men, and in the Netherlands 13 percent of women compared to nine percent of men. In others, a similar gap between women and men is noticed regarding opposition to premarital sex: in Poland 11 percent of women compared to seven percent of men, in South Korea 32 percent of women compared to 26 percent of men, in Colombia 24 percent of women compared to 19 percent of men.

In other states, the working class population is the group that is most opposed to abortion (e.g. U.S., Ghana, Iran, Nigeria, South Africa, India), to prostitution (e.g. Nigeria, South Africa, India) and to premarital sex (e.g. Nigeria, South Africa, India, and the U.S.).[32] In India, the working-class, religious groups, and female respondents were less willing to accept a liberal sexual morality, while more affluent and less religious individuals were more permissive.[33]

In the U.S. the wealthy top 20 percent of Americans tend to be more liberal than the general public on issues related to sexual morality, while also

31 All the data in this regard is available at: Inglehart, Haerpfer, and Moreno, "World Values Survey: Round Seven - Country-Pooled Datafile Version."

32 Inglehart, Haerpfer, and Moreno.

33 Chirodip Majumdar, "Attitudes Towards Premarital Sex in India: Traditionalism and Cultural Change," *Sexuality and Culture* 22, no. 1 (2018): 620.

they are more likely to influence public policy than the rest of the population.[34] Both in the U.S. and the U.K. the people from the lowest socioeconomic classes, with less educational attainment, and religious practitioners are the ones most opposed to a liberal sexual morality.[35]

Also, it is relevant to notice that an element that partly explains these variations is religion, for more religious groups share a more interdependent or traditional vision of sexuality, while more secularized societies opt for a more liberal view.[36] According to research, Western European states are outliers regarding their perceptions of religion, for these are deeply secularized societies, in contrast to the rest of the world that remains highly religious.[37]

Most of the world's population expresses a high level of trust in churches and religious organizations.[38] They also consider that religion is important in their lives, that it is a determinant element of their concept of morality,

34 Benjamin I. Page, Larry M. Bartels, and Jason Seawright, "Democracy and the Policy Preferences of Wealthy Americans," *Perspectives on Politics* 11, no. 1 (2013): 52.

35 See "Morality of Abortion, 2018–2020 Demographic Tables" (*Gallup*, 2020) <https://news.gallup.com/poll/244625/morality-abortion-2018-demographic-tables.aspx>. Consulted on 19 January 2020; Roger Harding, 'British Social Attitudes No. 34' (2017) <https://www.bsa.natcen.ac.uk/latest-report/british-social-attitudes-34/key-findings/context.aspx>. Consulted on January 8, 2020.

36 See in this regard: Ariana Salazar and Kelsey Jo Starr, "In the U.S. and Europe, Women Are about as Likely as Men to Favor Legal Abortion" (*Pew Research Center*, 2018) <https://www.pewresearch.org/fact-tank/2018/12/14/in-the-u-s-and-europe-women-are-about-as-likely-as-men-to-favor-legal-abortion/>. Consulted on 14 January 2020; Jacob Pushter and Janell Fetterolf, "A Changing World: Global Views on Diversity, Gender Equality, Family Life and the Importance of Religion" (*Pew Research Center*, 2019) <https://www.pewresearch.org/global/2019/04/22/a-changing-world-global-views-on-diversity-gender-equality-family-life-and-the-importance-of-religion/>. Consulted on January 8, 2020; 'The Changing Global Religious Landscape' (*Pew Research Center*, 2017) <http://assets.pewresearch.org/wp-content/uploads/sites/11/2017/04/07092755/FULL-REPORT-WITH-APPENDIXES-A-AND-B-APRIL-3.pdf>. Consulted on January 8, 2020.

37 See Inglehart and Norris, *Sacred and Secular: Religion and Politics Worldwide* (n 128); Harvey G Cox and Jan Swyngedouw, "The Myth of the Twentieth Century: The Rise and Fall of Secularization," *Japanese Journal of Religious Studies* 27 (2000): 1; Rodney Stark, "Secularization, R.I.P." *Sociology of Religion* 60 (1999): 249; "The Age Gap in Religion Around the World" (*Pew Research Center*, 2018) <https://www.pewforum.org/2018/06/13/how-religious-commitment-varies-by-country-among-people-of-all-ages/>. Consulted on January 8, 2020; 'The Changing Global Religious Landscape' (n 1370).

38 See Inglehart, Haerpfer, and Moreno, "World Values Survey: Round Seven—Country-Pooled Datafile Version."

and that it plays a relevant role in public life.[39] More than half of the global population considers that religious authorities give adequate answers to moral concerns, problems of family life, spiritual needs, and social problems in their countries.[40]

Thus, the data collected in these surveys and studies reveal that what is considered as acceptable and not in the sexual domain varies across different cultures in the world, and among socio-economic status, sex, and religious beliefs. Then, it is quite difficult to establish a uniform approach to SRHR, without disregarding the concerns and needs of different peoples (especially vulnerable groups like low socioeconomic classes and women). Disregarding this viewpoint diversity has only led to the implementation of policies that are not aligned with the needs and worldviews of people, and in the worst of cases, they have provoked gross human rights violations.

The Global Implementation of SRHR

Population policies became popular starting in the 1960s as mechanisms to regulate people's fertility through government-sponsored strategies to promote the use of contraception and to encourage small family sizes, through education and other means. They started in the wake of the "population problem" and the U.N. conferences on population. These policies constituted "a top-down, coercive and at times violent curtailment of fertility, most often targeting poor women of color, particularly in the global South".[41]

These policies responded to international pressure from Western states and local technocratic elites to reduce population growth and to "modernize"

39 See in this regard: Inglehart and Norris, *Sacred and Secular: Religion and Politics Worldwide* (n 128); "Religion" (*Atlas of European Values*, 2008) <http://www.atlasofeuropeanvalues.eu/new/ziewereld.php?year=2008>. Consulted on January 8, 2020; Inglehart and others (n 1329); Christine Tamir, Aidan Connaughton, and Ariana Slazar, "The Global God Divide" (*Pew Research Center*, 2020) <https://www.pewresearch.org/global/2020/07/20/the-global-god-divide/>. Consulted on January 8, 2020.

40 See Inglehart and Norris, *Sacred and Secular: Religion and Politics Worldwide*; "Religion"; Pushter and Fetterolf, "A Changing World: Global Views on Diversity, Gender Equality, Family Life and the Importance of Religion."

41 Anne Hendrixson et al., "Confronting Populationism: Feminist Challenges to Population Control in an Era of Climate Change," *Gender, Place and Culture* 27, no. 3 (March 3, 2020): 309, https://doi.org/10.1080/0966369X.2019.1639634.

society.[42] No population policy in the developing world was the result of people's wishes. As the political scientist Paige Eager comments: "while most Western women welcomed the liberation from unwanted, ill-timed, or too frequent childbearing, birth control in the Third World was often used coercively by governments to reduce population growth through family planning programmes".[43]

The same is true for the legalization of abortion. In most non-Western countries, the legalization or decriminalization of this practice was not a human rights' issue or the response to women's rights, rather it was part of a policy to reduce population growth. The best known example of this is China, but also there are the cases of Tunisia,[44] and Vietnam.[45] In the case of the former Soviet Union countries, the pioneers in this regard, abortion was also adopted as a population policy (for this reason it was constantly changed from being legal to illegal and finally legal again)[46] and as a form of social engineering to change the prevailing institutions, like marriage.[47]

Thus, all population policies responded to political and economic interests. Some examples are the one adopted in Colombia in 1966,[48] the 1970s family planning policies in Mexico[49], the project in Namibia,[50] the intervention

42 See Hartmann, *Reproductive Rights and Wrongs: The Global Politics of Population Control*, 1995, 54; Gwatkin, "The State of the World's Population Movement: Implications of the 1984 Mexico City Conference," 558.

43 Eager, "From Population Control to Reproductive Rights: Understanding Normative Change in Global Population Policy (1965–1994)," 151–152.

44 Irene Maffi and Malika Affes, "The Right to Abortion in Tunisia after the Revolution of 2011: Legal, Medical, and Social Arrangements as Seen through Seven Abortion Stories," *Health and Human Rights Journal* 21, no. 2 (2019).

45 Bussarawan Teerawichitchainan and Sajeda Amin, "The Role of Abortion in the Last Stage of Fertility Decline in Vietnam," *International Perspectives on Sexual and Reproductive Health* 36, no. 2 (2010).

46 See Mark Savage, "The Law of Abortion in the Union of Soviet Socialist Republics and the People's Republic of China: Women's Rights in Two Socialist Countries," *Stanford Law Review* 40, no. 4 (1988).

47 See Alexandra Kollontai, "The Labour of Women in the Evolution of the Economy," 1921, https://www.marxists.org/archive/kollonta/1921/evolution.htm.

48 Sánchez, "Population Discourse, Family Planning Policies, and Development in Colombia 1960-1969."

49 Jennifer Nelson, "Abortion Rights and Human Rights in Mexico," in *Reproductive Justice and Sexual Rights: Transnational Perspectives*, ed. Tanya Saroj Bakhru (Routledge, 2019).

50 Jennie Lindsay, "The Politics of Population Control in Namibia," *Review of African Political Economy* 36 (1986).

in Tanzania,[51] the one of Malawi[52], Puerto Rico[53], Bangladesh,[54] Indonesia,[55] and Uganda,[56] among others. By 1991, 69 countries had officially endorsed population policies with the support of international funding (Western states, Ford Foundation, IPPF, UNFPA, and the Population Council) and the elites of developing states.[57] The introduction of family planning services was an elite-driven process alienated from the people affected:

> The identification of population as a "problem" rested, to a very large degree, on the ideological assumptions of Western birth-control activists, population experts, and demographers. Without this epistemic community, which interpreted statistical evidence, developed theories, and devised action plans, it may well have been that population as a problem would have emerged much later.[58]

In Tanzania, for instance, contraception was presented as a service for the health of mothers and children, because it was considered as "much more palatable politically, and ignores the ambivalences behind the reasons donors are willing to fund planning in the first place".[59] These programs considered women as objects: as "targets of family planning services".[60]

In East Timor from 1975 to 1999 there were hundreds of allegations of forced sterilization and forced injections of Depo-Provera, where the

51 Richey, "Family Planning and the Politics of Population in Tanzania : International to Local Discourse."

52 Amy Kaler, "The Moral Lens of Population Control: Condoms and Controversies in Southern Malawi," *Studies in Family Planning* 35, no. 2 (2004).

53 Schoen, *Choice and Coercion: Birth Control, Sterilization, and Abortion in Public Health and Welfare*, 221–235; Dowbiggin, *The Sterilization Movement and Global Fertility in the Twentieth Century*, 81–83.

54 Hartmann, *Reproductive Rights and Wrongs: The Global Politics of Population Control*, 2016, chap. 12.

55 Terence H. Hull, ed., *People, Population, and Policy in Indonesia* (ISEAS, 2005).

56 Erin Heinz and Marie Louis Roth, "As Many as I Can Afford: Ideal Family Size in Contemporary Uganda," in *Reproductive Justice and Sexual Rights: Transnational Perspectives*, ed. Tanya Saroj Bakhru (Routledge, 2019), 193–194.

57 Hodgson and Watkins, "Feminists and Neo-Malthusians: Past and Present Alliances," 495.

58 Frey, "Neo-Malthusianism and Development: Shifting Interpretations of a Contested Paradigm," 79.

59 Richey, "Family Planning and the Politics of Population in Tanzania : International to Local Discourse," 479.

60 Eager, "From Population Control to Reproductive Rights: Understanding Normative Change in Global Population Policy (1965–1994)," 161.

Indonesian affiliate of IPPF was ahead of the contraceptive campaign.[61] In the Indonesian province of West Java the army was used to go from house to house to take women to centers for the forced insertion of IUDs, even at gunpoint if they refused.[62] The same situation also happened in Bangladesh, where military personnel forced local leaders with more than three children to undergo sterilization.[63]

In Singapore, the government enacted laws that penalized large families, by removing them from the priority list for housing and denying school choice to families of three or more children.[64] In Pakistan, the government and international donors implemented a mass campaign from 1965 to 1970 to insert thousands of IUDs.[65] The family planning personnel were given quotas of insertion for each month. In Vietnam, contraceptive campaigns were not welcomed by people. However, family planning workers were also expected to meet targets for IUD insertions.[66] Success was measured in terms of "numbers of acceptors and of targets met", not on whether people were satisfied by the delivered services.[67]

During the 1960s, the South African government funded an extensive population control policy, which focused on providing free contraception in hospitals.[68] This campaign in practice resulted in "pressuring Black women to accept contraceptive injections and devices, and promoting sterilisation among Blacks".[69]

The same program was extended to Namibia, where women were forced into accepting the injectable contraception Depo-Provera, which is associated with cancer and infertility problems.[70] In 1984 a school in the township

61 Dowbiggin, *The Sterilization Movement and Global Fertility in the Twentieth Century*, 220–221.
62 Hartmann, *Reproductive Rights and Wrongs: The Global Politics of Population Control*, 2016, 109.
63 Hartmann, 251.
64 Stephen L. Isaacs, "Incentives, Population Policy, and Reproductive Rights: Ethical Issues," *Studies in Family Planning* 26, no. 6 (1995): 363.
65 Bourbonnais, "Population Control, Family Planning, and Maternal Health Networks in the 1960s/70s: Diary of an International Consultant," 354.
66 Teerawichitchainan and Amin, "The Role of Abortion in the Last Stage of Fertility Decline in Vietnam," 81.
67 Hartmann, *Reproductive Rights and Wrongs: The Global Politics of Population Control*, 1995, 63.
68 Lindsay, "The Politics of Population Control in Namibia," 59.
69 Lindsay, 59.
70 Lindsay, 59.

of Katatura in Namibia "lined up the girls due to take matriculation and told them that they would not be entered for the exam unless they had contraceptive injections".[71] A supermarket in the Namibian city of Windhoek insisted that a condition for employment of women was to have Depo-Provera injections.[72]

In the state hospital of Katatura there were frequent reports of women who were given injections of Depo-Provera immediately after childbirth without their knowledge or consent.[73] This hospital has also received complaints of sterilizations and insertions of IUDs devices during the course of surgeries without the knowledge or consent of the patients.[74]

In Latin America, women in Mexico, Guatemala, Brazil, Chile and Puerto Rico were used as guinea pigs to test new contraceptives and sterilization methods.[75] In Brazil and Colombia low-income women represent the highest percentages of sterilization, which was caused by the strong emphasis that the family planning campaign put on this method, which targeted poor and rural women.[76] In 2018, the Brazilian President Jair Bolsonaro supported the sterilization of poor people to "combat misery and crime".[77] In the same year, a judge in Mococa, a small town in São Paulo, ordered the compulsory sterilization of Janaina Quirino.[78]

In the Caribbean, efforts to control population growth began in the 1930s, supported by British politicians. In Bermuda, the efforts were directed

71 Lindsay, 60.
72 Lindsay, 60.
73 Lindsay, 60.
74 Lindsay, 60–61.
75 Mass, *Population Target: The Political Economy of Population Control in Latin America*, 210–211.
76 Juan Chackiel and SU.S.na Schkolnik, "América Latina: Los Sectores Rezagados En La Transición de La Fecundidad," in *La fecundidad en América Latina: ¿Transición o revolución?*, eds. CELADE and CEPAL (CELADE-CEPAL 2003) 65 <https://repositorio.cepal.org/bitstream/handle/11362/6742/S043186_es.pdf?sequence=1&isAllowed=y>. Consulted on January 8, 2020; Caetano and Potter (n 95) 79.
77 Ranier Bragon, "Bolsonaro Defendeu Esterilização de Pobres Para Combater Miséria e Crime," *Folha de S.Paulo*, 2018, https://www1.folha.uol.com.br/poder/2018/06/bolsonaro-defendeu-esterilizacao-de-pobres-para-combater-miseria-e-crime.shtml. Consulted on January 8, 2020.
78 Jessica Carvalho Morris, "Who Decides over Janaina's Body? A Case of Forced Sterilization in Brazil," Open Democracy, 2018, https://www.opendemocracy.net/en/democraciaabierta/who-decides-over-janaina-s-body-case-of-forced-sterilizati/. Consulted on January 17, 2019.

to control the black population, which was considered to bear a lot of "illegitimate" children and that they were "lax in the sex code".[79] In 1935, Bermunda's legislature prepared a report recommending the compulsory sterilization of "mental defectives", women with more than one illegitimate children, and the castration of persons found guilty of rape or other sexual offences.[80]

Similar reasons were given in Barbados and Jamaica, where poor people were perceived as those that "produce children with reckless irresponsibility".[81] Some commentators in newspapers spoke about the "ignorant Jamaican mother" who was like "the old woman who lived in a shoe who had so many children because she didn't know what to do".[82] The family planning services included pamphlets to exert pressure on women to discourage large families.[83] Some technocrats even insisted on the participation of black nurses in Jamaica to administer contraceptive services, for "elite family planners saw these nurses as critical in a political sense, as it was believed the campaigns would be more successful if brought to the masses by those of 'their own colour'".[84]

In Haiti, nurses were trained in health clinics to encourage the use of contraception. Some scholars indicate that: "for every mother who had three children, the nurse had to clarify why repeated births were unhealthy. Then at the postnatal consultation and visits to the paediatrician, the nurse would emphasize how children are costly and pregnancy 'hinders' work".[85] The family planners also organized theatrical performances with actors who sang "we are educated", referring to people who used contraception, "to make our community more civilized"; and books were children sang "when we grow up, we will have only two children, two children, two children!"[86]

The most well-known case of forced contraception and abortion is China. In 1979 the government introduced the one-child policy and a broad system of incentives to promote small families through propaganda. The program

79 Nicole C Bourbonnais, *Birth Control in the Decolonizing Caribbean: Reproductive Politics and Practice on Four Islands, 1930–1970* (Cambridge University Press, 2016), 36.

80 Bourbonnais, 38.

81 Quoted in Bourbonnais, 55.

82 Quoted in Bourbonnais, 58.

83 Bourbonnais, 160–161.

84 Bourbonnais, 114.

85 Adam M Silvia, "Modern Mothers for Third World Nations: Population Control, Western Medical Imperialism, and Cold War Politics in Haiti," *Social History of Medicine* 27, no. 2 (2014): 273, https://doi.org/10.1093/shm/hku004.

86 Silvia, 274.

received funds from the UNFPA and the IPPF.[87] The Chinese government installed programs of incentives and disincentives to reduce women's fertility, like reduced food rations and no schooling for the third child.[88] The Chinese government promoted late marriage and introduced a rule of four to five years of interval between the first and second child.[89]

Regarding abortion in China, its coercive policy is a well-known one.[90] The abortion rate was of around 5 million per year in the early 1970s, then it "reached a combined total of more than 120 million in the decade between 1980 and 1990. IUD insertions stood at more than 10 million per year during this time, while tubal ligations were performed on a mass basis only in 1983 (with 16.4 million in that year)".[91]

These practices are not horrors of the past. In 2020, Uighur women denounced forced sterilization and forced insertion of IUDs as a population policy strategy to reduce the birthrates of Muslims in the area.[92] China has claimed that these methods have brought female "emancipation", for Uighur women are no longer "baby-making machines".[93]

The evidence that family planning did not respond to a desperate demand from the people can be perceived in the low percentages of acceptors and continuing users in the 1970s and 1980s. The research of sociologist Denis Hodgson shows that, as early as the 1950s, several prominent American demographers arrived at the conclusion that high fertility in the majority of

87 Patrick Goodenough, "'One-Child' Expert Urges Investigation Before UNFPA Funding Resumes," *CBS News*, 2009, https://www.cnsnews.com/news/article/one-child-expert-urges-investigation-unfpa-funding-resumes. Consulted on January 8, 2020.

88 Connelly, *Fatal Misconception: The Struggle to Control World Population*, 40–46.

89 Frey, "Neo-Malthusianism and Development: Shifting Interpretations of a Contested Paradigm," 94.

90 Max Fisher, "Why China's One-Child Policy Still Leads to Forced Abortions, and Always Will," *Washington Post*, 2013.

91 Frey, "Neo-Malthusianism and Development: Shifting Interpretations of a Contested Paradigm," 95.

92 Emma Harrison and Lily Kuo, "Uighur Muslim Teacher Tells of Forced Sterilisation in Xinjiang," *The Guardian*, 2020, https://www.theguardian.com/world/2020/sep/04/muslim-minority-teacher-50-tells-of-forced-sterilisation-in-xinjiang-china. Consulted on January 8, 2021.

93 Helen Davidson, "Twitter Removes China US Embassy Post Saying Uighur Women No Longer 'Baby-Making Machines,'" *The Guardian*, 2021, https://www.theguardian.com/world/2021/jan/10/twitter-removes-china-us-embassy-post-saying-uighur-women-no-longer-baby-making-machines. Consulted on August 8, 2021.

the developing world was not caused by an urgent "unmet demand" for contraception, but by a desire to have large families.[94] A study of 1974 revealed that

> About half the countries with family planning programs have acceptance rates of less than 5 percent per year. As an order of magnitude, there is a net annual addition of 2-3 percent of women, or couples, to the reproductive ages, and unless acceptance rates are appreciably above the additions to the reproductive ages through population growth, program accomplishments are very small.[95]

A 1988 article by Donald Warwick also indicates that the introduction of family planning programs in many countries (e.g. Philippines, Malaysia, South Africa, Indonesia, and India) found obstacles from the people themselves who were not interested in using them.[96] He highlights that while some governments in the developing world are interested in limiting fertility, there is a very low demand for contraceptives among the population.

In some cases the lack of an "unmet need" for contraception was so evident that the World Bank, the Food and Agriculture Organization (FAO) and UNFPA funded programs that distributed food as an incentive to increase the use and acceptance of contraception.[97] In Bangladesh, field-workers denied food to women who did not help them to meet their governmentally set sterilization targets.[98] In some countries, like Haiti (were one in eight children were severely malnourished) this kind of programs showed its ultimate rationale for population control and the manipulation of the poor, especially when fertility reduction was used to secure more funding for food programs.[99]

Taking into account this panorama, in 1967 demographer Kingsley Davis (member of the Advisory Committee on Population for the U.S.) argued that the problem of population growth in the developing countries was that more people preferred bigger family sizes than in Western societies.[100] Davis also

94 Dennis Hodgson, "Demography as Social Science and Policy Science," *Population and Development Review* 9, no. 1 (1983).

95 W. Parker Mauldin, "Assessment of National Family Planning Programs in Developing Countries," *Studies in Family Planning* 6, no. 2 (1975): 34.

96 Donald P. Warwick, "Culture and the Management of Family Planning Programs," *Studies in Family Planning* 19, no. 1 (1988): 2.

97 Connelly, *Fatal Misconception: The Struggle to Control World Population*, 246.

98 Connelly, 246.

99 Connelly, 246.

100 Kingsley Davis, "Population Policy: Will Current Programs Succeed?," *Science* 158 (1967): 732.

considered that access to contraception, with these prevailing preferences for large families, would not achieve the estimated goal:

> There is no reason to expect that the millions of decisions about family size made by couples in their own interest will automatically control population for the benefit of society. On the contrary, there are good reasons to think they will not do so. At most, family planning can reduce reproduction to the extent that unwanted births exceed wanted births.[101]

Regarding women's actual fertility desires, some surveys compared women's desired number of children and the actual fertility they had. They conclude that "excess fertility" or unwanted pregnancies are not higher in countries with high fertility rates.[102] Some scholars realized that "high fertility is explained almost completely by a high desire for children", in spite of available contraception methods.[103]

As most articles remarked: "since most of the world's people are having, and want to have, families larger than will ensure low or zero growth rates in the near future, policy makers must ultimately face the need to reduce family-size desires".[104] This means that "policy reflections on countries with low contraceptive prevalence and high fertility focus mainly on access to family planning services and ignore the large family size preferences".[105]

An article entitled *Can Family Planning Programs Reduce High Desired Family Size in Sub-Saharan Africa?* written by the vice-president of the Population Council, John Bongaarts, acknowledged this situation:

> The high desired family size that prevails in much of Sub-Saharan Africa hampers fertility decline. Even if the existing unmet need for contraceptives could be addressed, fertility would remain well above replacement levels. This raises the question: Can fertility preferences be influenced, and if so, how?[106]

101 Davis, 732.

102 Lant H. Pritchett, "Desired Fertility and the Impact of Population Policies," *Population and Development Review* 20, no. 1 (1994): 4 and 5.

103 Pritchett, 4.

104 Population Council, "Judith Blake on Fertility Control and the Problem of Voluntarism," *Population and Development Review* 20, no. 1 (1994): 168.

105 Charles Westoff, "Desired Number of Children: 2000–2008," Demographic and Health Surveys, 2010, 43, https://www.dhsprogram.com/pubs/pdf/CR25/CR25.pdf.

106 John Bongaarts, "Can Family Planning Programs Reduce High Desired Family Size in Sub-Saharan Africa?," *International Perspectives on Sexual and Reproductive Health* 37, no. 4 (2011): 209.

In this regard, the academic literature on contraception is full of articles that give advices about how to "persuade" people in developing countries to use contraception and to "desire" smaller families.[107] Several articles indicate the importance of public opinion and using mass media in order to influence people for these purposes.[108]

For this purpose, the Executive Director of the U.S. Commission on Population Growth, Charles Westoff suggested that "a demand for small families should be created".[109] He recommended:

> The use of the mass media to communicate the desirability of fertility control and small families […]. The most interesting approach is the production of soap operas to communicate in dramatic form the advantages of postponing pregnancy and marriage, of the spacing of births, of fewer children, and of gender equality. Such soap operas have been broadcast in Kenya, India, Mexico, Brazil, the Philippines, and elsewhere.[110]

An example of these efforts is the Entertainment-Education program of the John Hopkins University that promotes the small size family model through Third World media.[111] The U.S. government also pays popular singers to promote contraceptives on television and movies and it invests in broadcasting agencies of the non-Western countries to promote this publicity.[112]

Paul Ehrlich, the author of *The Population Bomb*, also proposed writing letters to editors to "complain bitterly about any positive treatment of large

107 See as some examples: Charles Westoff, "International Population Policy," *International Population Policy* 32, no. 4 (1995); John B. Casterline and Steven W. Sinding, "Unmet Need for Family Planning in Developing Countries and Implications for Population Policy," *Policy Research Division Working Paper No. 135*, 2000; John Cleland et al., "Family Planning: The Unfinished Agenda," *The Lancet Sexual and Reproductive Health Series* 368 (2006); Berelson and Lieberson, "Government Efforts to Influence Fertility: The Ethical Issues"; Council, "Judith Blake on Fertility Control and the Problem of Voluntarism"; W. Murray Todd, "Population Policy: Is It a Question of Voluntarism or Coercion?," *Boston College Environmental Affairs Law Review* I, no. 4 (1972).

108 Westoff, "Int. Popul. Policy"; Cleland et al., "Family Planning: The Unfinished Agenda"; Berelson and Lieberson, "Government Efforts to Influence Fertility: The Ethical Issues," 587–588.

109 Westoff, "Int. Popul. Policy," 14.

110 Westoff, 14.

111 "Family Planning," Johns Hopkins Center for Communication Programs, n.d., http://ccp.jhu.edu/health-areas/family-planning/. Consulted on January 8, 2020.

112 Hartmann, *Reproductive Rights and Wrongs: The Global Politics of Population Control*, 1995, 62.

families" in the media.[113] Even the least intrusive family planning programs focused on an "information-education-communication" component to change cultural patterns that welcomed large families and to "educate" people about the "correct" family size that they should desire.[114] In this regard Matthew Connelly indicates:

> All over the world, posters, films, flip charts, and folk performances depicted the "unplanned family" as unclean, unhealthy, violent, and ugly. This included the 1967 Disney film Family Planning, commissioned by the Population Council, which was translated into twenty-four languages […]. Planned families were not merely smaller, more beautiful, and athletic, but surrounded by consumer goods, and sometimes explicit promises of better housing, health care, and education—a veritable garden of earthly delights. Family planning promised miraculous results, to the point that the planned/unplanned family resembled nothing so much as a medieval altarpiece, with viewers offered the choice between heaven and hell.[115]

A very popular business technique called "social marketing" is also widely used in the family planning sector for the same purposes, which consists of creating a demand for contraception using marketing techniques employed for the promotion of other products, like Coca-Cola.[116]

Other demographic articles suggested more aggressive measures. Some promoted public policies that limit access to housing or to school to women with one or two children in order to discourage large families.[117] Other articles discussed the possibility of "compulsory birth controls".[118] Some organizations also suggested creating peer-pressure at the community level for limiting women's fertility, as suggested by Ernest Stern, the World Bank's vice president for South Asia.[119] Some even advocated creating a tax for children or to pay individuals to be sterilized.[120] In this regard, the World Bank,

113 Connelly, *Fatal Misconception: The Struggle to Control World Population*, 259.

114 See Connelly, 264; Todd, "Population Policy: Is It a Question of Voluntarism or Coercion?"

115 Connelly, *Fatal Misconception: The Struggle to Control World Population*, 264.

116 Green, *Broken Promises: How the AIDS Establishment Has Betrayed the Developing World.*

117 Jorge Rodríguez Vignoli, "La Fecundidad Alta En América Latina y El Caribe: Un Riesgo En Transición," in *La Fecundidad En América Latina: ¿Transición o Revolución?*, ed. CELADE and CEPAL (CELADE-CEPAL, 2003), https://repositorio.cepal.org/bitstream/handle/11362/6742/S043186_es.pdf?sequence=1&isAllowed=y. Consulted on March 23, 2020.

118 Todd, "Population Policy: Is It a Question of Voluntarism or Coercion?"

119 Connelly, *Fatal Misconception: The Struggle to Control World Population*, 335.

120 Hodgson and Watkins, "Feminists and Neo-Malthusians: Past and Present Alliances," 484.

UNFPA, and USAID supported a program of incentives for sterilization in Bangladesh.[121]

The adviser to the U.S. government, Kingsley Davis, insisted that abortion "is one of the surest means of controlling reproduction, and one that has been proved capable of reducing birth rates rapidly".[122] Regarding the situation of India and Pakistan, where family planning programs showed low levels of acceptance, Davis insisted that "no sharp decline in the birth rate can be expected until deliberate control by means of contraception, sterilization, abortion, etc. is inaugurated. Today there is no real evidence that such methods are being adopted by any wide sector of the population".[123]

Looking at the big picture, it is evident that contraception did not come from a popular demand of the developing world or from women's voices. Family planning services have been delivered in a top-down fashion and as part of economic and political interests, rather than for the well-being of people.

Thus, the interpretation of SRHR as part of the liberal paradigm will only further disconnect the views of human rights mechanisms from the grass-roots concerns of local populations. Such a reluctance to engage with the complexity of each context will only foster an environment that hinders dialogue with different worldviews and that reduces personal freedom, as the cases of India and Mexico demonstrate.

India's Family Planning Program

During the 1970s a massive government-sponsored campaign of forced sterilizations took place, leading to massive human rights violations, for the family planning program was not based on people's family needs and the acceptance of viewpoint diversity about reproduction and sexuality. This was a case of gross and systematic violations to human rights that has barely received the attention of Western NGOs, media, and human rits mechanisms.

In India, birth control was the proposal of urban-educated middle and upper-class Indians (influenced by Western elites). They considered that the rapid population growth, caused by the "irresponsible sexual breeding" of poor and marginal social groups prevented India's "modernization" and would lead

121 Hartmann, *Reproductive Rights and Wrongs: The Global Politics of Population Control*, 2016, 246.

122 Davis, "Population Policy: Will Current Programs Succeed?," 732.

123 Kingsley Davis, *The Population of India and Pakistan* (Princeton University Press, 1951), 82.

the country into a catastrophe.[124] Population policies started to be encouraged by eugenics and neo-Malthusian organizations like the Indian Eugenic Society and the Indian Birth Control Society.[125]

A key figure in these policies was the Indian economist Radhakamal Mukerjee. He considered that India's biggest problem was overpopulation and advocated for "an adaptative fertility" that was part of India's "modernization".[126] Another important supporter of birth control was professor of biology Gopaljee Ahluwalia, who claimed that India's poverty was caused by "thoughtless, irresponsible and extensive breeding, particularly among the middle and poor classes" and lamented that "racial defects and poisons are multiplying from day to day".[127]

Grounded on these ideas, the first official population policy was adopted by the Indian government in 1952. It received financial and technical support from the UNFPA, the Population Council, the Ford Foundation, USAID, IPPF and the Norwegian government.[128] The donors were aware that this did not respond to an urgent claim of Indian women. For this reason, officials at the Ford Foundation, UNFPA and the IPPF considered that incentives were necessary to "motivate" people to reduce the number of children they wanted to have.[129]

The program was then designed to "target" people, to increase the number of "acceptors", and to encourage small families.[130] They spread propaganda with cartoons and messages pointing out "small family: happiness" and "big family: problems in the way".[131] The program focused on providing contraception,

124 See Sanjam Ahluwalia, *Reproductive Restraints: Birth Control in India, 1877–1947* (University of Illinois Press, 2007), 24; Schoen, *Choice and Coercion: Birth Control, Sterilization, and Abortion in Public Health and Welfare*, 235–238; Connelly, *Fatal Misconception: The Struggle to Control World Population*, 91–94.

125 See Ahluwalia, *Reproductive Restraints: Birth Control in India, 1877–1947*, 27–30; Bashford, *Global Population: History, Geopolitics, and Life on Earth*, 220.

126 Bashford, *Global Population: History, Geopolitics, and Life on Earth*, 220.

127 Ahluwalia, *Reproductive Restraints: Birth Control in India, 1877–1947*, 31; Connelly, *Fatal Misconception: The Struggle to Control World Population*, 140–143.

128 Schoen, *Choice and Coercion: Birth Control, Sterilization, and Abortion in Public Health and Welfare*, 235–245; Dowbiggin, *The Sterilization Movement and Global Fertility in the Twentieth Century*, 122; Connelly, *Fatal Misconception: The Struggle to Control World Population*, 169–170.

129 Connelly, *Fatal Misconception: The Struggle to Control World Population*, 245–246.

130 Rao, *From Population Control to Reproductive Health: Malthusian Arithmetic*, 32.

131 Nilanjana Chatterjee and Nancy E. Riley, "Planning an Indian Modernity: The Gendered Politics of Fertility Control," *Signs* 26, no. 3 (2001): 814.

but also "education" and mass communication campaigns regarding the "correct" family size that should be desired by all Indians.[132] As some scholars have emphasized: "convincing people that small families are desirable has been the main focus of the Indian government's efforts in population control".[133]

However, low prevalence of contraceptive use and the reluctance of most women to use contraception in the future,[134] demonstrated that this was not a priority for people. A study concluded that

> The high proportion of women who do not intend to use family planning suggests that it will be difficult for the family planning program to succeed without a strong Information, Education and Communication (IEC) component to motivate couples to use contraception.[135]

The situation of the family planning program that took place in Uttar Pradesh supports this conclusion. In this region, people were interviewed to know their most urgent needs. The respondents indicated that the main problems of their villages where lack of infrastructure, like buildings, roads, irrigation, etc., but they did not consider that birth control or reduction of fertility was a problem.[136]

Therefore, supporters of population reduction advocated for more intrusive measures. The representative of the Ford Foundation in India, Douglas Ensminger, considered that if incentives to lower fertility failed then more "persuasive" measures needed to be taken. Ensminger insisted that the government of India should be entitled to prohibit parents from having more than three children.[137] He wanted "to make people ashamed of having more than three children".[138]

The idea to introduce sterilization as a contraceptive method was brought by Prime Minister Indira Gandhi's Minister of Health and Family Planning,

132 Chatterjee and Riley, 825–828; A. Dharmalingman, "The Social Context of Family Planning in a South Indian Village," *International Family Planning Perspectives* 21, no. 1 (1995).

133 Chatterjee and Riley, "Planning an Indian Modernity: The Gendered Politics of Fertility Control," 829.

134 "National Family Health Survey 1992–93," 1995, 130–148, https://dhsprogram.com/publications/publication-FRIND1-DHS-Final-Reports.cfm.

135 "National Family Health Survey 1992–93," 165.

136 Warwick, "Culture and the Management of Family Planning Programs," 7.

137 Connelly, *Fatal Misconception: The Struggle to Control World Population*, 245.

138 Connelly, 264.

Sripati Chandrasekher, who received financial aid from Alvin Kaufman, a well-known Canadian businessman promoter of family planning services.[139] Kaufman considered that sterilization should be the most promoted contraceptive method because he believed that people of India were "too poor, too ignorant, and too lazy to practice birth control".[140] With these ideas in mind, the sterilization program was adopted to reduce the fertility of the "abnormal" and "feebleminded" population.[141]

During the discussion and implementation of the program, there was wide opposition within Indian society, including health professionals. The economist Amartya Sen indicates that the family planning policies adopted in the 1970s were rejected by the vast majority of voters.[142] In this regard, Sen argues that these policies are not neutral and that they can manipulate people's choices regarding fertility, for they can only provide some options (to use contraception), while others are denied (the desire to have bigger families).[143]

Opposition also emerged from Muslim and Catholic sectors, especially from people of the rural areas where the vast majority of the population lived.[144] The head of the Family Planning Association in Ceylon explained in the 1950s:

> In the east just now there is violent dislike of "white" people telling us about a "better way" especially in regard to so intimate matters as family planning [...]. There is the feeling that the American more than any other will suggest things that are good for the world but not for the individual "black".[145]

Protests against family planning services emerged especially in rural areas. The village of Uttawar in Haryana was surrounded by the police and every eligible male was forced to undergo sterilization.[146] In other cases, like in the

139 Dowbiggin, *The Sterilization Movement and Global Fertility in the Twentieth Century*, 124–127.

140 Dowbiggin, 125.

141 Connelly, *Fatal Misconception: The Struggle to Control World Population*, 141.

142 Amartya Sen, "Population: Delusion and Reality," *New York Review of Books* 41, no. 15 (1994): 6, https://pdfs.semanticscholar.org/fa9e/62f54ea3b08e5aeeb6401598f7008a209f46.pdf.

143 Sen, 7.

144 Dowbiggin, *The Sterilization Movement and Global Fertility in the Twentieth Century*, 125.

145 Schoen, *Choice and Coercion: Birth Control, Sterilization, and Abortion in Public Health and Welfare*, 227.

146 Connelly, *Fatal Misconception: The Struggle to Control World Population*, 321.

city of Muzaffarnagar in Uttar Pradesh, the police either fired on or arrested the protesters. Between 50 and 150 people were killed during the riots.[147]

Family planning was not a proposal coming from women's organizations either, as "only a small minority of Indian women saw birth control as a means to greater female autonomy".[148] In fact, in the 1930s, women activists in support of contraception found internal opposition, because not all women agreed on this issue.[149] Some well-known feminists, like Rameshwari Nehru, Annie Besant and Khadijah Begum Ferozuddin opposed artificial contraception.[150]

Ferozuddin's opposition was based on Hindu and Islamic religious grounds, and she encouraged self-control as part of the teachings of both religions.[151] Mahatma Gandhi, in his interview with Margaret Sanger, explained his opposition to birth control in 1925, for he considered that the Indian virtue of self-control (*Brahmacharya*) was a better option than artificial contraception.[152]

In the early 1960s, the family planning services appeared to be a failure. Its supporters complained that Indian couples lacked interest in their services and contraceptives were mainly used by women at the end of their child-bearing years, but not by young newly married women.[153] Very few Indians wanted to have fewer children, some of them were even resentful when family planners did not help them with their desired family size bigger than liberal expectations.[154]

This scenario and the "success" of China's coercive one-child policy inspired Indian elites to advance coercive measures. The government led by Indira Gandhi decided to set "targets" and to provide incentives to halve the country's birthrate within the next decade by pushing IUDs and sterilization especially in rural areas.[155] The donors (the Ford Foundation, IPPF, UNFPA

147 Connelly, 324; Rao, *From Population Control to Reproductive Health: Malthusian Arithmetic*, 49.
148 Chatterjee and Riley, "Planning an Indian Modernity: The Gendered Politics of Fertility Control," 821.
149 See Ahluwalia, *Reproductive Restraints: Birth Control in India, 1877–1947*, 91.
150 Ahluwalia, 91–93.
151 Ahluwalia, 93.
152 Tobin, *Politics and Population Control: A Documentary History*, 114.
153 Schoen, *Choice and Coercion: Birth Control, Sterilization, and Abortion in Public Health and Welfare*, 230.
154 Connelly, *Fatal Misconception: The Struggle to Control World Population*, 172–173.
155 Schoen, *Choice and Coercion: Birth Control, Sterilization, and Abortion in Public Health and Welfare*, 250.

and the World Bank) suggested implementing a system of cash payment to motivate people to undergo sterilization or insertion of IUDs.[156]

Health professionals were required to fulfil sterilization quotas not to be penalized and to use incentives to convince men and women to undergo sterilization procedures.[157] The Indian government offered money and radios to "acceptors" of sterilization.[158] Women were paid 30 rupees to undergo sterilization and 15 more for every person they convinced.[159] Hartmann argues that "the emphasis on meeting targets means that people are often pushed into accepting contraception or sterilization against their will, so that family planning workers can fulfill the quotas on which their jobs depend".[160]

By 1967, over a million Indian women had been fitted with IUDs, but the rate was falling because of opposition from midwives and from women who suffered internal bleeding.[161] In view of the situation, Indira Gandhi decided to install an emergency rule from 1975 to 1977 during which she created a massive sterilization program. It performed two-thirds of the three million sterilization that were done from 1972 to 1973.[162] Among them, hundreds died due to lack of hygienic conditions and medicines during and after the surgical interventions.[163]

Norway contributed economically to the sterilization wards and to pay staff incentives to meet their quotas.[164] Just some months before the Third World Population Conference of Bucharest in 1974, UNFPA provided 40 million dollars to the family planning program of India, regardless of the abuses committed.[165]

As Connelly indicates, the main leaders of family planning in India supported compulsory sterilization and UNFPA and the World Bank did not oppose it, even though they were informed about the brutality of the

156 Connelly, *Fatal Misconception: The Struggle to Control World Population*, 224–225.
157 Connelly, 222–223.
158 Isaacs, "Incentives, Population Policy, and Reproductive Rights: Ethical Issues," 363.
159 Connelly, *Fatal Misconception: The Struggle to Control World Population*, 184.
160 Hartmann, *Reproductive Rights and Wrongs: The Global Politics of Population Control*, 2016, 94.
161 Dowbiggin, *The Sterilization Movement and Global Fertility in the Twentieth Century*, 139.
162 Rao, *From Population Control to Reproductive Health: Malthusian Arithmetic*, 39–40.
163 Hartmann, *Reproductive Rights and Wrongs: The Global Politics of Population Control*, 2016, 270–273.
164 Connelly, *Fatal Misconception: The Struggle to Control World Population*, 290.
165 Marika Vicziany, "Coercion in a Soft State: The Family-Planning Program of India: Part I: The Myth of Voluntarism," *Pacific Affairs* 55, no. 3 (1982): 397.

programs.[166] Even the UNFPA program director, Nafis Sadik, expressed her personal view that "compulsion may be needed at the expense of human rights, but that people should be provided with all types of contraceptive means. Without such a provision, compulsory sterilization seems 'unethical'".[167]

During the emergency rule, Gandhi authorized a program of disincentives to reduce fertility (like sanctions for parents with more than two children) and compulsory sterilization.[168] In that period around seven million Indians were sterilized and thousands died of complications from the surgeries.[169] The massive sterilization campaign was so aggressive that it led to the historical defeat of Gandhi's government. However, this seems to be a case of "success" for UNFPA, who in 1983 awarded Indira Gandhi with its Population Prize.[170]

Under this policy, families had to agree to sterilization if they wanted to keep their jobs or to receive medical treatment.[171] Matthew Connelly remarks that "those with three or more children had to produce a sterilization certificate to be eligible for new housing".[172] Sterilization became a condition for land allotments, irrigation water, electricity, ration cards, rickshaw licenses, and promotions.[173] A certificate of sterilization was required even to obtain fertilizers.[174] In the states of Maharashtra and Uttar Pradesh families with more than three children were barred from obtaining scholarships.[175] In 1976, the minister of health and family planning, Karan Singh, said that the government would not oppose the states, like Maharashtra, that wanted to send parents to prison with three or more children, if they refused to accept sterilization.[176] Sripati Chandrasekhar even proposed to make sterilization compulsory for every person with three or more children, but it was rejected for impractical, not for moral or legal reasons.[177]

166 Connelly, *Fatal Misconception: The Struggle to Control World Population*, 320–324.
167 Connelly, 323.
168 Connelly, 318.
169 Dowbiggin, *The Sterilization Movement and Global Fertility in the Twentieth Century*, 122.
170 Angus and Butler, *Too Many People? Population, Migration, and the Environmental Crisis*, 92.
171 Schoen, *Choice and Coercion: Birth Control, Sterilization, and Abortion in Public Health and Welfare*, 250; Rao, *From Population Control to Reproductive Health: Malthusian Arithmetic*, 45–50.
172 Connelly, *Fatal Misconception: The Struggle to Control World Population*, 321.
173 Rao, *From Population Control to Reproductive Health: Malthusian Arithmetic*, 48.
174 Rao, 48.
175 Connelly, *Fatal Misconception: The Struggle to Control World Population*, 229.
176 Connelly, 318.
177 Connelly, 230.

In 1971 the government approved the Medical Termination of Pregnancy Act to legalize abortion. This legislation was part of the population policy program of the government to reduce fertility in India,[178] though even today 58 percent of the population opposes abortion.[179]

Looking at the facts, it is no surprise that the most used contraceptive method in India is sterilization (around 39 percent among contraceptive users).[180] What is surprising is to see a joint statement of the WHO along with the U.N. Office of the High Commissioner on Human Rights (OHCHR), UNAIDS, United Nations Development Program, UNFPA, United Nations Children's Fund and U.N. Women against forced sterilization, which supports the continuation of sterilizations despite the evidence on its employment that can hardly be reconciled with human rights norms. The statement starts by affirming that "sterilization is one of the most widely used forms of contraception in the world" and that "sterilization as a method of contraception and family planning should be available, accessible to all, of good quality and free from discrimination, coercion or violence".[181] This seems to be a too soft approach to these kinds of human rights violations that can even amount to crimes against humanity or genocide.[182]

The Indian situation has not changed that much. By 1995 Indian women still complained that the insertion of IUD without their consent or knowledge was a routine practice in hospitals.[183] In 2006 teachers in Uttar Pradesh were ordered to find at least two "volunteers" for sterilization or face disciplinary

178 Sripati Chandrasekhar, *Abortion In A Crowded World: The Problem of Abortion With Special Reference to India* (University of Washington Press, 1974).

179 Pew Research Center "Global Morality."

180 "Trends in Contraceptive Use Worldwide 2015," 2015, 52, https://www.un.org/en/development/desa/population/publications/pdf/family/trendsContraceptiveUse2015Report.pdf.

181 U.N. Women, "UN organizations call for an end to forced, coercive and involuntary sterilization" (18 June 2014) <https://www.unwomen.org/en/news/stories/2014/6/joint-statement-on-forced-sterilizations>. Consulted on May 12, 2021.

182 Rome Statute of the International Criminal Court (1998): Article 7(g) establishes that enforced sterilization when "committed as part of a widespread or systematic attack directed against any civilian population, with knowledge of the attack" is a crime against humanity. Article 6(d) indicates that "imposing measures intended to prevent births within the group" when "committed with intent to destroy, in whole or in part, a national, ethnical, racial or religious group, as such" is a crime of genocide.

183 Cecilia Van Hollen, "Moving Targets: Routine IUD Insertion in Maternity Wards in Tamil Nadu, India," *Reproductive Health Matters* 6, no. 11 (1998): 100–103.

measures.[184] In the same district, in 2004 farm workers received guns and gun licenses in exchange for sterilizations.[185] As of 2021, there is a new governmental initiative to impose a two-child policy and further incentives to encourage more sterilizations.[186]

The Debate on Abortion in Mexico

Another category of SRHR that is also controversial is the issue of abortion. In the UDHR, this question was explicitly excluded, because some delegates from Western states, China and the Soviet Union supported it, but members from Latin American and Muslim countries wanted to protect life from conception.[187] The drafters decided to exclude the issue from the UDHR because there was no consensus on such a sensitive topic. For this same reason, abortion was also excluded during the drafting process of the Convention on the Rights of the Child[188] and of the ICCPR.[189]

This approach is consistent with the fact that there is no human rights treaty that includes access to abortion, except for the Protocol to the African Charter on Human and People's Rights on the Rights of Women in Africa of 2003 (the Maputo Protocol) that is a regional treaty. The Protocol has been ratified by 40 out of 55 states members of the African Union (with majoritarian populations that are opposed to abortion)[190] and six of them have expressed reservations.[191] Even in this case, this provision is not about

184 Dowbiggin, *The Sterilization Movement and Global Fertility in the Twentieth Century*, 228.

185 Randeep Ramesh, "Outrage at Guns for Sterilisation Policy," *The Guardian*, 2004, https://www.theguardian.com/world/2004/nov/01/india.randeepramesh. Consulted on March 23, 2020.

186 Hannah Ellis-Petersen, "India States Considering Two-Child Policy and Incentives for Sterilisation," *The Guardian*, 2021, https://www.theguardian.com/world/2021/jul/14/india-states-considering-two-child-policy-and-incentives-for-sterilisation. Consulted on August 23, 2021.

187 See Samnøy, *Human Rights as International Consensus: Making the Universal Declaration of Human Rights 1945–1948*, 90.

188 See Sharon Detrick, *A Commentary on the United Nations Convention on the Rights of the Child* (Martinus Nijhoff, 1999), 102.

189 See Bossuyt, *Guide to the "Travaux Préparatoires" of the International Covenant on Civil and Political Rights*, 121.

190 Inglehart, Haerpfer, and Moreno, "World Values Survey: Round Seven - Country-Pooled Datafile Version."

191 "High Level Consultation on the Ratification of the Maputo Protocol," African Union, 2020, https://au.int/en/newsevents/20180129/high-level-consultation-ratification-map

abortion on demand, but only "in cases of sexual assault, rape, incest, and where the continued pregnancy endangers the mental and physical health of the mother or the life of the mother or the foetus".[192]

In contrast, another regional instrument, the American Convention on Human Rights of 1969 protects life from conception,[193] and the Convention on the Rights of the Child protects unborn life in its preamble.[194] Also, the conferences on population and women expressly excluded the consideration of abortion as a human right or as a method of family planning.[195]

Moreover, the outcome documents of these conferences expressly insisted that "any measures or changes related to abortion within the health system can only be determined at the national or local level according to the national legislative process".[196] Therefore, legally speaking, there is no international human right to abortion, nor can abortion be considered as part of the content of any human right obligation.

Looking at state practice, 117 countries either totally ban abortion (24 countries) or allow it only in limited circumstances (93 countries), mainly to save the life of the mother or in case of rape or incest.[197] The first ground is legal in 98 percent of the countries worldwide, the second one amounts to 43 percent of legislations.[198] Also, it is relevant to remark that among the states that recognize abortion as legal, most of them have done so through the judicial rule of a court (which invoked human rights standards set by treaty

uto-protocol#:~:text=To date%2C out of 55,have not ratified the Protocol. Consulted on March 23, 2020.

192 Protocol to the African Charter on Human and People's Rights on the Rights of Women in Africa (2003), article 14.2.c <https://www.un.org/en/africa/osaa/pdf/au/protocol_rights_women_africa_2003.pdf>. Consulted on May 23, 2020.

193 American Convention on Human Rights (1969), article 4.1

194 Convention on the Rights of the Child (1980). Its preamble says: "the child, by reason of his physical and mental immaturity, needs special safeguards and care, including appropriate legal protection, before as well as after birth".

195 "Report of the International Conference on Population and Development," 46.

196 "Report of the International Conference on Population and Development," para. 8.25.

197 Theodorou and Sandstrom, "How Abortion Is Regulated around the World."

198 UK All-Party Parliamentary Group (APPG) on Population, Development and Reproductive Health, "Who Decides? We trust women Abortion in the developing world and the UK", (March 2018) p. 15 <https://static1.squarespace.com/static/5dc18cebdf3c7b576d0caacf/t/6018198ac5636e4cc26f08b7/1612192166560/Abortion+hearings+report+-+March+2018.PDF>. Consulted on February 23, 2021.

bodies)[199] and not as the result of a democratic dialogue that reflects the will of the people and in accordance with the national legislative process.[200]

Furthermore, in the majority of the states that permit abortion, this procedure is not established as a right, rather it is an exemption from criminal responsibility, which implies a totally different legal and moral status.[201] This means that in those countries, abortion is not framed as a legal entitlement that empowers women, not even as a morally acceptable action. Rather abortion, in those circumstances, is considered as not criminally punishable, which means that it is perceived as a morally wrongful action and a criminal offense, but one which will be tolerated or will not be sanctioned because of some specific circumstances.

Only around 30 percent of the countries in the world allow abortion on request (or almost totally on request), but with gestational limits.[202] Among these states, only Western European nations, the U.S., Canada and Australia (and recently Argentina) have legalized it based on feminists' demands. However, these modifications do not totally reflect people's opinion in those countries, where still a considerable part of the population holds a middle ground position on this debate.[203] Even in the West, it is far from settled that the abortion debate is finished. For instance, the American Supreme Court has just overruled the case that opened the door to abortion.[204]

199 Johanna B. Fine, Katherine Mayall, and Lilian Sepúlveda, "The Role of International Human Rights Norms in the Liberalization of Abortion Laws Globally," *Health and Human Rights Journal* June (2017).

200 See Pilar Zambrano and William Saunders, eds., Unborn Human Life and Fundamental Rights: Leading Constitutional Cases under Scrutiny (Peter Lang, 2020).

201 Alejandro González-Varas Ibáñez, "Aspectos Ético-Jurídicos de La Regulación Del Aborto En España," *Revista General de Derecho Canónico y Derecho Eclesiástico Del Estado*, no. 23 (2010).

202 UK All-Party Parliamentary Group (APPG) on Population, Development and Reproductive Health, "Who Decides? We trust women Abortion in the developing world and the UK", (March 2018) p. 15 <https://static1.squarespace.com/static/5dc18cebdf3c7b576d0caacf/t/6018198ac5636e4cc26f08b7/1612192166560/Abortion+hearings+report+-+March+2018.PDF>. Consulted on February 23, 2021.

203 Inglehart, Haerpfer, and Moreno, "World Values Survey: Round Seven - Country-Pooled Datafile Version."

204 Caroline Kelly, "More States Are Expected to Pass Anti-Abortion Bills Challenging Roe v. Wade Ahead of Monumental Supreme Court Case," *CNN*, 2021, https://edition.cnn.com/2021/05/18/politics/mississippi-abortion-case-impact-supreme-court-abortion-bans-activists/index.html. Consulted on March 23, 2021.

The majority of countries that belong to this 30 percent (among which there are some former Soviet Union states, Turkey, India, Tunisia, China, and Vietnam) have liberalized abortion not to champion women's rights, but as population control strategy to regulate fertility.[205] This statement is further confirmed by the fact that acceptance of abortion on demand in those countries remains low (in Albania two percent, Bosnia and Herzegovina eight percent, China two percent, Kazakhstan seven percent, Serbia seven percent, and Vietnam three percent), while percentages of total rejection remain high (in Armenia 54 percent, China 61 percent, Kyrgyzstan 76 percent, and Tunisia 55 percent).[206]

The idea of abortion as empowerment, as a human right, or as a key element of freedom for women can only make sense within a liberal worldview. Only within this narrative women's freedom and equality depends on the legalization of abortion as a means to "own" her body, for here a dignified life depends on pursuing individualistic lifestyles, absent of interdependent relationships or responsibilities. The "true" liberated woman is the one that pursues a liberal vision of human success: individualistic, secular, materialistic, and preference oriented.[207]

Only within this worldview, where women's bodies should be adapted to a male standard of reproduction (absent of the burdens of pregnancy and motherhood) instead of adapting society to the needs of women's bodies, can abortion be considered as a fundamental right. However, as surveys indicate,[208] not everybody shares this vision of what freedom, equality, and a dignified life means, both for women and men.

205 See Savage, "The Law of Abortion in the Union of Soviet Socialist Republics and the People's Republic of China: Women's Rights in Two Socialist Countries"; Donna Harsch, "Communism and Women," in *The Oxford Handbook of the History of Communism*, ed. Stephen A. Smith (Oxford University Press, 2013); Maffi and Affes, "The Right to Abortion in Tunisia after the Revolution of 2011: Legal, Medical, and Social Arrangements as Seen through Seven Abortion Stories"; Teerawichitchainan and Amin, "The Role of Abortion in the Last Stage of Fertility Decline in Vietnam"; Chandrasekhar, *Abortion In A Crowded World: The Problem of Abortion With Special Reference to India*.

206 Inglehart, Haerpfer, and Moreno, "World Values Survey: Round Seven—Country-Pooled Datafile Version."

207 See this argument as explained by the feminist scholar Erika Bachiochi, "The Troubling Ideals at the Heart of Abortion Rights," *The Atlantic*, 2020, https://www.theatlantic.com/ideas/archive/2020/01/equality-autonomy-abortion/605356/. Consulted on March 23, 2020.

208 See supra the first section of this chapter.

In recent years, attempts to legalize abortion in Mexico have increased, which for a foreign viewer might appear as a national claim from the people (especially women) that demand its legalization, or at least that is how Western media portrays the situation.[209] Nevertheless, a closer look at the situation reveals a different picture.

Before analyzing this case, some background about Mexico is required. Following the American model, Mexico was constituted as a federation with 32 states. According to the federal constitution, each state enjoys a broad degree of local autonomy to determine their own local legislation and constitution. Only specific issues are reserved to the federation, as established in the constitution.

Regarding the introduction of contraception and abortion in the public debate, the eugenic and neo-Malthusian philosophies permeated Mexican elites since the beginning of the nineteenth century, which culminated in the creation of several laws to regulate demographics, like the *Ley General de Población* [General Population Act].[210] In the context of the political pressure provoked by the "population problem", a national family planning program was installed in 1972 during the administration of president Luis Echeverría with the specific aim of reducing births among the country.[211]

In 1974, President Echeverría proposed an important reform to the legislation on this matter.[212] This initiative created the *Consejo Nacional de Población* [National Population Council] (CONAPO) and granted the faculty to the government to "regulate" and "stabilize" population growth with family planning strategies and to "influence population dynamics" through the educational system.[213]

Since then, the Mexican government has supported family planning and educational campaigns to reduce population growth and to encourage small families. Echeverría's campaign slogan "*la familia pequeña vive mejor*" [the small

209 For instance: "Mexican Women Demanding Legalization of Abortion Clash with Police," *Reuters*, 2020, https://www.reuters.com/article/us-mexico-abortion-protest-idUSKBN26J35Q. Consulted on March 23, 2021.

210 CONAPO, "Hacia Una Acción Internacional Para Frenar El Incremento de La Población," 89–96.

211 CONAPO, 100–101.

212 *Ley General de Población* (7 January 1974), arts. 3(II) and 3(IV). <http://www.diputados.gob.mx/LeyesBiblio/pdf/140_120718.pdf>. Consulted on January 12, 2021.

213 CONAPO, "Hacia Una Acción Internacional Para Frenar El Incremento de La Población," 122–131.

family lives better] and the message of cartoons "*vámonos haciendo menos*" [let's be less] were publicized in television and the radio for this objective.[214] In this context, some politicians started to wonder whether the legalization of abortion was adequate for these purposes.[215]

In Mexico, the first feminist groups that demanded the legalization of abortion were highly educated and economically privileged women.[216] Meanwhile, working class women's organizations focused on issues they considered more important for the daily life of most Mexicans: material needs, education, economic wellbeing, affordable housing, safety, childcare and health care.[217]

Regarding the opinion of the Mexican people, according to both the Pew Research Center and the World Values Survey more than half of the people are morally opposed to abortion in all circumstances.[218] A national survey of 2012 showed that 56 percent of Mexicans are opposed to abortion, while only 31 percent say they are in favor of it.[219] This survey revealed that even among the people that support abortion, most of them only agree to it when the life of the mother is in danger or as a result of rape, but support for abortion on request is acceptable only to 11 percent of the population.[220] According to the estimates of the World Values Survey that percentage is even lower: only 5 percent.[221]

Another national survey of 2019 conducted by the newspaper *El Financiero* showed that the majority of people in 30 out of the 32 states of the Mexican federation are opposed to abortion.[222] The results highlight that

214 Carlos Welti Chanes, "El Consejo Nacional de Población a 40 Años de Una Política Explícita de Población En México," *Papeles de Población* 20, no. 81 (2014).

215 CONAPO, "Hacia Una Acción Internacional Para Frenar El Incremento de La Población."

216 See Nelson, "Abortion Rights and Human Rights in Mexico," 129–131.

217 See Elizabeth Maier, "Documenting Mexico's Culture War," *Latin American Perspectives* 39, no. 6 (2012): 158.

218 See Pew Research Center "Global Morality"; Inglehart, Haerpfer, and Moreno, "World Values Survey: Round Seven - Country-Pooled Datafile Version."

219 Yamil Nares Feria, "¿Qué Pensamos Los Mexicanos Sobre El Aborto?," *Animal Político*, 2013, https://www.animalpolitico.com/la-ventana-indiscreta/que-pensamos-los-mexicanos-sobre-el-aborto/.

220 Nares Feria.

221 Inglehart, Haerpfer, and Moreno, "World Values Survey: Round Seven - Country-Pooled Datafile Version."

222 Alejandro Moreno, "Apoyo Mayoritario Al Aborto En CDMX y Baja California," *El Financiero*, 2019, https://www.elfinanciero.com.mx/nacional/apoyo-mayoritario-al-aborto-en-cdmx-y-bc.

63 percent of Mexicans are against the legalization of abortion, while only 32 percent of them agree that it should be legal and only in specific circumstances.[223] Only in Mexico City (where abortion was decriminalized in 2007) and Baja California, support for abortion was of 53 percent and 51 percent respectively.[224]

This survey indicated that in Chiapas (which is one of the states with the highest levels of poverty and with a majority indigenous population) 74 percent of the people are opposed to this practice.[225] It also demonstrated that in this state more women than men are opposed to it.[226] The same sex divide occurs at the national level. In 31 out of the 32 Mexican states, more women are opposed to abortion than men. While 38 percent of men agree with its legalization, only 27 percent of women share this position, and 69 percent of women do not even consider it as a women's rights issue.[227] In the state of Nayarit the gap between men (39 percent) and women (18 percent) who support abortion is of 21 points.

The most recent survey, conducted by Data Room in 2021, confirmed again that 57 percent of Mexicans are opposed to abortion, which means that two out of three persons are opposed to the legalization of this practice.[228] This study also indicated that 82 percent of Mexicans agree that life should be constitutionally protected from conception.[229] On the question about how to help a pregnant women in a situation of vulnerability, 62 percent of the people consider that the best aid is to provide her with free and accessible medical health services, 22 percent consider that economic support is key, 12 percent consider that emotional support is fundamental, and only two percent maintain that access to abortion is the best option that society can offer her.[230]

223 Moreno.

224 Moreno.

225 Moreno.

226 Alejandro Moreno, "OMG! La Mayoría de Las Mujeres En México Están En Contra Del Aborto," *Nación 321*, 2019, https://www.nacion321.com/encuestas/omg-la-mayoria-de-las-mujeres-en-mexico-estan-en-contra-del-aborto.

227 Moreno.

228 Wendy Roa, "SCJN Discutirá Validez de Leyes Sobre Aborto Aprobadas Por Varios Estados," *Excelsior*, 2021, https://www.excelsior.com.mx/nacional/scjn-discutira-validez-de-leyes-sobre-aborto-aprobadas-por-varios-estados/1469928. Consulted on September 23, 2021.

229 Roa.

230 Roa.

As this book is being written, abortion on demand (up to 12 weeks of gestation) has only been decriminalized (not recognized as a right)[231] in Mexico City (2007) and other nine states (Baja California, Baja California Sur, Oaxaca, Sinaloa, Guerrero, Quintana Roo, Colima, Hidalgo, and Veracruz), as a result of the judicial activism of the Mexican Supreme Court of Justice. Regarding the case of Mexico City, the reform to the Criminal Code was led by an alliance of five organizations (*La Alianza*) [The Alliance] financed and trained by the American organization IPPF.[232] The NGOs that created *La Alianza* have received more than 10 million dollars from IPPF just in the period of 2010–2014 to finance the promotion of abortion in Mexico.[233]

Following the "cultural sensitivity" approach of UNFPA, the organization that led the coalition, *Católicas por el derecho a decidir* [Catholics for the Right to Decide] (CDD), has been presented as a Mexican and Catholic institution that advocates for the right to abortion.[234] CDD (founded by an American pro-choice militant and currently directed by a British activist)[235] uses and distorts local religious beliefs so they can fit the liberal sexual paradigm promoted by this organization.[236] CDD uses Catholic symbols and false priests to confuse people, so they can be manipulated to think that the Catholic Church supports their agenda.[237] In this regard, there is a well-documented work by Keck and Sikkink that carefully studies the creation and operation of international networks of pressure groups that build transnational strategies to locally promote their agendas.[238]

231 See: *Código Penal para el Distrito Federal* (2002), arts. 144 and 145. <https://www.congresocdmx.gob.mx/media/documentos/9cd0cdef5d5adba1c8e25b34751cccfdcca80e2c.pdf>. Consulted on October 23, 2020.

232 See: IPPFWHR, México: *Católicas por el derecho a decidir* <https://www.ippfwhr.org/country/mexico/>; and IPPF, Financial statement 2008 <https://www.ippf.org/sites/default/files/ippf_financial_statements_2008.pdf>. Consulted on September 22, 2020.

233 All the financial statements of IPPF are available at: <https://www.ippf.org/resources?fpercent5B0percent5D=publication_seriespercent3A236&page=1>. Consulted on September 23, 2020.

234 See its webpage: <https://www.catolicasmexico.org/i/>. Consulted on January 26, 2021.

235 According to its website: CDD, *Quiénes somos* <https://www.catolicasmexico.org/i/quienes-somos/#valores-cdd>. Consulted on October 21, 2020.

236 See its webpage: <https://www.catolicasmexico.org/i/>. Consulted on January 26, 2021.

237 "Arquidiócesis Mexicana Alerta Sobre Falso Sacerdote a Favor Del Aborto," *Aciprensa*, 2014, https://www.aciprensa.com/noticias/arquidiocesis-mexicana-alerta-sobre-falso-sacerdote-a-favor-del-aborto-45121. Consulted on March 23, 2020.

238 See Keck and Sikkink, *Activists Beyond Borders: Advocacy Networks in International Politics*.

When abortion was partially decriminalized in Mexico City in 2007, only 38 percent of the population of this city supported the legislation.[239] Even among women that had aborted in Mexico City, 42 percent of them considered abortion should not be legalized.[240] As a reaction, at least 17 of the 32 states of Mexico have made amendments to protect the right to life since conception.

In 2008, another survey was conducted among the inhabitants of Mexico City. It revealed that support for abortion in the capital had raised to 63 percent since its decriminalization,[241] which indicates that the change was not a product of the free will of people, but rather an imposed social engineering process through a legislative change. In the meanwhile, the main cause of discrimination against women in the workplace in Mexico City is based on pregnancy,[242] an area that seems of little concern to abortion promoters and that is encouraged by the legalization of this practice.

As for the characteristics of abortion supporters in Mexico City, according to surveys, those with higher education, men, and those who did not attend religious services showed "significantly greater odds of supporting the Mexico City law, compared with those having less education, women, those who attended religious services more frequently, and those reporting no political party affiliation".[243] Survey after survey indicates that the majority of pro-choice people in Mexico are young (18–25 years old) cohorts, who are either students or work in the private sector, have higher education, possess high socioeconomic status, and do not attend religious services.[244]

239 Kate Wilson et al., "Public Opinion on Abortion in Mexico City after the Landmark Reform," *Studies in Family Planning* 42, no. 3 (2011): 178.

240 Benito Ramírez Valverde and Gustavo Suárez Vallejos, Pía F. Ramírez Valverde, "Opinión de Mujeres Con Interrupción Voluntaria de Embarazo Sobre La Legalización Del Aborto. Cuestionario Aplicado En La Ciudad de Puebla, México," *Boletín Mexicano de Derecho Comparado* 40, no. 120 (2007).

241 Wilson et al., "Public Opinion on Abortion in Mexico City after the Landmark Reform," 178.

242 Miguel Ángel Mancera Espinosa et al., "Discriminación Laboral Hacia La Mujer En La Ciudad de México: Despido Por Embarazo," 2015, http://data.copred.cdmx.gob.mx/wp-content/uploads/2015/08/Informe-Discriminación-Laboral-hacia-la-Mujer-Despido-por-Embarazo.pdf. Consulted on March 23, 2020.

243 Wilson et al., "Public Opinion on Abortion in Mexico City after the Landmark Reform," 179.

244 Nares Feria, "¿Qué Pensamos Los Mexicanos Sobre El Aborto?"

This implies that the archetypical profile of the abortion supporter is a person with an individualistic, secular and autonomy-oriented lifestyle. Thus, the legalization of abortion in Mexico does not follow from the call of vulnerable and marginalized women in a "backward" society. Rather, it is promoted by a minoritarian, but wealthy and powerful segment of the population.

Despite the evidence, some groups continue to pressure the government and the population to legalize and accept abortion. In 2020 the Mexican Supreme Court of Justice (SCJ) analyzed a case related to the legalization of abortion in the state of Veracruz. In view of the opportunity, 140 representatives of the Mexican Congress (from different political parties) showed their support for the legalization of abortion.[245] In respond to this action, around 237 other representatives, from different political parties (including some members of the ruling left-wing party) and 219 lawyers from all around the country submitted a letter requesting the SCJ to rule against the legalization of this practice.[246] The letter indicated that 98 percent of the people in prison for the crime of abortion are men that provoked forced abortions on women.[247] At the end, the Mexican SCJ decided not to rule on the merits of the issue because of procedural aspects.

In the legislative branch, there have also been a significant number of attempts to legalize this practice. Only in the past four years, initiatives for this purpose have been presented in several local congresses of the following states: in Guanajuato,[248] Jalisco,[249] Hidalgo, Guerrero,[250] Durango,[251]

245 Selene Flores, "Legisladores Piden a Corte 'Honrar División de Poderes' Por Despenalización de Aborto," *Milenio*, 2020, https://www.milenio.com/estados/veracruz-legisladores-scjn-honrar-division-poderes-aborto. Consulted on March 23, 2021.

246 Flores.

247 Flores.

248 "El Congreso de Guanajuato Cierra Las Puertas Al Aborto Legal," *Expansión*, 2020, https://politica.expansion.mx/estados/2020/05/26/diputados-guanajuato-desechan-despenalizar-aborto. Consulted on June 23, 2021.

249 "Presenta PRD Iniciativa Para Legalizar Aborto En Jalisco," *Proceso*, 2011, https://www.proceso.com.mx/265240/presenta-prd-iniciativa-para-legalizar-aborto-en-jalisco.

250 Rogelio Agustín Esteban, "Morena Propone Legalizar Aborto En Casos de Violación En Guerrero," *Milenio*, 2020, https://www.milenio.com/estados/morena-propone-legalizar-aborto-casos-violacion-guerrero.

251 Adriana Magallanes, "Durango Se Resiste a Garantizar Acceso Al Aborto Por Violación," *Milenio*, October 24, 2019, https://www.milenio.com/estados/durango-resiste-garantizar-acceso-aborto-violacion. Consulted on June 23, 2021.

Sonora,[252] Michoacán,[253] Sinaloa,[254] Quintana Roo,[255] Nuevo León,[256] and San Luis Potosi,[257] among others. In all these cases the local congresses have rejected the initiatives with votes against it from members of both left and right-wing political parties.

In 2014 an initiative to protect life from conception was presented in the congress of the state of Nuevo León. In response, the Mexican branch of the U.N. Office of the High Commissioner on Human Rights (OHCHR), U.N. Women and UNFPA presented a letter against the initiative. They maintained that according to the ICESCR, the CEDAW Convention, the recommendations of human rights treaty bodies, and the IACtHR, it was a violation of human rights to protect unborn life.[258] These agencies argued that the congress of Nuevo León was obliged to provide access to abortion as a human rights obligation.[259] These agencies presented this position, even though abortion is not part of their mandate, without any legal basis in human rights treaties, and regardless of the opinion of people in Nuevo León.

In August of 2019, an amendment to decriminalize abortion in the Criminal Code of the state of Oaxaca was presented in the local congress. Oaxaca is one of the poorest states of Mexico and the second state with the

252 "Desata Debate En Sonora Iniciativa Para Aborto Legal," *Milenio*, 2018, https://www.elimparcial.com/sonora/sonora/Desata-debate-en-Sonora-iniciativa-para-aborto-legal-20181004-0088.html.

253 Ernesto Martínez Elorriaga, "Diputados de Michoacán Rechazan Legalizar El Aborto," *La Jornada*, 2020, https://www.jornada.com.mx/ultimas/estados/2020/06/10/diputados-de-michoacan-rechazan-legalizar-el-aborto-5478.html. Consulted on June 23, 2021.

254 Luis Gerardo Beltrán López, "Presentan Iniciativa Para Despenalizar El Aborto En Sinaloa," *Debate*, 2020, https://www.debate.com.mx/culiacan/Presentan-iniciativa-para-despenalizar-el-aborto-en-Sinaloa-20200928-0181.html.

255 Larissa Makatia, "Despenalización Del Aborto En Q Roo, Congelada," *La Izquierda Diario*, 2020, http://www.laizquierdadiario.mx/Despenalizacion-del-aborto-en-Q-Roo-congelada. Consulted on June 23, 2021.

256 Yolanda Chio and Vicente Juárez, "Avalan En SLP y Nuevo León Leyes Contra El Aborto," *La Jornada*, 2020, https://www.jornada.com.mx/ultimas/estados/2020/05/23/avalan-en-slp-y-nuevo-leon-leyes-contra-el-aborto-750.html. Consulted on January 22, 2023.

257 "El Congreso de San Luis Potosí Rechaza La Legalización Del Aborto," *Expansión*, 2020, https://politica.expansion.mx/estados/2020/05/21/el-congreso-de-san-luis-potosi-rechaza-la-legalizacion-del-aborto. Consulted on June 23, 2021.

258 Adrián Rodríguez Alcocer and Marcelo Bartolini Esparza, "Las Recomendaciones de Los Organismos Internacionales Como Herramientas de Presión Política," *Derecho Público Iberiamericano*, no. 5 (2014): 234–35.

259 Rodríguez Alcocer and Bartolini Esparza, 234–35.

highest concentration of indigenous peoples.[260] Oaxaca is also a state where there have been repeated allegations of forced sterilization and contraception against indigenous women and men.[261]

These violations to human rights were pointed out by the Committee on the Elimination of Racial Discrimination (CERD) in its concluding observations of Mexico's report in 2006,[262] and by Mexico's National Commission on Human Rights in 2002.[263] In this regard, the CERD's member José Francisco Cali Tzay recalled that "the Convention on the Prevention and Punishment of the Crime of Genocide classified the imposition of measures intended to prevent births within a population group as a form of genocide".[264]

Regardless of this alarming situation which questions the environment of reproductive freedom in Oaxaca, the local congress voted the initiative to decriminalize abortion in the first trimester.[265] Many members of the congress remarked that the initiative was illegal, for it contradicts the local constitution, which in its article 12 protects human life from conception.[266] After

260 Senado de la Republica, "Población indígena de México con mayor probabilidad de caer en pobreza, destaca el IBD" (12 August 2017) <http://comunicacion.senado.gob.mx/index.php/informacion/boletines/38021-poblacion-indigena-de-mexico-con-mayor-probabilidad-de-caer-en-pobreza-destaca-el-ibd.html#:~:text=Elpercent2075percent20porpercent20cientopercent20de,percent2Cpercent20Guerreropercent2Cpercent20Hidalgopercent20ypercent20YucatpercentC3percentA1n>. Consulted on January 12, 2020.

261 Silvia Magally, "Esterilización Forzada: El Gobierno Admite El Exterminio," *Cimac Noticias*, 2002, https://cimacnoticias.com.mx/noticia/esterilizacion-forzada-el-gobierno-admite-el-exterminio/. Consulted on June 23, 2021.

262 CERD, Concluding observations of the Committee on the Elimination of Racial Discrimination Mexico, Sixty-eighth session20 February-10 March 2006, CERD/C/MEX/CO/15 (4 April 2006), para 17.

263 Comisión Nacional de los Derechos Humanos, Recomendación 46/2002 Caso de la señora Hermelinda del Valle Ojeda, indígena chinanteca de la comunidad Río Chiquito, Santiago Jocotepec, Oaxaca (2002) <https://www.cndh.org.mx/documento/recomendacion-462002>. Consulted on February 2, 2021.

264 CERD, Sixty-eighth session: Summary record of the 1731st meeting, Held at the Palais Wilson, Geneva, on Monday, 20 February 2006, CERD/C/SR.1731 (24 February 2006), para. 33.

265 "El Congreso de Oaxaca Aprueba La Despenalización Del Aborto," *Expansión*, 2019, https://politica.expansion.mx/estados/2019/09/25/la-ley-en-favor-del-aborto-en-oaxaca-avanza-es-aprobada-en-lo-general. Consulted on June 23, 2021.

266 Constitución Política del Estado Libre y Soberano de Oaxaca (1922), art. 12 <https://www.oaxaca.gob.mx/cocitei/wp-content/uploads/sites/48/2019/07/CONSTITUCION-POLITICA-DEL-ESTADO-LIBRE-Y-SOBERANO-DE-OAXACA.pdf>. Consulted on March 23, 2021.

interventions from positions in favor and against the amendment, and a pause provoked by a technical failure that turned off the electronic voting board, the initiative was approved by 24 votes in favor and 10 against it.[267]

However, the modification to the local constitution, which was previewed for the same session, was not voted. After the approval of the abortion initiative the congress abruptly decided to finish the session, without voting on the reform of the local constitution, which required a minimum of 28 votes,[268] compared to the 24 votes obtained.

In the case of Hidalgo, the project to decriminalize abortion was presented in December of 2019, just some months after the case of Oaxaca.[269] Nevertheless, the initiative failed to obtain the necessary votes because some members of the ruling left-wing political party (MORENA) voted against it. These members (among them four women) have been subjected to an internal disciplinary process in their political party for failing to vote in favor of the legalization of this procedure.[270]

Just a year and a half later, in June of 2021, a new bill to decriminalize abortion was presented in the congress of Hidalgo again and this time the project was approved with 16 votes from the MORENA (the minimal number of votes required to pass the bill) and 14 abstentions from all other political parties.[271] It seems that this pressure was also effective to approve the decriminalization of abortion on demand in the first trimester in the state of Veracruz just one month later, also thanks to the votes of the MORENA

267 Pedro Matias, "El Aborto Es Ley En Oaxaca: 'la Maternidad Será Elegida o No Será'," *Proceso*, 2019, https://www.proceso.com.mx/nacional/estados/2019/9/25/el-aborto-es-ley-en-oaxaca-la-maternidad-sera-elegida-no-sera-231728.html.

268 Constitución Política del Estado Libre y Soberano de Oaxaca (1922), art. 141 <https://www.oaxaca.gob.mx/cocitei/wp-content/uploads/sites/48/2019/07/CONSTITUCION-POLITICA-DEL-ESTADO-LIBRE-Y-SOBERANO-DE-OAXACA.pdf>. Consulted on March 23, 2021.

269 Karla Rodríguez, "Morena Abre Proceso a Diputados Que Votaron Contra Despenalización Del Aborto En Hidalgo," *El Universal*, 2019, https://www.eluniversal.com.mx/nacion/politica/morena-abre-proceso-diputados-que-votaron-contra-despenalizacion-del-aborto-en.

270 Rodríguez.

271 Juan Ricardo Montoya, "Aprueba Hidalgo Aborto Legal Hasta Las 12 Semanas de Gestación," *La Jornada*, 2021, https://www.jornada.com.mx/notas/2021/06/30/estados/congreso-de-hidalgo-aprueba-la-interrupcion-legal-del-embarazo/. Consulted on June 23, 2021.

deputies.[272] However, in this case, this bill is problematic, as in the case of Oaxaca (and other states, like Quintana Roo), for it contradicts the constitution of Veracruz that protects life from conception.[273]

At the national level, some members of the Mexican Federal Congress have also tried to legalize abortion through the *Ley General de Salud* [General Health Act], whose scope of application is for the whole federation.[274] This is a way of violating the constitutional autonomy of the federal entities and, at the local level, the will of the people who have rejected the legalization of abortion through democratic means. Nevertheless, the continuous opposition from some deputies and senators has impeded the progress of this initiatives.

This situation has instead prompted the action of the Mexican SCJ as a faster way to impose an unpopular agenda. Thus, in September of 2021 this judicial organ adopted the Mexican version of *Roe v. Wade*, which declared as unconstitutional some articles of the Criminal Code of the state of Coahuila that punish with prison women that have voluntarily aborted and the persons that assist them.[275]

This judgment is surprising, for this means that the justices assume that there is fundamental right to abortion, even though no article of the Mexican Constitution establishes so. Moreover, the judgment is primarily based on academic and opinion articles, which makes it look more like a treaty of philosophy exposing the justices' personal views on the human condition, freedom, and secularism, rather than a legal reasoning that confronts Coahuila's Criminal Code with the actual text of the Mexican Constitution.[276] The only legal references that are found on the judgment are the views adopted by human rights treaty bodies on the need to legalize abortion.[277]

272 Almudena Barragán, "El Estado de Veracruz Despenaliza El Aborto," *El País*, 2021, https://elpais.com/mexico/2021-07-20/el-estado-de-veracruz-despenaliza-el-aborto.html. Consulted on June 23, 2021.

273 Constitución Política del Estado Libre y Soberano de Veracruz (1917), article 4 <https://www.legisver.gob.mx/leyes/ConstitucionPDF/CONSTITUCION0407172.pdf>. Consulted on May 5, 2020.

274 Enrique Méndez and Roberto Garduño, "Proyecto a Favor Del Aborto, Avanza En Comisiones," *La Jornada*, 2020, https://www.jornada.com.mx/2020/02/07/politica/008n1pol. Consulted on June 23, 2021.

275 "Despenalización Del Aborto En Coahuila: Esto Es Lo Que Debes Saber Sobre La Resolución de La Corte."

276 Supreme Court of Justice of Mexico, *Acción de Inconstitucionalidad 148/2017, Pleno de la Suprema Corte de Justicia de la Nación* (7 September 2021).

277 Supreme Court of Justice of Mexico, *Acción de Inconstitucionalidad 148/2017*, paras 93–105.

Although this judgment does not imply that abortion has been legalized in the whole country, a decision of the Mexican SCJ is mandatory for all judges, which opens the door to the decriminalization of this practice through the judiciary. Furthermore, this ruling has been used as a political tool to pressure local congressess to modify their legislation, despite that the issue has already been discussed and the people and their representatives have decided not to legalize this practice (as is currently happeing in Cohauila and Aguascalientes).

This is the same technique that has been used in the American context to legalize controversial issues by avoiding the local, ordinary, and political process of bargaining, democratic participation, and solid argumentation that is required to decide controversial issues in democratic societies.[278] As pointed out by Mary Ann Glendon:

> With courts increasingly willing to nullify popular legislation and proclaim new rights, legislators are encouraged to avoid their responsibility for tackling controversial issues; interest groups are encouraged to take their cases to the courts rather than to try to persuade their fellow citizens; and citizens get the feeling that they have no say in setting the conditions under which they live, work, and raise their children. Political skills atrophy. We forget how to build coalitions, develop consensus, hammer out compromises, try out new ideas, learn from mistakes, and try again.[279]

State representatives are not free to exercise power as they wish, even if they have been democratically elected.[280] A political post is not a *carte blanche* to enact one's own personal preferences and policy choices, regardless of what people think. State representatives act on behalf of popular sovereignty, and they are supposed to represent it.

This problematic situation is even more evident at the international level. Regardless of their own people's ideas and the Federal Constitution, the Mexican representatives at different U.N. fora have presented a position in favor of abortion. They introduce this idea in the name of all Mexicans; this

278 See Glendon, *Rights Talk: The Impoverishment of Political Discourse*.

279 Mary Ann Glendon, "Reclaiming Human Rights," *First Things*, 2016, https://www.firstthings.com/article/2016/08/reclaim-human-rights. Consulted on June 23, 2021.

280 The HRC has determined in this regard that "it is also implicit that the representatives exercise only those powers which are allocated to them in accordance with constitutional provisions". HRC, General Comment No. 25: The right to participate in public affairs, voting rights and the right of equal access to public services (article 25), CCPR/C/21/Rev.1/Add.7 (1996), para. 7.

means, they are presenting their personal views as if they were the opinion of the 126 million Mexicans that they are supposed to democratically represent. They are presenting their policy preferences on behalf of a country without being held accountable for that. At the end, it is questionable whether international negotiations and agreements represent the ideas of the whole international community or only the views of a privileged-liberal-trained minority.

Some examples can be mentioned in this regard. In 2016, Mexico submitted its ninth periodic report to the CEDAW, regarding the implementation of the CEDAW Convention. This report highlighted the consultations that the Mexican government had held with members of civil society. These consultations determined Mexico's priorities for women rights, among which, access to abortion was a "*tema de especial preocupación*" [a topic of special concern];[281] while topics like violence provoked by organized crime, discrimination based on pregnancy, and the eradication of poverty are not part of this list. The report also remarks that one of the priorities of the Mexican "civil society" is to debate religious and cultural "barriers" for the acceptance of abortion.[282]

In 2018, during the consideration of this periodic report, an expert from the CEDAW requested information on the "harmonization" of abortion laws in all the country.[283] The Mexican delegate answered that "there was a need for national laws on abortion, as the procedure was only legal in Mexico City",[284] even though these initiatives have been constantly rejected by most people and local congresses.

In 2019, during the review of Mexico's periodic report submitted to the HRC, a member of this committee, Mr. Christopher Bulkan, also requested information on the advancement of abortion rights. He asked "what efforts had been made to ensure equal access to abortion in all states" and "what mechanisms were available to women in states where abortion was not permitted

281 Noveno informe periódico que los Estados Parte debían presentar en 2016, CEDAW/C/MEX/9, p. 8 and 10. <https://tbinternet.ohchr.org/Treaties/CEDAW/Sharedpercent20Documents/MEX/INT_CEDAW_ADR_MEX_26125_S.pdf>. Consulted on March 23, 2021.

282 Noveno informe periódico que los Estados Parte debían presentar en 2016, CEDAW/C/MEX/9, p. 28. <https://tbinternet.ohchr.org/Treaties/CEDAW/Sharedpercent20Documents/MEX/INT_CEDAW_ADR_MEX_26125_S.pdf>. Consulted on March 23, 2021.

283 "Committee on the Elimination of Discrimination against Women Reviews Report of Mexico," UN Human Rights Office of the High Commissioner, 2018, https://www.ohchr.org/EN/NewsEvents/Pages/DisplayNews.aspx?NewsID=23344.

284 "Committee on the Elimination of Discrimination against Women Reviews Report of Mexico."

under any circumstances".[285] In this regard, the Mexican delegate highlighted the advances made to promote access to abortion,[286] disregarding the internal conflict that is taking place in the country. The concluding observations on this report adopted by the HRC insisted on the need to legalize abortion as a human rights obligation.[287] The same recommendation regarding the "harmonization" of laws in Mexico to access abortion has been advanced by the CESCR in 2018.[288]

It is not only Mexican representatives who present their personal views as Mexico's claim, foreign NGOs also advocate in favor of their own interests, regardless of what local people want. During Mexico's Universal Periodic Review of 2019 at the Human Rights Council, some NGOs insisted on abortion as a "priority" for the Mexican population. The international provider of abortions IPPF and the Swedish Association for Sexuality Education insisted that Mexico should decriminalize abortion because it is "an important human rights principle".[289]

Mexico is not the only country were its liberal-trained elites are alienated from the rest of the population and use the state apparatus to simulate a climate of popular support for controversial positions. Anthropologist Sally Engle Merry concludes the following after observing the presentation of the state reports of Guinea, India and Egypt at the CEDAW:

> As the national elites participate in this international forum and construct a modern legal system they juxtapose their urban and educated world, in touch with the international community, to that of the apparently ancient and unchanging traditional culture of the rural areas,

285 HRC, Summary record of the 3653rd meeting 127th session (23 October 2019) CCPR/C/SR.3653, para 23.

286 U.N. Web TV, Consideration of Mexico - 3653rd Meeting, 127th Session of Human Rights Committee (16 October 2019) <http://webtv.un.org/meetings-events/human-rights-treaty-bodies/human-rights-committee/127th-session/watch/consideration-of-mexico-3653rd-meeting-127th-session-of-human-rights-committee/6095478655001/?term=&sort=date&page=2>. Consulted on May 4, 2021.

287 HRC, Concluding observations on the sixth periodic report of Mexico (4 December 2019) CCPR/C/MEX/CO/6, para 16.

288 CESCR, Concluding observations on the combined fifth and sixth periodic reports of Mexico (17 April 2018) E/C.12/MEX/CO/5-6, para 63.

289 "Human Rights Council Adopts the Universal Periodic Review Outcomes of Mexico, Mauritius, Jordan and Malaysia," Human Rights Council, 2019, https://www.ohchr.org/SP/HRBodies/HRC/Pages/NewsDetail.aspx?NewsID=24338&LangID=S.

> riddled with patriarchal culture. Such cultural framing resonates with the colonial past.[290]

A similar conclusion has been reached by the American/Sudanese scholar Abdullahi Ahmed An-Na'im at the end of the book *Human Rights in Cross-Cultural Perspectives: A Quest for Consensus*:

> I became more sensitive to the fact that Western hegemony (in the economic, technological, intellectual, and other fields) profoundly influences ruling elites, as well as scholars and activists in the South of the Third World [...]. It is misleading to assume genuine representation of popular perceptions and attitudes towards human rights in our countries from the formal participation of "our delegates" to international fora.[291]

290 Sally Engle Merry, "Constructing a Global Law-Violence against Women and the Human Rights System," *Law & Social Inquiry* 28, no. 4 (2003): 962.

291 Abdullahi Ahmed An-Na'im, "Conclusions," in *Human Rights in Cross-Cultural Perpestives: A Quest for Consensus*, ed. Abdullahi Ahmed An-Na'im (University of Pennsylvania Press, 1995), 428.

· 4 ·

THE PLURALISTIC UNIVERSALITY OF THE UDHR[1]

As can be perceived with the development of SRHR in the human rights sector, the prevailing liberal paradigm runs the risk of promoting an anthropological view that is not aligned with the real needs of people. Rather, the imposition of a specific paradigm about the good life that is not nourished by the complexity of reality could result in gross human rights violations, instead of protecting human dignity. Thus, good intentions are not enough, it is necessary to deeply scrutinize sensitive subjects.

It is with these premises in mind that this book proposes to analyze the pluralistic universality of the UDHR as an alternative interpretative framework that can help to reconnect the local and international spheres. This paradigm, based on dialogue and intercultural understanding, can foster a human rights setting process that looks for consensus and leaves space for reasonable disagreement in sensitive areas.

Before analyzing the UDHR, it is relevant to explain why this book uses this declaration as the starting point for the study of human rights universality. It is true that the UDHR is not a binding document and that it was

1 A preliminary version of this chapter can be seen in Gabriela García Escobar, "Human Rights Pluralistic Universality: A Bridge Between Global Norms and Cultural Diversity", *Nordic Journal of Human Rights* 41, no. 2 (2023).

adopted several decades ago. Nevertheless, its normative status is more complex, it is not equivalent to a simple political recommendation. The UDHR was adopted by consensus, with only eight abstentions that referred to specific articles and not the whole document in itself.[2] As Jack Donnelly recognizes, the UDHR "is unquestionably the foundational document of international human rights law. It establishes the basic parameters of the meaning of 'human rights' in contemporary international relations—and [...] in national discussions as well".[3]

Moreover, the UDHR was created to give content to one of the principles of the U.N. Charter.[4] The Commission on Human Rights, which was appointed to draft the UDHR, understood its mandate in this sense.[5] Actually, several experts on the UDHR consider that this declaration could constitute an authoritative interpretation of the U.N. Charter provisions on human rights.[6] Additionally, the two main human rights treaties of the U.N. system (the ICCPR and the ICESCR) were adopted with the intention to give effect to the principles of the UDHR.[7] For this reason, both treaties contain in their preambles an explicit reference to this declaration.[8] Similar references are also found in all other human rights conventions. Consequently, the UDHR is the moral, legal, and philosophical matrix from which all other human rights conventions, declarations, international norms, and standard-setting processes derive.

There is still another relevant aspect of this document that is barely mentioned in scholarship. The agreement reached in the UDHR, in a highly complicated political context, and the dedication of each drafter to seek common

2 Schmale, "Human Rights in the Intercultural Perspective and the Reorganization of the International Debate," 5.

3 Donnelly, *Universal Human Rights in Theory and Practice*, 26.

4 Charter of the United Nations (1945) article 1(3) <https://treaties.un.org/doc/publication/ctc/uncharter.pdf>. Consulted on November 19, 2019.

5 Quoted in Samnøy, *Human Rights as International Consensus: Making the Universal Declaration of Human Rights 1945–1948*, 69.

6 Nehemiah Robinson, *The Universal Declaration of Human Rights: Its Origins, Significance, Application and Interpretation* (Institute of Jewish Affairs, 1958); William A Schabas, *The Universal Declaration of Human Rights the Travaux Préparatoires: Volume 3* (Cambridge University Press, 2013).

7 Bossuyt, *Guide to the "Travaux Préparatoires" of the International Covenant on Civil and Political Rights*, 3.

8 ICCPR (1966) <https://www.ohchr.org/en/professionalinterest/pages/ccpr.aspx>. Consulted on November 19, 2019.

ground are paramount examples of a diplomatic effort that has no parallel in the seventy-eight years of existence of the U.N. system. During the drafting process there were representatives from very different backgrounds who were trying to reach a common commitment: 37 nations from Judeo-Christian tradition, 11 from Islamic ones, six from a Marxist vision, and four with a Buddhist background.[9]

One of the draft proposals that was the basis of the UDHR, the one presented by Panama's delegate, Ricardo Alfaro, and prepared by the American Law Institute, consulted experts from Arab, British, Chinese, Italians, indigenous, Latin-Americans, Polish, Soviet Russians and Spanish origins.[10] Also the first draft prepared by the Secretariat of the Drafting Committee, chaired by the British delegate John Humphrey, was based on a compilation of existing declarations and constitutions from all around the world.[11] The purpose was to test the extent to which cross-cultural consensus on human rights was possible.

The main drafters were not just pragmatic politicians; they combined distinct fields of knowledge and philosophies:[12] Carlos Romulo was a Filipino journalist who had won the Pulitzer Prize and was critical of colonialism. Hernán Santa Cruz was a Chilean left-wing politician who fought for the inclusion of economic and social rights. René Cassin was a French-Jewish expert in comparative law. Eleanor Roosevelt was well-known for her political skills. John Humphrey was a Canadian international lawyer. Hansa Mehta was the Indian delegate and a fierce defender of women's rights.[13]

The Chinese representative, Peng Chun Chang, was well instructed in Confucianism and had an especial commitment to education as a way to forge

9 See Johannes Morsink, *The Universal Declaration of Human Rights: Origins, Drafting and Intent* (Pensylvannia University Press, 1999), 21.

10 See Pedro Pallares Yabur, *Un Acuerdo En Las Raíces Los Fundamentos En La Declaración Universal de Derechos Humanos: De Jacques Maritain a Charles Malik* (2019) 54; and Åshild Samnøy, *Human Rights as International Consensus: Making the Universal Declaration of Human Rights 1945–1948* (Michelsen Institute 1993), 16.

11 Helle Kanger, *Human Rights in the UN Declaration* (Almqvist & Wiksell International, 1984), 18.

12 For a detailed description of the different personalities see: Glen Johnson and Janusz Symonides, *La Déclaration Universelle Des Droits de l'Homme: 40e Anniversaire—1948–1988* (L'Harmattan, 1990), 26–32; Glendon, A *World Made New: Eleanor Roosevelt and the Universal Declaration of Human Rights*, xx.

13 See Glendon, A *World Made New: Eleanor Roosevelt and the Universal Declaration of Human Rights*, 38.

virtues and solidarity.[14] He had wide experience of intercultural dialogue and exchange between Western and Eastern religious and social concepts.[15] Chang spent several years trying to make Chinese philosophy and traditions understandable for Western scholars and he had developed an interest in Islam and Latin American cultures.[16]

Charles Malik, the chair of the Economic and Social Council (ECOSOC), was a Christian Lebanese professor of philosophy, whose work was influenced by the ideas of Martin Heidegger. Together with Chang, he dominated the debate intellectually, although with opposite philosophical visions.[17] Mary Ann Glendon recounts how Chang and Malik debated about Thomism and Confucianism while having tea at Eleanor Roosevelt's apartment.[18] Glendon also comments about them: "each possessed an exceptional ability to understand other cultures, and to 'translate' concepts from one frame of reference to another".[19]

The figure of Malik and his relevance in the drafting process merits some considerations. Between 1935 and 1936, Malik spent some months in Germany. There he was surprised to see "how fragile reason could be when faced with the combined influence of mass media, rigid political censorship, and an anti-intellectual public culture".[20] This experience gave him a deeper sense of what was at stake when speaking about human rights. His intellectual path was dedicated to the understanding and integration of diverse cultural and philosophical perspectives and marked by the need for empathy to comprehend different arguments.[21] His work at the American University of Beirut was dedicated to the philosophical reconciliation between Western culture

14 As his biographer notes: Hans Ingvar Roth, *P. C. Chang and the Universal Declaration of Human Rights* (University of Pennsylvania Press, 2018), chap. 1.

15 Roth, chap. 1–8.

16 See Glendon, *A World Made New: Eleanor Roosevelt and the Universal Declaration of Human Rights*, 147.

17 See their discrepancies in John Humphrey, *Human Rights and the United Nations: A Great Adventure* (Transnational Publishers, 1984).

18 Glendon, "Knowing the Universal Declaration of Human Rights," 1159.

19 See Mary Ann Glendon, "Foundations of Human Rights: The Unfinished Business," *American Journal of Jurisprudence* 44, no. 1 (1999): 4.

20 See Glenn Mitoma, *Human Rights and the Negotiation of American Power* (University of Pennsylvania Press, 2013), 118.

21 See Pallares Yabur, *Un Acuerdo En Las Raíces Los Fundamentos En La Declaración Universal de Derechos Humanos: De Jacques Maritain a Charles Malik*, 94.

and Eastern traditions, which prevented him from acritical assimilationist positions during the drafting process of the UDHR.[22]

As Glendon narrates, as a professor of philosophy from 1937 to 1945, Malik organized gatherings with groups of young professors from all kinds of backgrounds (Islamic, Christian, Jewish, Marxist, radical secularists, etc.) in order to build bridges between different traditions.[23] Moreover, his knowledge of Western culture was not reduced to a "post-Enlightenment rational technocratic mastery of the material world".[24] He had a profound understanding of more ancient Eastern-Mediterranean interactions between the Greco-Roman philosophy and legal order, and Judeo-Christian theology.[25]

Malik knew that the most fundamental Western values were not reduced to the Enlightenment period and the scientific revolution. They were the result of the interaction of several cultural, philosophical, and religious traditions. He admired Western societies not for their economic success and their material prosperity, but for their commitment to individual freedom of conscience as the privileged place for moral discernment.[26]

Therefore, the intellectual diversity present in the drafting process was complex and rich. Humphrey writes that the ideological differences were not just between "communists and noncommunists"[27] as sometimes is simplified in Western academic circles. Intellectual, religious, and cultural diversity were taken seriously. As will be described in the following sections, debates took place even among defenders of traditional democracy themselves,[28] liberals

22 Pallares Yabur, 198.

23 See Glendon, *A World Made New: Eleanor Roosevelt and the Universal Declaration of Human Rights*, 126.

24 See Mitoma, *Human Rights and the Negotiation of American Power*, 2013, 126.

25 Glenn Mitoma, *Human Rights and the Negotiation of American Power* (University of Pennsylvania Press, 2013), 126.

26 Mitoma, 126. In this regard, Mitoma indicates that Malik proposed a "constructive program that could match the positive Soviet accomplishments in economic development and social justice, but without the loss of the higher values which constitute the very soul of the West. These values (…) maintained the priority of the mind and spirit over the material world. (…) If the West was not only going to win the Cold War, but also redeem itself and the rest of the world from the scourge of materialism of which communism was but a symptom, it needed to embrace and share this heritage".

27 See Humphrey, *Human Rights and the United Nations: A Great Adventure*.

28 See Samnøy, *Human Rights as International Consensus: Making the Universal Declaration of Human Rights 1945–1948*, 101.

(in its classic and other versions), communitarian perspectives, and religious worldviews, among others.

The debates that took place in Geneva and Paris where about the philosophical foundations of the declaration, the anthropological vision that underlies the human rights project, how to combine universality and local variations, and the risk of politicization and instrumentalization of human rights.[29] The non-binding nature of the declaration was a facilitator of this kind of discussion,[30] for it allowed the drafters to focus on the anthropological and ethical concerns, rather than on states obligations and political issues.

It was precisely this kind of less legalistic environment and the moral nature of the document which provided the basis for solving the deep intellectual and philosophical enterprise of structuring a truly universal project. In this regard, the drafters were "politically savvy, philosophically sophisticated creatures"[31] who were aware of the difficulty of proclaiming a specific doctrine as universal.

This kind of discussion can be hardly found in today's Human Rights Council sessions, where increasing tensions and polarization is evident once one enters the hall. Also, the way in which the drafting process was conducted presented not a vision of realpolitik, but rather a profound effort to reach a transcultural consensus. This can be perceived in one episode that Glendon narrates. During the period just before the adoption of the declaration Malik

> Made the most of the fact that the document reflected input from diverse sources, and he took pains to point each country to the places in the Declaration where it could either find its own contributions, or the influence of the culture to which it belonged.[32]

Malik and Romulo were especially concerned about not only including a diverse range of voices in the human rights debate, but also on deliberating towards consensus.[33] They were concerned about addressing everybody's arguments and concerns. They were not looking to build a paradigm according to

29 A detailed summary of these debates can be found in the three volumes of Schabas, *The Universal Declaration of Human Rights the Travaux Préparatoires: Volume 3.*

30 This aspect is brilliantly explained in Pallares Yabur, *Un Acuerdo En Las Raíces Los Fundamentos En La Declaración Universal de Derechos Humanos: De Jacques Maritain a Charles Malik*, 82–83.

31 Glendon, "Knowing the Universal Declaration of Human Rights," 1175.

32 Glendon, 1161.

33 See Mitoma, *Human Rights and the Negotiation of American Power*, 2013, 13.

their presuppositions and then to impose it upon all participants. Rather, they wanted to understand the world's diversity and to reach an agreement based on that real and pre-existing variety.

Actually, the idea of calling the document a "universal" declaration, instead of an "international" one, was because Cassin considered that "universal" meant that the UDHR was morally binding upon everyone, not only governments.[34] Chang also supported this idea, for he considered that the declaration should be "accessible to the citizens of the world rather than confined to the narrow sphere of intellectuals, philosophers, and jurists".[35]

Another event that points towards this deep diplomatic and intercultural effort is the work done by the United Nations Educational, Scientific and Cultural Organization (UNESCO). In 1947, the UNESCO conducted worldwide philosophical research on the foundations of the human rights project.[36] The director sent a questionnaire on the possibility of creating a universal human rights instrument based on different philosophies, cultures, and religions. The result were 54 responses from philosophers, scientists, and politicians representing a great intellectual diversity.[37]

Despite the unquestionable relevance of the UDHR and the importance of its uncommon drafting process, what seems inexplicable is the little attention dedicated to it and the widespread misconceptions about its nature. Johannes Morsink, one of the experts in the drafting history of the UDHR, expresses this critique in the following terms:

> The seminal texts that feed some of history's great movements make their impact and then take on a life of their own, without the movement members always taking the time to see what precisely their sacred text says or does not say, or how it was written and by whom and for what reasons. It was this kind of problem that in the 1980s led me to an investigation on how the Universal Declaration came to be written.[38]

34 Glendon, *A World Made New: Eleanor Roosevelt and the Universal Declaration of Human Rights*, 161.

35 Frédéric Krumbein, "P. C. Chang—The Chinese Father of Human Rights," *Journal of Human Rights* 14, no. 3 (2015): 339.

36 Glendon, *A World Made New: Eleanor Roosevelt and the Universal Declaration of Human Rights*, 73; Mark Goodale, ed., *Letters to the Contrary: A Curated History of the UNESCO Human Rights Survey* (Stanford University Press, 2018).

37 Goodale, *Letters to the Contrary: A Curated History of the UNESCO Human Rights Survey*, 21.

38 Johannes Morsink, *Inherent Human Rights : Philosophical Roots of the Universal Declaration* (University of Pennsylvania Press, 2009), 2.

Common wisdom assumptions about human rights are in general legally unfounded and far removed from what was originally agreed and achieved in the UDHR. As one of the experts in this document has pointed out: "rarely, in fact, has a text been so widely praised yet so little read or understood".[39] In this respect, Johannes Morsink adds: "very few people seem to know what was said and done during the drafting process [of the UDHR]. This ignorance has led to numerous misconceptions about how the document was written and what it and its various parts mean".[40] Another scholar expert on the subject, Tore Lindholm, has also expressed: "knowledge of the Universal Declaration of Human Rights –its content, intellectual background, and political context- is often surprisingly shallow".[41]

Therefore, the exploration of what was actually incorporated into this foundational document is of paramount relevance. This section provides some light on several topics that are important to the study of the concepts of universality and diversity. Accordingly, this analysis focuses on two main aspects that were established in the UDHR: (1) the philosophical foundations of the document, and (2) the anthropological premises underlying the declaration.

The Philosophical Foundations of the UDHR

The common wisdom shared by most human rights scholars is that the UDHR contained no specific philosophical foundation nor any anthropological assumptions. This combination of ideas renders the conclusion that the foundation of the UDHR is the paradigm liberal universality which is viewed as an agreement that was reached *beyond* culture and history or that *transcends* them, and consequently it is removed from local particularities and culturally neutral. Thus, while most scholars maintain that there is no foundational philosophy at the core of the UDHR, at the same time they embrace a very specific philosophical and cultural tradition as *the* universal one.

Although this narrative is barely challenged and often uncritically assumed, according to the experts in the drafting history of the UDHR, the

39 Glendon, *A World Made New: Eleanor Roosevelt and the Universal Declaration of Human Rights*, xvii.
40 Morsink, *The Universal Declaration of Human Rights: Origins, Drafting and Intent*, xiii.
41 Tore Lindholm, "The Cross-Cultural Legitimacy of Universal Human Rights: Plural Justification across Normative Divides," in *Cultural Human Rights*, eds. Francesco Francioni and Martin Scheinin (Martinus Nijhoff, 2008), 20, footnote 2.

foundations are different. The agreement was possible not because it was *above* all cultures, but rather because it was *cross-cultural* or *transcultural*. This change in perspective modifies the entire apparatus of the liberal philosophical justification, and therefore the way human rights were meant to be both interpreted and implemented.

During the drafting process of the UDHR, the question of the philosophy behind the project appeared from its earliest stages. The drafters were aware of the magnitude of this philosophical and cultural problem. John Humphrey remarked that in the first session of the Commission on Human Rights in 1946, when he was appointed Secretariat, Colonel Hodgson from Australia asked him: "what principles the Secretariat had used in the preparation of its draft and what was the philosophy behind it".[42] Humphrey answered that the project had no particular philosophy. He said that the declaration would include rights recognized in different national constitutions and the suggestions of delegations.[43] He added in his memoir that it was a combination of "humanitarian liberalism with social democracy".[44]

This statement was not received without criticism. Professor Koretsky, from the Soviet representation, accused the British draft as an attempt to "transfer certain principles of law accepted in the United Kingdom to other countries—not only principles but also the mechanisms of implementation. This system was not quite applicable to other countries whose historical development was different".[45]

Tore Lindholm remarks that many members of the Commission on Human Rights were alert "to various dangers involved in introducing philosophical, religious or ideologically 'deep' principles of human rights into the human rights instruments of the United Nations".[46] Mary Ann Glendon describes a session where Hansa Mehta, the Indian delegate, requested avoiding ideological disputes and concentrating on practical matters. Malik intervened and replied:

42 John Humphrey, *Human Rights and The United Nations: A Great Adventure* (Transnational Publishers, 1984), 39.

43 Humphrey, 39.

44 Humphrey, 40.

45 Humphrey, 41.

46 Tore Lindholm, "Article 1: A New Beginning," in *The Universal Declaration of Human Rights: A Commentary*, ed. Asbjørn Eide et al. (Scandinavian University Press, 1993), 35.

> Whatever you may say, Madam, must have ideological presuppositions [...] and no matter how much you may fight shy of them, they are there, and you either hide them or you are brave enough to bring them out in the open and see them and criticize them.[47]

The representatives were truly wary of including any metaphysical or philosophical tradition in the project because they knew that in a scenario of deep cultural, ideological, and philosophical divides theoretical agreement was not possible. The drafters maintained such a vision not as a pessimistic resignation, but as a philosophical and diplomatic reality.[48]

The Origin and Justification of Human Rights: Beyond Liberal Consensus?

In this complicated situation, the drafters decided to discuss the justification of the project in the preamble and in article 1, which explain why human beings have rights. Some delegates suggested relying on "Nature", "human nature", or "God", as foundations of why human beings "are born free and equal in dignity and rights".[49] None of these concepts were included, because there was no consensus.[50] This situation is usually interpreted as the acceptance of liberal universality.

However, a deeper analysis of the discussions reveals a different story. This deletion cannot be directly interpreted as a rejection of all these grounds for justification. The reasons not to include those were that not everybody agreed on them as *the universal* or official foundation of the project, although as Lindholm indicates, "none of these are outlawed, and each of them are welcomed, as it were, as optional rationales".[51] The same conclusion is reached by Mexican legal scholar Pedro Pallares Yabur in his recent study of the UDHR.[52]

47 Quoted in Glendon, *A World Made New: Eleanor Roosevelt and the Universal Declaration of Human Rights*, 41.

48 Actually, it is remarkable to notice the diplomatic efforts of Cassin to seek unanimity even when it was impossible, as highlighted in Humphrey, *Human Rights and the United Nations: A Great Adventure*.

49 UDHR (1948), article 1 <https://www.un.org/en/universal-declaration-human-rights/>. Consulted on February 23, 2019.

50 See Lindholm, "Article 1: A New Beginning," 50.

51 Lindholm, 50.

52 See Pallares Yabur, *Un Acuerdo En Las Raíces Los Fundamentos En La Declaración Universal de Derechos Humanos: De Jacques Maritain a Charles Malik*, chap. 4.

This detail is important, because the exclusion of these views would have already implied a non-neutral and anti-diversity position not shared by most of the countries and population of the world, as Pallares explains.[53] The drafters wanted to leave the justificatory process open to different worldviews as local interpretations. The drafters were aware that either the endorsement or exclusion of any philosophical, cultural or religious doctrine was neither neutral, nor universal.

This situation can be seen in the debates surrounding the inclusion of the word "God" in article 1. In one of the discussions, Chang requested avoiding using theological arguments and Western ideas not shared by all countries. He added that for Chinese people good manners, decorum, propriety and consideration for others are part of ethics, but he would not propose those aspects as universally shared for the declaration.[54] Mr. Beaufort from the Netherlands, the sponsor of the reference to God, responded that he did not want to impose God, but that those who want respect for their different beliefs, should also respect the religious convictions of others.[55]

Beaufort was aware that either decision, to include or erase religion, was not neutral and would exclude the vision of certain groups of people. Either position implied a "comprehensive"[56] or "thick" worldview that is not scientific, nor shared by everyone. Mr. Beaufort elaborated on this issue in the following terms:

> It had been said that no mention of God should be made in the declaration since there was a separation of Church and State in some countries. That argument had little foundation, for a reference to God would in no way contradict that separation. No one country should impose its religion upon another country but the reference to God could be interpreted by each country in accordance with its religious beliefs. It would, moreover, lend great weight to the article.[57]

53 Pallares Yabur, chap. 4.

54 Summary record ninety-sixth meeting Third Committee session, A/C.3/SR.96 (7 October 1948).

55 Summary records hundred and sixty-fourth Third Committee session, A/C.3/SR.164 (29 November 1948).

56 According to John Rawls, a comprehensive doctrine is a worldview that contains "conceptions of what is of value in human life, and ideals of personal character, as well as ideals of friendship and of familial and associational relationships, and much less that is to inform our conduct, and in the limit to our life as a whole". See Rawls, *Political Liberalism*, 13.

57 Summary Record of the Ninety-Eighth Meeting of the Third Committee, Held at the Palais de Chaillot, Paris (9 October 1948) A/C.3/SR.98.

The drafters avoided imposing a single philosophical foundation in order to respect the world's diversity: either religious or secular ones. It is in this sense that they looked for a "neutral" basis, but their way to frame "neutrality" was not in liberal terms for two reasons. The first is that the concept of liberal neutrality involves a series of philosophical and cultural presuppositions about the human condition that are not neutral, as explained in the previous chapter. The second is that they were seeking a cross-cultural or transcultural agreement, not one beyond or outside of culture, which involves a different philosophical starting point and conclusion.

Regarding the first point, the Cartesian rejection of all traditions is itself a tradition that involves a thick and culturally conditioned philosophical conception.[58] The Archimedean point of justification, used by the Enlightenment tradition requires a series of assumptions about human nature and society that are the product of specific historical, social, and religious events, as recognized by several philosophers.[59] Such a perspective would have implied a comprehensive doctrine not shared by everyone as *the* universal and only foundation of the human rights project. It would have been the ideological imposition of the culture of the most powerful Western states upon the rest of the world.

In this regard, the UNESCO's philosophers committee conducted its survey on the foundation of human rights by sending a questionnaire with some interesting assumptions. It indicated that human rights are based on the rationalistic natural law tradition of the XVIII century and on Marxist socio-economic structures.[60] However, French philosopher Jacques Maritain rightly argued that to trace human rights only to this tradition was an intellectual reductionism and led to a deformed vision of natural law,[61] which was a philosophical basis not shared by many cultures. Moreover, the eighteenth century philosophy of rights is based on the ideas of the middle-class emerging bourgeoisie in Europe, while the UDHR aimed towards the protection of the weak, the poor, and the marginalized.[62]

58 As thoroughly explained in MacIntyre, *Whose Justice? Which Rationality?*, 17.

59 As remarked by: MacIntyre, chap. 17; Charles Taylor, *Sources of the Self: The Making of the Modern Identity* (New York: Cambridge University Press, 1989); Habermas and Ratzinger, *Entre Razón y Religión: Dialéctica de La Secularización*.

60 See Goodale, *Letters to the Contrary: A Curated History of the UNESCO Human Rights Survey*, 48–50.

61 Jacques Maritain, *The Rights of Man and Natural Law* (The Century Press, 1944), 94; Pallares Yabur, *Un Acuerdo En Las Raíces Los Fundamentos En La Declaración Universal de Derechos Humanos: De Jacques Maritain a Charles Malik*, chap. 2.

62 Wiktor Osiatyński, *Human Rights and Their Limits* (Cambridge University Press, 2012), 27.

Therefore, the drafters considered the document a "neutral" one in the sense that "they did not think they had taken sides in the combat between liberal and conservative approaches to public policies or between proponents of planned or free economies".[63] The UDHR did not intend to establish any specific philosophical doctrine, not even liberalism. Instead of looking for an agreement beyond culture or out of it, the drafters sought a transcultural or cross-cultural one, which leads the discussion to the second reason.

In view of the philosophical challenge's magnitude, the objective of the UDHR was not to find the ultimate theoretical foundation acceptable to everybody. This was an impossible task without imposing a culture or ideology over the rest of the participants. Therefore, the goal of the drafters was more modest: to find instead a practical agreement.[64] The agreement was based on what was acceptable to different cultures according to daily experience. Maritain explains this perspective in the introduction to the UNESCO's Committee of Philosophers report:

> Practical goal, agreement between minds can be reached spontaneously, not on the basis of common speculative ideas, but on common practical ideas, not on the affirmation of one and the same conception of the world, of man and of knowledge, but upon the affirmation of a single body of beliefs for guidance in action.[65]

The drafters realized that it was possible to find common practical principles and convictions without maintaining a specific "comprehensive" theory. Cassin indicated that such a consensus "allowed the Committee to take no position on the nature of man and of society and to avoid metaphysical controversies, notably the conflicting doctrines of spiritualists, rationalists, and materialists regarding the origin of the rights of man".[66]

The state representatives realized that this agreement was based on general shared principles by different cultures and accessible through daily experience, but not on their theoretical foundation because each person came from different philosophical presuppositions about the good life. This meant that everybody could agree on the importance of "freedom" and "dignity" for human flourishing because everybody can find these values within their

63 Morsink, *The Universal Declaration of Human Rights: Origins, Drafting and Intent*, 327.

64 Glenn Hughes, "The Concept of Dignity in the Universal Declaration of Human Rights," *Journal of Religious Ethics* 39, no. 1 (2011): 2.

65 UNESCO, *Human Rights: Comments and Interpretations*, II.

66 Quoted in Morsink, *The Universal Declaration of Human Rights: Origins, Drafting and Intent*, 287.

specific cultural worldviews. However, every tradition will justify and interpret them according to different doctrines. Maritain famously said "we agree about the rights but on condition that no one asks us why".[67] In practice, this meant that each tradition was allowed to give life to these shared principles in very diverse manners.

The same was applicable to religion, which was considered another doctrine capable of giving content to the human goods inscribed in the UDHR. In the words of Christopher McCrudden, the UDHR did not intend to erase religion or to create a philosophical foundation either in confrontation or rejection of it, rather it "was not based on any particular set of religious principles or beliefs but is nevertheless consistent with them".[68] The human rights scholar Hans Ingvar Roth indicates that "the secularism that has often been associated with the document had more to do with pragmatism and a spirit of compromise than with any critical, Western view of religion with roots in Enlightenment thinking".[69]

In this sense, Lindholm indicates that the consensus reached with the UDHR provided a "cross-cultural intelligibility and justifiability".[70] The drafters looked for what different cultures and traditions shared to determine what was considered universal, and then left ample room to let each society to give life to those shared principles according to their own view of human flourishing. This means that it is possible to affirm that the "universal" philosophical foundation of the human rights project is a philosophy of plurality: a pluralism that involves taking into account all different world's cultures, religions, and traditions, and a diversity of forms to understand what the good life is.

This reasoning is confirmed in the letters received by the UNESCO's committee on the foundations of human rights. Most of the non-Western respondents recognized that in their own traditions it was possible to find the values and principles incorporated into the UDHR, although the language of "rights" was a modern European development.[71] This idea is also revealed in the speeches of several states. The delegate from the Soviet Union, Mr. Pavlov, acknowledged that:

67 UNESCO, *Human Rights: Comments and Interpretations*, I.

68 Christopher McCrudden, "Human Dignity and Judicial Interpretation of Human Rights," *The European Journal of International Law* 19 (2008):655, 677.

69 Roth, *P. C. Chang and the Universal Declaration of Human Rights*, 221–222.

70 Lindholm, "Article 1: A New Beginning," 52.

71 See Glendon, *A World Made New: Eleanor Roosevelt and the Universal Declaration of Human Rights*, 73.

> The Commission's discussion had clearly shown the divergences which existed between the members in the fields of philosophy and ideology; that difference of ideas had not prevented fruitful co-operation, because even though there had been disagreement on the nature of the rights, the Commission has, nevertheless, come to a satisfactory agreement as to their practicable application.[72]

The representative of Brazil, Mr. de Athayde, celebrated the success of the declaration on these grounds, highlighting that there was no single philosophical foundation:

> The draft declaration did not reflect the particular point of view of any one people or of any one group of peoples. Neither was it the expression of any one political doctrine or philosophical system. It was the result of the intellectual and moral cooperation of a large number of nations.[73]

Hernán Santa Cruz from Chile also remarked at the U.N. General Assembly the effort to find a transcultural consensus that took into account all different cultures and traditions:

> Tremendous difficulties had been involved in preparing a declaration of human rights which would meet the frequently divergent views of fifty-eight States. It had been necessary to reconcile the different ideologies of the Soviet Union and other Eastern European countries and of the other Members of the United Nations; the difference between the economic and social rights recognized by Christian Western civilization and those recognized by the Oriental civilization; the varying legal systems of Latin and Anglo-Saxon countries.[74]

Therefore, the UDHR relied on a philosophy of pluralism, which provided space for liberal ideas, but also to other less individualistic and more religiously oriented worldviews. The drafters intended a real-life and cross-cultural consensus, acceptable to a diversity of cultures and religions around the world. They did not disregard differences, instead they took diversity seriously into account as a fundamental part of their concept of universality.

72 Quoted in Morsink, *The Universal Declaration of Human Rights: Origins, Drafting and Intent*, 317.
73 Quoted in Morsink, 327.
74 Summary Record of the Ninety-First Meeting of the Third Committee, Held at the Palais de Chaillot, Paris (2 October 1948) A/C.3/SR.91.

Cross-Cultural or Transcultural Agreement

The emphasis on "cross-cultural" agreement is essential to understand the concept of pluralistic universality of the UDHR, for it is different from the liberal notion. The UDHR's agreement was not reached despite cultural and philosophical differences, but because from among those differences they borrowed parts of diverse cultures and traditions in order to construct a tradition with all the commonly shared aspects by all of them.[75] Even liberal scholars, like Jack Donnelly, recognize in this regard that the agreement was not based on the suppression of cultural, religious, or philosophical differences: "quite the contrary, the drafters saw the Declaration as emerging out of deeper foundations. Internationally recognized human rights stand 'above' these deeper foundations only in the sense that a house is 'above'–that is, constructed upon—its foundations".[76]

It is in this sense that the consensus was a transcultural or cross-cultural one. It was a horizontal exercise, which looked for commonalities among different traditions, instead of a liberal-vertical experiment that creates its own ideal of what should be the common ground, which is not corroborated by transcultural assessment.

Liberal universality defines what is acceptable as diversity in terms of what conceptions of the good are based on secularism, individualism, and the primacy of autonomy in all domains of life. On the contrary, a transcultural agreement does not set this pre-manufactured standard of acceptability, rather it builds its concept of legitimate diversity by looking at what different cultures and traditions consider as common and as different.

The drafters considered that these rights needed to be developed according to different worldviews, so that their idea of human flourishing could give shape and content to the thirty articles of the UDHR. In this sense, the process of theoretical justification was an unfinished business,[77] for it was left open, which is confirmed by the inclusion of the right to self-determination in the two treaties of 1966. This right, which is based on the recognition of pluralism and reasonable disagreement, allowed space for different human rights

75 See the argument in Glendon, "Knowing the Universal Declaration of Human Rights," 1161–1162; Asbjørn Eide, "Interdependence and Indivisibility of Human Rights," in *Human Rights in Education, Science and Culture: Legal Developments and Challenges*, ed. Yvonne Donders and Vladimir Volodin, 2007, 12–13.

76 Donnelly, *Universal Human Rights in Theory and Practice*, 60.

77 See Glendon, "Foundations of Human Rights: The Unfinished Business."

interpretations and implementations, according to the decisions taken by different peoples regarding their political, economic, social and cultural systems.

The chairman of the UNESCO's philosophers committee, Richard McKeon expressed the same idea in 1947:

> An agreement in the promulgation of those declarations of rights, far from signifying a general agreement on a single basic philosophy, provided a framework within which divergent philosophies, religious, and even economic social and political theories might be entertained and developed.[78]

Hans Ingvar Roth indicates that the UDHR was an intercultural document in three interrelated senses.[79] First, a range of people from all around the world worked on its content, which implied the encounter of different philosophical and cultural perspectives. Second, the declaration contains "principles that emphasize the importance of culture for people's self-identification and well-being as well as of understanding and tolerance".[80] Third, the document was the result of long and intensive intercultural dialogues, based on the pluralistic idea that "human rights should be able to be justified from several philosophical outlooks, not just one or two".[81]

These considerations take the analysis back to the abovementioned debate about "Nature", "human nature", and "God" as foundational concepts for the UDHR. The UDHR embraced both positions in a "benign secularism" that allows space for both foundations and a healthy interaction.[82] In words of Morsink, this situation revealed a middle ground between "atheistic materialism and overt propositional religiosity"[83] that provided space for both religious and non-religious justifications.

The reason why the reference to God was erased was to allow religious and non-religious people alike to interpret the foundations according to their own worldview, not to embrace a laicism hostile to religion.[84] Such a position

78 Quoted in Goodale, *Letters to the Contrary: A Curated History of the UNESCO Human Rights Survey*, 82.

79 See Roth, *P. C. Chang and the Universal Declaration of Human Rights*, 139–140.

80 Roth, 139.

81 Roth, 140.

82 Johannes Morsink, *The UDHR and The Holocaust: An Endangered Connection* (Georgetown University Press, 2019), 101.

83 Morsink, 105.

84 See Lydia H Liu, "Shadows of Universalism: The Untold Story of Human Rights around 1948," *Critical Inquiry* 40, no. 4 (2014): 409–410.

would have implied a non-neutral preference towards atheistic or materialistic visions of the human being, while it would have arbitrarily excluded religiously grounded views shared by a lot of people. This is corroborated in a speech of Eleanor Roosevelt in the University of Columbia in 1949:

> Perhaps one of the things that some of us learned was that in an international document you must try to find words that can be accepted by the greatest number of people. Not the words you would choose as the perfect words, but the words that most people can say and that will accomplish the ends you desire, and will be acceptable to practically everyone sitting round the table, no matter what their background, no matter what their beliefs may be. So that's what happened to us.
>
> [...]
>
> Now, I happen to believe that we are born free and equal in dignity and rights because there is a divine Creator, and there is a divine spark in men. But, there were other people around the table who wanted it expressed in such a way that they could think in their particular way about this question, and finally, these words were agreed upon because they stated the fact that all men were born free and equal, but they left it to each of us to put in our own reason, as we say, for that end.[85]

The reason for the adoption of this flexible approach in the UDHR is because the more specific the content of rights become, the more specific and "comprehensive" the philosophical underlying assumptions also becomes. And, therefore, the greater the probability of pushing for a very specific anthropological/philosophical conception and the greater the risk of imposing as universal a vision that is actually parochial.

Jacques Maritain was very aware of this danger: "where it is a question of rational interpretation and justification of speculation or theory, the problem of Human Rights involves the whole structure of moral and metaphysical (or anti-metaphysical) convictions held by each of us".[86] Accordingly, the agreement on the philosophical foundations was open to many different justifications because that was the limit of a universal declaration. To push for a stronger conception would be at the cost of the very universality of the project and a free or unforced consensus.[87]

Maritain explained in detail this issue. He remarked in the introduction of the philosophical UNESCO's compilation that an agreement based on

85 Eleanor Roosevelt, "Making human rights come alive. Speech to Pi Lambda Theta, Columbia University, March 30, 1949", Gifts of Speech (1949) in <http://gos.sbc.edu/r/eleanor1.html>. Consulted on May 23, 2019.

86 UNESCO, *Human Rights: Comments and Interpretations*, III.

87 See this point in Taylor, "Conditions of an Unforced Consensus on Human Rights."

what is considered as self-evident moral facts "is at every stage conditioned by the acquisitions, the constraints, the structure and the evolution of the social group".[88] He argued that an agreement on abstract principles implied that to give them substantive content meant that the rights would necessarily pass through cultural filters. Thus, there is a distinction between the general principles agreed in the UDHR and their transformation into concrete policies, the same as the distinction between internationally agreed human rights norms and their interpretations or standards.

This process of translation between the universal and abstract into the concrete and materialized is a culturally embedded one. The justification and implementation of common practical convictions will be interpreted in different manners depending on a diversity of cultural and social factors that influence human reasoning. There is no "pure" or "neutral" knowledge in human affairs. Pallares Yabur explains this in the following terms: "*el conocimiento espontáneo, elemental y primario de toda persona acierta en lo elemental, pero para justificarlo racionalmente necesitaría argumentarlo desde un sistema cultural*" [the spontaneous, elementary and primary knowledge of every person is correct in the elementary, but to justify it rationally it would need to be argued from a cultural system].[89]

Human rights principles were not conceived in terms of already completed, a priori determined, inflexible and deductible rules as envisaged in the rationalistic natural law tradition of the eighteenth century. As confirmed by the adoption of the right to self-determination, these principles needed to be adopted by each society according to their views of human flourishing and balancing different human goods. As Glendon states, "the framers of the Declaration did take account of the diversity of cultures by leaving room for a legitimate pluralism in interpreting and implementing its open-ended principles".[90]

Another important reason for this flexible approach was that the drafters were aware of the deep challenges that diversity poses. They knew that it is not reasonable nor open-minded to request people to waive the traditions where they find meaning and guidance. They accepted that space for reasonable and legitimate disagreement was not only healthy, but necessary to attain

88 UNESCO, *Human Rights: Comments and Interpretations*, IV.

89 Pallares Yabur, *Un Acuerdo En Las Raíces Los Fundamentos En La Declaración Universal de Derechos Humanos: De Jacques Maritain a Charles Malik*, 269.

90 Glendon, "Foundations of Human Rights: The Unfinished Business," 3.

an unforced consensus and not to detach people from their cherished attachments. Lindholm advances this argument in the following terms:

> Such a recalcitrance of peoples' commitments to their basic normative traditions is, I submit, neither irrational nor generally unreasonable. To the contrary, it is hardly ever reasonable, nor feasible, to suspend one's entire system of cognitive and normative beliefs, values, attitudes, sensibilities and loyalties. Reasonable change of beliefs and values must, most of the time, be piecemeal, and particularly if it is to be facilitated by the force of the better argument. It is not reasonable to expect agreement, all the way down, among reasonable people about the deepest grounds of their positions on human rights.[91]

However, this open-ended idea was not absolute, for an agreement in order to exist needs to set some limits on what can be acceptable and what will be excluded from it. The contrary leads to cultural and moral relativism. Thus, in spite of the intentions of the drafters, this cross-cultural universality did not mean that it was actually possible to draft an international document on human rights without installing into it some minimal presuppositions about the human condition.

Pallares Yabur indicates that the challenge for the drafters was how to affirm something that makes sense (about the human being and his rights), that is acceptable in practice to everyone, and that is sufficiently wide (philosophically speaking) to be received by every person.[92] The concern was that such an affirmation already implied taking a philosophical position at least regarding some aspects of the human condition. As human rights scholar Hans Ingvar Roth explains:

> Words such as "natural" and "inherent" had a special relevance in this context because they brought into focus the conditions for this moral and pedagogical project [the UDHR]. Nor is it entirely possible to dissociate oneself from metaphysical or philosophical anthropological assumptions about humanity if one's starting point is that humans have an inviolable value—or a dignity, a free will, and a moral conscience. Let us call this a "thin" metaphysics. It is possible to reach agreement about humanity's good side having these qualities or capacities without involving other metaphysical assumptions.[93]

91 Lindholm, "The Cross-Cultural Legitimacy of Universal Human Rights: Plural Justification across Normative Divides," 26.

92 Pallares Yabur, *Un Acuerdo En Las Raíces Los Fundamentos En La Declaración Universal de Derechos Humanos: De Jacques Maritain a Charles Malik*, 260.

93 Roth, *P. C. Chang and the Universal Declaration of Human Rights*, 165.

Thus, it is not possible to reach a practical agreement without postulating at least a "thin" conception of how society and the human being are portrayed.[94] Every practical agreement presupposes at least, the existence of "something" the participants agree on; the contrary would lead the UDHR to be a document of fantasy. It would imply that the agreement is not based on general principles about an objective reality (the human being and society), but rather an agreement to use those abstract or imaginary categories however one pleases.[95] Openness can only be absolute if it quits the very practical agreement in favor of relativism. Therefore, the philosophical pluralistic justification involves an implied "thin" or "minimal", but specific vision about certain aspects of the human being and of society.[96]

Consequently, such an agreement constrains the type of premises that can be used as theoretical foundations, because not every philosophical doctrine necessarily leads to the protection of human dignity in terms of the UDHR. The question that seems to follow is: what are the criteria to determine whether a justificatory tradition is acceptable or not for human rights?

The limits to this open-ended agreement can be found looking to its anthropological premises found in the debates regarding articles one and 29 of the UDHR and on the concept of freedom that permeates the declaration. These articles suggest a very different view of the human being than the model proposed by liberal universality.

This deeper analysis reveals that a more interdependent, religiously grounded, and duty-oriented vision of the human being was adopted as the basis of this cross-cultural consensus, because it was more compatible with non-Western cultures and with dignatarian legal traditions.

94 Pedro Pallares Yabur, "La Justificación Racional de Los Derechos Humanos En Los Redactores de La Declaración Universal de Los Derechos Humanos," *Persona y Derecho* (Pamplona, 2013), 156.

95 Pallares Yabur, *Un Acuerdo En Las Raíces Los Fundamentos En La Declaración Universal de Derechos Humanos: De Jacques Maritain a Charles Malik*, 260.

96 Glendon, *A World Made New: Eleanor Roosevelt and the Universal Declaration of Human Rights*, 67–69.

The Anthropological Premises Underlying the UDHR

To explore these anthropological premises, some context on the drafting process of the UDHR is required. The first draft of the UDHR was entrusted to the head of the Secretariat of the Commission on Human Rights, Canadian lawyer John Humphrey. For this task, he received initiatives from different delegations. Three of them were submitted by the Latin American representatives of Cuba, Chile, and Panama. The Cuban and Chilean drafts were the basis for the draft prepared by the Secretariat that served as the initial document for discussions.[97]

The Cuban draft was based on a barely known document that was adopted in Bogotá in May of 1948 by the Organization of American States (OAS) called the American Declaration of the Rights and Duties of Man (ADRDM).[98] Its preamble contains something similar to what was later adopted as article 1 of the UDHR: "all men are born free and equal, in dignity and in rights, and, being endowed by nature with reason and conscience, they should conduct themselves as brothers one to another".[99] Its preamble continues with different statements that provide a general vision on the human being shared by Latin American nations:

> The fulfillment of duty by each individual is a prerequisite to the rights of all.
>
> Rights and duties are interrelated in every social and political activity of man. While rights exalt individual liberty, duties express the dignity of that liberty.
>
> Duties of a juridical nature presuppose others of a moral nature which support them in principle and constitute their basis.
>
> Inasmuch as spiritual development is the supreme end of human existence and the highest expression thereof, it is the duty of man to serve that end with all his strength and resources.[100]

97 See Mary Ann Glendon, "The Forgotten Crucible: The Latin American Influence on the Universal Human Rights Idea," *Harvard Human Rights Journal* 16 (2003): 30–31; Álvaro Paúl, *Los Trabajos Preparatorios de La Declaración Americana de Los Derechos y Deberes Del Hombre y El Origen Remoto de La Corte Interamericana* (Instituto de Investigaciones Jurídicas UNAM, 2017), 2; Albert Verdoodt, *Naissance et Signification de La Déclaration Universel Des Droits de l'Homme* (Université Catholique de Lovain, 1964), 53–57.

98 The American Declaration of the Rights and Duties of Man (1948) <https://www.oas.org/dil/access_to_information_human_right_American_Declaration_of_the_Rights_and_Duties_of_Man.pdf>. Consulted on March 13, 2019.

99 The ADRM.

100 The ADRM.

These phrases are relevant because they provide the Latin American perspective on the rights holder of this declaration. These delegates did not envisage an individualistic being whose goal is liberal autonomy.[101] They presented a human being that is in relationship with other fellow beings (interdependent) and who has duties towards them as the best way of guaranteeing each other's rights (duty-oriented).

Such an idea was more in accordance with the constitutional, cultural, and religious traditions of Latin American states,[102] but also of many non-Western nations, as can be appreciated in the human rights declaration adopted by Asian and African countries.[103] The adoption of an individualistic-liberal anthropological model, shared only within the Anglo-Saxon legal tradition, would have been contrary to the spirit of inclusiveness of the UDHR. It would have implied the imposition of a minoritarian vision and the exclusion of most cultural and legal traditions of the world.[104] As remarked by the Chilean human rights scholar Álvaro Paúl:

> *El pensamiento latinoamericano sirvió como una suerte de bisagra entre las diversas visiones mundiales sobre los derechos humanos: la visión individualista liberal, más propia del mundo anglosajón occidental, y la visión más comunitaria, que hacía resonar concepciones de otras geografías.*[105]
>
> [Latin American thought served as a sort of hinge between the various world visions of human rights: the liberal individualistic vision, more typical of the Anglo-Saxon Western world, and the more communitarian vision, which resonated with conceptions from other geographies].

101 See the research of Chilean scholar Paúl, *Los Trabajos Preparatorios de La Declaración Americana de Los Derechos y Deberes Del Hombre y El Origen Remoto de La Corte Interamericana.*

102 As the research of Carozza points out: Paolo G. Carozza, "From Conquest to Constitutions: Retrieving a Latin American Tradition of the Idea of Human Rights," *Human Rights Quarterly* 25 (2003): 289–310.

103 African Charter on Human and Peoples' Rights (1981) <https://au.int/en/treaties/african-charter-human-and-peoples-rights>. Consulted on May 23, 2018; the Arab Charter of Human Rights (2004) <http://elearning.icrc.org/detention/es/story_content/external_files/Cartapercent20Arabepercent20depercent20Derechospercent20Humanospercent20(2004).pdf>. Consulted on May 23, 2019; and the ASEAN Human Rights Declaration (2013) <https://www.asean.org/storage/images/ASEAN_RTK_2014/6_AHRD_Booklet.pdf>. Consulted on May 23, 2019.

104 Glendon, *A World Made New: Eleanor Roosevelt and the Universal Declaration of Human Rights*, chap. 12.

105 Paúl, *Los Trabajos Preparatorios de La Declaración Americana de Los Derechos y Deberes Del Hombre y El Origen Remoto de La Corte Interamericana*, 3.

This anthropological vision was also discussed and incorporated into the UDHR. Seth Kaplan comments in this regard that

> The document itself [the UDHR] was influenced more by the dignitarian rights tradition of Latin America and continental Europe than by the more individualistic Anglo-American rights tradition, at least partly because this was necessary to gain acceptance in Asia and Africa. The former emphasizes social institutions such as the family and community and sees rights both as having clear limits and as being accompanied by responsibilities to other citizens and the state.[106]

An individualistic anthropological vision, as pointed out by Glendon, is alien to the continental civil law tradition (that represents the vast majority of legal systems in the world), which is rather influenced by "classical, biblical and socialist thought".[107] For this legal tradition, the inclusion of community, religiously grounded ideas, and duties is an essential part of rights interpretation. This can be appreciated in the speech of Mr. De Athayde from Brazil at the General Assembly, regarding the adoption of the UDHR:

> It had also been alleged that the declaration spoke only of human rights, without mentioning duties. That criticism was unfair. Article 30, in fact, imposed on all men the duty to respect the rights of others, public order, morality and the general welfare as provided for in a democratic society. Those were limitations justified by civilized life itself, as well as limitations of conscience. It was therefore unjust to say that all those duties, taken together with the rights proclaimed, did not form a coherent whole.[108]

Accordingly, the "everyone" envisioned in the UDHR is open to a human being constituted by relationships with others, solidarity, and mutual interdependency,[109] because it was the only way in which the document could have been accepted by non-Western cultures and dignatarian legal traditions.

Jack Donnelly acknowledges that the UDHR "envisions individuals deeply enmeshed in 'natural' and voluntary groups ranging from families through the state".[110] Louis Henkin notices that human rights did not establish

106 Kaplan, *Human Rights in Thick and Thin Societies: Universality without Uniformity*, 14.

107 Glendon, *A World Made New: Eleanor Roosevelt and the Universal Declaration of Human Rights*, 96.

108 Verbatim Record of the Hundred and Eighty-First Plenary Meeting of the General Assembly, Held at the Palais de Chaillot, Paris, on Friday, 10 December 1948, A/PV.181.

109 See the research of Glendon, *A World Made New: Eleanor Roosevelt and the Universal Declaration of Human Rights*, 227.

110 Donnelly, *Universal Human Rights in Theory and Practice*, 31.

a liberal and individualistic worldview.[111] Asbjørn Eide maintains that there is no atomistic individualism in the UDHR and that the free development of one's personality requires also the fulfillment of duties in community.[112] He further states that an extreme concept of autonomy "is alien to the Universal Declaration".[113] Lindholm goes further to the point of claiming that "human rights do not celebrate individual autonomy".[114] Wiktor Osiatyński argues that a radical individualism is inconsistent with the relational and interdependent idea of dignity and freedom that underlies the anthropological vision of the document.[115]

In this sense, the drafters of the UDHR included an anthropological vision of the human being as a relational and situated being, with duties towards other people. Even the responses received at the UNESCO's philosophers committee reveal that most opinions around the world coming from different approaches did not consider it possible to build the universal foundations of the document upon a radical individualism.[116] The contributions from classical liberal positions, such as the letter of Quincy Wright, considered that the human being possesses duties, lives in the context of a community, and that rights have limitations.[117] Similar concerns are expressed by Marxist and socialist,[118] Christian,[119] Confucian,[120] Islamic,[121] and Buddhist[122] perspectives.

A letter from Mahatma Gandhi indicated: "I learned from my illiterate but wise mother that all rights to be deserved and preserved came from duty well done".[123] He was aware that respect for rights "ultimately depends on

111 Louis Henkin, "Rights: American and Human," *Columbia Law Review* 79, no. 3 (1979).
112 Eide, "Interdependence and Indivisibility of Human Rights," 26.
113 Eide, 27.
114 Lindholm, "The Cross-Cultural Legitimacy of Universal Human Rights: Plural Justification across Normative Divides," 22.
115 Osiatyński, *Human Rights and Their Limits*, 26.
116 See all the documents and letters in Goodale, *Letters to the Contrary: A Curated History of the UNESCO Human Rights Survey*.
117 Goodale, 80, 91 and 98.
118 Goodale, 111, 114 and 172.
119 Goodale, 178–190.
120 Goodale, 192–195.
121 Goodale, 221.
122 Goodale, 238.
123 UNESCO, *Human Rights: Comments and Interpretations*, 4.

ingrained habits and attitudes having more to do with duty than entitlement".[124] Additionally, Chinese scholar Chung-Shu Lo, indicated that

> The basic ethical concept of Chinese social political relations is the fulfilment of the duty to one's neighbor, rather than the claiming of rights. The idea of mutual obligations is regarded as the fundamental teaching of Confucianism [...]. By the fulfilment of mutual obligations the infringement of the rights of the individual should be prevented.[125]

This vision of the human being is also confirmed by the interventions of some delegates. The representative of Australia, Colonel Hodgson, stated that no right is absolute and that each right has a corollary duty.[126] René Cassin (considered by some as the father of the UDHR) emphasized that human rights also depend on the role of the community and its rights.[127] Charles Dukes, member of the British Labour Party, declared that "unrestricted individual liberty was impossible in any modern community".[128] The same approach was followed by another British representative, Geoffrey Wilson, who insisted that the delegates "should avoid giving the reader the impression that the individual was granted unlimited rights".[129]

Professor Koretsky, from the Soviet delegation, insisted that the declaration "should not seek to separate man from his community; it should seek rather to create a man who is free in the framework of a free society".[130] Charles Malik, on his part, explained that he preferred to use the word "human person", not "individual", to highlight that the subject of human rights is not an isolated-autonomous being.[131] He wanted "to avoid connotations of radical autonomy and self-

124 Glendon, *A World Made New: Eleanor Roosevelt and the Universal Declaration of Human Rights*, 75.

125 Quoted in Goodale, *Letters to the Contrary: A Curated History of the UNESCO Human Rights Survey*, 193.

126 Summary record of the ninth meeting of the Commission on Human Rights (New York) E/CN.4/SR.9 (1 February 1947).

127 Summary record of the fourteenth meeting (New York) E/CN.4/SR.14 (4 February 1947).

128 Humphrey, *Human Rights and The United Nations: A Great Adventure*, 25.

129 Quoted in Morsink, *The Universal Declaration of Human Rights: Origins, Drafting and Intent*, 245.

130 Humphrey, *Human Rights and the United Nations: A Great Adventure*.

131 Pallares Yabur, *Un Acuerdo En Las Raíces Los Fundamentos En La Declaración Universal de Derechos Humanos: De Jacques Maritain a Charles Malik*, 207–209; Glendon, *A World Made New: Eleanor Roosevelt and the Universal Declaration of Human Rights*, 42.

sufficiency".[132] Pallares Yabur remarks:

> *Para describir al "ser-humano" de la declaración, los redactores deliberadamente prefirieron utilizar la palabra "persona" en lugar de "individuo", de "comunidad" en lugar de "sociedad"; describieron en el mismo nivel, los "derechos" y los "deberes", y equipararon los derechos civiles clásicos con los derechos sociales. Para los redactores el esquema "derechos-míos" enfrentados a "deberes-tuyos", no expresaba auténticamente las exigencias de la dignidad humana. La "persona" en la DUDH [Declaración Universal de los Derechos Humanos] no parte de una "pura autonomía" como condición para la autorrealización de libertad.*[133]
>
> [To describe the "human being" of the declaration, the drafters deliberately preferred to use the word "person" instead of "individual", "community" instead of "society"; they described "rights" and "duties" on the same level, and equated classical civil rights with social rights. For the drafters, the "my rights" versus "your duties" scheme did not authentically express the demands of human dignity. The "person" in the UDHR [Universal Declaration of Human Rights] does not start from a "pure autonomy" as a condition for the self-realization of freedom].

Morsink narrates an anecdote that is illustrative of these ideas. During the debates regarding article 28,[134] the representative of Australia, Alan Watt, suggested amending the article as follows: "everyone is entitled to a social and international order in which *alone* the full and freed development of his personality is possible".[135] Most delegates, both from Western and non-Western origin protested against this statement.[136] Glenn Mitoma remarks in his historical research of the UDHR, that these episodes reveal "how marginal classic liberalism was among most members of the UNCHR [United Nations Commission on Human Rights]".[137]

Thus, the UDHR embraces neither a "collectivistic" vision of human nature, nor a purely "individualistic one", for the drafters were able to avoid both "extremes of capitalist individualism and socialist collectivism".[138]

132 Glendon, *A World Made New: Eleanor Roosevelt and the Universal Declaration of Human Rights*, 42.
133 Pallares Yabur, "La Justificación Racional de Los Derechos Humanos En Los Redactores de La Declaración Universal de Los Derechos Humanos," 145.
134 "Article 28: Everyone is entitled to a social and international order in which the rights and freedoms set forth in this Declaration can be fully realized".
135 Quoted in Morsink, *The Universal Declaration of Human Rights: Origins, Drafting and Intent*, 245. The italics are from the author.
136 Morsink, 247.
137 Mitoma, *Human Rights and the Negotiation of American Power*, 2013, 116.
138 Glendon, *A World Made New: Eleanor Roosevelt and the Universal Declaration of Human Rights*, 68.

Rather, the drafters envisaged a relational concept of the human person, which in consequence also implied a relational notion of freedom, and the taking into account of duties and communities in giving content to human rights provisions. The relevance of these elements was not based on the liberal assumption that they are illegitimate restrictions to freedom, but rather they are part of human flourishing.

The Human Person Endowed with Reason and Conscience

> Article 1: All human beings are born free and equal in dignity and rights. They are endowed with reason and conscience and should act towards one another in a spirit of brotherhood.[139]

To begin with the analysis of this relational or interdependent concept of the human being, a close look at the first article of the declaration is necessary, for it is not a "right" to dignity, rather it justifies why human beings possess rights and sets the tone for the anthropological vision of the whole document.[140] The same applies to the prohibition of discrimination established in article two.[141] The two first articles are not rights, they are a "framework of reference" within which all other rights are contained.[142]

There is a commonly shared idea that the first article was a copy of the French Declaration on the Rights of Man of 1789. The French delegate Mr. Ordonneau maintained this affirmation.[143] However, the Dutch delegate, Mr. Beaufort, declared that he did not agree with eighteenth century philosophy as basis of the project because it had a "one-sided idea of man".[144] Lindholm

139 UDHR.

140 See McCrudden, "Human Dignity and Judicial Interpretation of Human Rights"; Robinson, *The Universal Declaration of Human Rights: Its Origins, Significance, Application and Interpretation*; Krumbein, "P. C. Chang—The Chinese Father of Human Rights."

141 "Article 2: Everyone is entitled to all the rights and freedoms set forth in this Declaration, without distinction of any kind, such as race, colour, sex, language, religion, political or other opinion, national or social origin, property, birth or other status. Furthermore, no distinction shall be made on the basis of the political, jurisdictional or international status of the country or territory to which a person belongs, whether it be independent, trust, non self-governing or under any other limitation of sovereignty".

142 Kanger, *Human Rights in the UN Declaration*, 78.

143 Summary record thirty-third meeting drafting committee E/CN.4/AC.1/SR.33 (14 May 1948).

144 Summary hundred and sixty-fourth third committee A/C.3/SR.164 (29 November 1948).

notes that article one is not "a commitment to an individualism at odds with people's legitimate attachments to community".[145]

The idea behind article one is more similar to the ADRDM than to the French version. Lindholm highlights that

> Interpreted in its proper context, article 1 is not a traditional Western natural rights foundation for a system of human rights to be implemented globally. It provides the thin, but crucially important normative basis, on which representatives of several cultures could reach agreement. But […] this commitment to inherent freedom and equal dignity is a part of a more complex, more realistic, and more "open-minded" scheme of justification of human rights.[146]

The notion of dignity was not understood as an expression of autonomy or as one's value in accordance with one's capacity for it, rather it was conceived as an ontological concept,[147] as part of the condition of being a person, which one can recognize only in a relational experience. This definition of dignity was especially welcomed by non-Western representatives.[148]

In this regard, Pallares Yabur points out that the word "dignity" was a novelty, because neither the American Declaration of Independence nor the French Declaration on the Rights of Man included such a concept, which means that the UDHR deviated from the liberal tradition.[149] The former document was founded on God and the later inscribed a too individualistic (and male) notion of the human being and a very specific and not universally shared philosophical school.[150]

Therefore, the foundations of the document were the idea of an ontological dignity that inscribes in each person an absolute value, beyond and despite his social, economic, or political utility.[151] No person is disposable, regardless of how "ineffective", "burdensome", or "unproductive" a human being might be considered by society, organizations, the market or the political power.

145 Lindholm, "The Cross-Cultural Legitimacy of Universal Human Rights: Plural Justification across Normative Divides," 22.
146 Lindholm, "Article 1: A New Beginning," 51.
147 See Hughes, "The Concept of Dignity in the Universal Declaration of Human Rights," 3.
148 Hughes, 5.
149 Pallares Yabur, *Un Acuerdo En Las Raíces Los Fundamentos En La Declaración Universal de Derechos Humanos: De Jacques Maritain a Charles Malik*, 204–209.
150 Pallares Yabur, 294–296.
151 Pallares Yabur, 296–299.

Accordingly, "dignity" in these terms was the basis of the UDHR, not individual autonomy.

The concept of dignity as the capacity to exercise personal autonomy has been legally developed in American jurisprudence, where unrestrained choice in every social dimension has been recently equated to freedom and equality.[152] This notion was not adopted by the UDHR, for it presupposes the rejection of a self with attachments and duties previous to any personal choice. This image is physically impossible because every human being is born free and equal, but always embedded in space and time: every human being is born in a certain social, economic, political, cultural, and religious context, which is the starting point of analysis of continental legal traditions.

The idea of the abstract and autonomous individual is "an ideological fiction", as remarked by Martti Koskenniemi.[153] It is "an analytical construct, not a description of social reality",[154] which runs in contradiction with a practical agreement as embedded in the UDHR that considers the human being as he or she exists in reality with his or her relations and context. As the psychological development of any human being reveals, it is impossible for a person to think or even exist "clean" of any philosophical or ideological influence.[155]

Besides the word "dignity", article one establishes a second sentence that reads "they [all human beings] are endowed with reason and conscience and should act towards one another in a spirit of brotherhood".[156] As Roth indicates, the word "endowed with" was also a way of implementing a pluralistic universality that welcomed both religious and non-religious perspectives:

> A formulation that almost all of the delegates could accept by virtue of the fact that it left open whether the endowing has been done by God, nature, or something else. [...] Those who believe in God could still find the idea of God in the powerful statement that all human beings are born free and equal and have been endowed with reason and conscience, even if the clause "by God" has been removed. Others would be able to interpret and accept the sentence in other ways.[157]

152 See in this regard: Mortimer Sellers, "Universal Human Rights in the Law of the United States," in *The Universalism of Human Rights*, ed. Rainer Arnold (Springer, 2013), 20.
153 Koskenniemi, "The Effects of Rights on Political Culture," 104.
154 Pollis, "New Universalism," 16.
155 See the anthropological work of Richard A. Shweder et al., "The Cultural Psychology of Development: One Mind, Many Mentalities," in *Handbook of Child Psychology Volume 1: Theoretical Models of Human Development*, ed. Richard Lerner, 6th edn (John Wiley & Sons, Inc, 2006).
156 UDHR.
157 Roth, *P. C. Chang and the Universal Declaration of Human Rights*, 197.

The words "endowed with reason and conscience" where suggested by Malik. He considered that through reason and conscience the human person can situate himself or herself in the world, in his or her relationships, and in his or her context, but without becoming absorbed or eliminated by them.[158] This was a conception that fostered respect towards the human person both as a social being and as a unique being with an unconditional dignity.[159] Pallares Yabur highlights the importance of these words because they involved a statement about the human being and reality itself. Human reason is capable of knowing certain demands of human dignity (as an objective fact) that are real, not the product of subjective interests, because the contrary would imply that the UDHR is a beautiful myth (like the goddess Venus), but a mere product of the imagination.[160]

The reason for choosing the word "conscience" was because Peng Chun Chang wanted to incorporate something more than reason, "something of a moral significance".[161] He chose the Chinese word *ren* (仁), whose translation to English is very difficult, but it would be something close to "two-man-mindedness" or "humaneness towards others".[162] Glendon indicates that *ren* refers to "the ability to see things from another's standpoint as well as one's own particular point of view".[163]

Roth remarks that this phrase "stands in contrast to that of one-man-mindedness, a designation for egoism, individualism, and selfishness".[164] Roth continues by stating that Chang used the concept *ren* "to emphasize a capacity to identify with other people's needs and interests and to show compassion and a more profound kind of engagement by which other people's worries and pleasures become one's own".[165] Hoover highlights that *ren* refers to the

158 See Pallares Yabur, "La Justificación Racional de Los Derechos Humanos En Los Redactores de La Declaración Universal de Los Derechos Humanos," 147–148.

159 Pallares Yabur, 147–48.

160 See the argument in Pallares Yabur, *Un Acuerdo En Las Raíces Los Fundamentos En La Declaración Universal de Derechos Humanos: De Jacques Maritain a Charles Malik*, 374–378.

161 Summary Record of the Thirteenth Meeting of the Drafting Committee of the Commission on Human Rights, Held at Lake Success, New York (20 June 1947) E/CN.4/AC.1/SR.13.

162 Tore Lindholm, "Article 1," in *The Universal Declaration of Human Rights: A Common Standard of Achievement*, ed. Asbjørn Eide and Gudmundur Alfredsson (Martinus Nijhoff, 1999), 43.

163 Glendon, *A World Made New: Eleanor Roosevelt and the Universal Declaration of Human Rights*, 67.

164 Roth, *P. C. Chang and the Universal Declaration of Human Rights*, 212.

165 Roth, 212–213.

recognition of mutual duties towards each other and to see things from the perspective of others.[166] Thus, it involves a notion much broader than liberal "equality", which does not require dialogue nor an effort to understand one another, but simply indifference towards other ideas.

Chang suggested this addition to emphasize that the recognition of each other's rights lies in mutual empathy and solidarity, rather than in a radical individualism. "Reason" and "conscience" indicate that the way to know our dignity and our duties towards other people does not happen through a speculative and abstract academic process.

Recognition of human dignity and its concomitant duties are perceived in an "experiential" process, in a relational interaction, where dignity is precisely relational, not the pure expression of autonomy. In the words of Pallares Yabur: "*el reconocimiento y la experiencia del propio 'ser-persona', se realiza no de forma autorreferencial, sino a partir del conocimiento empático de un 'tu-digno'*" [the recognition and experience of one's own "being a person" is not self-referential, but based on the empathic knowledge of a "worthy you"].[167] Therefore, the idea of the human being embedded in article 1 is far from being the replica of the individualistic liberal notion:

> *La Declaración espera, de manera contraria a lo que sostiene el modelo liberal, que la persona sea espoleada y salga de sí misma mediante la razón y conciencia, a través de la empatía, que la hacen consciente del bien real de lo que significa ser persona y que se comprometa con sus deberes.*[168]
>
> [The Declaration expects, contrary to the liberal model, that the person is spurred on and comes out of himself by reason and conscience, through empathy, which makes him aware of the real good of what it means to be a person and to commit himself to his duties].

It is precisely through a rational and empathetic act (reason and conscience/*ren*) that a person can recognize the value of another human being and that one finds oneself compelled to act in fraternity towards another person. This

166 See Joe Hoover, "Rereading the Universal Declaration of Human Rights : Plurality and Contestation, Not Consensus," *Journal of Human Rights* 12, no. 2 (2013): 229–230, https://doi.org/10.1080/14754835.2013.784663.

167 Pallares Yabur, "La Justificación Racional de Los Derechos Humanos En Los Redactores de La Declaración Universal de Los Derechos Humanos," 150.

168 Pallares Yabur, *Un Acuerdo En Las Raíces Los Fundamentos En La Declaración Universal de Derechos Humanos: De Jacques Maritain a Charles Malik*, 375.

idea is corroborated by what Chang expressed about the relationship between "conscience" and the duty to act in a "spirit of brotherhood":

> The second sentence of article 1 called upon men to act towards one another in a spirit of brotherhood. That attitude was perfectly consistent with the Chinese attitude towards manners and the importance of kindly and considerate treatment of others. It was only when man's social behavior rose to that level that he was truly human.[169]

Through a different line of reasoning, Lindholm arrives at a similar conclusion: "article 1 does not imply support of comprehensive individualist philosophies such as those propounded by Immanuel Kant or John Stuart Mill nor, for that matter, do human rights support more vulgar individualist ideologies".[170]

On the other hand, in Pallares Yabur's interpretation, this emphasis on reason and conscience as vehicles to recognize one's fraternal duties reveals another interesting characteristic of the rights holder in article one. The cognitive act through which the person can recognize human dignity in another fellow being does not involve the use of "reason" as understood in terms of the Enlightenment's legacy. This tradition conceives reason as instrumental and abstract. As a mechanical capacity to articulate premises that would accommodate the world to achieve one's interests. A reason that is devoid of substantive or moral content or that is only capable of discerning among means, but not objective ends.[171]

Neither does "conscience" refer to a purely emotive reaction, mostly related to German Romanticism. The capacity of "reason" and "conscience" involve a *moral reasoning* where the first realization is a duty towards an axiological fact: the dignity of another person and, in this act, the recognition of one's own worth. This statement involves the implicit rejection of a utilitarian or market-logic calculus and a merely instrumental rationality.

The logic of "reason" and "conscience" indicate a cognitive act accessible through an everyday moral experience that is able to grasp an axiological reality in the ontological constitution of the human person. An act that is not automatic (does not occur *ipso facto* or in every situation), but that highlights

169 See Krumbein, "P. C. Chang—The Chinese Father of Human Rights," 343.

170 Lindholm, "The Cross-Cultural Legitimacy of Universal Human Rights: Plural Justification across Normative Divides," 22.

171 See this point in Alasdair MacIntyre, *After Virtue: A Study in Moral Theory*, 3rd edn (Notre Dame: University of Notre Dame Press, 2011), chap. 5; Sandel, *Liberalism and the Limits of Justice*.

the human possibility to recognize dignity as an objective and inherent value in another person.[172] The contrary statement would devoid the UDHR of its moral force reducing its content to noble imagination, but as real as "witches and unicorns".[173] Nevertheless, this type of recognition is impossible through a merely instrumental or utilitarian rationality, which is the philosophical presupposition of an individualistic liberal conception of the human being.

The Concept of Freedom in the UDHR

The meaning of the word "freedom" might seem obvious for a Western-liberal-trained human rights activist, who will interpret it as individual autonomy or a negative freedom. However, from an intercultural and inter-philosophical perspective "freedom" can be understood in many ways, among which, the liberal tradition is only one option that is not considered as the broader one from the point of view of other philosophies.[174] During the drafting process, Eleanor Roosevelt noted this situation. In a speech she gave in 1949 at the University of Columbia, she narrated an episode that took place at the U.N.:

> In Japan, for instance, freedom only means license. There was no character in the Japanese language which meant freedom as we understand it, so that when we tried to explain what freedom meant, they had to evolve a new character, because when they speak of a child who acted with complete irresponsibility and complete license, they said he was acting with freedom.
>
> That is something we must remember, because when you argue with Mr. Vishinsky, he will say there is no such thing as absolute freedom, and of course you and I know that is true. All freedom is conditioned by the freedom of other people, but nevertheless there is for human beings something very precious, which we know

172 The word "objective" here is used to indicate that the quality of dignity is objective, in the sense that it exists independently of whether it is recognized or not by other people. The second sense is to indicate that dignity is an objective value in the sense that it is an ontological attribute of the person, it does not depend on the subjective perception of the person itself or on her particular characteristics, actions, or capacities.

173 As used by MacIntyre, *After Virtue: A Study in Moral Theory*, 83.

174 See this point in George Weigel, *The Cube and the Cathedral: Europe, America and Politics without God* (Basic Books, 2005); Michael J. Sandel, "The Procedural Republic and the Unencumbered Self," *Political Theory* 12, no. 1 (1984): 81–96; Taylor, *Sources of the Self: The Making of the Modern Identity*.

> as freedom, the freedom to help govern ourselves, the freedom to help develop the future.[175]

The chairman of the UNESCO's philosophers committee, Richard McKeon, explained that even within the Western culture there are different traditions: freedom can be understood as living according to what is truth (in Augustine) or freedom as the possibility to have different choices (in John Stuart Mill).[176]

It seems that there was no official agreement on the meaning of the word at the negotiations, as remarked by Malik. He noticed, during one of the sessions of the Drafting Committee, that the representatives of the United Kingdom and Yugoslavia were both speaking about freedom, but having different definitions of it: one was liberal, the other was Marxist.[177] Malik himself spoke about another way of understanding freedom: "today, men had no need for protection against kings or dictators, but rather against a new form of tyranny: that exercised by the masses and by the State".[178] He also insisted that

> Unless the proposed Bill of Rights can create conditions that will allow man to develop ultimate loyalties with respect to these intermediate sources of freedom [family, school and churches], over and above his loyalty to the state, we will have legislated not for man's freedom but for his virtual enslavement.[179]

The relevance of intermediary communities between the individual and the state for the development of personality and the respect of human dignity was highlighted also by the Dutch delegate Beaufort, who argued that the community included more groups and attachments than the state.[180] As Morsink indicates: "the absence of references to the state was in no way meant by the drafters to cut people off from their respective communities of birth and growth".[181] The UDHR was not created in a liberal fashion as a document to

175 Eleanor Roosevelt, "Making human rights come alive. Speech to Pi Lambda Theta, Columbia University, March 30, 1949", Gifts of Speech (1949) in <http://gos.sbc.edu/r/eleanor1.html>.

176 See it in Goodale, *Letters to the Contrary: A Curated History of the UNESCO Human Rights Survey*, 85.

177 Summary record of the ninth meeting of the Commission on Human Rights (New York) E/CN.4/SR.9 (1 February 1947).

178 Summary record of the ninth meeting of the Commission on Human Rights (New York) E/CN.4/SR.9 (1 February 1947).

179 Mitoma, *Human Rights and the Negotiation of American Power*, 2013, 119.

180 Verdoodt, *Naissance et Signification de La Déclaration Universel Des Droits de l'Homme*, 268.

181 Morsink, *The Universal Declaration of Human Rights: Origins, Drafting and Intent*, 240.

uproot the person from his or her relationships or context and to conceive him or her as a being that is alone in front of the political (state) and economic (market) power.

Thanks to Malik's sojourn in Germany, he was aware of the dangers of any entity that claimed absolute loyalty over the human person or that made such a request in order to provide security, peace, or food.[182] Based on this, he highlighted the relevance of protecting intermediary communities that limit the totalitarian temptation of political power (or market power in our times), because they are the source from which "real freedom" springs.[183] Cassin shared the same idea about the relevance of multiple loyalties of the human person towards these communities.[184] Having recently lived the dangers of totalitarianism, Malik was concerned about an all-powerful state:

> The world was faced with a tendency to "statism", or the determination by the state of all relations and ideas, thus supplanting all other sources of convictions. The state insisted on the individual's obligations and duties to it. This too was a grave danger, for man was not the slave of the state, and did not exist to serve the state only [...]. There were innumerable other intermediate loyalties which the individual must respect, such as those towards his family, his profession, his friends, and also towards his philosophical laws. The state could not be the exclusive arbiter of truth and beauty. Real freedom sprang from the loyalty of the individual not to the state but to these intermediate forms.[185]

For this reason, the UDHR recognizes the importance of the family (article 16) and the community (articles 18, 27 and 29) as institutions that establish duties, but whose purpose goes beyond that: they are needed for human flourishing and freedom. They are not reduced to "added" entities or necessary evils. They provide the tools and virtues that are needed for personal growth and maturity, but also to maintain a tolerant and healthy democracy, because

182 See Pallares Yabur, *Un Acuerdo En Las Raíces Los Fundamentos En La Declaración Universal de Derechos Humanos: De Jacques Maritain a Charles Malik*, 211–212.

183 As described in Glendon, *A World Made New: Eleanor Roosevelt and the Universal Declaration of Human Rights*, 113.

184 See Pallares Yabur, *Un Acuerdo En Las Raíces Los Fundamentos En La Declaración Universal de Derechos Humanos: De Jacques Maritain a Charles Malik*, 228.

185 Quoted in Morsink, *The Universal Declaration of Human Rights: Origins, Drafting and Intent*, 242.

it is through these networks that the human being builds his or her identity and learns solidarity, dialogue, and compassion with one another.[186]

Malik believed that in these places the human person learns to take a personal standing about the purpose and meaning of human existence, to act with freedom and to take responsibility.[187] Further attention to intermediary communities can be seen, as stated by Morsink, in the idea that the family is the main community to learn rights and duties, followed by the educational and religious ones.[188] Eleanor Roosevelt also shared the idea that human rights spring from the most fundamental and simple levels of community life:

> Where, after all, do universal human rights begin? In small places, close to home—so close and so small that they cannot be seen on any maps of the world. Yet they are the world of the individual person; the neighborhood he lives in; the school or college he attends; the factory, farm, or office where he works. Such are the places where every man, woman, and child seeks equal justice, equal opportunity, equal dignity without discrimination. Unless these rights have meaning there, they have little meaning anywhere. Without concerted citizen action to uphold them close to home, we shall look in vain for progress in the larger world.[189]

Thus, this provides a wider vision of "freedom", not only as detachment proper of the Enlightenment tradition, but also as a *relational* and positive attachment or the freedom to live according to a specific idea, religion, culture, or worldview. A freedom compatible with responsibility and context. As Malik remarked: "freedom was to be found in harmony between the individual and the community".[190]

On the other hand, from the discussions of the drafters, it seems that "freedom" was also understood in two different dimensions: an internal and an external one. The delegate of Lebanon, Karim Azkoul, considered that freedom of thought and conscience was to protect a person's "inner being" as "to determine his

186 As explained by Mary Ann Glendon, "Looking for Persons in the Law," *First Things*, no. December (2006), https://www.firstthings.com/article/2006/12/looking-forpersonsin-the-law; de Tocqueville, *Democracy in America*, chaps. 16 and 17.

187 See Pallares Yabur, *Un Acuerdo En Las Raíces Los Fundamentos En La Declaración Universal de Derechos Humanos: De Jacques Maritain a Charles Malik*, 216.

188 Morsink, *The Universal Declaration of Human Rights: Origins, Drafting and Intent*, 259.

189 Quoted in Glendon, *A World Made New: Eleanor Roosevelt and the Universal Declaration of Human Rights*, 239–240.

190 Summary Record of the Fourteenth Meeting of the Commission on Human Rights, Lake Success, New York (4 February 1947) E/CN.4/SR.14.

destiny".[191] Cassin also emphasized the importance of this inner freedom and its protection: "*le contraire de la liberté de pensée intérieur c'est l'obligation de professer une croyance qu'on n'a pas*" [the opposite of freedom of thought is the obligation to profess a belief that one does not have].[192] He insisted that this inner freedom was the pillar of the project, because it is: "*le fondement de tous les autres droits*" [the foundation of all other rights].[193] The same ideas were reiterated during the drafting process of the ICCPR, where the delegates referred to this right as "sacred" and "inviolable".[194]

For Cassin the idea of freedom of conscience was not reduced to a mere freedom to have different preferences or to imagine whatever one wants to. As specified in article 18 of the UDHR, internal freedom involves three different issues: thought, conscience, and religion. This article specifies three different inner categories that are protected. Imagination and preferences may involve freedom of thought, but not conscience and religion, which imply a moral discernment and commitment.

In this sense, freedom also entails the human capacity for moral reasoning that allows a person to reflect about reality and truth and to live according to it. In this regard, Pallares indicates that for Cassin: "*es gracias a la capacidad de vincularse en conciencia con aquello que se conoce como verdadero, como puede percibirse el valor de la dignidad de la persona*" [it is thanks to the capacity to link oneself in conscience to what is known to be true that the value of the dignity of the person can be perceived].[195] This idea of moral conscience was also incorporated in the ICCPR.[196]

Malik insisted that: "the human person's most sacred and inviolable possessions are his mind and his conscience, enabling him to perceive the truth, to choose freely, and to exist".[197] Malik further stated that this freedom

191 Quoted in Morsink, *The Universal Declaration of Human Rights: Origins, Drafting and Intent*, 25.

192 Quoted in Kanger, *Human Rights in the UN Declaration*, 120.

193 Quoted in Verdoodt, *Naissance et Signification de La Déclaration Universel Des Droits de l'Homme*, 181.

194 See Bossuyt, *Guide to the "Travaux Préparatoires" of the International Covenant on Civil and Political Rights*, 355.

195 Pallares Yabur, *Un Acuerdo En Las Raíces Los Fundamentos En La Declaración Universal de Derechos Humanos: De Jacques Maritain a Charles Malik*, 207.

196 See Bossuyt, *Guide to the "Travaux Préparatoires" of the International Covenant on Civil and Political Rights*, 355.

197 Summary Record of the Fourteenth Meeting of the Commission on Human Rights, Lake Success, New York (4 February 1947) E/CN.4/SR.14.

referred to the protection of a deep or robust diversity of viewpoints in all human concerns, it included: "the fact that a single nation is obligated, by international law, to recognize the diversity of fundamental points of view on ultimate matters should, he believed, be considered an essential and fundamental human right".[198]

Martin Scheinin argues that the importance of this dimension of freedom is linked to article 1, referring to the relevance of conscience and its close relationship to the recognition and protection of human dignity.[199] The categories included in article 18 reflect the rational and moral human capacities inscribed in the first article ("endowed with reason and conscience") to reason and act according to a moral reality found through conscience. In this regard, Malik envisaged the connection between "conscience" in article one and 18 as more than a simple "freedom to have opinions". In a meeting of the Commission on Human Rights, Malik declared the following:

> If we have any contribution to make, it is in the field of fundamental freedom, namely, freedom of thought, freedom of conscience and freedom of being. And there is one point on which we wish to insist more than anything else, namely that it is not enough to be, it is not enough to be free to be what you are. You must also be free to become what your conscience requires you to become in light of your best knowledge. It is therefore freedom of becoming, of change that we stress as much as freedom of being.[200]

As can be seen, the word "freedom" cannot be reduced to the parameters of liberal universality. Glendon remarks that the drafters "were comfortable with the idea that there would always be different visions of freedom within one human family".[201] A holistic and coherent reading of the document reveals that freedom was conceptualized as a relational concept with a positive and spiritual dimension. It involved the protection of intermediary communities, as spaces for human connectedness, flourishing and free from state oppression/politicization. Moreover, freedom also implied the protection of an inner

198 Summary Record of the Eighth Meeting of the Drafting Committee of the Commission on Human Rights, Held at Lake Success, New York (17 June 1947) E/CN.4/AC.1/SR.8.

199 Martin Scheinin, "Article 18," in *The Universal Declaration of Human Rights: A Commentary*, ed. Asbjørn Eide et al. (Scandinavian University Press, 1993), 266.

200 Hoover, "Rereading the Universal Declaration of Human Rights: Plurality and Contestation, Not Consensus," 228.

201 Quoted in Glendon, *A World Made New: Eleanor Roosevelt and the Universal Declaration of Human Rights*, 191.

place for moral discernment, that means, a freedom to act according to truth, as Vaclav Havel would call it.[202]

Connected to this broader notion of freedom, the UDH also incorporated the relevance of communities and dues as interpretative guidelines to give content to human rights norms. These provisions were more in line with dignatarian traditions and with the notion of human person as a being who has attachments and duties towards other fellow beings, as will be explained.

Community and Duties in the UDHR

> Article 29:
>
> (1) Everyone h duties to the community in which alone the free and full development of his personality is possible.
>
> (2) In the exercise of his rights and freedoms, everyone shall be subject only to such limitations as are determined by law solely for the purpose of securing due recognition and respect for the rights and freedoms of others and of meeting the just requirements of morality, public order and the general welfare in a democratic society.
>
> (3) These rights and freedoms may in no case be exercised contrary to the purposes and principles of the United Nations.[203]

Another element that provides a clearer picture of both the meaning of the first article and of "freedom" in the UDHR is article 29. Duties and responsibilities were understood as correlative to rights,[204] which is why they were also established in the preambles of the ICCPR and the ICESCR. However, for practical reasons, it was not possible to elaborate a list of the responsibilities that correspond to each of them.[205] The representatives agreed that the terms "morality", "duties", and "public order" should be left to be determined by each context.[206] For this reason, they decided to include a general article to be developed by each society.

202 Václav Havel, "The Power of the Powerless," in *The Power of the Powerless*, ed. Jhon Keane (New York: Routledge, 1985), http://www.vaclavhavel.cz/showtrans.php?cat=eseje&val=2_aj_eseje.html&typ=HTML.

203 UDHR, art. 29.

204 See Bossuyt, *Guide to the "Travaux Préparatoires" of the International Covenant on Civil and Political Rights*, 12–13.

205 See Eleanor Roosevelt, "Making human rights come alive. Speech to Pi Lambda Theta, Columbia University, March 30, 1949", Gifts of Speech (1949) in <http://gos.sbc.edu/r/eleanor1.html>.

206 See Kanger, *Human Rights in the UN Declaration*, 156.

As has been noted, duties and the community are an essential part of legal and cultural interpretations in all non-Western contexts and of the continental law tradition. It is no coincidence that this article was included at the request of Latin American delegations, with the specific intention to avoid a too individualistic declaration.[207] Or that the inclusion of duties was highly important to Chang, as explained by Roth: "Chang wanted the declaration to be imbued with duties in a number of ways, an ambition that has been surprisingly downplayed by some commentators".[208] On this point, the representative of Brazil, Austregesilio de Athayde argued that:

> It was impossible to draw up a declaration of rights without proclaiming the duties implicit in the concept of freedom which made it possible to set up a peaceful and democratic society. Article 29 was of great importance because without such a provision all freedom might lead to anarchy and tyranny.[209]

Considering this, the idea of article 29 indicates the importance of intermediary communities and duties of a moral nature (as stated in the preamble of the ADRDM)[210] on the part of individuals for the process of implementation and interpretation of human rights. Article 29 is not another human right, rather it is an interpretative guideline that gives shape to the scope, limitations and implementation of all other human rights.

This article sets the context where the human being lives and develops his personality, so that a balance of goods can be made in each case. It recognizes the social or relational nature of the rights holder. It helps to put the abstract principles into concrete existence. This article contributes to the pluralistic universality embedded in the declaration, for it allows different cultures to give content to human rights according to their notion of human flourishing, which includes duties, limitations, and other human goods. The same recognition of contextuality is required by the right to self-determination, where each society can decide their own political, economic, social and cultural orders.

This situation does not disregard that the UDHR surely received important influence from the Enlightenment and liberal traditions, for example in

207 Summary hundred and fifty-third meeting third committee, A/C.3/SR.153 (23 November 1948).

208 Roth, P. C. *Chang and the Universal Declaration of Human Rights*, 151.

209 Quoted in Morsink, *The Universal Declaration of Human Rights: Origins, Drafting and Intent*, 249.

210 The preamble states that the duties recognized in this document are not of legal nature, but rather of "a moral nature which supports them in principle and constitute their basis".

the inclusion of traditional civil and political rights[211], the words "inherent" and "inalienable" in the preamble,[212] and the idea itself of recognizing individual subjective rights. However, it is quite different to envisage a set of rights that are individual entitlements and another different thing is to interpret and implement them according to a purely individualistic paradigm about the nature of society.

Article 29, connected to the first article, indicates not just the relational concept of the human being incorporated in the UDHR, but also the nature of society. A society perceived as a space where persons have both rights and duties in their daily interactions. Article 29 is the shackle that unites rights and duties in a general sense, leaving space for local interpretation rather than for the exclusion of duties.

This article was included because for the drafters the ideas of rights and freedoms did not operate in a social or cultural vacuum, in contrast to the liberal narrative. For instance, Dukes, the representative from U.K., declared: "*il est inutile à mon avis de chercher à définir la liberté individuelle en la dissociant entièrement de l'obligation qui lie les individus soit à l'État, soit à des organisations volontaires*" [it is useless, in my opinion, to try to define individual freedom by dissociating it entirely from the obligation that binds individuals either to the State or to voluntary organizations].[213] The Dutch representative, Mr. Beaufort, also added: "*ce n'est que dans la communauté que l'individu peut trouver le cadre nécessaire au libre et plein développement de sa personnalité*" [it is only in the community that the individual can find the necessary framework for the free and full development of his personality].[214] Cassin and Roosevelt remarked that there was never an intention to deny the close relationship between rights and duties.[215]

Chang constantly emphasized that the recognition of rights was inseparable from the recognition of duties towards one another, the community, and the family:

211 Samnøy, *Human Rights as International Consensus: Making the Universal Declaration of Human Rights 1945–1948*, 81.

212 Morsink, *The Universal Declaration of Human Rights: Origins, Drafting and Intent*, 282.

213 Quoted in Verdoodt, *Naissance et Signification de La Déclaration Universel Des Droits de l'Homme*, 268.

214 Verdoodt, 270.

215 Summary hundred and fifty-third meeting third committee, A/C.3/SR.153 (23 November 1948).

> A human being had to be constantly conscious of other men, in whose society he lived. A lengthy process of education was required before men and women realized the full value and obligations of the rights granted to them in the declaration; it was only when that stage had been achieved that those rights could be realized in practice.[216]

The Belgian representative, Henry Carton de Wiart, stressed: "indeed, man had duties to his family, to his neighbor, and to himself".[217] In this respect, Chang considered that "the aim of the United Nations was not to ensure the selfish gains of the individual but to try and increase man's moral nature".[218] Carlos Romulo, from the Philippines also insisted that human rights should be based on an anticolonial tradition that must include balancing rights and responsibilities.[219] Lakshim Menon from India, during the adoption of the UDHR at the General Assembly, remarked that:

> As regards article 30, the Indian delegation had accepted the restrictions it imposed, since, as Mahatma Gandhi had said, all rights were born of obligations, and no man could claim the right to live unless he fulfilled his duties as a citizen of the world. From the very fact that it proclaimed rights, therefore, the declaration was a declaration of obligations.[220]

The way of framing duties was not aleatory. The first paragraph of article 29 specifically establishes that "everyone has duties to the community in which alone the free and full development of his personality is possible". In article 29 there is an explicit reference to the interdependence of the development of the personality and the existence of a community, for the sake of human flourishing.[221] Consequently, duties and life in community are intimately linked to the full development of one's own personality: they are not obstacles that must be eliminated. According to Wiktor Osiatyński the notion of "free and full development" of one's own personality is based on Jacques Maritain's personalism, which emphasizes the relational character of the human being and solidarity.[222]

216 Quoted in Krumbein, "P. C. Chang—The Chinese Father of Human Rights," 342.

217 Quoted in Morsink, *The Universal Declaration of Human Rights: Origins, Drafting and Intent*, 240.

218 idem.

219 Mitoma, *Human Rights and the Negotiation of American Power*, 2013, 4.

220 Verbatim Record of the Hundred and Eighty-Second Plenary Meeting of the General Assembly, Held at the Palais de Chaillot, Paris, on Friday (10 December 1948) A/PV.182.

221 Robinson, *The Universal Declaration of Human Rights: Its Origins, Significance, Application and Interpretation*, 141.

222 Osiatyński, *Human Rights and Their Limits*, 23.

The inclusion of the right to self-determination as a collective endeavor to decide the development of each society for the well-being of all its members is founded on the same idea. Accordingly, Mary Ann Glendon points out that the importance of self-determination was already incorporated into the UDHR in the preamble that states the purposes of the document: "to reaffirm our faith in fundamental human rights, in the dignity and worth of the human person, in the equal rights of men and women and of nations large and small".[223] This meant that equal rights in the preamble were reinforced by article one of the U.N. Charter that establishes as one of the U.N. principles the respect to self-determination of peoples and also for "human rights and for fundamental freedoms of all without distinction as to race, sex, language or religion".[224]

Thus, article 29 was also important because it incorporated the role and duties of the community in the UDHR, without providing any specific program on how this relationship should be framed. The relevance given to community and duties in states, based on dignitarian legal traditions,[225] led the drafters to consider that there are different ways through which the state can deliver the human good.[226]

In a "thick way" it encompasses "the meaning of life and typically involves religious, linguistic, or cultural practices that define the groups that feed and shape a person's identity".[227] The contrary case is when a government delivers the human good in a "thin" manner, which means that the state will only "set up a fair (legal) framework within which its people can, singly or in groups, pursue their own notions of the thick human good, as long as the limits of security and public order mentioned in article 29 are not violated".[228] Morsink points out that neither of these forms of government and of understanding the good life where prescribed by the drafters. The representatives were aware that cultural, religious, and philosophical diversity required leaving open the possibility of understanding the human good in different ways, which is in accordance with the right to self-determination.

223 UDHR.

224 UN Charter (1945), art. 1 <https://www.un.org/en/about-us/un-charter>. Consulted on May 23, 2020.

225 See Glendon, *A World Made New: Eleanor Roosevelt and the Universal Declaration of Human Rights*, 227.

226 See Osiatyński, *Human Rights and Their Limits*, chap. 1.

227 Morsink, *The Universal Declaration of Human Rights: Origins, Drafting and Intent*, 259.

228 Morsink, 259.

· 5 ·

THE INTERPRETATION AND IMPLEMENTATION OF THE UDHR

There is a widespread assumption that the UDHR did not set any specific way to read or interpret its provisions. Therefore, the document has been considered as separated clauses, as in the Anglo-Saxon legal tradition.[1] In this manner, there is a prevalent tendency to isolate specific human rights and to interpret them without considering the interdependency and deep interrelatedness of all thirty articles. It also disregards contextual interpretations and the relevance of local communities, duties, and other hierarchies of values. Nevertheless, the history of the UDHR reveals that the drafters had a different idea in mind.

A Holistic Reading of all Human Rights

The *travaux préparatoires* of the UDHR and the research of experts in this field, indicate that there is a specific legal and philosophical pluralistic vision inscribed into the document: it is a terminated, but open-ended system.[2] In

1 As criticized by Glendon, *Rights Talk: The Impoverishment of Political Discourse.*

2 See Pallares Yabur, "La Justificación Racional de Los Derechos Humanos En Los Redactores de La Declaración Universal de Los Derechos Humanos," 156.

other words, the drafters adopted a document with clearly specified values and principles (e.g. the right to education), but the agreement on those concepts was just made at a general level (practical agreement).

Nevertheless, this open-ended vision does not indicate that human rights can be interpreted at will. The substantive content of each human rights must consider all other rights, in order to avoid an imbalance among them or the deformation of a right for political convenience. To avoid these problems, the UDHR was conceived as a document that protects different aspects of every human life in an interrelated way: material, economic, intellectual, spiritual, social, political and cultural elements.

Human rights are grouped according to "the object of the rights".[3] Cassin stated that: "the declaration rested on four fundamental pillars: personal rights, relationships between man and his fellow men, public liberties and fundamental political rights, and economic and social rights".[4] All these dimensions of the human being are equally important. Cassin suggested the following way of reading the document:

> The two initial articles stated general principles within the framework of which individual rights were defined. There was a regular progression from individual rights to social rights. Between those two categories came, first a group of articles dealing with physical protection of the individual, then a group dealing with the relation of man to his fellow and to things –family, residence, frontiers, nationality, and finally property- then came articles dealing with the great public freedoms, including freedom of religion, and their external manifestations in such forms as freedom of expression; and last articles 22–27 provided guarantees of social security.[5]

This structure is also known as "Cassin's portico", where all rights and principles are interrelated. Mary Ann Glendon and Glen Johnson support Cassin's vision because this model is not aleatory.[6] Cassin was a pioneer in the study of comparative law and had extensive legislative experience.[7] He was aware that the document was not conceived as a mere list of rights, it had a structure. It involved a great deal of influence from the continental civil law tradition,

3 Kanger, *Human Rights in the UN Declaration*, 73.
4 Quoted in Schabas, *The Universal Declaration of Human Rights the Travaux Préparatoires: Volume 3*.
5 Morsink, *The Universal Declaration of Human Rights: Origins, Drafting and Intent*, 236.
6 Johnson and Symonides, *La Déclaration Universelle Des Droits de l'Homme: 40e Anniversaire—1948-1988*, 87.
7 Glendon, "Knowing the Universal Declaration of Human Rights," 1158.

rather than the Anglo-Saxon one. Glendon describes how this influence can be seen in its level of generality, the use of general clauses, and the mutual interrelatedness between different articles.[8]

Modeled in the image of this legal tradition, the document contains a preamble followed by a "general part" with six introductory principles to guide the interpretation of each legal provision.[9] The first two articles and the preamble embody the principles of equal rights and establish the concept of human being and society embedded into the document.[10] That is why articles one and two are not rights; they were conceived as general parts or principles through which the other articles must be interpreted.[11] The same happens with the last three articles (28, 29 and 30). They are not rights; they are interpretative clauses that provide context and limitations for the implementation of all other rights.[12]

The declaration was meant to be read not as isolated clauses, but as an integral document, where all rights are interdependent and indivisible.[13] By "interdependence" Donnelly interprets "a functional relation between rights: they interact with one another to produce a whole that is more than the sum of its parts".[14] Morsink indicates that

> The drafters wanted the readers of the Declaration to interpret each article in light of all the others. Most of them believed that the exact place of an article was not crucial to its meaning since it needed to be interpreted in the context of the whole anyway.[15]

The drafters specifically wanted the articles that touched on the same topic to be read together.[16] They did not consider that some rights were more important than others or that some rights could be legitimately suppressed in order to highlight others. Eide has emphasized that the UDHR "was conceived as a

8 Glendon, 1171.

9 Glendon, *A World Made New: Eleanor Roosevelt and the Universal Declaration of Human Rights*, 63.

10 Glendon, 64.

11 Sigrun Skogly, "Article 2," in *The Universal Declaration of Human Rights: A Common Standard of Achievement*, ed. Asbjørn Eide and Gudmundur Alfredsson (Martinus Nijhoff, 1999), 87.

12 Glendon, "Knowing the Universal Declaration of Human Rights," 1159.

13 Donnelly, *Universal Human Rights in Theory and Practice*, 28.

14 Donnelly, 31.

15 Morsink, *The Universal Declaration of Human Rights: Origins, Drafting and Intent*, 232.

16 Morsink, 238.

normative system of interrelated rights, not a menu from which states could pick and choose".[17]

Eide emphasizes that the position of the UDHR is that "states have to take all human rights into consideration when they deal with each one of the rights, otherwise respect for one right could become a violation of another right".[18] All categories of human rights are mutually supportive of each other and the very idea of universality of all rights involves the indivisibility and interdependent implementation of all of them.

Human Rights as General Principles: Context and Content

On the other hand, another relevant element regarding the interpretation of the UDHR has to do with considering the articles as a set of values or principles. The practical agreement of the UDHR was based on general values or principles as human rights because an absolute agreement was not possible regarding the detailed content of each right.

Åshild Samnøy narrates how there was deep-rooted disagreement on the Commission on Human Rights about the content of "democracy", discussions about marriage and the family, disagreement on the limits to freedom of thought and assembly, the system for labor rights, the rights of minorities, and the right to property.[19] Considering that reasonable disagreement was legitimate, the drafters agreed to use vague terms and wide limitation clauses to leave space for different interpretations.[20]

For example, regarding the meaning of "democracy" and "progress" there was no possibility of agreement between the U.S. and the Soviet Union, because each of them interpreted these words according to different philosophical worldviews. Because of this situation, Eleanor Roosevelt declared that these two words "applied to abstract ideas for which no uniform interpretation existed".[21]

17 Eide, "Interdependence and Indivisibility of Human Rights," 11.

18 Eide, 25.

19 Åshild Samnøy, "The Origins of the Universal Declaration of Human Rights," in *The Universal Declaration of Human Rights: A Common Standard of Achievement*, ed. Asbjørn Eide and Gudmundur Alfredsson (Martinus Nijhoff, 1999), 13.

20 Samnøy, *Human Rights as International Consensus: Making the Universal Declaration of Human Rights 1945–1948*, 15– 16.

21 Summary Record of the Hundred and Fiftieth Meeting of the Third Committee, Held at the Palais de Chaillot, Paris, 20 November 1948, A/C.3/SR.150.

Regarding the rights of minorities, this article was finally excluded because each delegate had a different vision about what was the best way to manage diversity within its frontiers: some considered that special rights should be granted (Soviet Union), others that assimilation was their national policy (France, U.S. and some Latin America countries), and some others that a multicultural state was better (Lebanon).[22] As the delegate of Haiti, Mr. Saint-Lot indicated each state proposed a different solution in this regard, "it was therefore impossible to establish a uniform rule for every country".[23]

There are further examples of this situation. Regarding article 26, on the right to education, there were discrepancies on the idea of education itself. Some delegations, especially the Latin American ones, emphasized the rights of parents and families to choose their children's education, others maintained the priority of the state as guarantor of this right. At the end, the representatives decided to take measures to avoid "Nazi-like schools"[24] or "Communistic training of youth",[25] where parents' concerns were ignored, and the state had a dangerous monopoly over education. The article incorporates both the rights and obligations of families and communities and states, giving priority to parents' rights and convictions.[26] But how to materialize and balance such premises was left open to each society.

Another important discussion on education was about its aims. Most delegates agreed that education was an integral aspect that included the intellectual, physical, emotional, and social dimensions of the person.[27] However,

22 See the discussions in: Summary Record of Eleventh Meeting [of the First Session of the Sub-Commission on Prevention of Discrimination and Protection of Minorities] Held at the Palais des Nations, Geneva, on Monday 1 December 1947, E/CN.4/Sub.2/SR.11; and Summary Record of the Seventy-Third Meeting [of the Commission on Human Rights] Held at Lake Success, New York, on Tuesday, 15 June 1948, E/CN.4/SR.73.

23 Summary Record of the Hundred and Sixty-First Meeting of the Third Committee, Held at the Palais de Chaillot, Paris, 27 November 1948, A/C.3/SR.161. Also see the General Assembly resolution A/C.3/376 (29 November 1948).

24 Kanger, *Human Rights in the UN Declaration*, 147; Robinson, *The Universal Declaration of Human Rights: Its Origins, Significance, Application and Interpretation*, 138.

25 Eleanor Roosevelt, "Making human rights come alive. Speech to Pi Lambda Theta, Columbia University, March 30, 1949", Gifts of Speech (1949) in <http://gos.sbc.edu/r/eleanor1.html>. Consulted on May 23, 2019.

26 Verdoodt, *Naissance et Signification de La Déclaration Universel Des Droits de l'Homme*, 252.

27 Pentti Arajarvi, "Article 26," in *The Universal Declaration of Human Rights: A Commentary*, ed. Asbjørn Eide et al. (Scandinavian University Press, 1993), 409.; and Summary record of the eight meeting Working group declaration (Geneva) E/CN.4/AC.2/SR.8 (10 December 1947).

there were two opposite visions: some representatives maintained that higher education was about technical and professional training, the other envisaged a more humanistic approach that stressed moral education and public virtues.[28]

In relation to this discussion, Pierre Lebar from the UNESCO remained the problems of an educational system that is only concerned with the development of technical skills: "where under Hitler regime, education had been admirably organized but had, nevertheless, produced disastrous results".[29] Therefore, state representatives agreed to include general guidelines about the moral and humanistic objectives of education, but leaving legitimate room for their interpretation and implementation.

Another relevant example of discrepancies is the heated discussions about family and marriage. Some delegations wanted to include the word "divorce", but it was not accepted by most states of Catholic tradition. The representatives did not try to impose their vision on these countries, rather the agreement was to replace it with the word "dissolution" in order to leave space to different worldviews.[30]

Thus, in view of these situations, the drafters envisaged the UDHR as a document containing principles and values, which involves a significant difference from the liberal approach.[31] The consideration of human rights as principles does not diminish their legal value, this distinction is not one between "soft" and "hard" law, nor one of "binding" versus "non-binding". The word "principles" is not used to excuse violations or non-implementation, rather it reveals the flexible and adaptive nature of the universal consensus. A too detailed description of what each right entailed would have created a too rigid document, unfit for dynamic human life, and it would have implied the imposition of a specific cultural view.

The drafters knew that they were making a declaration of principles and values, not a program of "a philosophy of life",[32] as was remarked by some delegates. According to this, principles meant that the rights contained in

28 Morsink, *The Universal Declaration of Human Rights: Origins, Drafting and Intent*, 213–215.

29 Morsink, 216.

30 Samnøy, *Human Rights as International Consensus: Making the Universal Declaration of Human Rights 1945–1948*, 96.

31 Humphrey, *Human Rights and the United Nations: A Great Adventure.*

32 Summary Record of the Ninetieth Meeting of the Third Committee, Held at the Palais de Chaillot, Paris (1 October 1948) A/C.3/SR.90.

the declaration were established to be interpreted and implemented in different ways. In this regard, the UNESCO's philosophers report stated that the UDHR:

> Must further be sufficiently definite to have real significance both as an inspiration and as a guide to practice, but also sufficiently general and flexible to apply to all men, and to be capable of modification to suit peoples of different stages of social and political development while yet retaining significance for them and their aspirations.[33]

Humphrey stated that "while there was deep disagreement on how they [human rights] should be implemented, there was substantial agreement on the stated objectives".[34] The representatives of Canada, United States, and the Netherlands emphasized that it was a difficult task to reconcile different philosophies and legal traditions, therefore a document with general guidelines was more appropriated for an international compromise.[35]

Jacques Maritain explained that "many different kinds of music could be played on the document's thirty strings".[36] This means that the interpretation of human rights inscribed in the UDHR provides cultural flexibility on the way the content of each universal right will be materialized. The objective was that the declaration would be enculturated in different contexts, taking different shapes, so that all states could learn from each other's experiences.[37] This is why the drafters decided to determine a general way of reading the document, an overview of the justification and anthropology underlying the project (article one), and interpretative guidelines (articles two, 27, 28 and 29) that would holistically frame and implement the rights of the document.

Cultural and philosophical differences where not despised by the UDHR; they were considered the soil, water, and sun required to plant the seed of human rights. The seed in abstract and without all these influences remains a "pure" but meaningless grain. However, with the necessary ingredients and patience (different traditions, the interpretative clauses, local and

33 Goodale, *Letters to the Contrary: A Curated History of the UNESCO Human Rights Survey*, 51.
34 Humphrey, *Human Rights and the United Nations: A Great Adventure*.
35 Comments of governments on the draft international declaration on human rights and the question of implementation, E/CN.4/82/Rev.1 (16 April 1948).
36 Glendon, *A World Made New: Eleanor Roosevelt and the Universal Declaration of Human Rights*, 230.
37 Glendon, "Foundations of Human Rights: The Unfinished Business," 7.

international dialogues) it will grow into different types of plants. Not every society has to cultivate orchids: there is a wide variety of plants.

The equation of universality with uniformity was an expressly rejected idea by the drafters of the UDHR. They did not create a one-size-fits-all model of moral behavior.[38] Glendon argues that the drafters "were not homogenizers, but they were universalists in the sense that they believed that human nature was everywhere the same and that the processes of experiencing, understanding, and judging were capable of leading everyone to certain basic truths".[39] The drafters started from the fact of a common human condition, but not a completed, unbiased, non-cultural or uniform understanding of it. Seth Kaplan remarks that

> The UDHR's flexibility is paralleled in how the drafters viewed implementation. It was understood that each country's circumstances would affect how they would fulfill their requirements. Developing countries would have fewer resources than developed countries. Communist states would emphasize different priorities than capitalist ones. Muslim states' values would vary from those of Western states. Each part of the world would have its particular concerns.[40]

During the adoption of the UDHR at the U.N. General Assembly, Lester Pearson from Canada indicated in his speech that "each nation would endeavor to implement it [the UDHR], in its own way and according to their own traditions".[41] Roosevelt remarked that implementation would necessarily vary from country to country, which "should be considered not only inevitable but salutary".[42] Chang also considered that

> The first condition for defence of the rights of man was tolerance towards the various opinions and beliefs held throughout the world. Uncompromising dogmatism had caused much harm, by accentuating disputes, and lending them an ideological basis. In the present times, [...] there had been a tendency to impose a standardized way of thinking and single way of life. With that approach, equilibrium could be reached

38 See Glendon, *A World Made New: Eleanor Roosevelt and the Universal Declaration of Human Rights*, xviii.
39 Glendon, 230.
40 Kaplan, "Will Human Rights Survive in a Multipolar World?," 116.
41 Verbatim Record of the Hundred and Eighty-Second Plenary Meeting of the General Assembly, Held at the Palais de Chaillot, Paris (10 December 1948) A/PV.182.
42 Summary Record of the Sixty-Fourth Meeting of the Commission on Human Rights, Held at Lake Success, New York, E/CN.4/SR.64 (8 June 1948).

only at the cost of moving away from the truth, or employing force. But, however violent the methods employed, equilibrium achieved in that way could never last.[43]

During the drafting process of the UDHR, state representatives were actually concerned with seeking consensus. They did not intend to create a speculative morality of self-righteousness that would be spread to change and shape societies all around the world according to their theoretical and cultural ideal.

Accordingly, the vision of the drafters of the UDHR is more accurately embraced in terms of what some scholars, like John Finnis[44] and Jacques Maritain,[45] present as basic goods and institutions that respond to the exigencies of a universally shared human dignity that take different forms in each community.

In this regard, the prevailing uniform approach of liberal universality puts the declaration's legitimacy in jeopardy. Today's problem is that the inclusion of duties, context, and cultural diversity were more welcomed by Chang and Malik than by contemporary activists, human rights courts, and treaty body mechanisms.[46]

The drafters knew that uniformity was the path that led to the destruction of the UDHR's universality. The drafters of the UDHR were not naïve. They knew that this kind of open-ended universality was the only possible one, but also it was one that could be either uniformly implemented under one single philosophy or politicized and instrumentalized. On the first problem, the American Anthropological Association warned against the expansion of an individualistic conception of human rights as universal that was only shared in Western Europe and the United States.[47] The representative of Saudi Arabia, Jamil Baroody, also stated that "it was not for the Committee to proclaim the superiority of one civilization over all the others or to establish uniform standards for all the countries of the world".[48]

Maritain cautioned about an absolutist interpretation of human rights based just on the Enlightenment paradigm.[49] Lindholm notices that "it is

43 Verbatim Record of the Hundred and Eighty-Second Plenary Meeting of the General Assembly, Held at the Palais de Chaillot, Paris, 10 December 1948, A/PV.182.

44 John Finnis, *Natural Law and Natural Rights* (New York: Clarendon Press, 1988).

45 Jacques Maritain, *Man and the State* (Chicago: The Chicago University Press, 1971).

46 Kaplan, *Human Rights in Thick and Thin Societies: Universality without Uniformity*, 18.

47 American Anthropological Association, "Statement on Human Rights," *American Anthropologist* 49, no. 4 (1947): 539–43.

48 Quoted in Morsink, *The Universal Declaration of Human Rights: Origins, Drafting and Intent*, 24.

49 UNESCO, *Human Rights: Comments and Interpretations*, VI.

potentially a much more serious matter if adherents of a particular religion, normative tradition, culture or ideology advance claims to public monopoly in the grounding of universally applicable human rights".[50]

On the second concern, Richard McKeon warned that different implementations and interpretations at the core relied on different conceptions about who the human being is and what are the purposes of society.[51] He declared that "difficulties will be discovered in the suspicions, suggested by these differences, concerning the tangential uses that might be made of a declaration of human rights for the purpose of advancing special interests rather than establishing universal truths or promoting general welfare".[52] Maritain acknowledged that "all depends on the ultimate value whereon those rights depend and in terms of which they are integrated by mutual limitations".[53]

The main problem is a profound international disagreement on the scale of values incorporated in the UDHR and about what is the good life. In this respect, Morsink recalls the dangers of a postmodernist way of thinking that denies access to objective truth and agreement.[54] Such an approach encourages opportunistic and non-universally shared interpretations that undermine the legitimacy of the whole human rights structure.

Considering the prevailing backlash against human rights, it seems evident that a "back to basics" approach is necessary. In this sense, the idea of universality envisaged by the UDHR's drafters provides a better understanding about what the possibilities and limitations of a universal agreement are. It can also provide a clearer picture about what was actually part of the consensus and what has to be left to a legitimate pluralism, which is not the same as cultural or moral relativism.

A human rights renewal based on this pluralistic universality can recover the legitimacy of the human rights project and provide a deeper reception of cultural diversity, paradoxically, as an essential part of a true universality.

50 Lindholm, "The Cross-Cultural Legitimacy of Universal Human Rights: Plural Justification across Normative Divides," 38.

51 Glendon, "Knowing the Universal Declaration of Human Rights," 1157.

52 Goodale, *Letters to the Contrary: A Curated History of the UNESCO Human Rights Survey*, 83.

53 UNESCO, *Human Rights: Comments and Interpretations*, VIII.

54 Morsink, *The UDHR and The Holocaust: An Endangered Connection.*

· 6 ·

THE RIGHT TO SELF-DETERMINATION: PLURALISTIC UNIVERSALITY IN ACTION

As argued throughout this book, the paradigm of liberal universality has resulted in the imposition of an interpretative framework for human rights that is not neutral, is legally unfounded, and is not shared by a large part of the global population. However, international law provides a tool that can help to change the prevailing paradigm and go back to the pluralistic universality of the UDHR: the right to self-determination.

As acknowledged by some scholars, the right to self-determination "is among the most commonly accepted principles of international ethical and legal thought".[1] Self-determination is a core component of the human rights corpus. It is the first article of the two main human rights treaties (the ICCPR and the ICESCR), but it is rarely addressed in a holistic manner in practice. Most scholarship works on the subject focusing on the decolonization process[2] and secessionist

1 Bas van der Vossen, "Self-Determination and Moral Variation," in *The Theory of Self-Determination*, ed. Fernando R Tesón (Cambridge University Press, 2016), 14.

2 See for instance: James R Crawford, "The Right to Self-Determination in International Law: Its Development and Future," in *Peoples' Rights*, ed. Philip Alston (Oxford University Press, 2001); Helen Quane, "The United Nations and the Evolving Right to Self-Determination," *The International and Comparative Law Quarterly* 47 (1998); Antonio

claims.[3]

Nevertheless, self-determination implies more than establishing an independent state or seceding from an existing one. It refers to the right of peoples to determine their own political regime, and their own economic, social and cultural development. This right enhances cultural diversity and recognizes that there are different legitimate ways of understanding human flourishing among diverse societies. Accordingly, it is a multidimensional right that involves taking people's claims and participation seriously in the conduct of public affairs, related to a wide spectrum of issues: cultural, social, and economic ones.

Following the spirit of the UDHR's pluralistic universality, a broad interpretation of the right to self-determination requires taking people's voices into account in the determination of international standards and interpretations adopted by human rights mechanisms, especially treaty bodies. Cross-cultural agreement in this regard is necessary for human rights universality.

This includes a change of paradigm in the standard-setting process, for the determination of whether a human rights interpretation is universal or not requires intercultural dialogue and mutual understanding of different perspectives. Thus, only interpretations that enjoy broad international support should be considered universal. Before explaining this proposal, the following section will introduce the historical development and legal nature of this right under international law.

Historical Background and Legal Status

The right to self-determination was initially envisaged as a principle of international law by Franklin Roosevelt and Winston Churchill in the Atlantic Charter of 1941.[4] It was then incorporated as a key principle of the U.N.

Cassese, "The Self-Determination of Peoples" in *The International Bill of Rights: The Covenant on Civil and Political Rights*, ed. Louis Henkin (Columbia University Press, 1981).

3 See for instance: Christian Walter, Antje von Ungern-Sternberg, and Kavus Abushov, eds., *Self-Determination and Secession in International Law* (Oxford University Press, 2014); Dietrich Murswiek, "The Issue of a Right of Secession – Reconsidered," in *Modern Law of Self-Determination*, ed. Christian Tomuschat (Martinus Nijhoff, 1993); Asbjørn Eide, "Peaceful Group Accommodation as an Alternative to Secession in Sovereign States" in *Self-Determination: International Perspectives*, eds. Donald Clark and Robert Williamson (Macmillan Press, 1996).

4 Paul Taylor, *A Commentary on the International Covenant on Civil and Political Rights: The UN Human Rights Committee's Monitoring of ICCPR Rights* (Cambridge University Press,

Charter, whose article 1.2 declares that "the principle of equal rights and self-determination of peoples" is necessary "to develop friendly relations among nations".[5]

This principle of political liberalism[6] has been mainly developed in the area of decolonization and embraced by the Third World. It was greatly used in this context as the legal vehicle to listen to people's claims in the developing world. The 1960 Declaration on the Granting of Independence to Colonial Countries and Peoples established that "all peoples have the right to self-determination; by virtue of that right they freely determine their political status and freely pursue their economic, social and cultural development".[7]

In 1970 the principle of equal rights and self-determination of peoples was incorporated in the Declaration on Principles of International law Concerning Friendly Relations and Co-operation among States in Accordance with the Charter of the United Nations (Declaration on Principles of International Law). This instrument emphasized that

> All peoples have the right freely to determine, without external interference, their political status and to pursue their economic, social and cultural development, and every State has the duty to respect this right in accordance with the provisions of the Charter.[8]

The document also indicates that sovereign equality includes the right of each state to freely "choose and develop its political, social, economic and cultural systems",[9] which constitutes an "inalienable right" and which must be done "without interference in any form by another State".[10] The declaration states

2020), 37; Thomas Musgrave, *Self-Determination and National Minorities* (Clarendon Press, 1997), 15–31.

5 U.N. Charter (1945) <https://www.un.org/en/sections/un-charter/chapter-i/index.html>. Consulted on December 10, 2019.

6 Different from the comprehensive form of liberalism that has been criticized in this research. See chapter one.

7 Declaration on the Granting of Independence to Colonial Countries and Peoples (1960), para 2 <https://www.ohchr.org/EN/ProfessionalInterest/Pages/Independence.aspx>. Consulted on January 7, 2019.

8 General Assembly, Resolution 2625(XXV), The Declaration on Principles of International law Concerning Friendly Relations and Co-operation among States in Accordance with the Charter of the United Nations (1970), p. 8 <https://www.un.org/ruleoflaw/files/3dda1f104.pdf>. Consulted on March 6, 2019.

9 The Declaration on Principles of International Law (1970), 10.

10 The Declaration on Principles of International Law (1970), 7.

that self-determination is based on having a representative government of the "whole people belonging to the territory without distinction as to race, creed or colour".[11] This paragraph indicates that self-determination requires a government that is legitimate and representative of the will of the people, in contrast with a self-serving one or one that serves foreign interests.[12]

Traditionally, this right has been divided into its external and internal dimensions. Regarding the first one, it refers to the right of peoples to decide their international political status and to be free from alien domination.[13] The latter aspect is "the right of a nation already constituted as a State to choose its own form of government and freely determine its own policies, free from outside interference".[14] According to scholarship, external self-determination is reserved to the process of decolonization, while internal self-determination is a right of all peoples and it involves "authentic self-government" or "the right for a people really and freely to choose its own political and economic regime".[15]

In the field of human rights, the UDHR did not incorporate an article that refers to self-determination, although the spirit of pluralistic universality is based on the same rationale. This right was included in the first article of both the ICCPR and the ICESCR. During the drafting process, some Western nations were reluctant to conceive a right to self-determination in the covenants. Nonetheless, self-determination was finally incorporated as a claim from Third World states motivated by the decolonization process.[16] The article as finally adopted establishes that "all peoples have the right of

11 The Declaration on Principles of International Law (1970), 10.

12 As argued by: James Summers, *Peoples and International law*, 2nd edn (Martinus Nijhoff, 2013), 230–238; James R Crawford, *The Creation of States in International law* (Oxford University Press, 2007), 118–122; David Raic, *Statehood and the Law of Self-Determination* (Kluwer Law International, 2002), 273–277.

13 James Summers, "The Internal and External Aspects of Self-Determination Reconsidered," in *Statehood and Self-Determination: Reconciling Tradition and Modernity in International law*, ed. Duncan French (Cambridge University Press, 2013).

14 Taylor, *A Commentary on the International Covenant on Civil and Political Rights: The UN Human Rights Committee's Monitoring of ICCPR Rights*, 42. Also see: CERD, General Recommendation No. XXI on the right to self-determination forty-eight session (1996), para 4.

15 Antonio Cassese, *Self-Determination of Peoples: A Legal Appraisal* (Cambridge University Press, 1995), 101.

16 Summers, *Peoples and International Law*, 303–307.

self-determination. By virtue of that right they freely determine their political status and freely pursue their economic, social and cultural development".[17]

This right was restated in the Vienna Declaration and Programme of Action of 1993.[18] This instrument links the right to self-determination with democratic principles: "democracy is based on the freely expressed will of the people to determine their own political, economic, social and cultural systems and their full participation in all aspects of their lives".[19] Therefore, self-determination requires taking people's opinions seriously in a democratic debate for the adoption of public decisions, so they can respond to the needs of society and not to the interests of other actors.

Thus, the inclusion of this right in human rights treaties indicates that self-determination is not restricted to the context of decolonization. Its scope has been broadened. As former Special rapporteur James Anaya indicates: "decolonization procedures did not themselves embody the substance of the norm of self-determination; rather they were measures to remedy a sui generis deviation from the norm that existed in the prior condition of colonialism".[20] As Rosalyn Higgins notes: "self-determination has never simply meant independence. It has meant the free choice of peoples".[21] Therefore, self-determination was not exhausted in the process of decolonization. It constituted just one of its multidimensional manifestations.

As some scholars indicate, the right to self-determination is a permanent one, which is not extinguished when independence is achieved,[22] for the actual object of protection is not the creation of a state, rather it is the permanent process of determining a people's political, economic, social and cultural development, according to the needs and claims of each society.[23] Then, its permanent nature is based on the continuous connection that should exist between policy decisions and people's needs. As stated during the drafting

17 ICCPR, article 1(1).

18 Vienna Declaration and Programme of Action (1993), para 2 <https://www.ohchr.org/en/professionalinterest/pages/vienna.aspx>. Consulted on May 7, 2019.

19 Vienna Declaration and Programme of Action, para 8.

20 See James Anaya, "A Contemporary Definition of the International Norm of Self-Determination," *Transnational Law & Contemporary Problems* 131, no. 3 (1993): 144.

21 Rosalyn Higgins, *Problems and Process: International law and How We Use It* (Oxford University Press, 1995) 120.

22 See Taylor, A *Commentary on the International Covenant on Civil and Political Rights: The UN Human Rights Committee's Monitoring of ICCPR Rights*, 46.

23 See Ulrike Barten, *Minorities, Minority Rights and Internal Self-Determination* (Springer, 2014), 201–202.

process of the covenants, self-determination was conceived as "a universal right and for all time".[24]

The HRC has issued a General Comment on this topic, which declares that self-determination "is of particular importance because its realization is an essential condition for the effective guarantee and observance of individual human rights and for the promotion and strengthening of those rights".[25] Special Rapporteur Héctor Gros Espiel has argued that self-determination is a precondition for enjoyment of all other human rights.[26] It has also been declared as a precondition for social progress and development in article three of the Declaration on Social Progress and Development of 1969.[27] In this way this right is "apart from and before all of the other rights in the two Covenants".[28] Thus, a society that is not able to decide on its own the most basic and daily aspects of their lives, is a society that is deprived of its human rights.

At the regional level, the ECHR does not contain a right to self-determination. However, the Helsinki Final Act of 1975, whose aim was to improve East and West relations during the Cold War, in its principle VIII addresses this right.[29] In the Western context, self-determination was equated to representative government and periodic elections, for the creation of independent states was limited to the decolonization process.[30] This right was later reaffirmed by the Organization for Security and Co-operation in Europe (OSCE) at the end of the Cold War in the Charter of Paris for a New Europe of 1990.[31]

24 Report of the Third Committee, Draft International Covenants on Human Rights, tenth session, A/3077, (8 December 1955), para 39.

25 HRC, General Comment No 12: Article 1 (Right to Self-Determination), twenty-first session (1984), para 1.

26 Héctor Gros Espiell (Special Rapporteur of the Sub-Commission on Prevention of Discrimination), The Right to Self-Determination: Implementation of United Nations Resolutions, E/CN.4/Sub.2/405/Rev.l (1980), 10.

27 General Assembly, Resolution 2542 (XXIV) Declaration on Social Progress and Development (11 December 1969) <https://www.ohchr.org/en/professionalinterest/pages/progressanddevelopment.aspx>. Consulted on March 4, 2019.

28 HRC, General Comment No 12: Article 1 (Right to Self-Determination), twenty-first session (1984), para 1.

29 Final Act of the Conference on Security and Co-operation in Europe, Part VIII (1975) <https://www.osce.org/files/f/documents/5/c/39501.pdf>. Consulted on May 13, 2019.

30 Musgrave, *Self-Determination and National Minorities*, 96–101.

31 Charter of Paris for a New Europe (1990) <https://www.osce.org/mc/39516>. Consulted on May 13, 2019.

The African Charter on Human and People's Rights also establishes in its article 20(1) that all peoples "shall have the unquestionable and inalienable right to self-determination. They shall freely determine their political status and shall pursue their economic and social development according to the policy they have freely chosen".[32] This paragraph means that the government should be a legitimate one and representative of the will of the people.[33]

In other words, the state apparatus should be at the service of people's needs, and not the other way around. The African Commission on Human Rights has also highlighted this aim of self-determination, by stating that this right "may be exercised in any of the following ways independence, selfgovernment, local government, federalism, confederalism, unitarism or any other form of relations that accords with the wishes of the people but fully cognisant of other recognised principles".[34]

Regarding the legal status of self-determination, it is both a right and a principle.[35] It is a principle of international law and a customary norm.[36] On the other hand, it is a human right as recognized in the ICCPR and the ICESCR. Commentators disagree on whether self-determination is a *ius cogens* norm or not.[37]

The International Law Commission (ILC) in the commentaries to the draft articles of 1966 on the Vienna Convention on the Law of Treaties (VCLT) cited self-determination as a *ius cogens* norm, but decided not to include any examples in the final article.[38] However, in 2022, the ILC adopted its conclusions on the identification of *ius cogens* norms and included the right to self-determination as an example of a rule that enjoys this legal status.[39]

32 African Charter on Human and People's Rights (1981), art. 30 <https://au.int/en/treaties/african-charter-human-and-peoples-rights> consulted on May 13, 2019.

33 Summers, *Peoples and International Law*, 230–238.

34 African Commission on Human Rights, *Katangese Peoples' Congress v. Zaire*, *African Commission on Human and Peoples' Rights*, Comm. No. 75/92 (1995), para 4

35 See Summers, *Peoples and International Law*, 70–78.

36 See Rüdiger Wolfrum, "Purposes and Principles," in *The Charter of the United Nations: A Commentary, Volume I*, ed. Bruno Simma et al., 3rd edn (Oxford University Press, n.d.), 108–109.

37 Summers, *Peoples and International Law*, 78–84; Cassese, *Self-Determination of Peoples: A Legal Appraisal*, 133–140.

38 ILC, Draft Articles on the Law of Treaties with commentaries 1966, p. 248 <https://legal.un.org/ilc/texts/instruments/english/commentaries/1_1_1966.pdf>. Consulted on May 7, 2019.

39 ILC, Draft Conclusions on Identification and Legal Consequences of Peremptory Norms of General International Law (*ius cogens*), with commentaries 2022, p. 89 < https://

Also, in the *East Timor Case*, the International Court of Justice (ICJ) has declared that the right to self-determination has an *erga omnes* character and is an essential principle of contemporary International law.[40]

Concerning the nature of this right, most scholars consider it a collective one,[41] but some maintain that self-determination is also an individual right, if it is equated to the democratic participation of every individual in the conduct of public affairs.[42] Special rapporteur Héctor Gros Espiell considers that this right is both collective and individual:

> Self-determination as a right of the human being is a consequence of the necessary recognition of the political rights of citizens and of the civil, economic, social and cultural rights of all individuals without any discrimination. The self-determination of citizens, individually, on the basis of the recognition of their political rights, is a prerequisite of the effective realization of self-determination as the people's collective right.[43]

Gros Espiell's assertion appears to be more in consonance with the anthropological vision of the UDHR, which conceived the human person both as an individual and as a member of society. It is also more coherent with a holistic interpretation of human rights based on their interdependence and indivisibility.

legal.un.org/ilc/texts/instruments/english/commentaries/1_14_2022.pdf>. Consulted on December 15, 2023.

40 ICJ, *East Timor (Portugal v. Australia)*, Judgment, I. C.J. Reports 1995, para 29. It was reiterated in ICJ, *Legal Consequences of the Construction of a Wall in the Occupied Palestinian Territory*, Advisory Opinion, I. C. J. Reports 2004, para 156.

41 See in this regard: Frank Przetacznik, "The Basic Collective Human Right to Self Determination of Peoples and Nations as a Prerequisite for Peace," *NYLS Journal of Human Rights* VIII (1990): 89–90; Isabelle Schulte-Tenckhoff, "Treaties, Peoplehood, and Self-Determination: Understanding the Language of Indigenous Rights" in *Indigenous Rights in the Age of the UN Declaration*, ed. Elvira Pulitano (Cambridge University Press, 2012), 79–80; Anaya, "A Contemporary Definition of the International Norm of Self-Determination" (n 1046), 137; Ian Brownlie, "The Rights of Peoples in Modern International law," *Bulletin of the Australian Society of Legal Philosophy* 9 (1985); James R Crawford, "The Rights of Peoples: Peoples or Governments," *Bulletin of the Australian Society of Legal Philosophy* 9 (1985).

42 See Marc Weller, *Escaping the Self-Determination Trap* (Martinus Nijhoff, 2008), 23.

43 Héctor Gros Espiell (Special Rapporteur of the Sub-Commission on Prevention of Discrimination), The Right to Self-Determination: Implementation of United Nations Resolutions, E/CN.4/Sub.2/405/Rev.l (1980), 10.

As declared by the HRC, self-determination in its collective dimension does not impel the fulfillment of individual rights, rather it is the precondition for their enjoyment. The protection of human rights, as envisaged by human rights treaties, can only occur where everyone can participate in the decisions of society. Moreover, individual human rights can only be protected through a government that is accountable to its people and acts according to popular will. A vision of the human person in these dual and complementary dimensions can better safeguard all human rights.

Self-Determination and Subsidiarity

Regarding the legal nature of the right to self-determination, it is relevant to mention its connection with one of the underpinning principles of public international law:[44] subsidiarity. The use of this concept is deeply rooted in Western political thought, especially in Europe.[45] It has also been developed in the context of federalism[46] and encouraged in the Catholic Church's social doctrine.[47]

The word subsidiarity has its roots in the Latin word *subsidum*, which refers to help or assistance.[48] As Samantha Besson argues, in broad terms, subsidiarity refers to two interrelated principles. First, "the individual/smaller/

44 Eirik Bjorge, "Been There, Done That: The Margin of Appreciation and International law," *Cambridge Journal of International and Comparative Law* 4, no. 1 (2015); Lukasz Gruszczynski and Wouter Werner, eds., *Deference in International Courts and Tribunals: Standard of Review and Margin of Appreciation* (Oxford University Press, 2014).

45 Chantal Millon-Delsol, *L'État Subsidiare: Ingérence et Non-Ingérence de l'Etat Le Principe de Subsidiarité Aux Fondements de l'histoire Européenne* (Presses Universitaires de France, 1992); Global Constitutionalism and Andreas Follesdal, "The Principle of Subsidiarity as a Constitutional Principle in International law" 2 (2013): 37–62, https://doi.org/10.1017/S2045381712000123.

46 George A. Bermann, "Taking Subsidiarity Seriously: Federalism in the European Community and the United States," *Columbia Law Review* 94, no. 2 (1994), https://doi.org/10.2307/1123200.

47 Thomas Kohler, "Quadragesimo Anno (1931)," in *A Century of Catholic Social Thought: Essays on "Rerum Novarum" and Nine Other Key Documents*, ed. Robert Royal and George Weigel (Ethics & Public Policy Center, 1991); Patrick McKinley Brennan, "Subsidiarity in the Tradition of Catholic Social Doctrine," in *Global Perspectives on Subsidiarity*, ed. Michelle Evans and Augusto Zimmermann (Springer, 2014).

48 Michelle Evans and Augusto Zimmermann, "The Global Relevance of Subsidiarity: An Overview," in *Global Perspectives on Subsidiarity*, ed. Michelle Evans and Augusto Zimmermann (Springer, 2014), 1.

lower/ internal unit or entity should have priority (or so-called 'primarity') in doing certain things". Second, "this priority may or should be reversed only when the individual/smaller/lower/internal unit or entity cannot do so, or not sufficiently well, and/or when the collective/larger/higher/external one can do so better".[49]

As developed in the Catholic Church's social doctrine, subsidiarity encompasses a wider perspective that involves different levels of society and communities within the state.[50] It fosters freedom and responsibility through different layers and communities in society. It requires that

> All societies of a superior order must adopt attitudes of help ("subsidium") — therefore of support, promotion, development — with respect to lower-order societies. In this way, intermediate social entities can properly perform the functions that fall to them without being required to hand them over unjustly to other social entities of a higher level, by which they would end up being absorbed and substituted, in the end seeing themselves denied their dignity and essential place.[51]

The legal development of this concept in international law can be traced to the European Union,[52] where the emphasis is seen in the suppletory character of higher political orders to avoid superseding lower forms of association. As developed in the European Union, subsidiarity means "to guarantee a degree of independence for a lower authority in relation to a higher body or for a local authority in relation to central government. It therefore involves the sharing of powers between several levels of authority".[53]

The Maastricht treaty on the European Union of 1992 incorporated this principle stating that the European Community should take action

49 Samantha Besson, "Subsidiarity in International Human Rights Law—What Is Subsidiary about Human Rights ?," *The American Journal of Jurisprudence* 61, no. 1 (2016): 86, https://doi.org/10.1093/ajj/auw009.

50 N. W. Barber, "The Limited Modesty of Subsidiarity," *European Law Journal* 11, no. 3 (2005).

51 Pontifical Council for Justice and Peace, Compendium of the Social Doctrine of the Church (2005) para 186.

52 Larry Cata Backer, "Harmonization, Subsidiarity and Cultural Difference: An Essay on the Dynamics of Opposition Within Federative and International Legal Systems," *Tulsa Journal of Comparative and International Law* 4, no. 2 (1997).

53 European Parliament, Fact Sheets on the European Union: The principle of subsidiarity (2020), 2 <https://www.europarl.europa.eu/factsheets/en/sheet/7/the-principle-of-subsidiarity>. Consulted on February 10, 2021.

> Only if and in so far as the objectives of the proposed action cannot be sufficiently achieved by the Member States and can therefore, by reason of the scale or effects of the proposed action, be better achieved by the Community.[54]

Article 5(3) of the Lisbon Treaty of 2007 formulated the concept in similar terms but specifies that the principle of subsidiarity becomes operative only regarding issues that are within the competence of the European Union.[55]

In IHRL, subsidiarity is first found in article 51 of the Fundamental Charter of the European Union, which establishes the principle of subsidiarity in the implementation of the instrument.[56] It was incorporated in 2013 in the preamble of the ECHR through the adoption of Protocol 15:

> Affirming that the High Contracting Parties, in accordance with the principle of subsidiarity, have the primary responsibility to secure the rights and freedoms defined in this Convention and the Protocols thereto, and that in doing so they enjoy a margin of appreciation, subject to the supervisory jurisdiction of the European Court of Human Rights established by this Convention.[57]

In this regime of international law, "the principle of subsidiarity is an express manifestation of the diversified character of the implementation of human rights guarantees at national level".[58] Subsidiarity as a structural principle of IHRL means that such an idea permeates the whole human rights system to its deepest roots.[59] Thus, subsidiarity, like self-determination and the pluralistic universality of the UDHR, are not accessory terms. Rather, they are rooted at the core of the project at different levels: procedural and substantive.

As for the procedural aspect, there are several principles grounded in the idea of subsidiarity. The requirement of the exhaustion of local remedies before bringing a claim to an international court, the "fourth instance" doctrine, and

54 Treaty on the European Union (1992), art. 3(b).
55 Treaty of Lisbon amending the Treaty on European Union and the Treaty establishing the European Community (2007), art. 5(3).
56 Charter of Fundamental Rights of the European Union (2000/C 364/01), article 51.
57 Protocol No. 15 amending the Convention on the Protection of Human Rights and Fundamental Freedoms (2013).
58 Robert Spano, "Universality or Diversity of Human Rights?: Strasbourg in the Age of Subsidiarity," *Human Rights Law Review* 14, no. 3 (2014): 491, https://doi.org/10.1093/hrlr/ngu021.
59 See Paolo G Carozza, "Subsidiarity as a Structural Principle of International Human Rights Law," *American Journal of International Law* 38 (2003).

remedial subsidiarity are examples of the application of this concept.[60] The "fourth instance" doctrine implies that international human rights mechanisms cannot assume the role of a first-instance national court.[61] The remedial subsidiarity protects states' options to decide how to remedy a human rights violation after an adverse judgment,[62] which also implies that international mechanisms are not empowered to order legislative modifications or the revocation of decisions.[63]

The best-known procedural development for the implementation of subsidiarity in IHRL is the margin of appreciation,[64] which has been embraced by the ECtHR, but barely used by the IACtHR and human rights treaty bodies.[65] This tool is an instrument of judicial self-restraint that establishes a methodology to delineate the degree of scrutiny that an international court may exercise.[66]

On the substantive aspects, this tool developed in the case-law of the ECtHR provides a normative latitude of maneuver for the state to decide how

60 Gerald Neuman, "Subsidiarity," in *The Oxford Handbook of Human Rights*, ed. Dinah Shelton (Oxford University Press, 2013).

61 ECtHR, *Austin and others v. UK* (Application nos. 39692/09, 40713/09 and 41008/09) 15 March 2012, para 61.

62 Besson, "Subsidiarity in International Human Rights Law — What Is Subsidiary about Human Rights ?," 82–83.

63 ECtHR, *Belilos v. Switzerland* (Application no. 10328/83) 29 April 1988, para 76 and 78: "The Court notes that the Convention does not give it jurisdiction to direct the Swiss State—even supposing that the latter could itself comply with such a direction—to cancel the applicant's conviction and sentence" and "The Court notes that the Convention does not empower it to order Switzerland to alter its legislation; the Court's judgment leaves to the State the choice of the means to be used in its domestic legal system to give effect to its obligation under Article 53".

64 Alastair Mowbray, "Subsidiarity and the European Convention on Human Rights," *Human Rights Law Review* 15, no. 2 (2015); Dean Spielmann, "Allowing the Right Margin: The European Court of Human Rights and The National Margin of Appreciation Doctrine: Waiver or Subsidiarity of European Review?," *Cambridge Yearbook of European Legal Studies* 14, no. 1 (2017).

65 Jorge Contesse, "Contestation and Deference in the Inter-American Human Rights System," *Law and Contemporary Problems* 79, no. 2 (2016); Dominic McGoldrick, "A Defence of the Margin of Appreciation and an Argument for Its Application by the Human Rights Committee," *International and Comparative Law Quarterly* 65, no. January (2016): 21–60, https://doi.org/10.1017/S0020589315000457.

66 Yuval Shany, "Toward a General Margin of Appreciation Doctrine in International law?," *European Journal of International Law* 16, no. 5 (2005): 909–910, https://doi.org/10.1093/ejil/chi149.

to comply with its international obligations.[67] It also circumscribes the degree and content of the judicial review conducted by international mechanisms.[68] The margin will be wider when the issue at stake involves matters where there is no consensus or cases about sensitive moral issues.[69]

The rationale behind this cautious self-restraint on the part of the regional court and the room provided for normative maneuver to the state is based on the open-ended nature of human rights norms[70] and the recognition of pluralism among different states.[71]

The synchronic interrelation between domestic and international planes is at the core of the human rights project, for their adoption relied on commonly shared principles among different legal regimes and their enforcement mechanism is also of a dual nature.[72] Human rights treaties were adopted as instruments to be further legislated, developed, and democratically implemented at the domestic level with the local participation of each state.[73]

The nature of these international norms is very peculiar, for their development was meant to spring from local practices.[74] Therefore, the process of human rights standard setting should also reflect this interdependency, which

67 Thomas A. O'Donnell, "The Margin of Appreciation Doctrine: Standards in the Jurisprudence of the European Court of Human Rights," *Human Rights Quarterly* 4, no. 4 (1982): 475.

68 Besson, "Subsidiarity in International Human Rights Law—What Is Subsidiary about Human Rights ?," 80–82.

69 ECtHR, *Dudgeon v. UK* (Application no. 7525/76) 22 October 1981, para 60–62; and ECtHR, *A, B, C v. Ireland*, para 222.

70 Shany, "Toward a General Margin of Appreciation Doctrine in International law?" Also, as recognized in ECtHR, Odièvre v. France (Application no. 42326/98) 13 February 2003, para 40.

71 Fabio Macioce, "Cultural Rights and the Margin of Appreciation Doctrine: A Legal Tool for Balancing Individual Rights and Traditional Rules," *Law, Culture and the Humanities* 13, no. 3 (2017): 458–461, https://doi.org/10.1177/1743872117732846.

72 Besson, "Subsidiarity in International Human Rights Law—What Is Subsidiary about Human Rights ?," 76; Neuman, "Subsidiarity."

73 Samantha Besson, "Human Rights and Constitutional Law: Patterns of Mutual Validation and Legitimation," in *Philosophical Foundations of Human Rights*, ed. Rowan Cruft (Oxford University Press, 2015); Grégoire Webber et al., *Legislated Rights: Securing Human Rights through Legislation* (Cambridge University Press, 2018); Andrew Legg, *The Margin of Appreciation in International Human Rights Law: Deference and Proportionality* (Oxford University Press, 2012), chap. 3.

74 Bosko Tripkovic, "A New Philosophy for the the Margin of Appreciation and European Consensus," *The Oxford Journal of Legal Studies* 42, no. 1 (2022).

is not reduced to a dialogue between state elites but is nurtured by the concerns of each society.

In this regard, subsidiarity requires giving priority to internal decision-making procedures for the implementation and interpretation of international norms.[75] This approach recognizes the importance of democratic dialogue and participation in the development of human rights norms, and therefore, a holistic view of self-determination. As stated by the ECtHR, "by reason of their direct and continuous contact with the vital forces of their countries, State authorities are in principle in a better position than the international judge" to assess the legitimacy of restrictions and interpretations.[76]

Due to this attention paid to local considerations, some scholars argue that subsidiarity prioritizes a *realpolitik* approach to uphold an abstract idea of sovereignty to the detriment of human rights and freedom.[77] Others consider that the motivation behind this idea is to avoid international scrutiny, which diminishes the functions of international courts.[78]

Nevertheless, as Dominic McGoldrick points out, the margin of appreciation is not a right of the state, nor does it entail an absence of international scrutiny.[79] The margin of appreciation goes hand in hand with international supervision,[80] because the assessment of interpretations is a joint task. In this sense, subsidiarity enhances the role of international courts, because their deference to local decisions fortifies the democratic legitimacy of their judicial review process.[81]

75 Laurence R. Helfer, "Redesigning the European Court of Human Rights: Embeddedness as a Deep Structural Principle of the European Human Rights Regime," *European Journal of International Law* 19, no. 1 (2008).

76 ECtHR, *Handyside v. UK* (Application no. 5493/72) 7 December 1976, para 48.

77 Marisa Iglesias Vila, "Subsidiarity, Margin of Appreciation and International Adjudication within a Cooperative Conception of Human Rights," *International Journal of Constitutional Law* 15, no. 2 (2017).

78 Eyal Benvenisti, "The Margin of Appreciation, Subsidiarity, and Global Challenges to Democracy," *GlobalTrust Working Paper Series 05/2016*, 2016, https://papers.ssrn.com/sol3/papers.cfm?abstract_id=3047237.

79 McGoldrick, "A Defence of the Margin of Appreciation and an Argument for Its Application by the Human Rights Committee," 22–23.

80 ECtHR, *Handyside v. UK*, para 48.

81 Andreas Von Staden, "The Democratic Legitimacy of Judicial Review Beyond the State: Normative Subsidiarity and Judicial Standards of Review," *International Journal of Constitutional Law* 10, no. 4 (2012): 1023–49, https://doi.org/10.1093/icon/mos032.

Furthermore, a holistic approach to self-determination means that the content of subsidiarity does not only refer to the review process or to the allocation of jurisdiction/powers between national authorities and international mechanisms. The aim of subsidiarity is to promote local participation and to give preference to the authorities that are closest to the citizens affected by a decision. The purpose of this approach is to avoid the alienation of people from decision-making processes that concern them and will affect their daily lives.[82]

The purpose of this principle is to nourish local freedoms by encouraging active and responsible participation in democratic decision-making processes.[83] As explained by Paolo Carozza, subsidiarity as a structural principle of human rights involves the prioritization of the human person and help/assistance to achieve human flourishing.[84]

Subsidiarity is based on the recognition of social pluralism, since the human being is part of different intermediate communities that contribute through different means to human flourishing.[85] Such premises run counter to a nationalistic-state-centric vision. Rather, they promote a person-centered approach both to subsidiarity and to self-determination as interpretative tools for the development of human rights standards.

The principle of subsidiarity in connection to the right to self-determination points towards another relevant aspect of this proposal. Subsidiarity means that the interpretation of human rights norms is not a process that only concerns either state authorities or human rights mechanisms. Rather, the process of interpretation should be owned by the people of each society, including the various intermediary communities, in order to achieve their vision of human flourishing. It is a shared task involving both local and international elements.

82 "Public responsibilities shall generally be exercised, in preference, by those authorities which are closest to the citizen", as stated in the European Charter of Local Self-Government (1985), article 4.3. Also see: European Parliament, Fact Sheets on the European Union: The principle of subsidiarity (2020), 1 <https://www.europarl.europa.eu/factsheets/en/sheet/7/the-principle-of-subsidiarity>. Consulted on February 10, 2021.

83 Besson, "Subsidiarity in International Human Rights Law—What Is Subsidiary about Human Rights ?," 93–98; Staden, "The Democratic Legitimacy of Judicial Review Beyond the State: Normative Subsidiarity and Judicial Standards of Review."

84 Carozza, "Subsidiarity as a Structural Principle of International Human Rights Law," 42–46 and 57–58.

85 Jonathan Chaplin, "Subsidiarity and Social Pluralism," in *Global Perspectives on Subsidiarity*, ed. Michelle Evans and Augusto Zimmermann (Springer, 2014).

A Holistic Approach to Self-Determination

Although it is clear that self-determination is a human right of all peoples, its holistic interpretation with all its political, economic, social and cultural elements has been barely studied. As scholar Ulrike Barten has stated "the overwhelming mass of literature on self-determination devotes much time and space on secession".[86] Most scholars have only addressed the political and external dimensions of this right.[87] The main research works on the subject have reduced this right to issues of secession or questions related to minorities and indigenous peoples as bearers of external self-determination.[88] Therefore, the development of the human right to self-determination in its broader political, social and cultural dimensions is still a pending task.

A holistic approach to self-determination allows each society not only to determine their own political, economic, social and cultural issues, but also to decide how to interpret and implement international human rights norms according to their own vision of human flourishing, as long as they include all

86 Barten, *Minorities, Minority Rights and Internal Self-Determination*, 194.

87 Some examples are: Joshua Castellino, "International law and Self-Determination," in *Self-Determination and Secession in International law*, eds. Christian Walter, Antje von Ungern-Sternberg, and Kavus Abushov (Oxford University Press 2014); Robert McCorquodale, "Self-Determination: A Human Rights Approach," The International and Comparative Law Quarterly 43 (1994); Quane (n 1028); Frederic L Kirgis, "The Degrees of Self-Determination in the United Nations Era," *The American Journal of International Law* 88 (1994) 88; Yoram Dinstein, "Collective Human Rights of Peoples and Minorities," *The International and Comparative Law Quarterly* 25 (1976).

88 See Joshua Castellino and Jeremie Gilbert, "Self-Determination, Indigenous Peoples and Minorities," *Macquarie Law Journal* 3 (2003); Peter Hilpold, ed., *Autonomy and Self-Determination: Between Legal Assertions and Utopian Aspirations* (Edward Elgar Publishing Limited, 2018); Hurst Hannum, *Autonomy, Sovereignty, and Self-Determination: The Accommodation of Conflicting Rights* (University of Pennsylvania Press 1990); Gaetano Pentassuglia, "Self-Determination, Human Rights, and the Nation-State," *International Community Law Review* 19 (2017); Norman J Padelford and K Gosta A Andersson, "The Aaland Islands Question," *The American Journal of International Law* 33 (1939); Schulte-Tenckhoff (n 1066); Walter, Ungern-Sternberg and Abushov (n 1029); Martti Koskenniemi, "National Self-Determination Today: Problems of Legal Theory and Practice," *The International and Comparative Law Quarterly* 43 (1994); BG Rancharan, "Peoples' Rights and Minorities' Rights," *Nordic Journal of International Law* 56 (1987); Gerry Simpson, "The Diffusion of Sovereignty: Self-Determination in the Post-Colonial Age," *Stanford Journal of International Law* 32 (1996); Weller (n 1067); Peter Hilpold, "Self-Determination and Autonomy: Between Secession and Internal Self-Determination," *International Journal on Minority and Group Rights* 24 (2017).

human rights. This right allows each people to democratically decide how to balance different interests and hierarchies of values, for it is far from evident how to determine the scope of each abstract human right in the concrete case, as explained in chapter one. In a clash of rights, other social and contextual elements play a primary role to discern how to balance the interests at stake.[89]

In this regard, as recognized by legal scholars and other scientific disciplines, there are different ways in which societies can be organized.[90] Some may choose a "thick way" to organize themselves, where the common good involves religiously grounded ideas or cultural practices.[91] Others would prefer a "thin" manner, where the state only sets a procedural legal framework in the public sphere.[92] Some societies, like Western ones, consider that the maximization of personal autonomy in all spheres of life is the most important goal of the state,[93] while many non-Western ones (and religious groups within the West) think that solid relationships and social institutions that promote different values are necessary for the common good.[94]

89 As argued by Koskenniemi, "The Effects of Rights on Political Culture"; MacIntyre, *Whose Justice? Which Rationality?*, chap. 17; Glendon, *Rights Talk: The Impoverishment of Political Discourse*.

90 See different sociological and anthropological works on this point: Henrich, Heine, and Norenzayan, "The Weirdest People in the World?"; Jonathan Haidt, *The Righteous Mind: Why Good People Are Divided by Politics and Religion* (New York: Random House, 2012); Richard Shweder, Nancy Much, Manamohan Nahapatra, et al., "The 'Big Three' of Morality (Autonomy, Community, Divinity) and the 'Big Three' Explanations of Suffering," in *Morality and Health*, ed. Paul Rozin and Allan Brandt (Routledge, 1997).

91 See this argument in Morsink, *The Universal Declaration of Human Rights: Origins, Drafting and Intent*, 259.

92 Morsink, 259.

93 See the research work of Henrich, Heine, and Norenzayan, "The Weirdest People in the World?," 74.

94 See the research work of Heejung S Kim and Smaranda Lawrie, "Culture and Motivation," in *Handbook of Cultural Psychology*, ed. Dov Cohen and Shinobu Kitayama (The Guilford Press, 2019); Shinobu Kitayama, Jiyoung Park, and Yay-hyung Cho, "Culture and Neuroplasticity," in *Handbook of Advances in Culture and Psychology: Volume 5*, ed. Michele J Gelfand, Chi-yue Chiu, and Ying-yi Hong (Oxford University Press, 2015); Marcelo Suárez-Orozco, "Everything You Ever Wanted to Know about Assimilation but Were Afraid to Ask," in *Engaging Cultural Differences: The Multicultural Challenge in Liberal Democracies*, eds. Richard A. Shweder, Martha Minow, and Hazel Rose Markus (Russell Sage Foundation, 2002); Kaplan, *Human Rights in Thick and Thin Societies: Universality without Uniformity*.

Thus, self-determination includes the right of people to organize themselves without external domination and the right to have a government that reflects their ideas and concerns.[95] The essence of self-determination is then "a free, genuine and voluntary choice in securing the continuing restructuring of human communities in accordance with the evolving aspirations of the members of such communities".[96]

As can be seen in the compilation of the *travaux préparatoires* of the ICCPR of Marc Bossuyt, the drafters of the ICCPR previewed a "very comprehensive definition", which included the right of a people "to establish its own political institutions, to develop its own economic resources, and to direct its own social and cultural evolution, without the interference of other peoples or nations".[97] Accordingly, this right has a multifaceted nature that comprises different elements of human life. Self-determination involves popular participation to determine broader aspects of the polis, which include economic, social, and cultural issues. As Special rapporteur Héctor Gros Espiell indicates

> For the right [of self-determination] to be fully effective, the existence of all these elements is required. The implementation of the right of peoples to self-determination involves not only the completion of the process of achieving independence or other appropriate legal status by the peoples under colonial and alien domination, but also the recognition of their right to maintain, assure and perfect their full legal, political, economic, social and cultural sovereignty.[98]

As Gros Espiell recalls the economic aspect of self-determination is stated in the second paragraph of common article one of the ICCPR and the ICESCR, and it refers to permanent sovereignty over natural resources.[99] In the social

95 See Hurst Hannum, "Self-Determination in the Post-Colonial Era," in *Self-Determination: International Perspectives*, ed. Donald Clark and Robert Williamson (Macmillan Press, 1996), 25.

96 Nihal Jayawickrama, *The Judicial Application of Human Rights Law: National, Regional and International Jurisprudence* (Cambridge University Press, 2017), 198.

97 Bossuyt, *Guide to the "Travaux Préparatoires" of the International Covenant on Civil and Political Rights*, 33.

98 Héctor Gros Espiell (Special Rapporteur of the Sub-Commission on Prevention of Discrimination), The Right to Self-Determination: Implementation of United Nations Resolutions, E/CN.4/Sub.2/405/Rev.l (1980), 8.

99 See also: Aureliu Cristescu (Special rapporteur of the Sub-Commission on Prevention of Discrimination), The Right to Self-Determination: Historical and Current Development on the Basis of the United Nations Instruments, E/CN.4/Sub.2/404/Rev. 1 (1981), 13–15; and Héctor Gros Espiell (Special Rapporteur of the Sub-Commission on Prevention of

aspects, it implies that each people has "the right to determine freely its own objectives of social development, to set its own priorities, and to decide the means and methods of their achievement without any external interference".[100] It also includes the right to choose their own social system, with due respect to their culture and traditions.[101] In the cultural sphere, it refers to "the right to determine and establish the cultural regime or system under which it is to live; this implies recognition of its right to regain, enjoy and enrich its cultural heritage, and the affirmation of the right of all its members to education and culture".[102]

The social and cultural aspects of self-determination acknowledge the right of peoples to freely pursue their cultural development, which involves respect for cultural diversity and to avoid homogenization or impositions.[103] As legal scholar Robert Araujo insists

> The right of political, cultural, and social self-determination is inextricably related to people exercising sovereignty. Efforts made to curtail this kind of sovereignty would deleteriously affect the exercise and protection of a wide variety of human rights. A sovereign nation is a community of people who exercise shared values concerning human dignities that shape and direct the particulars of their communitarian self-determination.[104]

Such a definition includes discerning the type of social and cultural development that each society wants to achieve. This determination will emerge from each people's conception of what constitutes human flourishing, which

Discrimination), The Right to Self-Determination: Implementation of United Nations Resolutions, E/CN.4/Sub.2/405/Rev.l (1980), 26–27.

100 Aureliu Cristescu (Special rapporteur of the Sub-Commission on Prevention of Discrimination), The Right to Self-Determination: Historical and Current Development on the Basis of the United Nations Instruments, E/CN.4/Sub.2/404/Rev. 1 (1981), 94.

101 See Héctor Gros Espiell (Special Rapporteur of the Sub-Commission on Prevention of Discrimination), The Right to Self-Determination: Implementation of United Nations Resolutions, E/CN.4/Sub.2/405/Rev.l (1980), 28

102 Héctor Gros Espiell, 28.

103 See Aureliu Cristescu (Special rapporteur of the Sub-Commission on Prevention of Discrimination), The Right to Self-Determination: Historical and Current Development on the Basis of the United Nations Instruments, E/CN.4/Sub.2/404/Rev. 1 (1981), 103–104.

104 Robert Araujo, "Sovereignty, Human Rights, and Self-Determination: The Meaning of International law," *Fordham International Law Journal* 1485 24 (2001).

at the same time depends on the cultural frame and concept of the self that each society embraces.

These other dimensions of self-determination are essential for the development of all peoples, although the social and cultural aspects are rarely addressed in scholarship. As Yale University professor of law Michael Reisman remarks: political self-determination and economic self-determination may be important, "but it is the integrity of the inner worlds of peoples—their rectitude systems or their sense of spirituality—that is their distinctive humanity. Without an opportunity to determine, sustain, and develop that integrity, their humanity—and ours—is denied".[105] Scholars Joshua Castellino and Cathal Doyle remark that the main driver of self-determination is to retain one's culture and identity, this means, to govern oneself instead of being culturally determined by an external power that fails to safeguard the most cherished values of the community.[106]

As for the interpretation and implementation of human rights, this aspect of self-determination becomes highly relevant. For this process must reflect the will and needs of the people of each society. Accordingly, state representatives should comply with this by consulting the people in all matters that affect them in the cultural, religious, social, and educational spheres, which are intimately related to human rights norms. In the words of Israeli scholar Yael Tamir:

> Individuals wish to be ruled by institutions imprinted by a culture that they find understandable and meaningful, and therefore allows a certain degree of transparency that facilitates their participation in public affairs. When one can identify one's own culture in the political framework, when political institutions reflect familiar norms of behavior, traditions, and historical interpretations, one's conception of oneself as a creator, or at least a carrier, of a valuable set of beliefs, is reinforced.[107]

Therefore, this right implies that although internationally recognized human rights norms are mandatory, the people cannot be alienated from the determination of their interpretations or standards, both at national and international

105 W Michael Reisman, "International law and the Inner Worlds of Others," *Saint Thomas Law Review* 25 (1996): 35.

106 Joshua Castellino and Cathal Doyle, "Who Are 'Indigenous Peoples'?," in *The UN Declaration on the Rights of Indigenous Peoples: A Commentary*, ed. Jessie Hohmann and Marc Weller (Oxford University Press, 2018), 8.

107 Yael Tamir, "The Right to National Self-Determination," *Social Research* 58, no. 3 (1991): 585.

levels. This means, that the process of interpretation should be a pluralistic, participative, and dialogical one between different conceptions of the good shared by a variety of peoples. For the determination of what is universal and what should be left to a legitimate space of diversity is in itself a joint and unfinished task, as established in the UDHR.[108]

For all these reasons, a multidimensional approach to self-determination protects freedom and plurality.[109] Self-determination "is often thought to be important precisely because it allows for moral variation between societies".[110] As Marc Weller recalls, it is a "right to be different".[111] While at the same time this right demands unity in diversity, for self-determination cannot be used to deny internationally recognized human rights.

Therefore, a holistic view of self-determination, as provided by the ICCPR and the ICESCR, is part of this internationally recognized human right, which includes at the same time the right to decide how to interpret and implement human rights norms. This approach then requires (1) implementing a robust understanding of self-determination including its social and cultural aspects; and (2) emphasizing that the rights holder is the people and not the states or any other international actor, which requires a truly representative government and robust democratic participation in the standard setting process conducted by human rights mechanisms.

Taking Democracy and Participation Seriously: Cultural and Social Decisions

Although common article 1 of the ICCPR and the ICESCR establishes that all peoples can decide their cultural and social development, the exploration of these broader elements in the literature has been limited to the rights of indigenous peoples.[112] Most scholars focus on autonomy arrangements or

108 See Glendon, "Foundations of Human Rights: The Unfinished Business."

109 See Tamir, "The Right to National Self-Determination"; Joseph Raz, "National Self-Determination," *The Journal of Philosophy* LXXXVII, no. 9 (1990); David Miller, *On Nationality* (Clarendon Press, 1995).

110 Vossen, "Self-Determination and Moral Variation," 14.

111 Marc Weller, "Self-Determination of Indigenous Peoples," in *The UN Declaration on the Rights of Indigenous Peoples: A Commentary*, ed. Jessie Hohmann and Marc Weller (Oxford University Press, 2018), 132.

112 See for instance: Erica-Irene A. Daes, "Some Considerations on the Right of Indigenous Peoples to Self-Determination," *Transnational Law & Contemporary Problems* 3, no. 1 (1993); Gudmundur Alfredsson, "The Right to Self-Determination and Indigenous Peoples," in *Modern Law of Self-Determination*, ed. Christian Tomuschat (Martinus Nijhoff,

different types of bilateral relations between indigenous peoples and the state that can be territorial and/or related to religious, linguistic or broad cultural matters.[113] However, as these two covenants indicate, a holistic development of these human rights requires extending this understanding as applicable to all different peoples.

Considering this, it is relevant to analyze how self-determination in these broader aspects has been developed regarding the rights of indigenous peoples. This category of rights holders involves a recent legal work within the U.N. system. There is no internationally agreed definition of indigenous peoples, but according to several instruments, they are broadly defined as

> Descendants of the peoples who inhabited the land or territory prior to colonization or the establishment of State borders; they possess distinct social, economic and political systems, languages, cultures and beliefs, and are determined to maintain and develop this distinct identity; they exhibit strong attachment to their ancestral lands and the natural resources contained therein; and/or they belong to the non-dominant groups of a society and identify themselves as indigenous peoples.[114]

The recognition of the right to self-determination as a right of indigenous peoples is found in the U.N. Declaration on the Rights of Indigenous Peoples of 2007. Its article 3 states their right to "freely determine their political status

1993); Castellino and Gilbert, "Self-Determination, Indigenous Peoples and Minorities"; Alexandra Xanthaki, *Indigenous Rights and United Nations Standards: Self-Determination, Culture and Land* (Cambridge University Press, 2007); S James Anaya, "The Right of Indigenous Peoples to Self-Determination in the Post-Declaration Era," in *Making the Declaration Work: The United Nations Declaration on the Rights of Indigenous Peoples*, eds. Claire Charters and Rodolfo Stavenhagen (IWGIA, 2009); Castellino, "International Law and Self-Determination"; Snezana Trifunovska, "One Theme in Two Variations—Self Determination for Minorities And Indigenous Peoples," *International Journal on Minority and Group Rights* 5, no. 2 (1997); Siegfried Wiessner, "Indigenous Self-Determination, Culture, and Land: A Reassessment in Light of the 2007 UN Declaration on the Rights of Indigenous Peoples," in *Indigenous Rights in the Age of the UN Declaration*, ed. Elvira Pulitano (Cambridge University Press, 2012).

113 See for instance: Xanthaki, *Indigenous Rights and United Nations Standards: Self-Determination, Culture and Land*, 131–173; Daes, "Some Considerations on the Right of Indigenous Peoples to Self-Determination"; Weller, *Escaping the Self-Determination Trap*, 78–90; Weller, "Self-Determination of Indigenous Peoples."

114 OHCHR, Minority Rights: International Standards and Guidance for Implementation (2010), 3 <https://www.ohchr.org/Documents/Publications/MinorityRights_en.pdf>. Consulted on January 14, 2019.

and freely pursue their economic, social and cultural development".[115] The conceptualization of this right is followed by article 4 that states "indigenous peoples, in exercising their right to self-determination, have the right to autonomy or self-government in matters relating to their internal and local affairs, as well as ways and means for financing their autonomous functions".[116]

Article 5 further indicates that indigenous peoples have the right "to maintain and strengthen their distinct political, legal, economic, social and cultural institutions, while retaining their right to participate fully, if they so choose, in the political, economic, social and cultural life of the State".[117] This means that indigenous peoples have "the right to participate in decision-making in matters which would affect their rights".[118] For this purpose, states are required to obtain their "free, prior and informed consent" before adopting measures that will affect them in different domains: cultural, political, religious, economic and social.[119]

As the expert on indigenous rights James Anaya remarks, "indigenous peoples with their own organic social and political fabrics, are to be full and equal participants at all levels in the construction and functioning of the governing institutions under which they live".[120] According to the Special rapporteur on the rights of indigenous peoples, these rights holders should be able "to become full participants in the life of the State with due regard for their own cultural patterns".[121] Therefore, this right permits indigenous peoples to configurate their own society in all aspects, without waiving their cultural identity or their most cherished beliefs.

As for cultural aspects, the Special rapporteur on the rights of indigenous peoples indicates that this right involves a "cultural self-determination", which implies "the right to recapture their identity, reinvigorate their ways of life, reconnect with the Earth, regain their traditional lands, protect their

115 U.N. Declaration on the Rights of Indigenous Peoples (2007), art. 3 <https://www.un.org/development/desa/indigenouspeoples/wp-content/uploads/sites/19/2018/11/UNDRIP_E_web.pdf>. Consulted on January 16, 2019.

116 U.N. Declaration on the Rights of Indigenous Peoples, art. 4.

117 U.N. Declaration on the Rights of Indigenous Peoples, art. 5.

118 U.N. Declaration on the Rights of Indigenous Peoples, art. 18.

119 U.N. Declaration on the Rights of Indigenous Peoples, art. 19.

120 Anaya, "The Right of Indigenous Peoples to Self-Determination in the Post-Declaration Era," 188.

121 James Anaya (Special rapporteur on the rights of indigenous peoples), Report on the Situation of Human Rights of Indigenous Peoples in Brazil, A/HRC/12/34/Add.2 (26 August 2009), p. 8.

heritage, revitalize their languages and manifest their culture".[122] James Anaya has suggested that in a human rights approach, self-determination can be understood as "a right of cultural groupings to the political institutions necessary to allow them to exist and develop according to their distinctive characteristics".[123] The Special rapporteur on the rights of indigenous peoples highlights that this dimension is very broad:

> The right to self-determination is understood as a right to control their past, present and future: control of the past, in the sense of developing their own narrative of their histories; control of the present, implying the power to maintain the elements that characterize them as distinct societies; and control of the future, referring to the security of knowing that they will be able to survive as diverse peoples on their own terms.[124]

In this regard, indigenous people enjoy cultural autonomy to decide several aspects of their daily life at large, including the fields of religion and education. Article 11 of the UN Declaration on the Rights of Indigenous Peoples establishes their right to practice and revitalize their culture and traditions.[125] Article 12 recognizes their right to practice their religion and to teach their spiritual traditions.[126] Article 14 recognizes their right to establish and control their own educational institutions.[127]

The IACtHR and the IACoHR have also recognized the rights of indigenous peoples in this wide sense. The IACoHR has established that indigenous peoples enjoy the right to use their own language, practice their religion, and all the characteristics that are necessary for the preservation of their cultural identity.[128] The IACtHR has recognized that human rights norms should be read according to the particular cultural characteristics and needs of indigenous peoples, taking into account their notion of communal property and the spiritual elements related to it.[129]

122 Victoria Tauli-Corpuz, (Special rapporteur on the rights of indigenous peoples), Rights of Indigenous Peoples, A/73/176 (17 July 2018), p. 9.

123 S. James Anaya, "The Capacity of International law to Advance Ethnic or Nationality Rights Claims," *Colorado Law Faculty Scholarship* 75 (1990): 842.

124 Victoria Tauli-Corpuz (Special rapporteur on the rights of indigenous peoples), Rights of Indigenous Peoples A/74/149 (17 July 2019), p. 7.

125 U.N. Declaration on the Rights of Indigenous Peoples, art. 11.

126 U.N. Declaration on the Rights of Indigenous Peoples, art. 12.

127 U.N. Declaration on the Rights of Indigenous Peoples, art. 14.

128 IACoHR, *Yanomami vs Brasil*, resolution N° 12/85, Case N° 7615 (5 March 1985), para 7.

129 IACtHR, *Case of the Mayagna (Sumo) Awas Tingni Community v. Nicaragua* (31 August 2001), paras 142–155; IACtHR, *Caso Comunidad indígena Yakye Axa vs. Paraguay* (17 June

Thus, as can be appreciated, in the domain of self-determination indigenous peoples enjoy the right to live according to their own cultural, religious, and social worldviews. They also have the right to be informed, consulted and to effectively participate in the public affairs that affect them and in the general decisions taken by society at large. Moreover, they have the right to participate in these processes with full respect of their particular identities.

However, self-determination as stated in article one of the two main human rights treaties implies that the right-holder is universal, in other words, that everyone is entitled to these aspects, which have only been developed with regard to indigenous peoples. Following the paradigm of pluralistic universality, this means that all peoples have the right to live according to their own cultural, religious and social worldviews, as long as they respect all internationally recognized human rights.[130]

Thus, regarding human rights interpretations, which are a matter of concern for society as a whole, self-determination requires popular participation and continuous dialogue to decide how to balance different interests. In this process, cultural and social self-determination and the identity of each people cannot be overlooked.

The Rights Holder: The People, not the State

To understand the relevance of this holistic approach to self-determination it is of utmost importance to recall that the rights holder is the "people", because some scholars have taken a state-centric approach,[131] based on the idea that the first international appearance of this right is in the U.N. Charter.

Looking at this approach and at state practice, it is pertinent to question whether self-determination reinforces or impels the enjoyment of human rights. A self-determination argument based primarily on the protection of state sovereignty and national interests can be used as an excuse for human rights violations without international surveillance. This claim can be presented by authoritarian governments as the representative voice of its people, while it is only serving the interests of a powerful minority. It can also be

2005), paras 123–156; and IACtHR, *Caso Comunidad Indígena Sawhoyamaxa vs. Paraguay* (29 March 2006), paras 116–126.

130 See this argument in Glendon and Kaplan, "Renewing Human Rights."

131 See Crawford, *The Creation of States in International law* (n 1038): 108–132.

used to advance human rights interpretations that are incompatible with the object and purposes of human rights treaties and render them ineffective.[132]

Nevertheless, there are some characteristics of this right that preserve it from being distorted into a state-centric tool. Self-determination as a human right has a special legal nature, which prevents these abuses. Human rights treaties are instruments that are not adopted for traditional reciprocal obligations between states for their own profit. They are rights recognized to a third-party beneficiary (the human person) for the protection of human dignity.[133] Accordingly, they require to be interpreted in the manner that is favorable to the rights holder and not to the interests of the state (generally, the ruling elite or political party).[134] James Anaya indicates that a focus on the state, instead of the people, rests on a

> State-centered vision of humanity and the world, that is, a vision of the world that considers the modern state—that institution of Western theoretical origin—as the most important and fundamental unit of human organization. This framework of thinking obscures the human rights character of self-determination, and it is blind to the contemporary realities of a world that is simultaneously moving toward greater interconnectedness and decentralization, a world in which the formal boundaries of statehood do not altogether determine the ordering of communities and authority.[135]

Therefore, the said criticism is only applicable if it is assumed that self-determination is for the sake of the state or the ruling elite. Nevertheless, as it has been stated in different international instruments, and consistent with the special legal nature of human rights treaties, the rights holder is not the state: it is the "people".

It is relevant to notice that the question of who is the "people" is a controversial one.[136] This subject will not be addressed here, for it is beyond the

132 An example is provided in An-Na'im, "The Cultural Mediation of Human Rights: The Al-Arqam Case in Malaysia."

133 IACtHR, *Advisory Opinion OC-3/83 (8 September 1993) Restrictions to the death penalty*, para 50.

134 Matthew Craven, *The International Covenant on Economic, Social and Cultural Rights: A Perspective on Its Development* (Clarendon Press, 1995), 3.

135 Anaya, "The Right of Indigenous Peoples to Self-Determination in the Post-Declaration Era," 188–189.

136 See on this discussion: Trifunovska, "One Theme in Two Variations—Self Determination for Minorities And Indigenous Peoples"; Xanthaki, *Indigenous Rights and United Nations Standards: Self-Determination, Culture and Land*, 132–140; Castellino and Gilbert, "Self-Determination, Indigenous Peoples and Minorities"; Musgrave, *Self-Determination and National Minorities*, 148–177.

scope of this book. Thus, for the sake of the argument, the "people" will be considered in its internationally accepted connotation: as the persons that inhabit a sovereign state or the whole people of a state.[137]

Consequently, self-determination is a right that is both related to the principles of sovereign equality and non-intervention, as stated in the U.N. Charter, but its goal goes beyond the survival of the state, because its foundation is in the will of the people.[138] The holder of the right is the people, which indicates that this right is not exhausted in its state-centric elements.[139] This right is not a prerogative of the state, rather it is held by the people *against* the abuses that the state can commit.[140] This right "is a human right, not a right of governments, whether they are headed by charismatic revolutionary leaders or military dictators".[141] Its purpose is to be a counterbalance to avoid abuses from state officials or the ruling elite against its own people,[142] and also abuses of powerful states against small ones.

Therefore, the key element of self-determination is *popular* sovereignty, instead of national sovereignty. While the latter is for the protection of the state apparatus (the political party in power, in many cases), popular sovereignty gives power to the people and it is at their service.[143] State sovereignty

137 As recognized by: Cassese (n 1028): 94; Quane (n 1028): 558–562; Patrick Thornberry, "Self-Determination, Minorities, Human Rights: A Review of International Instruments," *The International and Comparative Law Quarterly* 38 (1989); Malcolm Shaw, "Peoples, Territorialism and Boundaries," *European Journal of International Law* 3 (1997): 481; Christian Tomuschat, "Self-Determination in a Post-Colonial World" in *Modern Law of Self-Determination*, ed. Christian Tomuschat (Martinus Nijhoff, 1993), 16. Also see *Reference re Secession of Quebec*, 1998 CanLII 793 (SCC), [1998] 2 SCR 217, paras 113–146.

138 See Vladislav Tolstykh, "Three Ideas of Self-Determination in International law and the Reunification of Crimea with Russia," *Heidelberg Journal of International Law* 75 (2015): 119–134.

139 See Dorothée Cambou, "The UNDRIP and the Legal Significance of the Right of Indigenous Peoples to Self-Determination: A Human Rights Approach with a Multidimensional Perspective," *International Journal of Human Rights* 23, no. 1–2 (February 7, 2019): 37, https://doi.org/10.1080/13642987.2019.1585345.

140 See Summers, *Peoples and International Law*, 71; Allan Rosas, "Internal Self-Determination," in *Modern Law of Self-Determination*, ed. Christian Tomuschat (Martinus Nijhoff, 1993), 227.

141 Tesón, "International Human Rights and Cultural Relativism," 883.

142 See Raic, *Statehood and the Law of Self-Determination*, 199–225.

143 See Araujo, "Sovereignty, Human Rights, and Self-Determination: The Meaning of International Law."

can be used for the sake of the governmental system at the express of the dignity of its citizens. However, for popular sovereignty

> The object of protection is not the power base of the tyrant who rules directly by naked power or through the apparatus of a totalitarian political order, but the continuing capacity of a population freely to express and effect choices about the identities and policies of its governors.[144]

Such a vision is corroborated by most constitutions that express that sovereignty belongs to the people, not to the state apparatus or to the ruling political party.[145] It indicates that there is a difference between the state and its citizens, which is the classical legal relationship in IHRL: the individual rights holder *vis-à-vis* the state. It points out that the state, which is incarnated by the government in power, should represent the will of the people and not its own interests, for this is the *raison d'être* of the state and of the international legal system. The perversion of this public function corrupts the very essence of the international community.

The Westphalian model of the nation-state was built upon the idea of the protection of national self-interest (which does not necessarily correspond with popular will), but the world order funded with the U.N. Charter transformed the terms of the agreement. The preamble of the U.N. Charter that starts with the expression "we the people of the United Nations" is indicative of this change in paradigm. In the post 1945 world order, the states that participate in U.N. fora serve in the role of representing the people of their territory and to give voice to different local claims. Antonio Cassese remarks in this regard

> Self-determination was intended to brush aside the old, State-oriented approach prevailing in international dealings. Under this approach, the world community consisted of potentates: the sovereign States, each of them primarily concerned with the interests of its political elites […]. By contrast, selfdetermination meant that peoples and nations were to have a say in international dealings: sovereign Powers could no longer freely dispose of them [...]. Clearly, this set of principles was directed toward undermining the very core of the traditional principles on which international society had rested since its inception: dynastic legitimation of power, despotism (albeit

144 W Michael Reisman, "Sovereignty and Human Rights in Contemporary International law," *American Journal of International Law* 84 (1990): 872.

145 See Araujo, "Sovereignty, Human Rights, and Self-Determination: The Meaning of International Law," 1491.

in increasingly attenuated forms), and international dealings based on agreement between rulers only.[146]

Thus, regarding human rights interpretations, this right requires that the determination of the scope and limitations of rights responds to the concerns and the will of the people. For this purpose, self-determination requires (a) a representative government at the national level that truly responds to the needs and concerns of people, and (b) in the international plane, a human rights standard-setting process that is in permanent and constructive dialogue with the worldviews of different peoples to reach cross-cultural agreement.

Regarding the first element, although states are supposed to be the representatives of their population, the truth is that practice is not always so. Several ruling elites claim to speak on behalf of their people, while they are only representing their own interests.

Regarding the interpretation of human rights, this lack of connection between states representatives and the people reveals the need to emphasize that self-determination is the right of peoples and not of the state or the ruling political party. When ruling elites do not consult people and do not act according to the worldviews of the population in the determination of human rights interpretations and implementation, disastrous consequences take place.

This was illustrated in the case studies used in chapters two and three of the present work regarding the implementation of SRHR. As some human rights scholars have noticed, these are not isolated cases of lack of representation and connection between ruling elites and the population at large.[147]

Therefore, in order to respect the right to self-determination as a right of the people and not of the ruling elites, its deep link to democratic governance,[148] popular participation in public affairs, and a constitutional order needs to be re-emphasized.[149]

146 Cassese, *Self-Determination of Peoples: A Legal Appraisal*, 315–316.

147 Merry, "Constructing a Global Law-Violence against Women and the Human Rights System"; Makau Wa Mutua, "Standard Setting in Human Rights: Critique and Prognosis," *Human Rights Quarterly* 29 (2007); Glendon, "What Happened at Beijing"; Jane Haaland Matláry, *When Might Becomes Human Right: Essays on Democracy and the Crisis of Rationality* (Gracewing, 2007); An-Na'im, "Conclusions."

148 See Thomas Christiano, "Self-Determination and the Human Right to Democracy," in *Philosophical Foundations of Human Rights*, ed. Rowan Cruft, S. Matthew Liao, and Massimo Renzo (Oxford University Press, 2015).

149 See Summers (n 1039); Hannum, *Autonomy, Sovereignty, and Self-Determination: The Accommodation of Conflicting Rights* (n 1073); Steven Wheatley, "Democracy in

Cassese remarks that there has been a growing tendency to conceive self-determination in terms of democratic representation of the interests of people within the boundaries of independent states.[150] Unfortunately, scholarship work on this issue mainly focuses on democratic elections of political representatives,[151] disregarding a wider participation of people in all other aspects.

A deeper insight into this right reveals that participation and democratic governance are not exhausted in public elections. It requires "authentic self-government" or "the right for a people really and freely to choose its own political and economic regime".[152] There is no definition of self-government that has been developed in relation to self-determination, but in the context of minority rights it is framed as "a measure of control by a community over matters affecting it".[153] It is a way to encourage local forms of government or the decentralization of power to allow each society to take ownership of the political decision-making process.[154]

Thus, self-determination demands a robust and permanent participation in all decision-making processes that affect each society, including human rights interpretations, and especially in relation to controversial or sensitive topics. In this regard, the participatory political rights established in article 21 of the UDHR[155] and article 25 of the

International law: A European Perspective," *International and Comparative Law Quarterly* 51 (2002); Daniel Philpott, "In Defence of Self-Determination" (1995) 105 Ethics; Simpson (n 1073); Alfredsson (n 1097); Patrick Thornberry, "The Democratic or Internal Aspect of Self-Determination with Some Remarks on Federalism" in *Modern Law of Self-Determination*, ed. Christian Tomuschat (Martinus Nijhoff, 1993); Crawford, "The Right to Self-Determination in International law: Its Development and Future" (n 1028); Steven Wheatley, *The Democratic Legitimacy of International law* (Hart Publishing 2010).

150 Cassese, *Self-Determination of Peoples: A Legal Appraisal*, chap. 11.

151 Some examples are: Thomas Franck, "The Emerging Right to Democratic Governance," *The American Journal of International Law* 86 (1992) 86; James R Crawford, "Democracy and the Body of International law" in *Democratic Governance and International law*, eds. Gregory Fox and Brad Roth (Cambridge University Press, 2010).

152 Cassese, *Self-Determination of Peoples: A Legal Appraisal*, 101.

153 OSCE, The Lund Recommendations on the Effective Participation of National Minorities in Public Life & Explanatory Note (1999), 26.

154 See in this regard: Working Group on Minorities, Commentary of the Working Group on Minorities to the United Nations Declaration on the Rights of Persons belonging to National or Ethnic, Religious and Linguistic Minorities, E/CN.4/Sub.2/AC.5/2005/2 (2005), para 46.

155 "Article 21: 1. Everyone has the right to take part in the government of his country, directly or through freely chosen representatives. 2. Everyone has the right of equal access to public service in his country. 3. The will of the people shall be the basis of the authority

ICCPR[156] in light of the right to self-determination point towards an important statement: the will of the people is the basis of governmental authority in general.

The same basis of legitimatization of public authority is expressed by the ICJ in the *Namibia* Advisory Opinion, where it is argued that the principle of self-determination means to give effect to "the clearly expressed wishes of the people of the territory".[157] In the *Western Sahara* Advisory Opinion, the ICJ has also emphasized that self-determination requires "a free and genuine expression of the will of the peoples concerned".[158]

This means that popular participation is not only related to voting in each elections period and then being forgotten or excluded from the public sphere. It requires a deeper form of representation and power decentralization that consults people in all the issues that will affect them.[159] As Jan Klabbers argues self-determination is the right "to be taken seriously" when decisions that concern one's life are taken.[160] Resolution 19/20 of the Human Rights Council indicates that good governance responds to the needs and aspirations of peoples, especially to those of vulnerable members of society.[161]

of government; this will shall be expressed in periodic and genuine elections which shall be by universal and equal suffrage and shall be held by secret vote or by equivalent free voting procedures". UDHR.

156 "Article 25: Every citizen shall have the right and the opportunity, without any of the distinctions mentioned in article 2 and without unreasonable restrictions: (a) To take part in the conduct of public affairs, directly or through freely chosen representatives; (b) To vote and to be elected at genuine periodic elections which shall be by universal and equal suffrage and shall be held by secret ballot, guaranteeing the free expression of the will of the electors; (c) To have access, on general terms of equality, to public service in his country". ICCPR.

157 ICJ, *Legal Consequences for States of the Continued Presence of South Africa in Namibia (South West Africa) notwithstanding Security Council Resolution 276 (1970)*, Advisory Opinion, I.C.J. Reports 1971, 52. Also see Héctor Gros Espiell (Special Rapporteur of the Sub-Commission on Prevention of Discrimination), The Right to Self-Determination: Implementation of United Nations Resolutions, E/CN.4/Sub.2/405/Rev.l (1980), 11.

158 ICJ, *Western Sahara, Advisory Opinion*, I.C.J. Reports 1975, para 55.

159 Hannum, *Autonomy, Sovereignty, and Self-Determination: The Accommodation of Conflicting Rights*; Anaya, "A Contemporary Definition of the International Norm of Self-Determination."

160 Jan Klabbers, "The Right to Be Taken Seriously: Self-Determination in International law," *Human Rights Quarterly* 28 (2006).

161 Human Rights Council, Resolution 19/20 The Role of Governance in the Promotion and Protection of Human Rights, A/HRC/19/L.26 (19 March 2012).

The HRC in its General Comment on article 25 of the ICCPR has determined that "the conduct of public affairs" is a broad concept that includes "the exercise of political power, in particular the exercise of legislative, executive and administrative powers. It covers all aspects of public administration, and the formulation and implementation of policy at international, national, regional and local levels".[162] The right to participate in public affairs requires a robust participation in public debates, dialogue, freedom of expression, assembly and association.[163] Self-determination in terms of democratic governance requires a meaningful participation in all social, cultural, political, and economic matters that affect society.

For the purpose of human rights interpretations, self-determination implies that the people of a state should be effectively taken into account in this process, without excluding the views of those that disagree with the ruling political party. As envisaged by the UDHR, the universal abstract values incorporated into this document and into human rights treaties should pass through a process of cultural appropriation that gives them concrete content. This process should include different perspectives and respect diverse cultural approaches to the definition of what is human flourishing, instead of a unilateral imposition from the ruling elites upon the rest of the population (see chapter three), even if the policy is supported by foreign states or by human rights mechanisms.

For this reason, each society should be able to define and prioritize their own views on the human condition, as long as their concept of the good life respects the rules of interpretation and the limits set by the UDHR. As explained in the previous chapter, these restrictions are broader than what liberal universalism purports, for they provide space for duty-oriented ideas, an interdependent notion of the self, religiously grounded worldviews, and different value hierarchies.

Human rights interpretations, especially regarding sensitive issues, involve policy decisions based on different ideas about the good life, rather than neutral-legal determinations. The drafters of the UDHR were aware of this situation and for this reason they adopted an open-ended document of principles, instead of specific interpretations.

162 HRC, General Comment No. 25: The right to participate in public affairs, voting rights and the right of equal access to public services (article 25), CCPR/C/21/Rev.1/Add.7 (1996), para 5.

163 As noticed by the HRC itself: HRC, General Comment No. 25, para 8.

Self-determination means that the state's decisions should actually reflect the needs, aspirations, and the idea of human flourishing embraced by all people in society. Instead of being a protector of collective interests that oppresses human dignity, it is a safeguard against the imposition of a vision of the common good, in the name of the people, but that actually has been decided without them. The self-determination of peoples (not the state) requires consultation and deep engagement with the human beings that compose each society and to avoid populist initiatives that pretend to speak on their behalf.

Moving to the human rights standard-setting process conducted by human rights mechanisms, the right to self-determination also requires a change of paradigm on their behalf. This process was originally conceived as a deeply democratic and participatory endeavor. This dialogical task of mutual understanding can be better accomplished by effectively implementing the right to self-determination in this broad manner. Such a view especially emphasizes the aspects of social and cultural self-determination, which are essential for an intercultural dialogue and for taking people's concerns and ideas seriously, so that human rights interpretations could be more acceptable to different societies.

Thus, the standard-setting process adopted by human rights treaty bodies and regional courts should be based on the same democratic, dialogical, and consensus-based logic. Human rights mechanisms cannot determine the content of norms in a unilateral and top-down fashion, without taking into account how different cultures and societies understand these shared principles. This attitude will only encourage resentment and backlash.

To illustrate this problem the case of human rights treaty bodies will be explored. These are committees of experts created by human rights treaties and mandated to monitor the implementation of states' obligations regarding these treaties.[164] There are ten human rights treaty bodies. These mechanisms monitor the main human rights treaties on civil and political rights, economic, social and cultural rights, women's rights, children's rights, the elimination of racial discrimination, the elimination of torture, the rights of people with disabilities, enforced disappearances, and the rights of migrant workers.

Their main function is to assess states parties' reports on the implementation of their human rights obligations through a process of "constructive

164 See OHCHR, "Human Rights Treaty Bodies" <https://www.ohchr.org/EN/HRBodies/Pages/TreatyBodies.aspx>. Consulted on May 27, 2021.

dialogue" and the adoption of "concluding observations", which are recommendations on how to improve compliance with human rights obligations. The notion of "constructive dialogue" emphasizes the non-judicial character of the treaty bodies' functions and the cooperative approach of this process, for states are invited to send their delegations to discuss their reports submitted on the implementation of their international obligations.[165]

In addition to this function, treaty bodies can also receive individual complaints and adopt views in a quasi-judicial process, if the state at stake has ratified the corresponding protocol. There is another practice that has been extended among treaty bodies that consists of the adoption of "General Comments" or "General Recommendations" which have been described as "a treaty body's interpretation of human rights treaty provisions, thematic issues or its methods of work", which "seek to clarify the reporting duties of State parties with respect to certain provisions and suggest approaches to implementing treaty provisions".[166] These General Comments are highly relevant, for treaty bodies generally refer to them to determine the scope of specific rights and the existence of violations.[167]

Treaty bodies have increased democratic participation in the determination of human rights standards with different mechanisms, like the intervention of NGOs. Another example is holding days of general discussion, where treaty bodies extend an open invitation to states, NGOs, or any expert to discuss the adoption of a General Comment on the content of specific rights. The aim of these events is to gather ideas, opinions, and perspectives from different states and members of the civil society, so they can contribute to the process of interpretations.[168]

However, still there is a pending task to transform the standard-setting process, so it can be more grassroot-based, which can help to adopt standards that enjoy cross-cultural legitimacy and are acceptable to a broader audience and not only to the actors that can access the debates in New York or Geneva.

As mentioned earlier, the practice of state delegates that present positions in international forums that are removed from the local perceptions create a problem because they forge a false consensus on how to interpret human

165 OHCHR, "Human Rights Treaty Bodies".
166 OHCHR, "Human Rights Treaty Bodies".
167 Schlütter, "Aspects of Human Rights Interpretation by the UN Treaty Bodies," 290–291.
168 Sepúlveda, *The Nature of the Obligations under the International Covenant on Economic, Social and Cultural Rights*, 42.

rights, for these representatives distort the real situation of controversial topics. The same can occur with the standards-setting process of treaty body mechanisms if resolutions that exclude certain views are adopted, especially on controversial and sensitive topics, which will undermine trust in the international community and treaty body mechanisms themselves.

This problem has been highlighted by some scholars, such as the Kenyan-American human rights lawyer from the University of Buffalo Makau W. Mutua:

> There is no direct democracy in standard setting at the UN. The people are out of sight, but represented usually by self-chosen, or self-imposed, proxies. Do these self-professed representatives of the victims actually represent the aggrieved, or do they fight for their vision of society? Often, INGOs, [international NGOs] who are the most powerful brokers for standards, claim to be working in what they call "international civil society" or a "coalition" of NGOs from across the world. But how democratic is this global coalition of international civil society? Who dominates and controls it?[169]

There is still a pending task of making the process of human rights standard-setting a more democratic and cross-cultural one, whose outcome reflects broad international consensus and space for dissenting opinions on sensitive issues. Nevertheless, some scholars disagree with this because they consider that treaty body mechanisms alone should have the last word on how to interpret human rights, regardless of what other states and peoples think.[170] This strategy seems unwise, for a unilateral determination of standards becomes self-referential among different human rights mechanisms, loses contact with

169 Mutua, *Human Rights Standards: Hegemony, Law, and Politics*, 63.

170 See for instance: Gabriella Citroni, "The Human Rights Committee and Its Role in Interpreting the International Covenant on Civil and Political Rights Vis-à-Vis States Parties," *EJIL: Talk!*, 2015, https://www.ejiltalk.org/the-human-rights-committee-and-its-role-in-interpreting-the-international-covenant-on-civil-and-political-rights-vis-a-vis-states-parties/; Kerstin Mechlem, "Treaty Bodies and the Interpretation of Human Rights," *Vanderbilt Journal o Transnational Law* 42 (2007): 905–47; Caroline Dommen, "Claiming Environmental Rights: Some Possibilities Offered by the United Nations' Human Rights Mechanisms," *Georgetown International Environmental Law Review* 11 (1998); Craven, *The International Covenant on Economic, Social and Cultural Rights: A Perspective on Its Development*; Gerald Neuman, "Giving Meaning and Effect to Human Rights," in *The Human Rights Covenants at 50: Their Past, Present, and Future*, ed. Daniel Moeckli, Helen Keller, and Corina Heri (Oxford University Press, n.d.).

local viewpoints, and will only provoke more resistance to international norms that will be perceived as foreign impositions.

From a legal point of view, the position of these scholars also presents some problems. According to the rules of interpretation of international law, states parties to a convention have the main competence to interpret a treaty.[171] This exercise should be conducted according to the rules of interpretation of the VCLT and it "must be based above all upon the text of the treaty", as the ICJ has declared.[172] The HRC itself has indicated that its General Comments "did not purport to be limitative or to attribute any priority as between different aspects of the implementation of the Covenant".[173] Its original aim was to draw attention to the insufficiencies of the states' reports, to suggest improvements in the reporting procedure, and to promote the implementation of the ICCPR.[174]

Even the ICJ has recognized that it should "ascribe great weight" to the interpretations developed by human rights treaty body mechanisms, for they have been created to supervise the application of their founding treaty.[175] However, the ICJ declared that it is "in no way obliged, in the exercise of its judicial functions, to model its own interpretation of the Covenant on that of the Committee", especially when "the relevant customary rules on treaty interpretation" point towards a different conclusion.[176]

In its early beginnings, the HRC and states understood the mandate of this committee as a faculty to issue non-country specific suggestions, mainly procedural, and of general nature,[177] without establishing any hierarchy of

171 James R Crawford, *Brownlie's Principles of Public International law* (9th ed, Oxford University Press, 2019), 365.

172 ICJ, *Territorial Dispute (Libyan Arab Jamahiriya/Chad)*, Judgment, ICJ Reports 1994, para 41.

173 General Assembly, Report of the Human Rights Committee, General Assembly Official Records, 39th session, A/39/40 (1984), 107.

174 General Assembly, Report of the Human Rights Committee, General Assembly Official Records, 39th session, 107.

175 ICJ, *Application of the International Convention on the Elimination of All Forms of Racial Discrimination (Qatar v. United Arab Emirates)*, Judgment preliminary objections of 4 February 2021, para 101. Also see: ICJ, *Ahmadou Sadio Diallo (Republic of Guinea v. Democratic Republic of the Congo)*, Merits, Judgment, I.C.J. Reports 2010, para 66.

176 ICJ, *Application of the International Convention on the Elimination of All Forms of Racial Discrimination (Qatar v. United Arab Emirates)*, para 101.

177 See Joanne Pedone and Andrew Kloster, "New Proposals for Human Rights Treaty Body Reform" 22 Journal of Transnational Law & Policy 29, 38; Geir Ulfstein, "Law-Making by

values or interpretations.[178] As some scholars noted: "for much of the over forty year history of the treaty body system, treaty bodies did not issue comments on any State Party in particular, with many members concluding they lacked the authority to do so".[179] The same is true of concluding observations on states' reports, which started to be adopted in 1992 (although still in terms of broad and flexible recommendations).[180]

The members of the HRC understood their role as one of constructive dialogue, conciliation and cooperation with states to determine the content of human rights interpretations, which followed the spirit of pluralism of the UDHR, instead of acting as a supra-national organ.[181] For that reason, the HRC assumed in its beginning a more flexible approach, which relied on looking for cross-cultural consensus for human rights interpretations.

Nevertheless, in the last two decades, human rights treaty bodies have become bolder in their role of monitoring and giving detailed content to human rights provisions both through the reporting system and General Comments. This has increased their relevance, but it has also diminished the flexibility and diversity allowed to states in the interpretation and implementation of rights.

For instance, the HRC, during the consideration of the sixth periodic report of Canada on the implementation of the ICCPR in 2015, had a disagreement with the Canadian delegate over the extraterritorial application of the treaty. The Committee Chairperson, Fabian Omar Salvioli, concluded that "the final arbiter for interpreting the Covenant was the Committee and not individual States".[182] Similar remarks have been made in other sessions. During the review of the sixth periodic report of Spain, the Chairperson

Human Rights Treaty Bodies" in *International law-making: Essays in Honour of Jan Klabbers*, Rain eds. Liivoja and Jarna Petman (Routledge, 2013), 251–252.

178 See Helen Keller and Leena Grover, "General Comments of the Human Rights Committee and Their Legitimacy," in *UN Human Rights Treaty Bodies: Law and Legitimacy*, ed. Helen Keller and Geir Ulfstein (Cambridge University Press, 2012), 123–124.

179 Pedone and Kloster, "New Proposals for Human Rights Treaty Body Reform," 39.

180 See Keller and Grover, "General Comments of the Human Rights Committee and Their Legitimacy," 123.

181 Makau Wa Mutua, "Looking Past the Human Rights Committee: An Argument for DeMarginalizing Enforcement," *Buffalo Journal of International Law* 4 (1998): 224–228.

182 "Human Rights Committee Discusses the Report of Canada," OHCHR, 2015, https://www.ohchr.org/EN/NewsEvents/Pages/DisplayNews.aspx?NewsID=16215&LangID=E. Consulted on May 4, 2021.

emphasized that "only the Committee could interpret the Covenant".[183] On another occasion, the HRC ordered states to amend the Optional Protocol to the ICCPR to transform the views adopted under the petition system into binding decisions.[184]

According to the mandates of treaty body mechanisms, they were not provided with the function to issue authoritative interpretations regarding human rights instruments. As the human rights expert Matthew Cravens has acknowledged "no body has the ability to interpret the Covenant in a manner that binds States Parties".[185] It was not envisaged that any of the human rights treaty bodies "would involve themselves in standard-setting or normative development".[186] From the standpoint of international law, there is no obligation for a domestic court to interpret any human rights treaty according to the standards provided by a treaty monitoring body,[187] although they have an obligation to comply with their obligations as established in human rights treaties.

Human rights treaty bodies have self-allocated an interpretative function by issuing General Comments or General Recommendations, which establish guidelines and requirements about how a specific human right should be interpreted and implemented.[188] Article 40 of the ICCPR, (that has been used to justify this function) does not provide any such role of a *super partes* interpreter to the HRC.

This provision does not grant any ultimate interpretative faculty to the HRC, nor does it establish that the HRC is free to determine the correct interpretation of its articles without any legal restrains. It does not allow the HRC to unilaterally determine the content of human rights norms, disregarding

183 HRC, Summary record of the 3175th meeting (114th session) CCPR/C/SR.3175 (13 July 2015), para 61.

184 Laurence R. Helfer and Anne-Marie Slaughter, "Toward a Theory of Effective Supranational Adjudication," *The Yale Law Journal* 107 (1997): 351.

185 Matthew Craven, "The UN Committee on ESCR," in *Economic, Social, and Cultural Rights: A Textbook*, ed. Asbjorn Eide, Caterina Krause, and Allan Rosas (Martinus Nijhoff, 2001), 458.

186 Craven, 458.

187 Matthew Craven, "The Domestic Application of the International Covenant on Economic, Social and Cultural Rights," in *Economic, Social and Cultural Rights as Human Rights*, ed. Olivier de Schutter (Edward Elgar Publishing Limited, 2013), 83–84.

188 Keller and Grover, "General Comments of the Human Rights Committee and Their Legitimacy," 117.

the perspectives of state parties to the ICCPR. Moreover, the rules of treaty interpretation of the VCLT do not authorize adopting interpretations which depart from state practice, the agreement of states, and the text itself of a treaty (including its context, preparatory works, preamble, object and purpose).[189]

Since the beginning of this interpretation of article 40(4), regarding issuing authoritative interpretations of human rights norms, states have expressed their concern about the activity of the HRC acting beyond its mandate.[190] Several scholars have criticized the ultra vires nature of these acts in different treaty body mechanisms and the lack of legal analysis, methodological and technical rigor that generally accompanies them.[191] Other scholars also criticize the superficial examination of reports, the failure to establish legal and accurate standards of evaluation, and the lack of consistency of interpretations regarding the rules set out in the VCLT.[192]

The report system was not envisaged as a judicial or quasi-judicial tool.[193] Nor was it conceived as a method of treaty enforcement.[194] Even the petition

189 As established in articles 31 and 32 that establish the rules of treaty interpretation: Vienna Convention on the Law of Treaties (1969) <https://treaties.un.org/doc/publication/unts/volumepercent201155/volume-1155-i-18232-english.pdf>. Consulted on June 10, 2021.

190 General Assembly, Report of the Human Rights Committee, General Assembly Official Records, 39th session, A/39/40 (1984), p. 4.

191 See for instance: Craven, "The UN Committee on ESCR," 45 and 46; Michael J. Dennis and David P. Stewart, "Justiciability of Economic, Social and Cultural Rights: Should There Be an International Complaints Mechanism to Adjudicate the Rights to Food, Water, Housing, and Health?," in *Economic, Social and Cultural Rights as Human Rights*, ed. Olivier De Schutter (Edward Elgar Publishing Limited, 2013); Michael O'Flaherty, "Towards Integration of United Nations Human Rights Treaty Body Recommendations: The Rights-Based Approach Model," in *Economic, Social and Cultural Rights in Action*, ed. Mashood A. Baderin and Robert McCorquodale (Oxford University Press, 2007), 29; Mechlem, "Treaty Bodies and the Interpretation of Human Rights," 908.

192 See for instance: Craven, *The International Covenant on Economic, Social and Cultural Rights: A Perspective on Its Development*, 40–41; Marco Odello and Francesco Seatzu, *The UN Committee on Economic, Social and Cultural Rights: The Law, Process and Practice* (Routledge, 2013), 34 and 128–129; Michael O'Flaherty, "The Concluding Observations of United Nations Human Rights Treaty Bodies," *Human Rights Law Review* 6, no. 1 (2006): 39–41; de Casas, "¿Qué Son Los Estándares de Derechos Humanos?"; Schlütter, "Aspects of Human Rights Interpretation by the UN Treaty Bodies."

193 Phillip Alston and Ryan Goodman, *International Human Rights: The Sucessor to International Human Rights in Context* (Oxford University Press, 2013), 776.

194 Michael O'Flaherty, "The Reporting Obligation under Article 40 of the International Covenant on Civil and Political Rights: Lessons to Be Learned from Consideration by

system provided by the Optional Protocol to the ICCPR is of a quasi-judicial and non-binding nature, which permits the HRC to analyze communications related only to the violation of rights established in the ICCPR.[195] It does not involve a law-making faculty.

The extension of treaty bodies mandates has not been an agreement of states, but rather a demand from scholars.[196] State practice that continuously reject controversial interpretations, as the case of SRHR, supports this point. As University of Alberta law professor Joanna Harrington indicates:

> The States parties have not relinquished their ability to determine the meaning of a treaty as between themselves to a part-time treaty-monitoring body tasked primarily to review State reports, and subject to additional State consent, receive and consider individual complaints. (The making of general comments was not a function envisioned by States parties, but a function derived by the Committee itself from a reading of article 40(4) back in 1981).[197]

The treaty body mechanisms were originally created to monitor state compliance with treaty obligations in a cooperative and ongoing dialogue.[198] This point does not diminish the relevance and contributions of the monitoring system. States are obliged to comply with their treaty obligations in good faith, which requires them to take seriously the recommendations of the HRC.

The treaty monitoring bodies play a key role in the promotion of intercultural and constructive dialogue to advance human rights, to look for common

the Human Rights Committee of Ireland's First Report," *Human Rights Quarterly* 16, no. 3 (1994): 519.

195 Helfer and Slaughter, "Toward a Theory of Effective Supranational Adjudication," 341–344; Ludovic Hennebel, "The Human Rigths Committee," in *The United Nations and Human Rights: A Critical Appraisal*, ed. Frédéric Mégret and Philip Alston (Oxford University Press, 2009), 350–355.

196 Martin Scheinin, "The Proposed Optional Protocol to the Covenant on Economic, Social and Cultural Rights: A Blueprint for UN Human Rights Treaty Body Reform Without Amending the Existing Treaties," *Human Rights Law Review* 6, no. 1 (2006); Mutua, "Looking Past the Human Rights Committee: An Argument for DeMarginalizing Enforcement."

197 Joanna Harrington, "The Human Rights Committee, Treaty Interpretation, and the Last Word," *EJIL: Talk!*, 2015, https://www.ejiltalk.org/the-human-rights-committee-treaty-interpretation-and-the-last-word/. Consulted on May 4, 2021.

198 The Permanent Court of International Justice (PCIJ) has determined that "it is an established principle that the right of giving an authoritative interpretation of a legal rule belongs solely to the person or body who has the power to modify or suppress it." In PCIJ, *Question of Jaworzina*, Advisory Opinion of 6 December 1923, PCIJ Series B, No. 8, at 37.

ground, and to find consensus among different visions of human flourishing. But these objectives cannot justify the adoption of interpretations that do not follow the rules of international law and that ignore lack of agreement on controversial subjects.

Practical Implications of Pluralistic Universality in Action

The institutionalization of this proposal in the work of human rights mechanisms will require a more critical analysis of their decision-making processes regarding the adoption of interpretations. Some concrete steps that can help to implement the paradigm of pluralistic universality is to conduct detailed assessments of cross-cultural consensus. The general norms of international law in relation to sources and rules of interpretation are useful guidance for this purpose.

Just as "new" human rights cannot be created out of nowhere, the interpretation of norms that extend their content (and possibly create new rights) should also be legally justified. Human rights mechanisms should be more careful by thoroughly using the main sources of international law: treaties and custom,[199] for IHRL is part of public international law and therefore follows the same general rules.[200]

Accordingly, if a specific interpretation cannot be adequately grounded according to "the ordinary meaning"[201] of the terms of a treaty or in customary law, then such a proposal should be dismissed. The identification of customary law requires to look for general practice accepted as law (*opinion iuris*). This practice should be sufficiently widespread and representative among states,[202] not among other actors.[203] It is not enough for human rights standards to be adopted based on the majoritarian views of treaty body members, which is a very small audience and will only make these interpretations self-referential

199 As recognized in article 38 of the Statute of the ICJ.

200 Samantha Besson, "The Sources of International Human Rights Law : How General Is General International law?" in *The Oxford Handbook of the Sources of International law*, eds. Samantha Besson and Jean D'Aspremont (Oxford University Press, 2017).

201 As required by the rules of interpretation in the VCLT art. 31(1).

202 ILC, Draft Conclusions on the Identification of Customary International law session (2018) A/73/10, conclusion 8.

203 ILC, Draft Conclusions on the Identification of Customary International law session (2018) A/73/10, conclusion 4(3).

statements.[204] Human rights standards should reflect shared practices and understanding among different cultures, not among NGOs or human rights mechanisms.

Also, practice within each state should be assessed carefully and as a whole, considering the overall context,[205] which includes local views and internal debates. To avoid either a state-centric approach or an elite-driven one that does not reflect the views of society,[206] state practice cannot be deduced from isolated acts of state officials, while the wider context indicates that there is no consensus, as is the case of SRHR.

In this regard, human rights mechanisms should be careful when using non-binding instruments as sources of IHRL or as evidence of practice.[207] Some soft law instruments are adopted for political or economic reasons and in a context of deep disagreement (e.g. the Beijing Platform for Action and the ICDP) which can hardly amount to general state practice, and especially, *opinion iuris*. Hence, the normative value of this kind of documents should be assessed in light of the content, its conditions of adoption, the votes, and the dissenting opinions.[208]

The same reasoning is applicable regarding the rules of interpretation. As established in article 31(3) of the VCLT, a human rights treaty should be interpreted considering "any subsequent agreement between the parties regarding the interpretation of the treaty" and "any subsequent practice in the application of the treaty which establishes the agreement of the parties regarding its interpretation".[209] An agreement in terms of article 31(3) of the VCLT requires "a common understanding regarding the interpretation of a treaty which the parties are aware of and accept".[210] This shared agreement or practice refers to the conduct of the state and not of other actors.[211]

204 As criticized by Harrington, "The Human Rights Committee, Treaty Interpretation, and the Last Word."

205 ILC, Draft Conclusions on the Identification of Customary International law, conclusions 3 and 7.

206 See Chapters two and three.

207 ILC, Draft Conclusions on the Identification of Customary International law session (2018) A/73/10, conclusion 12.

208 See ICJ, *Legality of the Threat or Use of Nuclear Weapons Advisory Opinion*, Reports 1996, para 70–73.

209 VCLT article 31(3).

210 ILC, Draft conclusions on subsequent agreements and subsequent practice in relation to the interpretation of treaties (2018) A/73/10, conclusion 10.

211 ILC, Draft conclusions on subsequent agreements and subsequent practice in relation to the interpretation of treaties, conclusion 5.

Accordingly, for an action to be considered subsequent practice or agreement for treaty interpretation, regard must be given to the overall context and circumstances. Such an assessment would also be necessary when considering non-binding instruments adopted by international organizations,[212] and pronouncements of treaty monitoring bodies.[213]

Thus, in the spirit of subsidiarity, the role of human rights mechanisms is to adopt interpretations that are solidly grounded on transnational practice and common ground, and to leave a "margin of appreciation" to domestic decision-making processes on the rest of issues.[214] As demanded by the right to self-determination, the purpose of this approach is not to protect states' sovereignty, but rather to improve the quality of human rights standards in order to avoid an arbitrary proliferation of interpretations that are not grounded on shared principles by different societies, as the pluralistic universality of the UDHR demands.

Accordingly, in the spirit of pluralistic universality and respecting the right to self-determination, the standard-setting process should be framed as a joint enterprise. The interpretations adopted by human rights mechanisms must reflect the consensus and cross-cultural agreement that created them.[215] The non-binding nature of the treaty bodies' procedures indicate that cooperation, dialogue, and mutual understanding should be prioritized over unilateral legal or political decisions. This statement is supported by the fact that treaty-monitoring bodies are not required to be made up of jurists or technical experts (e.g. biologists or economists), nor to operate like a court by guaranteeing a fair submission of evidence and arguments by all parties.[216]

The standard-setting process cannot adopt human rights interpretations as universal if they are based on paradigms or definitions which do not enjoy

212 See ICJ, *Whaling in the Antarctic (Australia v. Japan: New Zealand intervening)*, Judgment, Reports 2014, para 78–83; and ILC, Draft conclusions on subsequent agreements and subsequent practice in relation to the interpretation of treaties, conclusion 11.

213 ILC, Draft conclusions on subsequent agreements and subsequent practice in relation to the interpretation of treaties, conclusion 13.

214 Besson, "The Sources of International Human Rights Law: How General Is General International law?" (n 1238) 860.

215 See Geir Ulfstein, "Institutions and Competences" in *The Constitutionalization of International law*, eds. Jan Klabbers and Geir Ulfstein, (Oxford University Press, 2009), 75–80.

216 Richard Stith, "If Dorothy Had Not Had Toto to Pull Back the Wizard's Curtain: The Fabrication of Human Rights as a World Religion," *Valparaiso University Law Review* 44 (2010): 852–853.

broad international and popular support. This has been agreed since 1986 in the General Assembly resolution 41/120 entitled "Setting international standards in the field of human rights". This document establishes some guidelines for the development of human rights standards, among which it requires that they should be consistent "with the existing body of international human rights law" and attract "broad international support".[217] The same conclusion was also reached by the American Commission on Unalienable Rights of 2020.[218]

Making cross-cultural assessments of universality is especially important regarding sensitive issues, where no international agreement has been reached, as in the field of sexuality. The contrary would imply that human rights mechanisms are selectively choosing some human goods and definitions, which resonate with their personal preferences and cultural visions, but that ignore the desires of different peoples around the world. Such an approach arbitrarily discriminates against other viewpoints, treats other cultures as inferior, and curtails the freedom of dissenting voices who have a different worldview.

The consensus reached in 1948 indicates that not every social or cultural issue can be determined through international agreements. Human rights were not conceived as a theory of justice or of the good life, as Louis Henkin remarks.[219] Some deeply divisive topics should be left to local determination and debate.[220]

This approach is not a way of justifying human rights violations. Some liberal scholars give preference to the policy choices made by human rights mechanisms over the ones of states, because the latter have abused the faculty to determine human rights interpretations as an excuse to violate these norms or to avoid their effective implementation.[221]

217 U.N. General Assembly, Resolution 41/120 Setting international standards in the field of human rights (4 December 1986), para 4.

218 "Report of the Commission on Unalienable Rights," 2020, https://www.state.gov/wp-content/uploads/2020/08/Report-of-the-Commission-on-Unalienable-Rights.pdf.

219 Henkin, "Rights: American and Human."

220 Brems, *Human Rights: Universality and Diversity*, 382.

221 Citroni (n 1156); Kasey L McCall-Smith, "Interpreting International Human Rights Standards: Treaty Body General Comments as a Chisel or a Hammer" in *Tracing the Roles of Soft Law in Human Rights*, eds. Stéphanie Lagoutte, Thomas Gammeltoft-Hansen and John Cerone (Oxford University Press, 2016); Douglas Lee Donoho, "Relativism Versus Universalism in Human Rights: The Search for Meaningful Standards," *Stanford Journal of International Law* 27 (1991); Tesón (n 63).

This criticism is a legitimate concern. However, as mentioned earlier, a preference for human rights treaty bodies does not remedy this situation. Impositions alien to the concerns of peoples can come from all different international actors, not just states. The objective of self-determination is to build human rights standards that are actually decided by people, not the ruling political party of a state, not even by human rights mechanisms alone. The indeterminacy of human rights can be manipulated by any individual or institution. Nobody is exempt from cognitive bias or personal interests.

Therefore, human rights interpretations should be decided by all international actors in a joint task, but mainly responding to the needs of the human person. This means that human rights should be truly owned by each society, which seems to be the best (although imperfect) safeguard against manipulation.

Limitations and Challenges

This paradigm, like any proposal, has its limitations and challenges. The unrestricted use of self-determination without any objective parameters would destroy the pluralistic universality of human rights norm, as feared by some scholars.[222] For this reason, although the purpose of self-determination is to provide a legitimate space for pluralism and reasonable disagreement in the development of human rights interpretations, this freedom is not absolute.

The purpose of a treaty is to reach some degree of basic agreement between the parties, the contrary would render the instrument meaningless. Thus, following the rules of the VCLT, states are not allowed to adopt interpretations that contradict the ordinary meaning of a human rights treaty,[223] or the guidelines provided by the *travaux préparatoires*.[224] Another relevant limitation, already pointed out by some scholars,[225] is that any interpretative framework should include in its vision of human flourishing all internationally recognized human rights in an interdependent manner.

Another important concern is the abuse of self-determination to absolutize a culture or a state in detriment of human dignity.[226] The holistic approach

222 William M. Carter Jr., "Rethinking Subsidiarity in International Human Rights Adjudication," *Hamline Journal of Public Law & Policy* 30, no. 319 (2008).

223 VCLT, art. 31(1).

224 VCLT, art. 32.

225 Glendon and Kaplan, "Renewing Human Rights."

226 As seen in: Isabelle Schulte-Tenckhoff, "Treaties, Peoplehood, and Self-Determination: Understanding the Language of Indigenous Rights," in *Indigenous Rights in the Age of the UN Declaration*, ed. Elena Pulitano (Cambridge University Press, 2012), 67.

to self-determination does not mean the essentialization of culture as a frozen and out of history reality. No tradition is static, for they are lived and owned by people, which applies to liberalism, but also to all other worldviews. As already articulated by German philosopher of hermeneutics Hans-Georg Gadamer, all traditions are dynamic because people are not passive objects: they decide to embrace, reject, or modify their heritage.[227] Self-determination provides in this regard "a space for a relatively autonomous transformation" of cultures, instead of "the preservation of cultures as static systems".[228]

As the ICJ has remarked, the essence of the right to self-determination is to provide people with the opportunity to discuss and decide the matters are going to affect their daily lives.[229] In this sense, the objective of a people-centered approach to self-determination is to provide a space for deliberation on the development of human rights interpretations. Thus, the purpose of self-determination is in direct opposition to a monolithic and static vision of society.

On the other hand, the aim of self-determination is not to encourage the tyranny of majorities either,[230] where minorities and dissenting voices can be discriminated against and ostracized. The human rights architecture already provides some safeguards against this problem, as explained in the interpretative guidelines provided by the UDHR.[231] No human right was conceived as a concept to be constructed in the vacuum, which includes self-determination. Human rights were conceived in a holistic manner. For this reason, self-determination is not an invitation to cherry-pick among human rights and to disregard others.

The rights of minorities, the principle of non-discrimination and freedom of conscience, thought and religion guarantee the protection of all members of society against majoritarian decisions contrary to human dignity.

227 See this argument in Hans-Georg Gadamer, *Truth and Method*, erd (London: Continuum, 2004), chap. 4.

228 Stephen Marglin, "Towards the Decolonization of the Mind," in *Dominating Knowledge: Development, Culture, and Resistance*, ed. Frédérique Apffel Marglin and Stephen Marglin (Clarendon Press, 1990), 16.

229 ICJ, *Legal Consequences for States of the Continued Presence of South Africa in Namibia (South West Africa) notwithstanding Security Council Resolution 276 (1970)*, Advisory Opinion, I.C.J. Reports 1971, 52; and ICJ, Western Sahara, Advisory Opinion, I.C.J. Reports 1975, para 55.

230 A concept used by de Tocqueville, *Democracy in America*, chaps. 15 and 16.

231 See Chapter five.

However, the main challenge of this paradigm is the adequate balance of different demands and goods necessary for the common good. There is no one-size-fits-all solution, nor a deductive and ready-made answer. Self-determination requires a constant dialogue to reexamine the balance between general welfare and the rights of individuals, it does not imply homogenization or stagnation. There is no ready-made recipe in this regard, it is rather a constant and dynamic exercise of trial and error, both at the national and international levels.

· 7 ·

CONCLUSIONS: TOWARDS A CHANGE OF INTERPRETATIVE PARADIGM

Liberal universality has become the main interpretative framework that has been used by human rights mechanisms and scholars alike to determine the scope and limits of internationally recognized human rights norms. This analytical tool has prioritized the values of secularism, individualism, and personal autonomy above everything else and has demanded the implementation of these premises in all domains of life and in all societies.

This has led to frame universality in terms of a liberal worldview and relativism as all other anthropological views that disagree with the dominant paradigm. This situation has even led to other views being considered inadmissible in the human rights debate, as seen in the development of SRHR. Such a paradigm has produced clashes with religious groups within Western nations and tensions between non-Western societies and a liberally oriented human rights sector.

The problem of this prevailing paradigm is that although its intentions are to provide freedom and equality for everyone, in practice it has not delivered these results. The reason why this happens is that the supporters of this framework consider it neutral, universal and legally founded, while they ignore that all three statements are deeply questionable.

Regarding its alleged neutrality, even liberal philosophers themselves recognize that a comprehensive liberalism relies on the unconditional acceptance of some values and specific philosophical assumptions about the human being and society. As many scholars have pointed out, this paradigm emerged out of specific cultural, historical, and religious events that took place in Western nations, which gave origin to the idea of the abstract, secular, and autonomous individual.[1] Thus, it is hard to argue that these ideas are the product of "pure" reasoning and independent of a cultural and philosophical background, which automatically undermines its universality.

Furthermore, this interpretative framework does not welcome a lot of different conceptions of the good life, as it purports to do. Rather, it only accepts lifestyles that prioritize its pillar values (autonomy, individualism, and secularism) in all domains of life. This means that traditions and lifestyles that are more interdependent and religiously grounded do not enjoy the same level of respect, acceptance, and tolerance, although many Western and non-Western persons cherish them.

Regarding the universal acceptance of this paradigm, the case of SRHR challenges this premise. The constant opposition to it is seen in the different positions of state representatives and the surveys conducted by the World Values Survey and the Pew Research Center, which indicate that a large part of the global population disagrees with a liberal view of the family, sexuality, and reproduction. Moreover, the implementation of SRHR, which in many countries resulted in massive and forced interventions also demonstrate that not everybody agrees with the anthropological premises of this paradigm. Rather, its universal imposition has resulted in gross human rights violations.

On this point, it is relevant to highlight that when universality is understood as a strategy or methodology to implement a ready-made human rights doctrine, it will always result in a top-down intervention that does not treat local people as equal, rational, and free beings capable of making their own decisions.

A "culturally sensitive" approach, based on this framework, will only result in the manipulation and analysis of local practices and beliefs in order to adopt them according to the ready-made liberal agenda. Such a perspective avoids a real intercultural dialogue and exchange of views on how to better promote human dignity, for it assumes that the local population has nothing

1 See Alain Papaux and Eric Wyler, *L'etique Du Droit International* (Paris: Presses Universitaires de France, 1997), 60.

relevant to contribute to the discussion. This kind of intervention relies on the unquestionable superiority of the liberal paradigm, so its supporters do not consider that they need to be self-critical with their own assumptions and that openness to other views is necessary.

Then, in this paradigm, the adoption of human rights interpretations or standards becomes a top-down monologue, instead of a democratic and respectful dialogue, which will only provoke more backlash against human rights. This is what can be appreciated in relation to the implementation of SRHR and the imposition of certain ideas as human rights obligations, without any legal foundation or even concern for what people think and their real needs.

This situation is in stark contradiction to what happened during the drafting process of the UDHR, where the delegates were deeply committed to looking for common ground among different cultures. They incorporated into the document only concepts that were acceptable to everyone, for a universal declaration can only be "universal" if it establishes ideas shared by all major cultures and religions. Consensus and dialogue, rather than imposition and exclusion, was their goal. Also, they were careful to leave ample space for reasonable disagreement on controversial, sensitive, and non-universal issues. This is why the UDHR enjoys broad international support and legitimacy, while controversial and legally unfounded human rights interpretations are experiencing resistance and backlash.

Looking at this situation, liberal universality appears to be a doctrine deeply limited for a dialogical and bottom-up approach for the determination of human rights interpretations or standards. It suffers from a deep problem, which cannot be remedied unless liberalism renounces its foundational anthropological premises and opens itself to the acceptance of other lifestyles that are less individualistic and religiously grounded.

Also, it seems that its premises of individualism and autonomy impel to acquire the virtues that are needed for tolerance, and mutual understanding: humility to listen to others, to recognize that one is not morally and intellectually superior to others, and to recognize when one is mistaken.[2] As Mahatma Gandhi indicated in his letter to the UNESCO, a self-referential

2 See Gabriela García Escobar, "How (Not) to Promote Human Dignity through Higher Education," *The Public Discourse*, 2021, https://www.thepublicdiscourse.com/2021/06/76365/.

framework for human rights that forgets about duties towards others, dialogue, and humility is not the best way to protect human dignity.[3]

Thus, according to this analysis, liberal universality does not necessarily encourage more equality and freedom than other doctrines, for it discriminates against certain worldviews, while it prioritizes others. This paradigm already sets the groundwork of what will be included and excluded, which provides no space for negotiations on the underlying presuppositions of the debate, which challenge the core problem of this framework: its lack of universality.

There are other alternatives that can be explored, which also seek equality, freedom, and respect for human dignity, but that frame those concepts in less individualistic terms. Here, it is pertinent to highlight again that the rejection of liberal universality does not mean encouragement of illiberal or authoritarian views; rather it looks for other more effective and diversity-friendly forms of promoting human dignity that are acceptable to a wider audience than just liberal-trained elite professionals.

An example of such other approaches is the pluralistic universality of the UDHR, which provides an interpretative framework that welcomes different worldviews for the development of human rights interpretations. This paradigm enjoys wide international support and can trace its legal foundations to the document that is the matrix of the whole human rights system.

Pluralistic universality accepts that it is not a neutral vision, for this is an impossible task. The drafters of the UDHR did not intend to erase all cultural, social, religious, and moral attachments to build an allegedly "neutral" vision of the human being, following the Enlightened ideas. Rather, they opted for a practical and cross-cultural agreement, which means that they looked for what was commonly shared among many different traditions. Thus, the idea of what is "universal" did not emerge from a decontextualization and abstraction of the human being, but from looking at the human condition as it is presented in practical terms in different cultures, with all its attachments.

In this regard it is relevant to highlight the anthropological premises which were the basis of this project. Although the drafters consciously tried to avoid making any type of philosophical assumptions, they realized that it was impossible not to include at least some minimal characteristics about the human condition, for the contrary would have meant that there is an agreement to agree on nothing. Therefore, the drafters relied on a "thin" but specific anthropological vision, whose analysis is highly relevant for it will

3 UNESCO, *Human Rights: Comments and Interpretations*, 4.

determine the acceptable worldviews that can serve as interpretative frameworks to develop the content of human rights norms.

Articles one and 29 of the UDHR indicate that the human rights holder was conceived as a human person, who is a relational or interdependent being (rather than as an abstract individual) endowed with a capacity for moral reasoning and to discover his own humanity through the humanity of other persons (*ren*). Through these faculties the human person is able to grasp that he or she has a duty of fraternity towards another fellow being, which is the path that allows him or her to discover and respect human dignity.

Furthermore, the UDHR envisaged a situated being who develops the full potential of his or her personality in community, as part of a family, and through the fulfillment of duties. Contrary to the liberal narrative, for the drafters, these elements make human existence richer and full of meaning. These places where not seen as arbitrary limitations and restrains to one's autonomy, rather they are part of human flourishing. Thus, the concept of freedom itself was understood in a relational and contextualized manner that is compatible with duties and consideration for other human goods (rather than as abstract autonomy).

This anthropological vision was adopted because most cultures and traditions of the world agreed that these elements were evident and necessary in every human life (although understood in different terms and to diverse degrees). It is according to this cross-cultural endeavor that the drafters developed a model of pluralistic universality, for they realized that there are some commonly shared values among very different societies, but that the content and interpretation of those varies from culture to culture. Therefore, in order to avoid the imposition of a specific cultural or philosophical vision not shared by the rest of the world, the UDHR was conceived as a set of principles that would be understood and implemented in a diversity of legitimate forms according to the idea of human flourishing of each society.

It is for these reasons that the drafters considered that the interpretation and implementation of the document required taking context into account, a holistic reading that includes all human rights, and some interpretative guidelines to give content to the rights (articles two, 28 and 29). They also considered that the human rights norms should be framed as open-ended principles to provide ample room for different interpretations and ways of implementing them.

Accordingly, the UDHR conceived human rights as a deeply local and grass-root project, not as a top-down intervention decided by remote elites. It is on this point that the right to self-determination results relevant as a continuation and way of implementing this idea if pluralistic universality.

Although the right to self-determination is one of the main principles of the whole U.N. system and a human right as recognized by the ICCPR, the ICESCR, and the African Charter on Human and People's Rights, this right has been reduced to questions of decolonization and secessionist claims. However, this provision refers to the right of people to determine their own political status, as well as their social, economic, and cultural development.

This means that the right to self-determination possesses a multidimensional nature, for it encompasses the capacity to decide very broad issues related to culture, economy and social aspects. It is in this holistic approach that self-determination is a form of pluralistic universality in action because it follows the same rationale of the UDHR of encouraging a local and grass-roots determination of how to build a just society.

These larger aspects of self-determination have only been developed in relation to indigenous communities. However, there is a pending job to extend this perspective to all peoples, as the legal nature of a human right requires. Accordingly, this holistic approach to self-determination is open to viewpoint and worldview diversity and requires popular and democratic participation in the process of human rights interpretations, for human rights are part of the social, cultural, and economic aspects that affect the daily lives of peoples.

This broader vision of self-determination encourages the construction of human rights interpretations from below and contributes to better *internationalize* the field of IHRL, so it can reflect the concerns and needs of all peoples. Thus, the proposal of this book implies a change of paradigm at two interrelated levels: national and international.

Regarding the national sphere, it is pertinent to emphasize that self-determination is the right of the "people", not of the state, the ruling elites, some NGOs, or Western governments. This means that at the local level, the debates on how to interpret and implement human rights should actually reflect the concerns of the people, instead of the personal views or ideals of a minoritarian (but powerful) and liberal-oriented ruling elite, who might be totally disconnected from the real demands of the people, as explained in the case studies of India and Mexico.

Thus, the right to self-determination requires taking people seriously and respecting democratic channels that promote participation, dialogue, tolerance, and deliberation for the adoption of decisions regarding the interpretation of human rights norms. The contrary will make human rights standards an elite-driven social engineering process that tells people how to behave in order to comply with a top-down opinion about what is human flourishing. It will amount to the prevailing situation that Glendon and Kaplan describe: "today, human rights activists declare: 'Here is how you need to change to join us'. Instead, they should begin by asking: 'What does human flourishing look like in your society or community, and how can we support you in encouraging it?'"[4]

The respect of self-determination at the national level is the core aspect of this right, for if it cannot be protected by local elites, there is little that can be done at the international level. If freedom and equality are to be considered essential values, then they should be respected in their most elemental expressions: allowing peoples to decide how to interpret human rights norms, as long as all human rights are embedded in their concept of human flourishing.

The second aspect of this proposal refers to the international plane. Here, state representatives are also required to truly act on behalf of the needs and views of their people in international fora. A state representative is not supposed to be acting according to his personal policy preferences. The U.N. system is designed to be a mechanism through which different peoples can be represented by their mandataries in international conferences, so their views can find a channel through which they can be heard in New York or Geneva.

The contrary would result in a self-serving system, where state representatives act on their own personal behalf and in an anti-democratic way. This creates a dangerous and misleading consensus on controversial issues because many states, where there is widespread internal disagreement, falsely indicate that all their population is in favor of their proposals.

The continuation of this practice that disconnects the local from the international will only further deepen the backlash against human rights, for what has been "agreed" in the international plane is just a fictious consensus forged among like-minded elites that has nothing to do with the global reality. This creates dangerous bubbles of "echo chambers",[5] which result in close intellectual environments that when confronted with the global viewpoint diversity will perceive these disagreements as unacceptable ideas that should be banished from the human rights debate.

4 See Glendon and Kaplan, "Renewing Human Rights."

5 Nicholas Kristof, "The Dangers of Echo Chambers on Campus," *The New York Times*, 2016, https://www.nytimes.com/2016/12/10/opinion/sunday/the-dangers-of-echo-chambers-on-campus.html.

This is precisely what happened when this book was presented as a PhD thesis in a prestigious Western university. Some professors felt "threatened" by it because they had never been exposed to a different vision regarding human rights interpretations (or even regarding the human condition). They have always lived among like-minded colleagues and students in a highly secularized and individualistic society, where their only window to other societies is reduced to contact with minoritarian liberal-oriented elites in the non-Western world. Such a situation indicates that they have lost touch with reality.

It should be noticed that the blame is not only to be found on state representatives, but also on the members of human rights mechanisms themselves, because they have unquestionably embraced the paradigm of liberal universality. Thus, they have constantly maintained that controversial and unsettled issues, like contraception and abortion, are international human rights obligations.

This type of judgments adopted by human rights mechanisms do not help to conduct a tolerant, open, and democratic debate. Rather, they contribute to further polarization and intolerance within societies, and backlash against international organs. For such rulings impose only one possible outcome on the debate and paralyze the normal political and democratic process of decision-making. If human rights mechanisms continue to follow this path, they will only risk calling into question their own legitimacy and impartiality.

In order to remedy this situation, human rights mechanisms should review their process of interpretation, by making it more legally based, respectful of legitimate disagreement on issues not established in human rights treaties, and grounded on cross-cultural assessments. This means that to determine that a specific interpretation of human rights norms is universal, it requires to be based on broad international support (among different cultures and traditions) and respond to the mandate of each organ as established in human rights treaties. For this process, local views and concerns cannot be disregarded. On sensitive and controversial issues, human rights mechanisms should recognize that no universal interpretation can be adopted and that the system itself was designed to avoid uniformity, for this would be contrary to the idea of pluralistic universality and the right to self-determination. Only through this interpretative framework, where pluralism is the core of human rights universalism, the project of human rights can be renewed.

BIBLIOGRAPHY

Books and Articles

Adaji, Sunday E, Linnea U Warenius, Antony A Ong'any, and Elisabeth A Faxelid. "The Attitudes of Kenyan In-School Adolescents Toward Sexual Autonomy." *African Journal of Reproductive Health* 14, no. 1 (2010).

Ahluwalia, Sanjam. *Reproductive Restraints: Birth Control in India, 1877–1947*. University of Illinois Press, 2007.

Al-Gharbi, Musa. "A Lack of Ideological Diversity Is Killing Social Research." *Times Higher Education*, no. March (2017): 26–30.

Alexy, Robert. *Teoría de Los Derechos Fundamentales*. 2nd ed. Centro de Estudios Políticos y Constitucionales, 2007.

Alfredsson, Gudmundur. "The Right to Self-Determination and Indigenous Peoples." In *Modern Law of Self-Determination*, edited by Christian Tomuschat. Martinus Nijhoff, 1993.

Almqvist, Jessica. *Human Rights, Culture, and the Rule of Law*. Vol. 6. Oxford: Hart Publishing, 2005.

Alston, Phillip. "Conjuring Up New Human Rights: A Proposal For Quality Control." *American Journal of International Law* 78, no. 3 (1984).

Alston, Phillip, and Ryan Goodman. *International Human Rights: The Sucessor to International Human Rights in Context*. Oxford University Press, 2013.

An-Na'im, Abdullahi Ahmed. "Conclusions." In *Human Rights in Cross-Cultural Perpestives: A Quest for Consensus*, edited by Abdullahi Ahmed An-Na'im. University of Pennsylvania Press, 1995.

———. *Human Rights in Cross-Cultural Perspectives: A Quest for Consensus*. Edited by Abdullahi Ahmed An-Na'im. Pensylvannia University Press, 1995.

———. "Problems of Universal Cultural Legitimacy for Human Rights." In *Human Rights in Africa: Cross-Cultural Perspectives*, edited by Abdullahi Ahmed An-Na'im and Francis Deng. The Brookings Institution, 1990.

———. "The Cultural Mediation of Human Rights: The Al-Arqam Case in Malaysia." In *The East Asian Challenge for Human Rights*, edited by Joanne Bauer and Daniel Bell. Cambridge University Press, 1999.

Anaya, S James. "A Contemporary Definition of the International Norm of Self-Determination." *Transnational Law & Contemporary Problems* 131, no. 3 (1993).

———. "The Capacity of International Law to Advance Ethnic or Nationality Rights Claims." *Colorado Law Faculty Scholarship* 75, no. 837 (1990).

———. "The Right of Indigenous Peoples to Self-Determination in the Post-Declaration Era." In *Making the Declaration Work: The United Nations Declaration on the Rights of Indigenous Peoples*, edited by Claire Charters and Rodolfo Stavenhagen. IWGIA, 2009.

Angus, Ian, and Simon Butler. *Too Many People? Population, Migration, and the Environmental Crisis*. Haymarket Books, 2011.

Arajarvi, Pentti. "Article 26." In *The Universal Declaration of Human Rights: A Commentary*, edited by Asbjørn Eide, Gudmundur Alfredsson, Goran Melander, Allan Rosas, and Lars Adam Rehof. Scandinavian University Press, 1993.

Araujo, Robert. "Sovereignty, Human Rights, and Self-Determination: The Meaning of International Law." *Fordham International Law Journal* 24, no. 5 (2001).

Association, American Anthropological. "Statement on Human Rights." *American Anthropologist* 49, no. 4 (1947): 539–43.

Attar, Mohsen al. "Subverting Racism in / through International Law Scholarship." Opinio Juris, 2021. http://opiniojuris.org/2021/03/03/subverting-racism-in-international-law-scholarship/.

Avonius, Leena, and Damien Kingsbury. "Introduction." In *Human Rights in Asia: Reassessment of the Asian Values Debate*, edited by Leena Avonius and Damien Kingsbury. Palgrave, 2008.

Bachiochi, Erika. "The Troubling Ideals at the Heart of Abortion Rights." *The Atlantic*, 2020. https://www.theatlantic.com/ideas/archive/2020/01/equality-autonomy-abortion/605356/.

Backer, Larry Cata. "Harmonization, Subsidiarity and Cultural Difference: An Essay on the Dynamics of Opposition Within Federative and International Legal Systems." *Tulsa Journal of Comparative and International Law* 4, no. 2 (1997).

Baderin, Mashood A. *International Human Rights and Islamic Law*. Oxford University Press, 2003.

Bantekas, Ilias, and Lutz Oette. *International Human Rights: Law and Practice*. Cambridge University Press, 2013.

Barber, N. W. "The Limited Modesty of Subsidiarity." *European Law Journal* 11, no. 3 (2005).

Barten, Ulrike. *Minorities, Minority Rights and Internal Self-Determination*. Springer, 2014.

Bary, Theodore de. *Asian Values and Human Rights: A Confucian Communitarian Perspective.* Harvard University Press, 1998.

Bashford, Alison. *Global Population: History, Geopolitics, and Life on Earth.* Columbia University Press, 2014.

Bayefsky, Anne. "Cultural Sovereignty, Relativism, and International Human Rights: New Excuses for Old Strategies." *Ratio Juris* 9, no. 1 (1996).

Bearce, David, and Brandy J. Jolliff Scott. "Popular Non-Support for International Organizations: How Extensive and What Does This Represent?" *The Review of International Organizations* 14 (2019).

Benvenisti, Eyal. "The Margin of Appreciation, Subsidiarity, and Global Challenges to Democracy." *GlobalTrust Working Paper Series 05/2016*, 2016. https://papers.ssrn.com/sol3/papers.cfm?abstract_id=3047237.

Berelson, Bernard, and Jonathan Lieberson. "Government Efforts to Influence Fertility: The Ethical Issues." *Population and Development Review* 5, no. 4 (1979): 581–613.

Berger, Peter, Grace Davie, and Effie Fokas. *Religious America, Secular Europe? A Theme and Variation.* Ashgate, 2008.

Bermann, George A. "Taking Subsidiarity Seriously: Federalism in the European Community and the United States." *Columbia Law Review* 94, no. 2 (1994). https://doi.org/10.2307/1123200.

Besson, Samantha. "Human Rights and Constitutional Law: Patterns of Mutual Validation and Legitimation." In *Philosophical Foundations of Human Rights*, edited by Rowan Cruft. Oxford University Press, 2015.

———. "Subsidiarity in International Human Rights Law — What Is Subsidiary about Human Rights ?" *The American Journal of Jurisprudence* 61, no. 1 (2016). https://doi.org/10.1093/ajj/auw009.

———. "The Sources of International Human Rights Law: How General Is General International Law?" In *The Oxford Handbook of the Sources of International Law*, edited by Samantha Besson and Jean D'Aspremont. Oxford University Press, 2017.

Bjorge, Eirik. "Been There, Done That: The Margin of Appreciation and International Law." *Cambridge Journal of International and Comparative Law* 4, no. 1 (2015).

Bogdandy, Armin von, and Ingo Venzke. *In Whose Name? A Public Law Theory of International Adjudication.* Oxford University Press, 2014.

Borelli, Silvia. "Of Veils, Crosses and Turbans: The European Court of Human Rights and Religious Practices as Manifestations of Cultural Diversity." In *Cultural Heritage, Cultural Rights, Cultural Diversity: New Developments in International Law*, edited by Silvia Borelli and Federico Lenzerini. Martinus Nijhoff, 2002.

Bossuyt, Marc. *Guide to the "Travaux Préparatoires" of the International Covenant on Civil and Political Rights.* Martinus Nijhoff, 1987.

———. "The Court of Strasbourg Acting as an Asylum Court." *European Constitutional Law Review* 8, no. 2 (2012).

Bourbonnais, Nicole C. *Birth Control in the Decolonizing Caribbean: Reproductive Politics and Practice on Four Islands, 1930–1970.* Cambridge University Press, 2016.

———. "Population Control, Family Planning, and Maternal Health Networks in the 1960s/70s: Diary of an International Consultant." *Bulletin of the History of Medicine* 93, no. 3 (2019): 335–64.

Brems, Eva. "Enemies or Allies—Feminism and Cultural Relativism as Dissident Voices in Human Rights Discourse." *Human Rights Quarterly* 19, no. 1 (1997).

———. *Human Rights: Universality and Diversity*. Martinus Nijhoff, 2001.

Brennan, Patrick McKinley. "Subsidiarity in the Tradition of Catholic Social Doctrine." In *Global Perspectives on Subsidiarity*, edited by Michelle Evans and Augusto Zimmermann. Springer, 2014.

Broberg, Gunnar, and Nils Roll-Hansen. *Eugenics and the Welfare State: Norway, Sweden, Denmark, and Finland*. Michigan State University Press, 2005.

Brownlie, Ian. "The Rights of Peoples in Modern International Law." *Bulletin of the Australian Society of Legal Philosophy* 9, no. 2 (1985).

Bunch, Charlotte. "Women's Rights as Human Rights: Toward a Re-Vision of Human Rights." *Human Rights Quarterly* 12, no. 4 (1990).

Caetano, André J., and Joseph E. Potter. "Politics and Female Sterilization in Northeast Brazil." *Population and Development Review* 30, no. 1 (2004).

Cambou, Dorothée. "The UNDRIP and the Legal Significance of the Right of Indigenous Peoples to Self-Determination: A Human Rights Approach with a Multidimensional Perspective." *International Journal of Human Rights* 23, no. 1–2 (February 7, 2019): 34–50. https://doi.org/10.1080/13642987.2019.1585345.

Carl, Noah. "Lackademia: Why Do Academics Lean Left?" *Briefing Paper*. March 2, 2017. https://www.nas.org/academic-questions/31/2/homogenous_the_political_affiliations_of_elite_liberal_arts_college_faculty.

Carozza, Paolo G. "From Conquest to Constitutions: Retrieving a Latin American Tradition of the Idea of Human Rights." *Human Rights Quarterly* 25 (2003): 281–313.

Carozza, Paolo G. "Subsidiarity as a Structural Principle of International Human Rights Law." *American Journal of International Law* 38 (2003).

Cartabia, Marta. "The Age of 'New Rights.'" *Straus Institute Working Paper* 03/10 (2010).

Carter Jr., William M. "Rethinking Subsidiarity in International Human Rights Adjudication." *Hamline Journal of Public Law & Policy* 30, no. 319 (2008).

Casas, Ignacio de. "¿Qué Son Los Estándares de Derechos Humanos?" *Revista Internacional de Derechos Humanos* 9, no. 2 (2019).

Cassese, Antonio. *Self-Determination of Peoples: A Legal Appraisal*. Cambridge University Press, 1995.

———. "The Self-Determination of Peoples." In *The International Bill of Rights: The Covenant on Civil and Political Rights*, edited by Louis Henkin. Columbia University Press, 1981.

Castellino, Joshua. "International Law and Self-Determination." In *Self-Determination and Secession in International Law*, edited by Christian Walter, Antje von Ungern-Sternberg, and Kavus Abushov. Oxford University Press, 2014.

Castellino, Joshua, and Cathal Doyle. "Who Are 'Indigenous Peoples'?" In *The UN Declaration on the Rights of Indigenous Peoples: A Commentary*, edited by Jessie Hohmann and Marc Weller. Oxford University Press, 2018.

Castellino, Joshua, and Jeremie Gilbert. "Self-Determination, Indigenous Peoples and Minorities." *Macquarie Law Journal* 3 (2003).

Casterline, John B., and Steven W. Sinding. "Unmet Need for Family Planning in Developing Countries and Implications for Population Policy." *Policy Research Division Working Paper No. 135*, 2000.

Chackiel, Juan, and Susana Schkolnik. "América Latina: Los Sectores Rezagados En La Transición de La Fecundidad." In *La Fecundidad En América Latina: ¿Transición o Revolución?*, edited by CELADE and CEPAL. CELADE-CEPAL, 2003. https://repositorio.cepal.org/bitstream/handle/11362/6742/S043186_es.pdf?sequence=1&isAllowed=y.

Chae, Sophia, Sheila Desai, Marjorie Crowell, and Gilda Sedgh. "Reasons Why Women Have Induced Abortions: A Synthesis of Findings from 14 Countries." *Contraception* 96, no. 4 (2017): 233–41. https://doi.org/10.1016/j.contraception.2017.06.014.Reasons.

Chan, Joseph. "The Asian Challenge to Universal Human Rights: A Philosophical Appraisal." In *Human Rights in Asia and the Pacific*, edited by Ben Saul and Catherine Renshaw. Routledge, 2014.

Chandrasekhar, Sripati. *Abortion In A Crowded World: The Problem of Abortion With Special Reference to India*. University of Washington Press, 1974.

Chaplin, Jonathan. "Subsidiarity and Social Pluralism." In *Global Perspectives on Subsidiarity*, edited by Michelle Evans and Augusto Zimmermann. Springer, 2014.

Charlesworth, Hilary, Christine Chinkin, and Shelley Wright. "Feminist Approaches to International Law." *American Journal of International Law* 85, no. 4 (2017).

Chatterjee, Nilanjana, and Nancy E. Riley. "Planning an Indian Modernity: The Gendered Politics of Fertility Control." *Signs* 26, no. 3 (2001).

Chimni, B S. "Third World Approaches to International Law: A Manifesto." *International Community Law Review* 8 (2006).

Christiano, Thomas. "Self-Determination and the Human Right to Democracy." In *Philosophical Foundations of Human Rights*, edited by Rowan Cruft, S. Matthew Liao, and Massimo Renzo. Oxford University Press, 2015.

Citernesi, Angela, Valeria Dubini, Anna Uglietti, and Elena Ricci. "Intimate Partner Violence and Repeat Induced Abortion in Italy: A Cross Sectional Study." *The European Journal of Contraception & Reproductive Health Care* 20, no. 5 (2015).

Citroni, Gabriella. "The Human Rights Committee and Its Role in Interpreting the International Covenant on Civil and Political Rights Vis-à-Vis States Parties." *EJIL: Talk!*, 2015. https://www.ejiltalk.org/the-human-rights-committee-and-its-role-in-interpreting-the-international-covenant-on-civil-and-political-rights-vis-a-vis-states-parties/.

Cleland, John, Stan Bernstein, Alex Ezeh, Anibal Faundes, Anna Glasier, and Jolene Innis. "Family Planning: The Unfinished Agenda." *The Lancet Sexual and Reproductive Health Series* 368 (2006).

Close, C. F. "The World Population Conference of 1927." *The Geographical Journal* 70, no. 5 (1927).

Cobbah, Josiah A. M. "African Values and the Human Rights Debate: An African Perspective." *Human Rights Quarterly*, 1987. https://doi.org/10.2307/761878.

Connelly, Matthew. *Fatal Misconception: The Struggle to Control World Population*. Harvard University Press, 2008.

———. "Population Control Is History: New Perspectives on the International Campaign to Limit Population Growth." *Comparative Studies in Society and History* 45, no. 1 (2003).

Constitutionalism, Global, and Andreas Follesdal. "The Principle of Subsidiarity as a Constitutional Principle in International Law" 2 (2013): 37–62. https://doi.org/10.1017/S2045381712000123.

Contesse, Jorge. "Contestation and Deference in the Inter-American Human Rights System." *Law and Contemporary Problems* 79, no. 2 (2016).

Cose, Paul, and David Askew. *Asia Pacific and Human Rights: A Global Political Economy Perspective*. Ashgate, 2004.

Council, Population. "Judith Blake on Fertility Control and the Problem of Voluntarism." *Population and Development Review* 20, no. 1 (1994).

Cox, Harvey G, and Jan Swyngedouw. "The Myth of the Twentieth Century: The Rise and Fall of Secularization." *Japanese Journal of Religious Studies* 27, no. 1 (2000): 1–13.

Cox, Peter. "World Population Conference 1954." *The Eugenics Review* 46, no. 4 (1955).

Cox, Peter, Peel John, and Thomas Clifford. "The World Population Conference Belgrade, 1965." *The Eugenics Review* 51, no. 1 (1966).

Craven, Matthew. "The Domestic Application of the International Covenant on Economic, Social and Cultural Rights." In *Economic, Social and Cultural Rights as Human Rights*, edited by Olivier de Schutter. Edward Elgar Publishing Limited, 2013.

———. *The International Covenant on Economic, Social and Cultural Rights: A Perspective on Its Development*. Clarendon Press, 1995.

———. "The UN Committee on ESCR." In *Economic, Social, and Cultural Rights: A Textbook*, edited by Asbjorn Eide, Caterina Krause, and Allan Rosas. Martinus Nijhoff, 2001.

Crawford, James R. *Brownlie's Principles of Public International Law*. 9th ed. Oxford University Press, 2019.

———. "Democracy and the Body of International Law." In *Democratic Governance and International Law*, edited by Gregory Fox and Brad Roth. Cambridge University Press, 2010.

———. *The Creation of States in International Law*. Oxford University Press, 2007.

———. "The Right to Self-Determination in International Law: Its Development and Future." In *Peoples' Rights*, edited by Philip Alston. Oxford University Press, 2001.

———. "The Rights of Peoples: Peoples or Governments." *Bulletin of the Australian Society of Legal Philosophy* 9, no. 2 (1985).

Critchlow, Donald. "Birth Control, Population Control, and Family Planning: An Overview." *Journal of Policy History* 7, no. 1 (1995).

Critchlow, Donald T. *Intended Consequences: Birth Control, Abortion and the Federal Government in Modern America*. Oxford University Press, 1999.

Daes, Erica-Irene A. "Some Considerations on the Right of Indigenous Peoples to Self-Determination." *Transnational Law & Contemporary Problems* 3, no. 1 (1993).

Davis, Kingsley. "Population Policy: Will Current Programs Succeed?" *Science* 158 (1967).

———. *The Population of India and Pakistan*. Princeton University Press, 1951.

Dawson, Christopher. *The Dynamics of World History*. Sheed and Ward, 1956.

DeJong, Jocelyn. "The Role and Limitations of the Cairo InternationalConference on Population and Developmen." *Social Science and Medicine* 51 (2000).

Demery, Ahmed El. *The Arab Charter of Human Rights: A Voice for Sharia in the Modern World.* Council on International Law and Politics, 2015.

Dennis, Michael J., and David P. Stewart. "Justiciability of Economic, Social and Cultural Rights: Should There Be an International Complaints Mechanism to Adjudicate the Rights to Food, Water, Housing, and Health?" In *Economic, Social and Cultural Rights as Human Rights*, edited by Olivier De Schutter. Edward Elgar Publishing Limited, 2013.

Detrick, Sharon. *A Commentary on the United Nations Convention on the Rights of the Child.* Martinus Nijhoff, 1999.

Dharmalingman, A. "The Social Context of Family Planning in a South Indian Village." *International Family Planning Perspectives* 21, no. 1 (1995).

Dijk, Peter van. "A Common Standard of Achievement: About Universal Validity and Uniform Interpretation of International Human Rights Norms." In *Human Rights: Chinese and Dutch Perspectives*, edited by Peter Baehr, Fried van Hoof, Liu Nanlai, Tao Zhenghua, and Jaqueline Smith. Martinus Nijhoff, 1996.

Dinstein, Yoram. "Collective Human Rights of Peoples and Minorities." *The International and Comparative Law Quarterly* 25, no. 1 (1976).

Dommen, Caroline. "Claiming Environmental Rights: Some Possibilities Offered by the United Nations' Human Rights Mechanisms." *Georgetown International Environmental Law Review* 11 (1998).

Donders, Yvonne. "Human Rights and Cultural Diversity: Too Hot to Handle?" *Netherlands Quarterly of Human Rights* 30, no. 4 (2012).

Donnelly, Jack. "Cultural Relativism and Universal Human Rights." *Human Rights Quarterly* 6, no. 4 (1984): 400–419.

———. "Human Rights and Asian Values: A Defense of 'Western' Universalism." In *Human Rights in Asia and the Pacific*, edited by Ben Saul and Catherine Renshaw. Routledge, 2014.

———. *Universal Human Rights in Theory and Practice*. 3rd ed. New York: Cornell University Press, 2013.

Donoho, Douglas Lee. "Relativism Versus Universalism in Human Rights: The Search for Meaningful Standards." *Stanford Journal of International Law* 27, no. 2 (1991).

Douzinas, Costas. *Human Rights and Empire: The Political Philosophy of Cosmopolitanism.* Routledge, 2007.

———. *The End of Human Rights: Critical Legal Thought at the Turn of the Century*. Portland: Hart Publishing, 2000.

Dowbiggin, Ian R. *The Sterilization Movement and Global Fertility in the Twentieth Century.* Oxford University Press, 2008.

Dundes Renteln, Alison. *International Human Rights: Universalism versus Relativism*. SAGE, 1990.

Dworkin, Ronald. *Life's Dominion: An Argument about Abortion, Euthanasia, and Individual Freedom.* Harper Collins, 1993.

———. *Taking Rights Seriously*. 5th edn. London: Duckworth, 2009.

Eager, Paige Whaley. "From Population Control to Reproductive Rights: Understanding Normative Change in Global Population Policy (1965–1994)." *Global Society* 18, no. 2 (2004). https://doi.org/10.1080/1360082042000207483.

Ehrlich, Paul. *The Population Bomb*. Ballantine Books, 1986.

Eide, Asbjørn. "Interdependence and Indivisibility of Human Rights." In *Human Rights in Education, Science and Culture: Legal Developments and Challenges*, edited by Yvonne Donders and Vladimir Volodin, 2007.

———. "Peaceful Group Accommodation as an Alternative to Secession in Sovereign States." In *Self-Determination: International Perspectives*, edited by Donald Clark and Robert Williamson. Macmillan Press, 1996.

Ellis-Petersen, Hannah. "India States Considering Two-Child Policy and Incentives for Sterilisation." *The Guardian*, 2021. https://www.theguardian.com/world/2021/jul/14/india-states-considering-two-child-policy-and-incentives-for-sterilisation.

Elorriaga, Ernesto Martínez. "Diputados de Michoacán Rechazan Legalizar El Aborto." *La Jornada*, 2020. https://www.jornada.com.mx/ultimas/estados/2020/06/10/diputados-de-michoacan-rechazan-legalizar-el-aborto-5478.html.

Emtseva, Julia. "Practicing Reflexivity in International Law: Running a Never-Ending Race to Catch up with the Western International Lawyers." MPIL Research Paper Series, 2021. https://papers.ssrn.com/sol3/papers.cfm?abstract_id=3837283.

Eslava, Luis, and Sundhya Pahuja. "Between Resistance and Reform: TWAIL and the Universality of International Law." *Trade, Law and Development* 3 (2011).

Evans, Michelle, and Augusto Zimmermann. "The Global Relevance of Subsidiarity: An Overview." In *Global Perspectives on Subsidiarity*, edited by Michelle Evans and Augusto Zimmermann. Springer, 2014.

Fachin, Melina Girardi, and Bruna Nowak. "The Joint Declaration to the Inter-American System of Human Rights: Backlash or Contestation?" Blog of the International Journal of Constitutional Law, 2019. http://www.iconnectblog.com/2019/12/the-joint-declaration-to-the-inter-american-system-of-human-rights-backlash-or-contestation/.

Farmer, Ann. *By Their Fruits: Eugenics, Population Control, and the Abortion Campaign*. Catholic University of America Press, 2008.

Fernández, Alfred. "De La Idea a La Cultura de Los Derechos Humanos: Los Derechos Humanos En El Siglo XXI." *Anuario de Derechos Humanos* 3 (2002).

Fine, Johanna B., Katherine Mayall, and Lilian Sepúlveda. "The Role of International Human Rights Norms in the Liberalization of Abortion Laws Globally." *Health and Human Rights Journal* June (2017).

Finkle, Jason L, and Barbara B Crane. "The Politics of Bucharest: Population, Development, and the New International Economic Order." *Population and Development Review* 1, no. 1 (1975): 87–114.

Finnis, John. *Natural Law and Natural Rights*. New York: Clarendon Press, 1988.

Franck, Thomas. "The Emerging Right to Democratic Governance." *The American Journal of International Law* 86, no. 1 (1992).

Freeman, Michael. *Human Rights: An Interdisciplinary Approach*. 2nd ed. Polity Press, 2011.

Frey, Marc. "Neo-Malthusianism and Development: Shifting Interpretations of a Contested Paradigm." *Journal of Global History* 6, no. 1 (2011).

Gadamer, Hans-Georg. *Truth and Method*. Erd. London: Continuum, 2004.

García Escobar, Gabriela. "Human Rights Pluralistic Universality: A Bridge Between Global Norms and Cultural Diversity", Nordic Journal of Human Rights 41, no. 2 (2023).

Ghuman, Sharon, Vu Manh Loi, Vu Tuan Huy, and John Knodel. "Continuity and Change in Premarital Sex in Vietnam." *International Perspectives on Sexual and Reproductive Health* 32, no. 4 (2006).

Glendon, Mary Ann. *A World Made New: Eleanor Roosevelt and the Universal Declaration of Human Rights*. New York: Random House Trade Paperbacks, 2002.

———. "Foundations of Human Rights: The Unfinished Business." *American Journal of Jurisprudence* 44, no. 1 (1999).

———. "Knowing the Universal Declaration of Human Rights." *Notre Dame Law Review* 73, no. 5 (1998).

———. "La Soportable Levedad de La Dignidad." *Persona y Derecho* 67, no. 2 (2012): 41–45.

———. "Looking for Persons in the Law." *First Things*, no. December (2006). https://www.firstthings.com/article/2006/12/looking-forpersonsin-the-law.

———. "Reclaiming Human Rights." *First Things*, 2016. https://www.firstthings.com/article/2016/08/reclaim-human-rights.

———. *Rights Talk: The Impoverishment of Political Discourse*. New York: The Free Press, 1991.

———. "The Forgotten Crucible: The Latin American Influence on the Universal Human Rights Idea." *Harvard Human Rights Journal* 16 (2003).

———. "What Happened at Beijing." *First Things*, 2019. https://www.firstthings.com/article/1996/01/005-what-happened-at-beijing.

Glendon, Mary Ann, and Seth Kaplan. "Renewing Human Rights." *First Things*, 2019. https://www.firstthings.com/article/2019/02/renewing-human-rights.

González-Varas Ibáñez, Alejandro. "Aspectos Ético-Jurídicos de La Regulación Del Aborto En España." *Revista General de Derecho Canónico y Derecho Eclesiástico Del Estado*, no. 23 (2010).

Goodale, Mark, ed. *Letters to the Contrary: A Curated History of the UNESCO Human Rights Survey*. Stanford University Press, 2018.

Grant, Burke. "The World Population Conference: An Overview." *Journal of International Law and Economics* 9, no. 1 (1974).

Green, Edward C. *Broken Promises: How the AIDS Establishment Has Betrayed the Developing World*. Routledge, 2017.

Green, Marshall. "The Evolution of US International Population Policy, 1965-92: A Chronological Account." *Population and Development Review* 19, no. 2 (1993): 303–21.

Griffin, James. *On Human Rights*. Oxford: Oxford University Press, 2008.

Grimes, Seamus. "From Population Control to 'Reproductive Rights': Ideological Influences in Population Policy." *Third World Quarterly* 19, no. 3 (1998).

———. "The Ideology of Population Control in the UN Draft Plan for Cairo." *Population Research and Policy Review* 13 (1994).

Gross, Neil, and Solon Simmons, eds. *Professors and Their Politics*. Johns Hopkins University Press, 2014.

Gruszczynski, Lukasz, and Wouter Werner, eds. *Deference in International Courts and Tribunals: Standard of Review and Margin of Appreciation*. Oxford University Press, 2014.

Guerra López, Rodrigo. *Afirmar a La Persona Por Sí Misma: La Dignidad Como Fundamento de Los Derechos de La Persona*. Mexico City: Comisión Nacional de los Derechos Humanos, 2003.

Gunnar, Broberg, and Mattias Tydén. "Eugenics in Sweden: Efficient Care." In *Eugenics and the Welfare State: Norway, Sweden, Denmark and Finland*, edited by Gunnar Broberg and Nils Roll-Hansen. Michigan State University Press, 2005.

Gwatkin, Davidson. "The State of the World's Population Movement: Implications of the 1984 Mexico City Conference." *World Development* 13, no. 4 (1985).

Haarscher, Guy. "Con Human Rights Be 'Contextualized'?" In *Human Rights with Modesty: The Problem of Universalism*, edited by András Sajó. Martinus Nijhoff, 2004.

Habermas, Jürgen. "Reconciliation Through the Public Use of Reason: Remarks on John Rawls's Political Liberalism." *The Journal of Philosophy* 92, no. 3 (1995).

Habermas, Jürgen, and Joseph Ratzinger. *Entre Razón y Religión: Dialéctica de La Secularización*. Fondo de Cultura Económica, 2008.

Hafner - Burton, Emilie M., and Kiyoteru Tsutsui. "Human Rights in a Globalizing World: The Paradox of Empty Promises." *American Journal of Sociology* 110, no. 5 (2005).

Haidt, Jonathan. *The Righteous Mind: Why Good People Are Divided by Politics and Religion*. New York: Random House, 2012.

Hannum, Hurst. *Autonomy, Sovereignty, and Self-Determination: The Accommodation of Conflicting Rights*. University of Pennsylvania Press, 1990.

———. "Reinvigorating Human Rights for the Twenty-First Century." *Human Rights Law Review* 16, no. 3 (2016).

———. "Self-Determination in the Post-Colonial Era." In *Self-Determination: International Perspectives*, edited by Donald Clark and Robert Williamson. Macmillan Press, 1996.

Harrington, Joanna. "The Human Rights Committee, Treaty Interpretation, and the Last Word." *EJIL: Talk!*, 2015. https://www.ejiltalk.org/the-human-rights-committee-treaty-interpretation-and-the-last-word/.

Harsch, Donna. "Communism and Women." In *The Oxford Handbook of the History of Communism*, edited by Stephen A. Smith. Oxford University Press, 2013.

Hartmann, Betsy. "Liberal Ends, Illiberal Means: National Security, 'Environmental Conflict' and the Making of the Cairo Consensus." *Indian Journal of Gender Studies* 12, no. 2 (2006): 195–227. https://doi.org/10.1177/097152150601300204.

———. *Reproductive Rights and Wrongs: The Global Politics of Population Control*. South End Press, 1995.

———. *Reproductive Rights and Wrongs: The Global Politics of Population Control*. 3rd ed. Haymarker Books, 2016.

Heinz, Erin, and Marie Louis Roth. "As Many as I Can Afford: Ideal Family Size in Contemporary Uganda." In *Reproductive Justice and Sexual Rights: Transnational Perspectives*, edited by Tanya Saroj Bakhru. Routledge, 2019.

Helfer, Laurence R. "Redesigning the European Court of Human Rights: Embeddedness as a Deep Structural Principle of the European Human Rights Regime." *European Journal of International Law* 19, no. 1 (2008).

Helfer, Laurence R., and Anne-Marie Slaughter. "Toward a Theory of Effective Supranational Adjudication." *The Yale Law Journal* 107 (1997).

Helle, Horst. *China: Promise or Threat?* Brill, 2017. https://doi.org/10.1163/9789004330603.

Hendrixson, Anne, Diana Ojeda, Jade S. Sasser, Sarojini Nadimpally, Ellen E. Foley, and Rajani Bhatia. "Confronting Populationism: Feminist Challenges to Population Control in an Era of Climate Change." *Gender, Place and Culture* 27, no. 3 (March 3, 2020): 307–15. https://doi.org/10.1080/0966369X.2019.1639634.

Henkin, Louis. "Rights: American and Human." *Columbia Law Review* 79, no. 3 (1979).

Hennebel, Ludovic. "The Human Rigths Committee." In *The United Nations and Human Rights: A Critical Appraisal*, edited by Frédéric Mégret and Philip Alston. Oxford University Press, 2009.

Henrich, Joseph, Steven J Heine, and Ara Norenzayan. "The Weirdest People in the World?" *Behavioral and Brain Sciences* 33, no. 2 (2010): 61–135.

Henríquez, Tomás. "La Política y Politización de Los Derechos Humanos." In *Desarrollo Humano y Solidario: Nuevas Ideas Para Chile*, edited by Diego Schalper. Fundación IdeaPaís, 2017.

Henry, P. J., and Jaime L Napier. "Education Is Related to Greater Ideological Prejudice." *Public Opinion Quarterly* 81, no. 4 (2017): 930–42. https://doi.org/10.1093/poq/nfx038.

Hickey, Colin, Travis N Rieder, and Jake Earl. "Population Engineering and the Fight against Climate Change." *Social Theory and Practice* 42, no. 4 (2016).

Higgins, Rosalyn. *Problems and Process: International Law and How We Use It*. Oxford University Press, 1995.

Hilpold, Peter, ed. *Autonomy and Self-Determination: Between Legal Assertions and Utopian Aspirations*. Edward Elgar Publishing Limited, 2018.

———. "Self-Determination and Autonomy: Between Secession and Internal Self-Determination." *International Journal on Minority and Group Rights* 24 (2017).

Hodgson, Dennis. "Demography as Social Science and Policy Science." *Population and Development Review* 9, no. 1 (1983).

Hodgson, Dennis, and Susan Cotts Watkins. "Feminists and Neo-Malthusians: Past and Present Alliances." *Population and Development Review* 23, no. 3 (1997): 469–523.

Hollen, Cecilia Van. "Moving Targets: Routine IUD Insertion in Maternity Wards in Tamil Nadu, India." *Reproductive Health Matters* 6, no. 11 (1998).

Honeycutt, Nathan, and Laura Freberg. "The Liberal and Conservative Experience Across Academic Disciplines: An Extension of Inbar and Lammers." *Social Psychological and Personality Science* 8, no. 2 (2017): 115–23. https://doi.org/10.1177/1948550616667617.

Hoover, Joe. "Rereading the Universal Declaration of Human Rights: Plurality and Contestation, Not Consensus." *Journal of Human Rights* 12, no. 2 (2013). https://doi.org/10.1080/14754835.2013.784663.

Hopgood, Stephen. *The Endtimes of Human Rights*. Cornell University Press, 2015.

Howard-hassmann, Rhoda E, and Rhoda E Howard. "Cultural Absolutism and the Nostalgia for Community Cultural Absolutism and the Nostalgia for Community," 1993.

Hughes, Glenn. "The Concept of Dignity in the Universal Declaration of Human Rights." *Journal of Religious Ethics* 39, no. 1 (2011).

Hull, Terence H., ed. *People, Population, and Policy in Indonesia*. ISEAS, 2005.

Humphrey, John. *Human Rights and the United Nations: A Great Adventure*. Transnational Publishers, 1984.

———. *Human Rights and The United Nations: A Great Adventure*. Transnational Publishers, 1984.

Iglesias Vila, Marisa. "Subsidiarity, Margin of Appreciation and International Adjudication within a Cooperative Conception of Human Rights." *International Journal of Constitutional Law* 15, no. 2 (2017).

Inbar, Yoel, and Joris Lammers. "Political Diversity in Social and Personality Psychology." *Perspectives on Psychological Science* 7, no. 5 (2012). https://doi.org/10.1177/1745691612448792.

Inglehart, Ronald, and Pippa Norris. *Rising Tide: Gender Equality and Cultural Change Around the World*. Cambridge University Press, 2003.

———. *Sacred and Secular: Religion and Politics Worldwide*. Cambridge University Press, 2011.

———. "The True Clash of Civilizations." *Foreign Policy*, no. 135 (2003): 63–70. https://doi.org/10.2307/3183594.

Isaacs, Stephen L. "Incentives, Population Policy, and Reproductive Rights: Ethical Issues." *Studies in Family Planning* 26, no. 6 (1995).

Jayawickrama, Nihal. *The Judicial Application of Human Rights Law: National, Regional and International Jurisprudence*. Cambridge University Press, 2017.

Jensen, Lene Arnett. "Coming of Age in a Multicultural World: Globalization and Adolescent Cultural Identity Formation." *Applied Developmental Science* 7, no. 3 (2003). https://doi.org/10.1207/S1532480XADS0703.

John Bongaarts. "Can Family Planning Programs Reduce High Desired Family Size in Sub-Saharan Africa?" *International Perspectives on Sexual and Reproductive Health* 37, no. 4 (2011).

Johnson, Glen, and Janusz Symonides. *La Déclaration Universelle Des Droits de l'Homme: 40e Anniversaire—1948–1988*. L'Harmattan, 1990.

Jones, Rachel K, Lori Frohwirth, and Ann M Moore. "More than Poverty: Disruptive Events among Women Having Abortions in the USA." *BMJ Sexual and Reproductive Health* 39, no. 1 (2013).

Kaler, Amy. "The Moral Lens of Population Control: Condoms and Controversies in Southern Malawi." *Studies in Family Planning* 35, no. 2 (2004).

Kälin, Walter, and Jörg Künzli. *The Law of International Human Rights Protection*. Oxford University Press, 2009.

Kanger, Helle. *Human Rights in the UN Declaration*. Almqvist & Wiksell International, 1984.

Kaplan, Seth. "Will Human Rights Survive in a Multipolar World?" *The Washington Quarterly* 42, no. 1 (2019).

Kaplan, Seth Daniel. *Human Rights in Thick and Thin Societies: Universality without Uniformity*. Cambridge University Press, 2018.

Kausikan, Bilahari. "An East Asian Approach to Human Rights." *Buffalo Journal of International Law* 2, no. 2 (1996).

Keck, Margaret E., and Kathryn Sikkink. *Activists Beyond Borders: Advocacy Networks in International Politics*. Cornell University Press, 1998.

Keller, Helen, and Leena Grover. "General Comments of the Human Rights Committee and Their Legitimacy." In *UN Human Rights Treaty Bodies: Law and Legitimacy*, edited by Helen Keller and Geir Ulfstein. Cambridge University Press, 2012.

Kennedy, David. *The Dark Sides of Virtue: Reassessing International Humanitarianism*. Princeton: Princeton University Press, 2004.

Kim, Heejung S, and Smaranda Lawrie. "Culture and Motivation." In *Handbook of Cultural Psychology*, edited by Dov Cohen and Shinobu Kitayama. The Guilford Press, 2019.

Kirgis, Frederic L. "The Degrees of Self-Determination in the United Nations Era." *The American Journal of International Law* 88, no. 2 (1994).

Kitayama, Shinobu, Jiyoung Park, and Yay-hyung Cho. "Culture and Neuroplasticity." In *Handbook of Advances in Culture and Psychology: Volume 5*, edited by Michele J Gelfand, Chi-yue Chiu, and Ying-yi Hong. Oxford University Press, 2015.

Kitayama, Shinobu, and Ayse K Uskul. "Culture, Mind, and the Brain: Current Evidence and Future Directions." *Annual Review of Psychology* 62 (2011): 419–52. https://doi.org/10.1146/annurev-psych-120709-145357.

Klabbers, Jan. "On Epistemic Universalism and the Melancholy of International Law." *European Journal of International Law* 29, no. 4 (2018).

———. "The Right to Be Taken Seriously: Self-Determination in International Law." *Human Rights Quarterly* 28, no. 1 (2006).

Koch, Elard, Monique Chireau, Fernando Pliego, Joseph Stanford, Sebastian Haddad, Byron Calhoun, Paula Aracena, Miguel Bravo, Sebastián Gatica, and John Thorp. "Abortion Legislation, Maternal Healthcare, Fertility, Female Literacy, Sanitation, Violence against Women and Maternal Deaths: A Natural Experiment in 32 Mexican States." *BMJ Open* 5, no. 2 (February 1, 2015). https://doi.org/10.1136/bmjopen-2014-006013.

Kohler, Thomas. "Quadragesimo Anno (1931)." In *A Century of Catholic Social Thought: Essays on "Rerum Novarum" and Nine Other Key Documents*, edited by Robert Royal and George Weigel. Ethics & Public Policy Center, 1991.

Koskenniemi, Martti. *From Apology to Utopia: The Structure of International Legal Argument*. Cambridge University Press, 2006.

———. "National Self-Determination Today: Problems of Legal Theory and Practice." *The International and Comparative Law Quarterly* 43, no. 2 (1994).

———. "The Effects of Rights on Political Culture." In *The European Union and Human Rights*, edited by Phillip Alston. Oxford University Press, 1999.

———. "The Politics of International Law." *European Journal of International Law* 4 (1990): 58–63.

———. "Whose Intolerance, Which Democracy?" In *Democratic Governance and International Law*, edited by Gregory H. Fox and Brad Roth. Cambridge University Press, 2010.

Krisch, Nico. "The Backlash against International Courts." Verfassungsblog, 2014. https://verfassungsblog.de/backlash-international-courts-2/.

Krumbein, Frédéric. "P. C. Chang—The Chinese Father of Human Rights." *Journal of Human Rights* 14, no. 3 (2015).

la Torre Rangel, José Antonio De. "Sobre El Origen de La Tradición Iberoamericana de Derechos Humanos." In *Tradición Iberoamericana de Derechos Humanos*. Mexico City: Porrúa, 2014.

Lange, Felix. "Hard Times for Voices from the Global South." Völkerrechtsblog, 2019. https://voelkerrechtsblog.org/de/hard-times-for-voices-from-the-global-south/.

Lauren, Paul Gordon. *The Evolution of International Human Rights: Visions Seen*. University of Pennsylvania Press, 2003.

Leary, Virginia. "Postliberal Strands in Western Human Rights Theory: Personalist-Communitarian Perspectives." In *Human Rights in Cross-Cultural Perpestives: A Quest for Consensus*, edited by Abdullahi Ahmed An-Na'im, 1995.

Legg, Andrew. *The Margin of Appreciation in International Human Rights Law: Deference and Proportionality*. Oxford University Press, 2012.

Lenzerini, Federico. *The Culturalization of Human Rights Law*. Oxford University Press, 2014.

Letsas, George. *A Theory of Interpretation of the European Convention on Human Rights*. Oxford University Press, 2007.

Li, Xiaorong. "'Asian Values' and the Universality of Human Rights." *Philosophical Dimensions of Public Policy*, 2019, 171–79. https://doi.org/10.4324/9781315126357-17.

Lindholm, Tore. "Article 1: A New Beginning." In *The Universal Declaration of Human Rights: A Commentary*, edited by Asbjørn Eide, Gudmundur Alfredsson, Goran Melander, Allan Rosas, and Lars Adam Rehof. Scandinavian University Press, 1993.

———. "Article 1." In *The Universal Declaration of Human Rights: A Common Standard of Achievement*, edited by Asbjørn Eide and Gudmundur Alfredsson. Martinus Nijhoff, 1999.

———. "The Cross-Cultural Legitimacy of Universal Human Rights: Plural Justification across Normative Divides." In *Cultural Human Rights*, edited by Francesco Francioni and Martin Scheinin. Martinus Nijhoff, 2008.

Lindsay, Jennie. "The Politics of Population Control in Namibia." *Review of African Political Economy* 36 (1986).

Liu, Lydia H. "Shadows of Universalism: The Untold Story of Human Rights around 1948." *Critical Inquiry* 40, no. 4 (2014): 385–417.

Llewellyn, Jennifer, and Daniel Philpott, eds. *Restorative Justice, Reconciliation, and Peacebuilding*. Oxford University Press, 2014.

Lloyd, Cynthia, ed. *Growing Up Global: The Changing Transitions to Adulthood in Developing Countries*. National Research Council, 2005.

Lorimer, Frank, Carmen Miró, Wilson H. Grabill, and Vasilios Valaoras. "The Role of the International Union for the Scientific Study of Population." *The Milbank Memorial Fund Quarterly* 49, no. 4 (1971).

Lukianoff, Greg, and Jonathan Haidt. *The Coddling of the American Mind: How Good Intentions and Bad Ideas Are Setting up a Generation for Failure*. Penguin Press, 2018.

MacIntyre, Alasdair. *After Virtue: A Study in Moral Theory*. 3rd edn. Notre Dame: University of Notre Dame Press, 2011.

———. *Whose Justice? Which Rationality?* Notre Dame: University of Notre Dame Press, 1988.

Macioce, Fabio. "Cultural Rights and the Margin of Appreciation Doctrine: A Legal Tool for Balancing Individual Rights and Traditional Rules." *Law, Culture and the Humanities* 13, no. 3 (2017). https://doi.org/10.1177/1743872117732846.

Madsen, Mikael Rask. "Who Rules the World? The Educational Capital of the International Judiciary." *University of California Journal of International, Transnational, and Comparative Law*, 2018.

Maffi, Irene, and Malika Affes. "The Right to Abortion in Tunisia after the Revolution of 2011: Legal, Medical, and Social Arrangements as Seen through Seven Abortion Stories." *Health and Human Rights Journal* 21, no. 2 (2019).

Maier, Elizabeth. "Documenting Mexico's Culture War." *Latin American Perspectives* 39, no. 6 (2012).

Majumdar, Chirodip. "Attitudes Towards Premarital Sex in India: Traditionalism and Cultural Change." *Sexuality and Culture* 22, no. 1 (2018).

Marglin, Stephen. "Towards the Decolonization of the Mind." In *Dominating Knowledge: Development, Culture, and Resistance*, edited by Frédérique Apffel Marglin and Stephen Marglin. Clarendon Press, 1990.

Maritain, Jacques. *Man and the State*. Chicago: The Chicago University Press, 1971.

———. *The Rights of Man and Natural Law*. The Century Press, 1944.

Mass, Bonnie. *Population Target: The Political Economy of Population Control in Latin America.* Charters Publishing, 1976.

Massini Correa, Carlos Ignacio. *La Ley y Su Interpretación Contemporánea*. EUNSA, 2006.

Mathews, Jud, and Alec Stone Sweet. "Proportionality Balancing and Global Constitutionalism." *Columbia Journal of Transnational Law* 47, no. 72 (2008).

Matláry, Jane Haaland. *When Might Becomes Human Right: Essays on Democracy and the Crisis of Rationality*. Gracewing, 2007.

Mauldin, W. Parker. "Assessment of National Family Planning Programs in Developing Countries." *Studies in Family Planning* 6, no. 2 (1975).

McCall-Smith, Kasey L. "Interpreting International Human Rights Standards: Treaty Body General Comments as a Chisel or a Hammer." In *Tracing the Roles of Soft Law in Human Rights*, edited by Stéphanie Lagoutte, Thomas Gammeltoft-Hansen, and John Cerone. Oxford University Press, 2016.

McCorquodale, Robert. "Self-Determination: A Human Rights Approach." *The International and Comparative Law Quarterly* 43, no. 4 (1994).

McCrudden, Christopher. "Human Dignity and Judicial Interpretation of Human Rights." *The European Journal of International Law* 19, no. 4 (2008): 655–724. https://doi.org/10.1093/ejil/chn043.

Mcgoldrick, Dominic. "Religion in the European Public Square and in European Public Life - Crucifixes in the Classroom ?" *Human Rights Law Review* 11, no. 3 (2011). https://doi.org/10.1093/hrlr/ngr024.

McGoldrick, Dominic. "A Defence of the Margin of Appreciation and an Argument for Its Application by the Human Rights Committee." *International and Comparative Law Quarterly* 65, no. January (2016): 21–60. https://doi.org/10.1017/S0020589315000457.

McIntosh, C. Alison, and Jason L. Finkle. "The Cairo Conference on Population and Development: A New Paradigm?" *Population and Development Review* 21, no. 2 (1995).

Mechlem, Kerstin. "Treaty Bodies and the Interpretation of Human Rights." *Vanderbilt Journal o Transnational Law* 42 (2007): 905–47.

Merry, Sally Engle. "Constructing a Global Law-Violence against Women and the Human Rights System." *Law & Social Inquiry* 28, no. 4 (2003).

———. "Human Rights Law and the Demonization of Culture (And Anthropology Along the Way)." *Political and Legal Anthropology Review* 26, no. 1 (2003): 55–76.

Miller, David. *On Nationality*. Clarendon Press, 1995.

Millon-Delsol, Chantal. *L'État Subsidiare: Ingérence et Non-Ingérence de l'Etat Le Principe de Subsidiarité Aux Fondements de l'histoire Européenne*. Presses Universitaires de France, 1992.

Mitoma, Glenn. *Human Rights and the Negotiation of American Power*. University of Pennsylvania Press, 2013.

———. *Human Rights and the Negotiation of American Power*. University of Pennsylvania Press, 2013.

Morelli, Gilda A, Nandita Chaudhary, Alma Gottlieb, Heidi Keller, Marjorie Murray, Naomi Quinn, Mariano Rosabal-Coto, Gabriel Scheidecker, Akira Takada, and Marga Vicedo. "Taking Culture Seriously: A Pluralistic Approach to Attachment." In *The Cultural Nature of Attachment: Contextualizing Relationships and Development*, edited by Heidi Keller and Kim Bard, Vol. 22. MIT Press, 2017.

Morsink, Johannes. *Inherent Human Rights : Philosophical Roots of the Universal Declaration*. University of Pennsylvania Press, 2009.

———. *The UDHR and The Holocaust: An Endangered Connection*. Georgetown University Press, 2019.

———. *The Universal Declaration of Human Rights: Origins, Drafting and Intent*. Pensylvannia University Press, 1999.

Mowbray, Alastair. "Subsidiarity and the European Convention on Human Rights." *Human Rights Law Review* 15, no. 2 (2015).

Moyn, Samuel. "Beyond the Human Rights Measurement Controversy." *Law and Contemporary Problems* 81, no. 121 (2018).

———. "Personalism, Community, and the Origins of Human Rights." In *Human Rights in the Twentieth Century*, edited by Stefan-Ludwig Hoffmann. Cambridge University Press, 2012.

Murswiek, Dietrich. "The Issue of a Right of Secession—Reconsidered." In *Modern Law of Self-Determination*, edited by Christian Tomuschat. Martinus Nijhoff, 1993.

Musgrave, Thomas. *Self-Determination and National Minorities*. Clarendon Press, 1997.

Mutua, Makau Wa. *Human Rights Standards: Hegemony, Law, and Politics*. State University of New York Press, 2016.

———. "Looking Past the Human Rights Committee: An Argument for DeMarginalizing Enforcement." *Buffalo Journal of International Law* 4 (1998).

———. "Standard Setting in Human Rights: Critique and Prognosis." *Human Rights Quarterly* 29 (2007).

———. "The Complexity of Universalism in Human Rights." In *Human Rights with Modesty: The Problem of Universalism*, edited by András Sajó. Martinus Nijhoff, 2004.

———. "What Is TWAIL?" *Proceedings of the Annual Meeting (American Society of International Law)* 31 (2000).

Nagel, Thomas. "Rawls on Justice." In *Reading Rawls*, edited by Jonathan Daniels. Blackwell Publishing, 1989.

Neier, Aryeh. *The International Human Rights Movement: A History*. Princeton University Press, 2012.

Nelson, Jennifer. "Abortion Rights and Human Rights in Mexico." In *Reproductive Justice and Sexual Rights: Transnational Perspectives*, edited by Tanya Saroj Bakhru. Routledge, 2019.

Neuman, Gerald. "Giving Meaning and Effect to Human Rights." In *The Human Rights Covenants at 50: Their Past, Present, and Future*, edited by Daniel Moeckli, Helen Keller, and Corina Heri. Oxford University Press, n.d.

———. "Subsidiarity." In *The Oxford Handbook of Human Rights*, edited by Dinah Shelton. Oxford University Press, 2013.

Nussbaum, Martha. "Perfectionist Liberalism and Political Liberalism." *Philosophy & Public Affairs* 39, no. 1 (2011).

O'Donnell, Thomas A. "The Margin of Appreciation Doctrine: Standards in the Jurisprudence of the European Court of Human Rights." *Human Rights Quarterly* 4, no. 4 (1982).

O'Flaherty, Michael. "The Concluding Observations of United Nations Human Rights Treaty Bodies." *Human Rights Law Review* 6, no. 1 (2006).

———. "The Reporting Obligation under Article 40 of the International Covenant on Civil and Political Rights: Lessons to Be Learned from Consideration by the Human Rights Committee of Ireland's First Report." *Human Rights Quarterly* 16, no. 3 (1994).

———. "Towards Integration of United Nations Human Rights Treaty Body Recommendations: The Rights-Based Approach Model." In *Economic, Social and Cultural Rights in Action*, edited by Mashood A. Baderin and Robert McCorquodale. Oxford University Press, 2007.

Odello, Marco, and Francesco Seatzu. *The UN Committee on Economic, Social and Cultural Rights: The Law, Process and Practice*. Routledge, 2013.

Okin, Susan, Joshua Cohen, and Matthew Howard, eds. *Is Multiculturalism Bad for Women?* Princeton University Press, 1999.

Okin, Susan Moller. "Is Multiculturalism Bad for Women?" In *Is Multiculturalism Bad for Women?*, edited by Susan Moller Okin. Princeton University Press, 1999.

Osiatynski, Wiktor. "On the Universality of the Universal Declaration of Human Rights." In *Human Rights with Modesty: The Problem of Universalism*, edited by András Sajó. Martinus Nijhoff, 2004.

Osiatyński, Wiktor. *Human Rights and Their Limits*. Cambridge University Press, 2012.

Oyserman, Daphna, Heather M Coon, and Markus Kemmelmeier. "Rethinking Individualism and Collectivism: Evaluation of Theoretical Assumptions and Meta-Analyses." *Psychological Bulletin* 128, no. 1 (2002): 3–72. https://doi.org/10.1037//0033-2909.128.1.3.

Padelford, Norman J., and K. Gosta A. Andersson. "The Aaland Islands Question." *The American Journal of International Law* 33, no. 3 (1939).

Page, Benjamin I., Larry M. Bartels, and Jason Seawright. "Democracy and the Policy Preferences of Wealthy Americans." *Perspectives on Politics* 11, no. 1 (2013).

Pallares Yabur, Pedro. "La Justificación Racional de Los Derechos Humanos En Los Redactores de La Declaración Universal de Los Derechos Humanos." *Persona y Derecho*. Pamplona, 2013.

———. *Un Acuerdo En Las Raíces Los Fundamentos En La Declaración Universal de Derechos Humanos: De Jacques Maritain a Charles Malik*. Instituto de Investigaciones Jurídicas UNAM, 2020.

Panikkar, R. "Is the Notion of Human Rights a Western Concept?" *Diogenes* 30, no. 120 (1982): 75–102.

Papaux, Alain, and Eric Wyler. *L'etique Du Droit International*. Paris: Presses Universitaires de France, 1997.

Patel, Cynthia, and Trisha Kooverjee. "Abortion and Contraception: Attitudes of South African University Students." *Health Care for Women International* 30, no. 6 (2009).

Paúl, Álvaro. *Los Trabajos Preparatorios de La Declaración Americana de Los Derechos y Deberes Del Hombre y El Origen Remoto de La Corte Interamericana*. Instituto de Investigaciones Jurídicas UNAM, 2017.

Pedone, Joanne, and Andrew Kloster. "New Proposals for Human Rights Treaty Body Reform." *Journal of Transnational Law & Policy* 22 (n.d.): 29–84.

Pentassuglia, Gaetano. "Self-Determination, Human Rights, and the Nation-State." *International Community Law Review* 19, no. 443 (2017).

Philipov, Dimiter. "Fertility Intentions and Outcomes: The Role of Policies to Close the Gap." *European Journal of Population* 25 (2009).

Philpott, Daniel. "In Defence of Self-Determination." *Ethics* 105, no. 2 (1995).

———. *Just and Unjust Peace: An Ethic of Political Reconciliation*. Oxford University Press, 2012.

Philpott, Daniel, and Gerard Powers. *Strategies of Peace: Transforming Conflict in a Violent World*. Oxford University Press, 2010.

Pollis, Adamantia. "New Universalism." In *Human Rights: New Perspectives, New Realities*, edited by Adamantia Pollis and Peter Schwab. Lynne Rienner, 2000.

Pritchett, Lant H. "Desired Fertility and the Impact of Population Policies." *Population and Development Review* 20, no. 1 (1994).

Przetacznik, Frank. "The Basic Collective Human Right to Self Determination of Peoples and Nations as a Prerequisite for Peace." *NYLS Journal of Human Rights* VIII, no. 1 (1990).

Quane, Helen. "The United Nations and the Evolving Right to Self-Determination." *The International and Comparative Law Quarterly* 47, no. 3 (1998).

Raic, David. *Statehood and the Law of Self-Determination*. Kluwer Law International, 2002.

Ramesh, Randeep. "Outrage at Guns for Sterilisation Policy." *The Guardian*, 2004. https://www.theguardian.com/world/2004/nov/01/india.randeepramesh.

Ramírez Valverde, Benito, and Gustavo Suárez Vallejos, Pía F. Ramírez Valverde. "Opinión de Mujeres Con Interrupción Voluntaria de Embarazo Sobre La Legalización Del Aborto. Cuestionario Aplicado En La Ciudad de Puebla, México." *Boletín Mexicano de Derecho Comparado* 40, no. 120 (2007).

Rancharan, B. G. "Peoples' Rights and Minorities' Rights." *Nordic Journal of International Law* 56, no. 1 (1987).

Rao, Mohan. *From Population Control to Reproductive Health: Malthusian Arithmetic*. SAGE, 2004.

Rawls, John. "Justice as Fairness: Political Not Metaphysical." *Philosophy & Public Affairs* 14, no. 3 (1985).

———. *Political Liberalism*. Columbia University Press, 1993.

Raz, Joseph. "Facing Diversity: The Case of Epistemic Abstinence." *Philosophy and Public Affairs* 19, no. 1 (1990).

———. "National Self-Determination." *The Journal of Philosophy* LXXXVII, no. 9 (1990).

Reed, James. "The Birth Control Movement Before Roe v. Wade." *Journal of Policy History* 7, no. 1 (1995).

Régnier-Loilier, Arnaud, and Daniele Vignoli. "Fertility Intentions and Obstacles to Their Realization in France and Italy." *Population* 66, no. 2 (2011).

Reisman, W Michael. "International Law and the Inner Worlds of Others." *Saint Thomas Law Review* 25, no. 9 (1996).

———. "Sovereignty and Human Rights in Contemporary International Law." *American Journal of International Law* 84, no. 4 (1990).

Richey, Lisa. "Family Planning and the Politics of Population in Tanzania : International to Local Discourse." *The Journal of Modern African Studies* 37, no. 3 (1999).

Roberts, Anthea. *Is International Law International?* Oxford University Press, 2017.

Robinson, Nehemiah. *The Universal Declaration of Human Rights: Its Origins, Significance, Application and Interpretation*. Institute of Jewish Affairs, 1958.

Rodríguez Alcocer, Adrián, and Marcelo Bartolini Esparza. "Las Recomendaciones de Los Organismos Internacionales Como Herramientas de Presión Política." *Derecho Público Iberiamericano*, no. 5 (2014): 231–49.

Rosas, Allan. "Internal Self-Determination." In *Modern Law of Self-Determination*, edited by Christian Tomuschat. Martinus Nijhoff, 1993.

Roth, Hans Ingvar. *P. C. Chang and the Universal Declaration of Human Rights*. University of Pennsylvania Press, 2018.

Ruiz-Chiriboga, Oswaldo. "Indigenous Corporal Punishment in Ecuador and the Prohibition of Torture and Il Treatment." *American University International Law Review* 28, no. 5 (2013): 975–1016.

Rüsen, Jörn. "Human Rights from the Perspective of a Universal History." In *Human Rights and Cultural Diversity: Europe, Arabic-Islam World, Africa, China*, edited by Wolfgang Schmale. Kelp Publishing, 1993.

Sajó, András. "Introduction." In *Human Rights with Modesty: The Problem of Universalism*, edited by András Sajó. Martinus Nijhoff, 2004.

Samnøy, Åshild. *Human Rights as International Consensus: Making the Universal Declaration of Human Rights 1945–1948*. Michelsen Institute, 1993.

———. "The Origins of the Universal Declaration of Human Rights." In *The Universal Declaration of Human Rights: A Common Standard of Achievement*, edited by Asbjørn Eide and Gudmundur Alfredsson. Martinus Nijhoff, 1999.

Sánchez, Alisa. "Population Discourse, Family Planning Policies, and Development in Colombia 1960–1969." In *Reproductive Justice and Sexual Rights: Transnational Perspectives*, edited by Tanya Saroj Bakhru. Routledge, 2019.

Sandel, Michael J. *Democracy's Discontent: America in Search of a Public Philosophy*. Harvard University Press, 1996.

———. *Justice: What's the Right Thing to Do?* New York: Farrar. Straus and Giroux, 2010.

———. *Liberalism and the Limits of Justice*. New York: Cambridge University Press, 1982.

———. "The Procedural Republic and the Unencumbered Self." *Political Theory* 12, no. 1 (1984): 81–96.

Sanger, Margaret. *The Pivot of Civilization*, 1922. http://www.gutenberg.org/files/1689/1689-h/1689-h.htm#link2HCH0004.

Saul, Ben, Jacqueline Mowbray, and Irene Baghoomians. "Resistance to Regional Human Rights Cooperation in the Asia-Pacific: Demythologizing Regional Exceptionalism by Learning from the Americas, Europe and Africa." In *Human Rights in the Asia-Pacific Region: Towards Institution Building*, edited by Hitoshi Nasu and Ben Saul. Routledge, 2011.

Savage, Mark. "The Law of Abortion in the Union of Soviet Socialist Republics and the People's Republic of China: Women's Rights in Two Socialist Countries." *Stanford Law Review* 40, no. 4 (1988).

Schabas, William A. *The Universal Declaration of Human Rights the Travaux Préparatoires: Volume 3*. Cambridge University Press, 2013.

Schachter, Oscar. "The Invisible College of International Lawyers." *Northwestern University Law Review* 72 (1977).

Scheinin, Martin. "Article 18." In *The Universal Declaration of Human Rights: A Commentary*, edited by Asbjørn Eide, Gudmundur Alfredsson, Goran Melander, Allan Rosas, and Lars Adam Rehof. Scandinavian University Press, 1993.

———. "The Proposed Optional Protocol to the Covenant on Economic, Social and Cultural Rights: A Blueprint for UN Human Rights Treaty Body Reform Without Amending the Existing Treaties." *Human Rights Law Review* 6, no. 1 (2006).

Schlütter, Birgit. "Aspects of Human Rights Interpretation by the UN Treaty Bodies." In *UN Human Rights Treaty Bodies: Law and Legitimacy*, edited by Helen Keller and Geir Ulfstein. Cambridge University Press, 2012.

Schmale, Wolfgang. "Human Rights in the Intercultural Perspective and the Reorganization of the International Debate." In *Human Rights and Cultural Diversity: Europe, Arabic-Islam World, Africa, China*, edited by Wolfgang Schmale. Kelp Publishing, 1993.

Schoen, Johanna. *Choice and Coercion: Birth Control, Sterilization, and Abortion in Public Health and Welfare*. The University of North Carolina Press, 2005.

Schulte-Tenckhoff, Isabelle. "Treaties, Peoplehood, and Self-Determination: Understanding the Language of Indigenous Rights." In *Indigenous Rights in the Age of the UN Declaration*, edited by Elvira Pulitano. Cambridge University Press, 2012.

———. "Treaties, Peoplehood, and Self-Determination: Understanding the Language of Indigenous Rights." In *Indigenous Rights in the Age of the UN Declaration*, edited by Elena Pulitano. Cambridge University Press, 2012.

Schutter, Olivier de. "Universalité Des Droits de l'homme et Mondialisation: La Question Des 'Valeurs Asiatiques.'" In *Droits Humains et Valeurs Asiatiques: Un Dialogue Possible?*, edited by Thierry Marrès and Paul Servais. Bruylant, 2002.

Sellers, Mortimer. "Universal Human Rights in the Law of the United States." In *The Universalism of Human Rights*, edited by Rainer Arnold. Springer, 2013.
Sen, Amartya. *Human Rights and Asian Values*. Carnegie Council on Ethics and International Affairs, 1997.
Sepúlveda, Magdalena. *The Nature of the Obligations under the International Covenant on Economic, Social and Cultural Rights*. Intersentia, 2003.
Shany, Yuval. "Toward a General Margin of Appreciation Doctrine in International Law?" *European Journal of International Law* 16, no. 5 (2005): 907–40. https://doi.org/10.1093/ejil/chi149.
Shaw, Malcolm. "Peoples, Territorialism and Boundaries." *European Journal of International Law* 3 (1997).
Sherwood, Harriet. "Oxford Students Call for Professor's Removal over Alleged Homophobia." *The Guardian*, 2019. https://www.theguardian.com/education/2019/jan/09/oxford-students-call-for-professors-removal-over-alleged-homophobia.
Shweder, Richard. "Moral Realism without the Ethnocentrism: Is It Just a List of Empty Truisms?" In *Human Rights with Modesty: The Problem of Universalism*, edited by András Sajó. Leiden: Martinus Nijhoff, 2004.
Shweder, Richard A. "'What About Female Genital Mutilation?' And Why Understanding Culture Matters in the First Place." In *Engaging Cultural Differences: The Multicultural Challenge in Liberal Democracies*, edited by Martha Minow, Richard A Shweder, and Hazel Rose Markus. SAGE, 2020.
Shweder, Richard A., Jacqueline Goodnow, Giyoo Hatano, Robert LeVine, Hazel Rose Markus, and Peggy Miller. "The Cultural Psychology of Development: One Mind, Many Mentalities." In *Handbook of Child Psychology Volume 1: Theoretical Models of Human Development*, edited by Richard Lerner, 6th ed. John Wiley & Sons, Inc., 2006.
Shweder, Richard, Nancy Much, Manamohan Mahapatra, and Lawrence Park. "The 'Big Three' of Morality (Autonomy, Community, Divinity) and the 'Big Three' Explanations of Suffering." In *Morality and Health*, edited by Paul Rozin and Allan Brandt. Routledge, 1997.
Shweder, Richard, Nancy Much, Manamohan Nahapatra, and Lawrence Park. "The 'Big Three' of Morality (Autonomy, Community, Divinity) and the 'Big Three' Explanations of Suffering." In *Morality and Health*, edited by Paul Rozin and Allan Brandt. Routledge, 1997.
Silliman, Jael. "Making the Connections: Women's Health and Environmental Justice." *Race, Gender & Class* 5, no. 1 (1997).
Silverman, Jay G., Michele R. Decker, Heather L. McCauley, and Jhumka Gupta. "Male Perpetration of Intimate Partner Violence and Involvement in Abortions and Abortion-Related Conflict." *American Journal of Public Health* 100, no. 8 (2010).
Silvia, Adam M. "Modern Mothers for Third World Nations: Population Control, Western Medical Imperialism, and Cold War Politics in Haiti." *Social History of Medicine* 27, no. 2 (2014): 260–80. https://doi.org/10.1093/shm/hku004.
Simmons, Beth. *Mobilizing for Human Rights: International Law in Domestic Politics*. Cambridge University Press, 2012.
Simpson, Gerry. "The Diffusion of Sovereignty: Self-Determination in the Post-Colonial Age." *Stanford Journal of International Law* 32, no. 2 (1996).

Skogly, Sigrun. "Article 2." In *The Universal Declaration of Human Rights: A Common Standard of Achievement*, edited by Asbjørn Eide and Gudmundur Alfredsson. Martinus Nijhoff, 1999.

Soares Pereira, Luiza Leão, and Niccolò Ridi. "Mapping the 'Invisible College of International Lawyers' through Obituaries." *Leiden Journal of International Law* 34 (2021).

Spano, Robert. "Universality or Diversity of Human Rights?: Strasbourg in the Age of Subsidiarity." *Human Rights Law Review* 14, no. 3 (2014). https://doi.org/10.1093/hrlr/ngu021.

Spielmann, Dean. "Allowing the Right Margin: The European Court of Human Rights and The National Margin of Appreciation Doctrine: Waiver or Subsidiarity of European Review?" *Cambridge Yearbook of European Legal Studies* 14, no. 1 (2017).

Staden, Andreas Von. "The Democratic Legitimacy of Judicial Review Beyond the State: Normative Subsidiarity and Judicial Standards of Review." *International Journal of Constitutional Law* 10, no. 4 (2012): 1023–49. https://doi.org/10.1093/icon/mos032.

Stark, Rodney. "Secularization, R.I.P." *Sociology of Religion* 60, no. 3 (1999): 249–73.

Stepan, Nancy Leys. *The Hour of Eugenics: Race, Gender, and Nation in Latin America*. Cornell University Press, 1991.

Stith, Richard. "If Dorothy Had Not Had Toto to Pull Back the Wizard's Curtain: The Fabrication of Human Rights as a World Religion." *Valparaiso University Law Review* 44 (2010).

Suárez-Orozco, Marcelo. "Everything You Ever Wanted to Know about Assimilation but Were Afraid to Ask." In *Engaging Cultural Differences: The Multicultural Challenge in Liberal Democracies*, edited by Richard A. Shweder, Martha Minow, and Hazel Rose Markus. Russell Sage Foundation, 2002.

Summers, James. *Peoples and International Law*. 2nd ed. Martinus Nijhoff, 2013.

———. "The Internal and External Aspects of Self-Determination Reconsidered." In *Statehood and Self-Determination: Reconciling Tradition and Modernity in International Law*, edited by Duncan French. Cambridge University Press, 2013.

Swigart, Leigh. "National Judge: Some Reflections on Diversity in International Courts and Tribunals." *McGeorge Law Review* 42, no. 1 (2017).

Tamir, Yael. "The Right to National Self-Determination." *Social Research* 58, no. 3 (1991).

Taylor, Charles. "Conditions of an Unforced Consensus on Human Rights." In *The East Asian Challenge for Human Rights*, edited by Joanne Bauer and Daniel Bell. Cambridge University Press, 1999.

———. *Philosophy and the Human Sciences: Philosophical Papers 2*. Cambridge, United Kingdom: Cambridge University Press, 1985.

———. *Sources of the Self: The Making of the Modern Identity*. New York: Cambridge University Press, 1989.

Taylor, Paul. *A Commentary on the International Covenant on Civil and Political Rights: The UN Human Rights Committee's Monitoring of ICCPR Rights*. Cambridge University Press, 2020.

Teerawichitchainan, Bussarawan, and Sajeda Amin. "The Role of Abortion in the Last Stage of Fertility Decline in Vietnam." *International Perspectives on Sexual and Reproductive Health* 36, no. 2 (2010).

Tesón, Fernando R. "International Human Rights and Cultural Relativism." *Virginia Journal of International Law* 25, no. 4 (n.d.).

Tharoor, Shashi. "The Universality of Human Rigths and Their Relevance to Developing Countries." *Nordic Journal of International Law* 59, no. 1 (1990).

"The Independence of UN Human Rights Treaty Body Members," Geneva Academy of International Humanitarian Law and Human Rights, 2012. https://www.geneva-academy.ch/joomlatools-files/docman-files/The Independence of UN Human Rights Treaty Body MembersGenevaAcademGeneva (1).pdf.

Thornberry, Patrick. "Self-Determination, Minorities, Human Rights: A Review of International Instruments." *The International and Comparative Law Quarterly* 38, no. 4 (1989).

———. "The Democratic or Internal Aspect of Self-Determination with Some Remarks on Federalism." In *Modern Law of Self-Determination*, edited by Christian Tomuschat. Martinus Nijhoff, 1993.

Tobin, Kathleen. *Politics and Population Control: A Documentary History*. Greenwood, 2004.

Tocqueville, Alexis de. *Democracy in America*. 2nd ed. Chicago University Press, 2002.

Todd, W. Murray. "Population Policy: Is It a Question of Voluntarism or Coercion?" *Boston College Environmental Affairs Law Review* I, no. 4 (1972).

Tolstykh, Vladislav. "Three Ideas of Self-Determination in International Law and the Reunification of Crimea with Russia." *Heidelberg Journal of International Law* 75 (2015).

Tomuschat, Christian. "Self-Determination in a Post-Colonial World." In *Modern Law of Self-Determination*, edited by Christian Tomuschat. Martinus Nijhoff, 1993.

Trifunovska, Snezana. "One Theme in Two Variations—Self Determination for Minorities And Indigenous Peoples." *International Journal on Minority and Group Rights* 5, no. 2 (1997).

Tripkovic, Bosko. "A New Philosophy for the the Margin of Appreciation and European Consensus." *The Oxford Journal of Legal Studies* 42, no. 1 (2022).

Twining, William. *General Jurisprudence: Understanding Law from a Global Perspective*. Cambridge University Press, 2012.

Ulfstein, Geir. "Institutions and Competences." In *The Constitutionalization of International Law*, edited by Jan Klabbers and Geir Ulfstein. Oxford University Press, 2009.

———. "Law-Making by Human Rights Treaty Bodies." In *International Law-Making: Essays in Honour of Jan Klabbers*, edited by Rain Liivoja and Jarna Petman. Routledge, 2013.

UNESCO. *Human Rights: Comments and Interpretations*, 1948.

UNFPA. *Integrating Human Rights, Culture and Gender in Programming*. UNFPA, 2009. https://doi.org/10.1080/03064228208533447.

"Universality of Human Rights: Principles, Practice and Prospects." The Hague, 2008.

Verdoodt, Albert. *Naissance et Signification de La Déclaration Universel Des Droits de l'Homme*. Université Catholique de Lovain, 1964.

Vicziany, Marika. "Coercion in a Soft State: The Family-Planning Program of India: Part I: The Myth of Voluntarism." *Pacific Affairs* 55, no. 3 (1982).

Vignoli, Jorge Rodríguez. "La Fecundidad Alta En América Latina y El Caribe: Un Riesgo En Transición." In *La Fecundidad En América Latina: ¿Transición o Revolución?*, edited by CELADE and CEPAL. CELADE-CEPAL, 2003. https://repositorio.cepal.org/bitstream/handle/11362/6742/S043186_es.pdf?sequence=1&isAllowed=y.

Vigo, Rodolfo L. *El Iusnaturalismo Actual: De M. Villey a J. Finnis*. Mexico City: Fontanamara, 2007.

Vinjamuri, Leslie. "Human Rights Backlash." In *Human Rights Futures*, edited by Stephen Hopgood, Jack Snyder, and Leslie Vinjamuri. Cambridge University Press, 2017.

Viola, Francesco. *Derecho e Interpretación: Elementos de Teoría Hermenéutica Del Derecho*. Dykinson, 2000.

Vítolo, Alfredo. "El Valor de Las Opiniones Consultivas de La Corte Interamericana de Derechos Humanos a La Luz de Las OC-21/14 y 23/17." *Revista Jurídica Austral* 1, no. 1 (2020).

Vossen, Bas van der. "Self-Determination and Moral Variation." In *The Theory of Self-Determination*, edited by Fernando R Tesón. Cambridge University Press, 2016.

Walter, Christian, Antje von Ungern-Sternberg, and Kavus Abushov, eds. *Self-Determination and Secession in International Law*. Oxford University Press, 2014.

Walter, Stefanie. "The Backlash Against Globalization." *Annual Review of Political Science* 24 (2021).

Walzer, Michael. *Spheres of Justice*. Blackwell Publishing, 1983.

Warwick, Donald P. "Culture and the Management of Family Planning Programs." *Studies in Family Planning* 19, no. 1 (1988).

Webber, Grégoire, Paul Yowell, Richard Ekins, Maris Köpcke, Bradley W. Miller, and Francisco J. Urbina. *Legislated Rights: Securing Human Rights through Legislation*. Cambridge University Press, 2018.

Weigel, George. *The Cube and the Cathedral: Europe, America and Politics without God*. Basic Books, 2005.

Weiler, Joseph H. H. "Je Suis Achbita!" *EJIL: Talk!*, 2018. https://www.ejiltalk.org/je-suis-achbita/.

———. "Lautsi: A Reply." *International Journal of Constitutional Law* 11, no. 1 (2013).

Weller, Marc. *Escaping the Self-Determination Trap*. Martinus Nijhoff, 2008.

———. "Self-Determination of Indigenous Peoples." In *The UN Declaration on the Rights of Indigenous Peoples: A Commentary*, edited by Jessie Hohmann and Marc Weller. Oxford University Press, 2018.

Wellings, Kaye, Martine Collumbien, Emma Slaymaker, Susheela Singh, Zoé Hodges, Dhaval Patel, and Nathalie Bajos. "Sexual Behaviour in Context: A Global Perspective." *Lancet*, 2006. https://doi.org/10.1016/S0140-6736(06)69479-8.

Welti Chanes, Carlos. "El Consejo Nacional de Población a 40 Años de Una Política Explícita de Población En México." *Papeles de Población* 20, no. 81 (2014).

Westoff, Charles. "International Population Policy." *International Population Policy* 32, no. 4 (1995).

Wheatley, Steven. "Democracy in International Law: A European Perspective." *International and Comparative Law Quarterly* 51 (2002).

———. *The Democratic Legitimacy of International Law*. Hart Publishing, 2010.

Widmer, Eric D., Judith Treas, and Robert Newcomb. "Attitudes Toward Nonmarital Sex in 24 Countries." *The Journal of Sex Research* 35, no. 4 (1998).

Wiessner, Siegfried. "Indigenous Self-Determination, Culture, and Land: A Reassessment in Light of the 2007 UN Declaration on the Rights of Indigenous Peoples." In *Indigenous*

Rights in the Age of the UN Declaration, edited by Elvira Pulitano. Cambridge University Press, 2012.

Wilson, Kate, Sandra García, Claudia Díaz Olavarrieta, Aremis Villalobos-Hernández, and Jorge Valencia. "Public Opinion on Abortion in Mexico City after the Landmark Reform." *Studies in Family Planning* 42, no. 3 (2011).

Wolfrum, Rüdiger. "Purposes and Principles." In *The Charter of the United Nations: A Commentary, Volume I*, edited by Bruno Simma, Daniel-Erasmus Khan, Georg Nolte, Andreas Paulus, and Nikolai Wessendorf, 3rd ed. Oxford University Press, n.d.

Xanthaki, Alexandra. *Indigenous Rights and United Nations Standards: Self-Determination, Culture and Land*. Cambridge University Press, 2007.

Yancey, George, Sam Reimer, and Jake O'Connell. "How Academics View Conservative Protestants." *Sociology of Religion* 76, no. 3 (2015).

Yasuaki, Onuma. "Toward an Intercivilizational Approach to Human Rights." In *The East Asian Challenge for Human Rights*, edited by Joanna Bauer and Daniel Bell. Cambridge University Press, 1999.

Zorkin, Valery. "The Extent of Flexibility." *Rossiskaya Gazeta*, 2010.

Zucca, Lorenzo. "Lautsi: A Commentary on a Decision by the ECtHR Grand Chamber." *International Journal of Constitutional Law* 11, no. 1 (2013).

Zwart, Tom. "Balancing Yin and Yang in the International Human Rights Debate." Collected Papers of the Sixth Beijing Forum on Human Rights. Beijing, 2013. http://www.chinahumanrights.org/html/2014/PAPERS_1102/1096.html.

———. "More Human Rights than Court: Why the Legitimacy of the European Court of Human Rights Is in Need of Repair and How It Can Be Done." In *The European Court of Human Rights and Its Discontents*, edited by Spyridon Flogaitis, Tom Zwart, and Julie Fraser. Edward Elgar Publishing Limited, 2013.

Documents of International Organizations:

Aureliu Cristescu (Special rapporteur of the Sub-Commission on Prevention of Discrimination), The Right to Self-Determination: Historical and Current Development on the Basis of the United Nations Instruments, E/CN.4/Sub.2/404/Rev. 1 (1981).

"Backlash against Women's Rights Progress Hurts Us All—Zeid." *OHCHR*, 2017. https://www.ohchr.org/EN/NewsEvents/Pages/DisplayNews.aspx?NewsID=21305.

"Beijing Declaration and Platform for Action." Beijing, 1995. https://www.un.org/womenwatch/daw/beijing/platform/index.html.

CAT, Concluding observations on the seventh periodic report of Peru (18 December 2018) CAT/C/PER/CO/7.

CAT, Concluding observations on the seventh periodic report of Poland (29 August 2019) CAT/C/POL/CO/7.

Catherine d'Arcangues, "Sexual and reproductive health and human rights" (15 November 2010) <https://www.ohchr.org/Documents/HRBodies/CESCR/Discussions/2010/CatherineArcangues.pdf> (consulted on January 6, 2021)

CEDAW, Concluding observations on the combined seventh and eighth periodic reports of Hungary, adopted by the Committee at its fifty-fourth session (11 February–1 March 2013) CEDAW/C/HUN/CO/7-8, 26 March 2013.

CEDAW, Concluding observations on the fifth periodic report of Pakistan (10 March 2020) CEDAW/C/PAK/CO/5.

CEDAW, Concluding observations on the fourth periodic report of Côte d'Ivoire (30 July 2019) CEDAW/C/CIV/CO/4.

CEDAW, Concluding observations on the sixth periodic report of Eritrea (10 March 2020) CEDAW/C/ERI/CO/6.

CEDAW, Concluding observations on the sixth periodic report of Zimbabwe (10 March 2020) CEDAW/C/ZWE/CO/6.

CEDAW, Concluding observations on the third periodic report of Afghanistan (10 March 2020) CEDAW/C/AFG/CO/3.

CEDAW, General Recommendation No. 19: Violence against women, eleventh session (1992)

CEDAW, General Recommendation No. 21: Equality in marriage and family relations, thirteenth session (1994).

CEDAW, General Recommendation No. 28 on the core obligations of States parties under article 2 of the Convention on the Elimination of All Forms of Discrimination against Women (16 December 2010) CEDAW/C/GC/28.

CEDAW, General Recommendation No. 30 on women in conflict prevention, conflict and post-conflict situations (1 November 2013) CEDAW/C/GC/30.

CEDAW, General Recommendation No. 34 (2016) on the rights of rural women (7 March 2016) CEDAW/C/GC/34.

CEDAW, General Recommendation No. 35 on gender based violence against women, updating general recommendation No. 19 (26 July 2017) CEDAW/C/GC/35.

CEDAW, General Recommendation No. 37 (2018) on the gender-related dimensions of disaster risk reduction in the context of climate change (13 March 2018) CEDAW/C/GC/37.

CEDAW, General Recommendation No. 38 (2020) on trafficking in women and girls in the context of global migration, CEDAW/C/GC/38 (6 November 2020).

CEDAW, General Recommendation on article 16 of the Convention on the Elimination of All Forms of Discrimination against Women (Economic consequences of marriage, family relations and their dissolution), CEDAW/C/GC/29 (30 October 2013).

CEDAW, Summary record of the 884th meeting, forty-third session, CEDAW/C/SR.884, (27 May 2009).

CERD, Concluding observations of the Committee on the Elimination of Racial Discrimination Mexico, Sixty-eighth session20 February-10 March 2006, CERD/C/MEX/CO/15 (4 April 2006).

CERD, General Recommendation No. XXI on the right to self-determination forty-eight session (1996).

CERD, Sixty-eighth session: Summary record of the 1731st meeting, Held at the Palais Wilson, Geneva, 20 February 2006, CERD/C/SR.1731 (24 February 2006).

CESCR, Concluding observations of the Committee on Economic, Social and Cultural Rights on Sri Lanka, 9 December 2010, E/C.12/LKA/CO/2-4.

CESCR, Concluding observations of the Committee on Economic, Social and Cultural Rights on Uruguay, 1 December 2010, E/C.12/URY/CO/3-4.
CESCR, Concluding observations on the combined fifth and sixth periodic reports of the Philippines, 26 October 2016, E/C.12/PHL/CO/5-6.
CESCR, Concluding observations on the combined fifth and sixth periodic reports of Mexico (17 April 2018) E/C.12/MEX/CO/5-6.
CESCR, Concluding observations on the combined second to fifth periodic reports of Kenya, 6 April 2016, E/C.12/KEN/CO/2-5.
CESCR, Concluding observations on the combined second to fourth periodic reports of Egypt, 13 December 2013, E/C.12/EGY/CO/2-4.
CESCR, Concluding observations on the combined third, fourth and fifth periodic reports of El Salvador, 19 June 2014, E/C.12/SLV/CO/3-5.
CESCR, Concluding observations on the fifth periodic report of Italy, 28 October 2015, E/C.12/ITA/CO/5.
CESCR, Concluding observations on the fifth periodic report of Mauritius, 5 April 2019, E/C.12/MUS/CO/5.
CESCR, Concluding observations on the fourth periodic report of Argentina, 1 November 2018, E/C.12/ARG/CO/4.
CESCR, Concluding observations on the fourth periodic report of Cameroon, 25 March 2019, E/C.12/CMR/CO/4.
CESCR, Concluding observations on the fourth periodic report of Chile, 7 July 2015, E/C.12/CHL/CO/4.
CESCR, Concluding observations on the fourth periodic report of Ecuador, 14 November 2019, E/C.12/ECU/CO/4.
CESCR, Concluding observations on the fourth periodic report of Morocco, 22 October 2015, E/C.12/MAR/CO/4.
CESCR, Concluding observations on the fourth periodic report of Paraguay, 20 March 2015, E/C.12/PRY/CO/4.
CESCR, Concluding observations on the fourth periodic report of the Dominican Republic, 21 October 2016, E/C.12/DOM/CO/4.
CESCR, Concluding observations on the initial report of Burkina Faso, 12 July 2016, E/C.12/BFA/CO/1.
CESCR, Concluding observations on the initial report of Burundi, 16 October 2015, E/C.12/BDI/CO/1.
CESCR, Concluding observations on the initial report of Guinea, 30 March 2020, E/C.12/GIN/CO/1.
CESCR, Concluding observations on the initial report of Pakistan, 20 July 2017, E/C.12/PAK/CO/1.
CESCR, Concluding observations on the initial report of South Africa, 29 November 2018, E/C.12/ZAF/CO/1.
CESCR, Concluding observations on the initial report of Uganda, 8 July 2015, E/C.12/UGA/CO/1.

CESCR, Concluding observations on the second periodic report of Honduras, 11 July 2016, E/C.12/HND/CO/2.

CESCR, Concluding observations on the second periodic report of the Islamic Republic of Iran, adopted by the Committee at its fiftieth session, 10 June 2013, E/C.12/IRN/CO/2.

CESCR, Concluding observations on the second to fourth periodic report of Rwanda, adopted by the Committee at its fiftieth session, 10 June 2013, E/C.12/RWA/CO/2-4.

CESCR, Concluding observations on the sixth periodic report of Canada, 23 March 2016, E/C.12/CAN/CO/6.

CESCR, Concluding observations on the sixth periodic report of Poland, 26 October 2016, E/C.12/POL/CO/6.

CESCR, Concluding observations on the sixth periodic report of Spain, 25 April 2018, E/C.12/ESP/CO/6.

CESCR, Concluding observations on the third periodic report of Guatemala, 9 December 2014, E/C.12/GTM/CO/3.

CESCR, Concluding observations on the third periodic report of Ireland (8 July 2015) E/C.12/IRL/CO/3.

CESCR, Concluding observations on the third periodic report of Nepal, 12 December 2014, E/C.12/NPL/CO/3.

CESCR, Concluding observations on the third periodic report of Senegal, 13 November 2019, E/C.12/SEN/CO/3.

CESCR, Concluding observations on the third periodic report of the Bolivarian Republic of Venezuela, 7 July 2015, E/C.12/VEN/CO/3.

CESCR, General Comment 22 (2016) on the right to sexual and reproductive health (article 12 of the International Covenant on Economic, Social and Cultural Rights), 2 May 2016, E/C.12/GC/22.

CESCR, General Comment No. 14 (2000) The right to the highest attainable standard of health (article 12 of the International Covenant on Economic, Social and Cultural Rights), 11 August 2000, E/C.12/2000/4.

CESCR, General Comment No. 20 Non-discrimination in economic, social and cultural rights (art. 2, para. 2, of the International Covenant on Economic, Social and Cultural Right), 2 July 2009, E/C.12/GC/20.

"Committee on the Elimination of Discrimination against Women Reviews Report of Mexico." UN Human Rights Office of the High Commissioner, 2018. https://www.ohchr.org/EN/NewsEvents/Pages/DisplayNews.aspx?NewsID=23344.

Council of Europe/ECHR, The admissibility of an application (2015) Human Rights Education for Legal Professionals <https://www.echr.coe.int/Documents/COURtalks_Inad_Talk_ENG.PDF> (consulted on October 3, 2020)

CRC, Concluding observations on the combined fifth and sixth periodic reports of Rwanda (28 February 2020) CRC/C/RWA/CO/5-6.

CRC, Concluding observations on the combined third to fifth periodic reports of Kenya (21 March 2016) CRC/C/KEN/CO/3-5.

CRC, Concluding observations on the fifth periodic report of Pakistan (11 July 2016) CRC/C/PAK/CO/5.

CRC, Concluding observations on the second periodic report of South Africa, (27 October 2016) CRC/C/ZAF/CO/2.

CRC, General comment No. 15 (2013) on the right of the child to the enjoyment of the highest attainable standard of health (art. 24), CRC/C/GC/15 (17 April 2013).

CRPD, General comment No. 3 (2016) on women and girls with disabilities (25 November 2016) CRPD/C/GC/3.

CSCE Document of the Copenhagen Meeting of the Conference on the Human Dimension (1990) <https://www.osce.org/files/f/documents/9/c/14304.pdf> (consulted on January 14, 2019)

CSCE Document of the Copenhagen Meeting of the Conference on the Human Dimension (1990).

Dasgupta ANZ, Ueffing P and Kantorová V, 'Sexual Activity by Marital Status and Age: A Comparative Perspective' (2018) 2017/11 <https://www.un.org/en/development/desa/population/publications/pdf/technical/TP2017-11.pdf> (consulted on May 8, 2021)

"Day of General Discussion on 'the Right to Sexual and Reproductive Health', 15 November 2010." UNHCHR, n.d. https://www.ohchr.org/EN/HRBodies/CESCR/Pages/Discussion2010.aspx.

Declaration on the Granting of Independence to Colonial Countries and Peoples (1960) <https://www.ohchr.org/EN/ProfessionalInterest/Pages/Independence.aspx> (consulted on January 7, 2019)

European Parliament, Fact Sheets on the European Union: The principle of subsidiarity (2020) <https://www.europarl.europa.eu/factsheets/en/sheet/7/the-principle-of-subsidiarity>. (consulted on February 10, 2019)

Final Declaration of the Regional Meeting for Asia of the World Conference on Human Rights (1993).

Francesco Capotori (Special Rapporteur of the UN Sub-Commission on Prevention of Discrimination and Protection of Minorities), Study on the Rights of Persons belonging to Ethnic, Religious and Linguistic Minorities, E/CN.4/Sub.2/384/Rev.1 (1977).

General Assembly Resolution 47/135, UN Declaration on the Rights of Persons Belonging to National or Ethnic, Religious and Linguistic Minorities (18 December 1992).

General Assembly resolution A/C.3/376 (29 November 1948) https://undocs.org/A/C.3/376.

General Assembly, Report of the Human Rights Committee, General Assembly Official Records, 39th session, A/39/40 (1984).

General Assembly, Report of the Human Rights Committee, General Assembly Official Records, fiftieth session, A/50/40 (3 October 1995).

General Assembly, Resolution 2542 (XXIV) Declaration on Social Progress and Development (11 December 1969) <https://www.ohchr.org/en/professionalinterest/pages/progressanddevelopment.aspx> (consulted on March 4, 2019)

General Assembly, Resolution 2625(XXV), The Declaration on Principles of International law Concerning Friendly Relations and Co-operation among States in Accordance with the Charter of the United Nations (1970) <https://www.un.org/ruleoflaw/files/3dda1f104.pdf> (consulted on March 6, 2019)

"General Comment No. 36 on Article 6 of the International Covenant on Civil and Political Rights—Right to Life." OHCHR, n.d. https://www.ohchr.org/EN/HRBodies/CCPR/Pages/GC36-Article6Righttolife.aspx.

"Global Status Report on Violence Prevention 2014," World Health Organization, 2014. https://www.who.int/publications/i/item/9789241564793.

Héctor Gros Espiell (Special Rapporteur of the Sub-Commission on Prevention of Discrimination), The Right to Self-Determination: Implementation of United Nations Resolutions, E/CN.4/Sub.2/405/Rev.l (1980).

HRC, Concluding observations on Nigeria in the absence of its second periodic report (29 August 2019), CCPR/C/NGA/CO/2.

HRC, Concluding observations on the fifth periodic report of Senegal (11 December 2019) CCPR/C/SEN/CO/5.

HRC, Concluding observations on the initial report of Pakistan (23 August 2017) CCPR/C/PAK/CO/1.

HRC, Concluding observations on the initial reports of Ghana (9 August 2016) CCPR/C/GHA/CO/1.

HRC, Concluding observations on the seventh periodic report of El Salvador (9 May 2018) CCPR/C/SLV/CO/7.

HRC, Concluding observations on the seventh periodic report of Ukraine, (22 August 2013) CCPR/C/UKR/CO/7

HRC, Concluding observations on the sixth periodic report of Mexico (4 December 2019) CCPR/C/MEX/CO/6.

HRC, Concluding observations on the sixth periodic report of Tunisia (24 April 2020) CCPR/C/TUN/CO/6.

HRC, Concluding observations on the third periodic report of the Central African Republic (30 April 2020) CCPR/C/CAF/CO/3.

HRC, General Comment No 12: Article 1 (Right to Self-Determination), twenty-first session (1984).

HRC, General comment No. 16: Article 17 (Right to privacy), thirty-second session (1988).

HRC, General comment No. 20: Article 7 (Prohibition of torture, or other cruel, inhuman or degrading treatment or punishment), forty-fourth session (1992).

HRC, General Comment No. 23 on article 27: Rights of minorities, CCPR/C/21/Rev.1/Add.5 (1994).

HRC, General Comment No. 25: The right to participate in public affairs, voting rights and the right of equal access to public services (article 25), CCPR/C/21/Rev.1/Add.7 (1996).

HRC, Summary record of the 3175th meeting (114th session) CCPR/C/SR.3175 (13 July 2015).

HRC, Summary record of the 3653rd meeting 127th session (23 October 2019) CCPR/C/SR.3653.

"Human Rights Committee Discusses the Report of Canada." OHCHR, 2015. https://www.ohchr.org/EN/NewsEvents/Pages/DisplayNews.aspx?NewsID=16215&LangID=E.

Human Rights Commission, Conscientious objection to military service (1989/59).

Human Rights Committee, General Comment No. 22: Article 18 (Freedom of Thought, Conscience or Religion), (CCPR/C/21/Rev.1/Add.4).

"Human Rights Council Adopts the Universal Periodic Review Outcomes of Mexico, Mauritius, Jordan and Malaysia." Human Rights Council, 2019. https://www.ohchr.org/SP/HRBodies/HRC/Pages/NewsDetail.aspx?NewsID=24338&LangID=S.

Human Rights Council, Resolution 12/21 (12 October 2009) A/HRC/RES/12/21.

Human Rights Council, Resolution 16/3 (8 April 2011) A/HRC/RES/16/3.

Human Rights Council, Resolution 19/20 The Role of Governance in the Promotion and Protection of Human Rights, A/HRC/19/L.26 (19 March 2012).

Human Rights Council, Study of the Human Rights Council Advisory Committee on promoting human rights and fundamental freedoms through a better understanding of traditional values of humankind (6 December 2012) A/HRC/22/71

IACoHR, *Comunicado de Prensa No. 171/18. CIDH concluye su visita a Honduras y presenta sus Observaciones Preliminares* (3 August 2018) <https://www.oas.org/es/cidh/prensa/comunicados/2018/171.asp>. (consulted on October 4, 2019)

IACoHR, *Informe Anual 2018—Capítulo IV.B República Dominicana* (2018) <https://www.oas.org/es/cidh/docs/anual/2018/docs/IA2018cap.5RD-es.pdf>. (consulted on October 4, 2019)

IACoHR, *Violencia y discriminación contra mujeres, niñas y adolescentes: Buenas prácticas y desafíos en América Latina y en el Caribe*, OEA/Ser.L/V/II (14 November 2019).

IACoHR. *Anexo al Comunicado No. 011/18. Conclusiones y observaciones sobre la visita de trabajo de la Comisión Interamericana de Derechos Humanos a El Salvador* (29 January 2018) <http://www.oas.org/es/cidh/prensa/comunicados/2018/011.asp>. (consulted on October 4, 2019)

IACtHR, *Medidas cautelares respecto de El Salvador Asunto B* (29 May 2013).

ICL, Draft Articles on the Law of Treaties with commentaries 1966 <https://legal.un.org/ilc/texts/instruments/english/commentaries/1_1_1966.pdf> (consulted on May 7, 2019)

ILC, Draft conclusions on subsequent agreements and subsequent practice in relation to the interpretation of treaties (2018) A/73/10

ILC, Draft Conclusions on the Identification of Customary International law session (2018) A/73/10

ILC, Draft Conclusions on Identification and Legal Consequences of Peremptory Norms of General International Law (*ius cogens*), with commentaries (2022)

"Informe de La Conferencia Mundial de Población," 1975. https://repositorio.cepal.org/bitstream/handle/11362/21970/S7500346_es.pdf?sequence=2&isAllowed=y.

"Joint Statement on the Nairobi Summit," 2019. https://www.hhs.gov/about/agencies/oga/global-health-diplomacy/protecting-life-global-health-policy/joint-statement-on-the-nairobi-summit-on-the-icpd25.html.

Noveno informe periódico que los Estados Parte debían presentar en 2016, CEDAW/C/MEX/9 <https://tbinternet.ohchr.org/Treaties/CEDAW/Sharedpercent20Documents/MEX/INT_CEDAW_ADR_MEX_26125_S.pdf>. (consulted on March 23, 2021)

OHCHR, "Human Rights Treaty Bodies—Glossary of technical terms related to the treaty bodies" https://www.ohchr.org/EN/HRBodies/Pages/TBGlossary.aspx#cd>. (consulted on May 27, 2021)

OHCHR, "Human Rights Treaty Bodies" <https://www.ohchr.org/EN/HRBodies/Pages/TreatyBodies.aspx>. (consulted on May 27, 2021)

OHCHR, "The global backlash against human rights", Edited text of a lecture by Andrew Gilmour, United Nations Assistant Secretary-General for Human Rights (12 and 13 March 2018) <https://www.ohchr.org/EN/NewsEvents/Pages/DisplayNews.aspx?NewsID=23202&LangID=E>. (consulted on January 5, 2020)

OHCHR, Workshop on traditional values of humankind (13 December 2010) A/HRC/16/37.

OHCHR, Minority Rights: International Standards and Guidance for Implementation (2010) <https://www.ohchr.org/Documents/Publications/MinorityRights_en.pdf> (consulted on January 14, 2019)

OSCE, The Bolzano/Bozen Recommendations on National Minorities in Inter-State Relations & Explanatory Note (2008).

OSCE, The Lund Recommendations on the Effective Participation of National Minorities in Public Life & Explanatory Note (1999) <https://www.osce.org/files/f/documents/0/9/32240.pdf> (consulted on January 14, 2019)

Parliamentary Assembly of the Council of Europe, Resolution 1763 (2010) "The right to conscientious objection in lawful medical care", 35th sitting, 7 October 2010.

"Programme of Action of the International Conference on Population Development: 20th Anniversary Edition," 2014. https://www.unfpa.org/sites/default/files/pub-pdf/programme_of_action_Web ENGLISH.pdf.

"Recommendations for Implementation of World Population Plan of Action," 1984. https://www.unfpa.org/sites/default/files/event-pdf/Recommendations for implementation of World Population Plan of Action_1.pdf.

Regional Meeting for Latin America and the Caribbean for the World Conference on Human Rights (San José, 11 February 1993) <https://undocs.org/A/CONF.157/LACRM/15>. (consulted on January 23, 2021)

"Report of the Fourth World Conference on Women." Beijing, 1995. https://www.un.org/womenwatch/daw/beijing/pdf/Beijing full report E.pdf.

"Report of the International Conference on Population and Development." Cairo, 1995. https://documents-dds-ny.un.org/doc/UNDOC/GEN/N95/231/26/IMG/N9523126.pdf?OpenElement.

"Report of the World Conference of the United Nations Decade for Women: Equality, Development and Peace." Copenhagen, 1980. https://www.un.org/womenwatch/daw/beijing/otherconferences/Copenhagen/Copenhagen Full Optimized.pdf.

Report of the Regional Meeting for Africa of the World Conference on Human Rights (Tunis, 24 November 1992) <https://undocs.org/A/CONF.157/AFRM/14>. (consulted on January 3, 2020)

Report of the Third Committee, Draft International Covenants on Human Rights, tenth session, A/3077 (8 December 1955).

Special Rapporteur (Paul Hunt), The right of everyone to the enjoyment of the highest attainable standard of physical and mental health (16 February 2014) E/CN.4/2004/49.

Special rapporteur on cultural rights (Karima Bennouna), Report of the Special Rapporteur in the field of cultural rights (17 July 2017) A/72/155.

Special rapporteur on cultural rights (Karima Bennouna), Report of the Special Rapporteur in the field of cultural rights (16 January 2017) A/HRC/34/56.

Special rapporteur on cultural rights (Karima Bennouna), Report of the Special Rapporteur in the field of cultural rights (17 July 2017) A/72/155.
Special rapporteur on cultural rights (Karima Bennoune), "Universality, cultural diversity and cultural rights" (25 July 2018) A/73/227.
Special rapporteur on religious freedom (Abdelfattah Amor), Study on freedom of religion or belief and the status of women in the light of religion and traditions (24 April 2009) E/CN.4/2002/73/Add.2.
Special rapporteur on religious freedom (Ahmed Shaheed), Report of the Special Rapporteur on freedom of religion or belief (27 February 2020) A/HRC/43/48.
Special rapporteur on the right to development, Report of the Special Rapporteur on the Right to Development (2 August 2017) A/HRC/36/49.
Special rapporteur on the right to health (Anand Grover), Right of everyone to the enjoyment of the highest attainable standard of physical and mental health (3 August 2011) A/66/254.
Special rapporteur on the right to health (Paul Hunt), The right of everyone to the enjoyment of the highest attainable standard of physical and mental health (13 September 2006) A/61/338.
Special rapporteur on the right to privacy (Joseph Cannataci), Report of the Special Rapporteur on the right to privacy (24 November 2016) A/HRC/31/64.
Special rapporteur on the rights of persons with disabilities (Catalina Devandas), Sexual and reproductive health and rights of girls and young women with disabilities (14 July 2017) A/72/133.
Special rapporteur on violence against women (Dubravka Šimonović), Report of the Special Rapporteur on violence against women, its causes and consequences on online violence against women and girls from a human rights perspective, A/HRC/38/47 (18 June 2018).
Special rapporteur on violence against women (Dubravka Šimonović), A human rights-based approach to mistreatment and violence against women in reproductive health services with a focus on childbirth and obstetric violence (11 July 2019) A/74/137.
Special rapporteur on violence against women (Radhika Coomaraswamy), Cultural practices in the family that are violent towards women, E/CN.4/2002/83 (31 January 2002).
Special rapporteur on violence against women (Yakin Ertürk), Intersections between culture and violence against women, A/HRC/4/34 (17 January 2007).
"Trends in Contraceptive Use Worldwide 2015," 2015. https://www.un.org/en/development/desa/population/publications/pdf/family/trendsContraceptiveUse2015Report.pdf.
UN Declaration on the Rights of Indigenous Peoples (2007) <https://www.un.org/development/desa/indigenouspeoples/wp-content/uploads/sites/19/2018/11/UNDRIP_E_web.pdf> (consulted on January 16, 2019)
UN General Assembly, Plan of Action to Prevent Violent Extremism: Report of the Secretary-General (24 December 2015) A/70/674.
UN General Assembly, Resolution 41/120 Setting international standards in the field of human rights (December 1986).
UN General Assembly, Resolution 41/128 Declaration on the Right to Development (December 1986).

UN Population Division, 'What Would It Take to Accelerate Fertility Decline in the Least Developed Countries?' (2009) No. 2009/1 <http://www.upc.apgdm.org/en/content/what-would-it-take-accelerate-fertility-decline-least-developed-countries> (consulted on May 8, 2021)

UN Security Council, Resolution 2250 (2015), S/RES/2250 (9 December 2015).

UN Web TV, Consideration of Mexico—3653rd Meeting, 127th Session of Human Rights Committee (16 October 2019) <http://webtv.un.org/meetings-events/human-rights-treaty-bodies/human-rights-committee/127th-session/watch/consideration-of-mexico-3653rd-meeting-127th-session-of-human-rights-committee/6095478655001/?term=&sort=date&page=2>. (consulted on May 4, 2021)

UN Women, "UN organizations call for an end to forced, coercive and involuntary sterilization" (18 June 2014) <https://www.unwomen.org/en/news/stories/2014/6/joint-statement-on-forced-sterilizations>. (consulted on May 12, 2021)

UNFPA, "About Us" <https://www.unfpa.org/about-us>. Consulted on February 12, 2021.

UNFPA, "Indonesia Continues Commitment to Universal Access to Family Planning Services" (30 September 2020) <https://indonesia.unfpa.org/en/news/indonesia-continues-commitment-universal-access-family-planning-services>. (consulted on October 4, 2020)

UNFPA, "Nairobi Summit on ICPD25 ends with a clear path forward to transform the world for women and girls" (14 November 2019) <https://www.unfpa.org/press/nairobi-summit-icpd25-ends-clear-path-forward-transform-world-women-and-girls> (consulted on May 20, 2020)

UNFPA, *6 Billion: A Time for Choices* (1999).

UNFPA, *Against my will: Defying the practices that harm women and girls and undermine equality* (2020).

UNFPA, *From conflict and crisis to renewal: generations of change* (2010).

UNFPA, *Integrating Human Rights, Culture and Gender in Programming* (2009)

UNFPA, *Lives Together, Worlds Apart* (2000).

UNFPA, *Shelter from the Storm: A transformative agenda for women and girls in a crisis-prone world* (2015).

UNFPA, *The Promise of Equality: Gender Equity, Reproductive Health, and the Millennium Development Goals* (2005).

Victoria Tauli-Corpuz (Special rapporteur on the rights of indigenous peoples), Rights of Indigenous Peoples, A/74/149 (17 July 2019).

Victoria Tauli-Corpuz, (Special rapporteur on the rights of indigenous peoples), Rigths of Indigenous Poeples, A/73/176 (17 July 2018).

WHO, "Accelerating uptake of voluntary, rights-based family planning in developing countries" (2018) WHO/RHR/18.26 <https://www.who.int/reproductivehealth/publications/family_planning/financing-family-planning/en/>. (consulted on September 3, 2020)

WHO, 'Global Status Report on Violence Prevention 2014' (2014) <https://www.who.int/publications/i/item/WHO-NMH-NVI-14.2>. (consulted on September 4, 2020)

Working group on discrimination against women in law and in practice, Report of the Working Group on the issue of discrimination against women in law and in practice, A/HRC/29/40 (2 April 2015).

Working Group on Minorities, Commentary of the Working Group on Minorities to the United Nations Declaration on the Rights of Persons belonging to National or Ethnic, Religious and Linguistic Minorities, E/CN.4/Sub.2/AC.5/2005/2 (2005).

Working Group on the issue of discrimination against women in law and in practice, Report of the Working Group on the issue of discrimination against women in law and in practice, A/HRC/29/40 (2 April 2015).

"World Fertility and Family Planning 2020," 2020. https://www.un.org/en/development/desa/population/publications/pdf/family/World_Fertility_and_Family_Planning_2020_Highlights.pdf.

Treaties:

African Charter on Human and People's Rights (1981) <https://au.int/en/treaties/african-charter-human-and-peoples-rights> consulted on May 13, 2019.

American Declaration of the Rights and Duties of Man (1948) <https://www.oas.org/dil/access_to_information_human_right_American_Declaration_of_the_Rights_and_Duties_of_Man.pdf>. Consulted on March 13, 2019.

Arab Charter of Human Rights (2004) <http://elearning.icrc.org/detention/es/story_content/external_files/Cartapercent20Arabepercent20depercent20Derechospercent20Humanospercent20(2004).pdf>. Consulted on February 3, 2020

ASEAN Human Rights Declaration (2013) <https://www.asean.org/storage/images/ASEAN_RTK_2014/6_AHRD_Booklet.pdf>. Consulted on February 3, 2020

Charter of Fundamental Rights of the European Union (2000/C 364/01)

Charter of Paris for a New Europe (1990) <https://www.osce.org/mc/39516> consulted on May 13, 2019

Convention against Torture and Other Cruel, Inhuman or Degrading Treatment or Punishment (1984) <https://www.ohchr.org/en/professionalinterest/pages/cat.aspx>. Consulted on June 8, 2020

Convention on the Elimination of all forms of Discrimination against Women (1979) <https://www.ohchr.org/documents/professionalinterest/cedaw.pdf>. Consulted on September 20, 2020.

Convention on the Rights of the Child (1980) <https://www.ohchr.org/en/professionalinterest/pages/crc.aspx>. Consulted on June 9, 2020.

European Charter of Local Self-Government (1985) <https://www.coe.int/en/web/conventions/full-list/-/conventions/treaty/122#:~:text=Thepercent20Charterpercent20commitspercent20thepercent20Parties,wherepercent20practicablepercent2Cpercent20inpercent20thepercent20constitution>. Consulted on May 11, 2021.

European Convention on Human Rights (1950) <https://www.echr.coe.int/documents/convention_eng.pdf>. Consulted on March 23, 2019.

Final Act of the Conference on Security and Co-operation in Europe (1975) <https://www.osce.org/files/f/documents/5/c/39501.pdf> consulted on May 13, 2019

Framework Convention for the Protection of National Minorities (1995) <https://www.coe.int/en/web/conventions/full-list/conventions/rms/090000168007cdac>. Consulted on May 17, 2019.

Indigenous and Tribal Peoples Convention, 1989 (No. 169) <https://www.ilo.org/dyn/normlex/en/f?p=NORMLEXPUB:12100:0::NO::P12100_ILO_CODE:C169>. Consulted on November 23, 2020.

International Covenant on Civil and Political Rights (1966), <https://www.ohchr.org/EN/ProfessionalInterest/Pages/CCPR.aspx>. Consulted on February 14, 2019

Rome Statute of the International Criminal Court (2002).

Protocol No. 15 amending the Convention on the Protection of Human Rights and Fundamental Freedoms (2013)

Protocol to the African Charter on Human and People's Rights on the Rights of Women in Africa (2003) <https://www.un.org/en/africa/osaa/pdf/au/protocol_rights_women_africa_2003.pdf>. Consulted on May 23, 2020.

Statute of the International Court of Justice (1946)

Treaty of Lisbon amending the Treaty on European Union and the Treaty establishing the European Community (2007)

Treaty on the European Union (1992)

United Nations Charter (1945) <https://www.un.org/en/sections/un-charter/chapter-i/index.html> consulted on December 10, 2019.

Universal Declaration of Human Rights (1948) <https://www.un.org/en/universal-declaration-human-rights/>. Consulted on February 23, 2019

Vienna Convention on the Law of Treaties (1969)

Vienna Declaration and Programme of Action, World Conference on Human Rights in Vienna (25 June 1993) <https://www.ohchr.org/en/professionalinterest/pages/vienna.aspx>. Consulted on June 14, 2020

Case-law

African Commission on Human Rights, *Katangese Peoples' Congress v. Zaire*, Comm. No. 75/92 (1995)

CAT, *Mayantie Jasmina Soumahoro v. the Netherlands* (3 May 2019) CAT/C/66/D/757/2016

CAT, *Y. H. G. v. Australia* (14 November 2013) CAT/C/51/D/434/2010.

CEDAW, *Andrea Szijjarto v. Hungary* (14 August 2006) CEDAW/C/36/D/4/2004

CEDAW, *J. I. v. Finland* (5 May 2018) CEDAW/C/69/D/103/2016

CEDAW, *J.D. et al. V. Czech Republic* (16 July 2019) CEDAW/C/73/D/102/2016

CEDAW, *L.C. v. Peru* (17 October 2011) CEDAW/C/50/D/22/2009

Court of Justice of the European Union, *Judgment in Joined Cases C-804/18 and C-341/19 Wabe and MH Müller Handel* (15 July 2021).

ECtHR, *A, B, C v. Ireland* (Grand Chamber), 16 December 2010

ECtHR, *Austin and others v. UK* (Application nos. 39692/09, 40713/09 and 41008/09) 15 March 2012

ECtHR, *Belilos v. Switzerland* (Application no. 10328/83) 29 April 1988
ECtHR, *Bruno Pichon and Marie-Line Sajous v. France*, (Application n° 49853/99) 2 October 2001
ECtHR, *Dudgeon v. UK* (Application no. 7525/76) 22 October 1981
ECtHR, *Lautsi v. Italy* (Application no. 30814/06), Grand Chamber Judgement 18 March 2011
ECtHR, *Leyla Sahin v. Turkey* (Application no. 44774/98) 10 November 2005
ECtHR, *P. and S. v Poland* (Application no. 57375/08) 30 January 2013
ECtHR, *R.R. v. Poland*, (Application no. 27617/04) 28 November 2011
ECtHR, *Tysiąc v. Poland* (Application no. 5410/03) 24 September 2007
EuCSR, *International Planned Parenthood Federation—European Network (IPPF EN) v. Italy (merits)*, 10 September 2013
HRC, *Apirana Mahuika et al. v. New Zealand*, Communication No. 547/1993, U.N. Doc. CCPR/C/70/D/547/1993 (2000)
HRC, *Khairullo Saidov v. Tajikistan* (4 April 2018) CCPR/C/122/D/2680/2015
HRC, *L. M. R. v. Argentina* (29 March 2011) CCPR/C/101/D/1608/2007.
HRC, *Länsman et al. v. Finland*, Communication No. 511/1992, U.N. Doc. CCPR/C/52/D/511/1992 (1994)
HRC, *Mellet v. Ireland* (17 November 2016) CCPR/C/116/D/2324/2013
HRC, *Sandra Lovelace v. Canada*, Communication No. R.6/24, U.N. Doc. Supp. No. 40 (A/36/40) at 166 (1981).
HRC, *Whelan v. Ireland* (17 March 2017) CCPR/C/119/D/2425/2014
IACoHR, *Beatriz v. El Salvador, Informe* 9/20, Caso 13.378 (3 March 2020)
IACoHR, *Informe N° 71/03 María Mamérita Mestaza Chávez* (10 October 2003)
IACoHR, *Yanomami vs Brasil*, resolution N° 12/85, Case N° 7615 (5 March 1985)
IACtHR, *Advisory Opinion OC-24/17 on gender identity, and equality, and non-discrimination of same-sex couples* (24 November 2017).
IACtHR, *Advisory Opinion OC-3/83 Restrictions to the death penalty* (8 September 1993)
IACtHR, *Case of the Mayagna (Sumo) Awas Tingni Community vs. Nicaragua* (31 August 2001)
IACtHR, *Caso Comunidad indígena Sawhoyamaxa vs. Paraguay* (29 March 2006)
IACtHR, *Caso Comunidad indígena Yakye Axa vs. Paraguay* (17 June 2005)
IACtHR, *Manuela v. El Salvador* (Judgment of 2 November 2021)
ICJ, *Ahmadou Sadio Diallo (Republic of Guinea v. Democratic Republic of the Congo)*, Merits, Judgment, I.C.J. Reports 2010
ICJ, *Application of the International Convention on the Elimination of All Forms of Racial Discrimination (Qatar v. United Arab Emirates)*, Judgment preliminary objections of 4 February 2021
ICJ, *East Timor (Portugal v. Australia)*, Judgment, I. C.J. Reports 1995
ICJ, *Legal Consequences for States of the Continued Presence of South Africa in Namibia (South West Africa) notwithstanding Security Council Resolution 276 (1970)*, Advisory Opinion, I.C.J. Reports 1971
ICJ, *Legal Consequences of the Construction of a Wall in the Occupied Palestinian Territory*, Advisory Opinion, I. C. J. Reports 2004.
ICJ, *Legality of the Threat or Use of Nuclear Weapons Advisory Opinion*, Reports 1996

ICJ, *Territorial Dispute (Libyan Arab Jamahiriya/Chad)*, Judgment, ICJ Reports 1994

ICJ, *Western Sahara, Advisory Opinion*, I.C.J. Reports 1975

ICJ, *Whaling in the Antarctic (Australia v. Japan: New Zealand intervening)*, Judgment, Reports 2014

PCIJ, *Question of Jaworzina*, Advisory Opinion of 6 December 1923, PCIJ Series B, No. 8

Supreme Court of Canada, *Reference re Secession of Quebec*, 1998 CanLII 793 (SCC), [1998] 2 SCR 217

Supreme Court of Justice of Mexico, *Acción de Inconstitucionalidad 148/2017*, *Pleno de la Suprema Corte de Justicia de la Nación* (7 September 2021)

U.S. Supreme Court of Justice, *Buck v. Bell* 274 U.S. 200 (1927)

U.S. Supreme Court of Justice, *Roe v. Wade* 410 U.S. 113 (1973)

Archives of the UDHR:

A/C.3/SR.153, 23 November 1948, summary hundred and fifty-third meeting third committee.

A/C.3/SR.153, 23 November 1948, summary hundred and fifty-third meeting third committee

A/C.3/SR.164, 29 November 1948, summary hundred and sixty-fourth third committee.

A/C.3/SR.96, 7 October 1948, Summary record ninety-sixth meeting third committee.

Comments from Governments on the Draft International Declaration of Human Rights, Draft International Covenant on Human Rights and the Question of Implementation, E/CN.4/82/Add.1, (16 April 1948).

E/CN.4/AC.1/SR.33, 14 May 1948, summary record thirty-third meeting drafting committee.

E/CN.4/AC.2/SR.8, 10 December 1947, summary record of the eight meeting Working group declaration (Geneva).

E/CN.4/SR.14, 4 February 1947, Summary record of the fourteenth meeting (New York).

E/CN.4/SR.9, 1 February 1947, Summary record of the ninth meeting of the Commission on Human Rights (New York).

E/CN.4/SR.9, 1 February 1947, Summary record of the ninth meeting of the Commission on Human Rights (New York).

Summary Record of Eleventh Meeting of the First Session of the Sub-Commission on Prevention of Discrimination and Protection of Minorities. Held at the Palais des Nations, Geneva, on Monday 1 December 1947, E/CN.4/Sub.2/SR.11.

Summary Record of the Eighth Meeting of the Drafting Committee of the Commission on Human Rights, Held at Lake Success, New York, 17 June 1947, E/CN.4/AC.1/SR.8.

Summary Record of the Fourteenth Meeting of the Commission on Human Rights, Lake Success, New York, 4 February 1947, E/CN.4/SR.14.

Summary Record of the Hundred and Sixty-First Meeting of the Third Committee, Held at the Palais de Chaillot, Paris, 27 November 1948, A/C.3/SR.161.

Summary Record of the Ninetieth Meeting of the Third Committee, Held at the Palais de Chaillot, Paris, 1 October 1948, A/C.3/SR.90.

Summary Record of the Ninety-Eighth Meeting of the Third Committee, Held at the Palais de Chaillot, Paris, 9 October 1948, A/C.3/SR.98.

Summary Record of the Ninety-First Meeting of the Third Committee, Held at the Palais de Chaillot, Paris, 2 October 1948, A/C.3/SR.91.

Summary Record of the Ninety-Ninth Meeting [of the Third Committee] Held at the Palais de Chaillot, Paris, 11 October 1948, A/C.3/SR.99.

Summary Record of the Ninth Meeting of the Commission on Human Rights, Held at Lake Success, New York, 1 February 1947, E/CN.4/SR.9.

Summary Record of the Seventy-Third Meeting [of the Commission on Human Rights] Held at Lake Success, New York, on Tuesday, 15 June 1948, E/CN.4/SR.73.

Summary Record of the Sixty-Fourth Meeting of the Commission on Human Rights, Held at Lake Success, New York, 8 June 1948, E/CN.4/SR.64.

Summary Record of the Thirteenth Meeting of the Drafting Committee of the Commission on Human Rights, Held at Lake Success, New York, 20 June 1947, E/CN.4/AC.1/SR.13.

Verbatim Record of the Hundred and Eighty-First Plenary Meeting of the General Assembly, Held at the Palais de Chaillot, Paris, on Friday, 10 December 1948, A/PV.181.

Verbatim Record of the Hundred and Eighty-Second Plenary Meeting of the General Assembly, Held at the Palais de Chaillot, Paris, on Friday, 10 December 1948, A/PV.182.

Other Documents

"Accelerating the Promise: The Report of the Nirobi Summit on ICPD25," 2019. https://www.unfpa.org/sites/default/files/pub-pdf/Nairobi_Summit_Report_on_ICPD25.pdf.

Adams, Edith G. "World Population Conference, Belgrade August 30-September 10." *Population Index* 31, no. 4 (1965).

Agustín Esteban, Rogelio. "Morena Propone Legalizar Aborto En Casos de Violación En Guerrero." *Milenio*, 2020. https://www.milenio.com/estados/morena-propone-legalizar-aborto-casos-violacion-guerrero.

Al-Gharbi, Musa. "Data on How Ideological (under)Representation Compares to (under) Representation along the Lines of Race, Gender or Sexuality." Heterodox Academy, 2018. https://heterodoxacademy.org/ideological-underrepresentation-compared-to-race-gender-sexuality/.

"Arquidiócesis Mexicana Alerta Sobre Falso Sacerdote a Favor Del Aborto." *Aciprensa*, 2014. https://www.aciprensa.com/noticias/arquidiocesis-mexicana-alerta-sobre-falso-sacerdote-a-favor-del-aborto-45121.

Barragán, Almudena. "El Estado de Veracruz Despenaliza El Aborto." *El País*, 2021. https://elpais.com/mexico/2021-07-20/el-estado-de-veracruz-despenaliza-el-aborto.html.

Beltrán López, Luis Gerardo. "Presentan Iniciativa Para Despenalizar El Aborto En Sinaloa." *Debate*, 2020. https://www.debate.com.mx/culiacan/Presentan-iniciativa-para-despenalizar-el-aborto-en-Sinaloa-20200928-0181.html.

Bennett, Rosemary. "Trans Rights Activists Halt Gender Debate at Essex University." *The Times*, 2019. https://www.thetimes.co.uk/article/trans-rights-activists-halt-gender-debate-at-essex-university-qf9sh5r3q.

Borrego Borrego, Javier. "Estrasburgo y El Crucifijo En Las Escuelas." *El Mundo*, 2009. https://www.elmundo.es/opinion/tribuna-libre/2009/12/21559042.html.

Bot, Olivier. "Polémique Sur La Venue d'un Populiste à Genève." *Tribune de Genève*, 2016. https://www.tdg.ch/monde/polemique-venue-populiste-geneve/story/13374260.

Bragon, Ranier. "Bolsonaro Defendeu Esterilização de Pobres Para Combater Miséria e Crime." *Folha de S.Paulo*, 2018. https://www1.folha.uol.com.br/poder/2018/06/bolsonaro-defendeu-esterilizacao-de-pobres-para-combater-miseria-e-crime.shtml.

Carvalho Morris, Jessica. "Who Decides over Janaina's Body? A Case of Forced Sterilization in Brazil." Open Democracy, 2018. https://www.opendemocracy.net/en/democraciaabierta/who-decides-over-janaina-s-body-case-of-forced-sterilizati/.

Chio, Yolanda, and Vicente Juárez. "Avalan En SLP y Nuevo León Leyes Contra El Aborto." *La Jornada*, 2020. https://www.jornada.com.mx/ultimas/estados/2020/05/23/avalan-en-slp-y-nuevo-leon-leyes-contra-el-aborto-750.html.

"Commission on Unalienable Rights." U.S. Department of State, 2019. https://www.state.gov/commission-on-unalienable-rights-member-bio.

CONAPO. "Hacia Una Acción Internacional Para Frenar El Incremento de La Población," 1999. https://www.gob.mx/cms/uploads/attachment/file/187565/Parte_III_-_Parte_VII.pdf.

Davidson, Helen. "Twitter Removes China US Embassy Post Saying Uighur Women No Longer 'Baby-Making Machines.'" *The Guardian*, 2021. https://www.theguardian.com/world/2021/jan/10/twitter-removes-china-us-embassy-post-saying-uighur-women-no-longer-baby-making-machines.

"Desata Debate En Sonora Iniciativa Para Aborto Legal." *Milenio*, 2018. https://www.elimparcial.com/sonora/sonora/Desata-debate-en-Sonora-iniciativa-para-aborto-legal-20181004-0088.html.

"Despenalización Del Aborto En Coahuila: Esto Es Lo Que Debes Saber Sobre La Resolución de La Corte." *El Financiero*, 2021. https://www.elfinanciero.com.mx/nacional/2021/09/08/despenalizacion-del-aborto-en-coahuila-esto-es-lo-que-debes-saber-sobre-la-resolucion-de-la-corte/.

"Eastern and Western Europeans Differ on Importance of Religion, Views of Minorities, and Key Social Issues." Pew Research Center, 2018. https://www.pewforum.org/2018/10/29/eastern-and-western-europeans-differ-on-importance-of-religion-views-of-minorities-and-key-social-issues/.

"El Congreso de Guanajuato Cierra Las Puertas Al Aborto Legal." *Expansión*. 2020. https://politica.expansion.mx/estados/2020/05/26/diputados-guanajuato-desechan-despenalizar-aborto.

"El Congreso de Oaxaca Aprueba La Despenalización Del Aborto." *Expansión*, 2019. https://politica.expansion.mx/estados/2019/09/25/la-ley-en-favor-del-aborto-en-oaxaca-avanza-es-aprobada-en-lo-general.

"El Congreso de San Luis Potosí Rechaza La Legalización Del Aborto." *Expansión*, 2020. https://politica.expansion.mx/estados/2020/05/21/el-congreso-de-san-luis-potosi-rechaza-la-legalizacion-del-aborto.

"El PSOE Propone Penas de Cárcel Para Los Grupos Provida Que «obstaculicen El Derecho Al Aborto»." *ABC*, 2021. https://www.abc.es/sociedad/abci-psoe-propone-penas-carcel-para-grupos-provida-obstaculicen-derecho-aborto-202105301905_noticia.html.

Ernst, Douglas. "Pinterest Blocks Pro-Life Group Live Action from Platform over 'public Safety' Guidelines." *The Washington Times*, 2019. https://www.washingtontimes.com/news/2019/jun/11/lila-roses-pro-life-live-action-content-banned-fro/.

Eunjung, Ariana. "U.S. Joins 19 Nations, Including Saudi Arabia and Russia: 'There Is No International Right to an Abortion.'" *The Washington Post*, 2019. https://www.washingtonpost.com/health/2019/09/24/us-joins-nations-including-saudi-arabia-russia-there-is-no-international-right-an-abortion/.

European Parliament, Fact Sheets on the European Union: The principle of subsidiarity (2020), 2 <https://www.europarl.europa.eu/factsheets/en/sheet/7/the-principle-of-subsidiarity>. Consulted on February 10, 2021

"Family Planning." Johns Hopkins Center for Communication Programs, n.d. http://ccp.jhu.edu/health-areas/family-planning/.

Ferguson, Donna. "'We Can't Give in': The Birmingham School on the Frontline of Anti-LGBT Protests." *The Guardian*, 2019. https://www.theguardian.com/uk-news/2019/may/26/birmingham-anderton-park-primary-muslim-protests-lgbt-teaching-rights.

Fisher, Max. "Why China's One-Child Policy Still Leads to Forced Abortions, and Always Will,." *Washington Post*, 2013.

Flores, Selene. "Legisladores Piden a Corte 'Honrar División de Poderes' Por Despenalización de Aborto." *Milenio*. 2020. https://www.milenio.com/estados/veracruz-legisladores-scjn-honrar-division-poderes-aborto.

Ford, Liz. "US Abortion Policy Is 'extremist Hate' and 'Torture', Says UN Commissioner." *The Guardian*, 2019. https://www.theguardian.com/global-development/2019/jun/04/us-abortion-policy-extremist-hate-torture-un-commissioner-kate-gilmore.

García Escobar, Gabriela. "How (Not) to Promote Human Dignity through Higher Education." *The Public Discourse*, 2021. https://www.thepublicdiscourse.com/2021/06/76365/.

García, Jacobo. "Derrotada La Iniciativa Encabezada Por Colombia Para Reformar La Defensa de Derechos Humanos En La OEA." *El País*, 2019. https://elpais.com/internacional/2019/06/27/america/1561672485_548623.html.

"Germany: Headscarf Bans Violate Rights." *Human Rights Watch*, 2009. https://www.hrw.org/news/2009/02/26/germany-headscarf-bans-violate-rights.

"Global Morality." Pew Research Center, 2014. https://www.pewresearch.org/global/interactives/global-morality/.

"Global Views on Premarital Sex 2013." Statista, 2013. https://www.statista.com/statistics/297288/global-views-on-premarital-sex/.

Goodenough, Patrick. "'One-Child' Expert Urges Investigation Before UNFPA Funding Resumes." *CBS News*, 2009. https://www.cnsnews.com/news/article/one-child-expert-urges-investigation-unfpa-funding-resumes.

Hammer, Joshua. "Anti-Semitism and Germany's Movement Against Circumcision." *The Atlantic*, 2013. https://www.theatlantic.com/health/archive/2013/01/anti-semitism-and-germanys-movement-against-circumcision/266794/.

Harding, Roger. "British Social Attitudes No. 34," 2017. https://www.bsa.natcen.ac.uk/latest-report/british-social-attitudes-34/key-findings/context.aspx.

Harris, Paul. "They're Called the Good Club—and They Want to Save the World." *The Guardian*, 2009. https://www.theguardian.com/world/2009/may/31/new-york-billionaire-philanthropists.

Harrison, Emma, and Lily Kuo. "Uighur Muslim Teacher Tells of Forced Sterilisation in Xinjiang." *The Guardian*, 2020. https://www.theguardian.com/world/2020/sep/04/muslim-minority-teacher-50-tells-of-forced-sterilisation-in-xinjiang-china.

Havel, Václav. "The Power of the Powerless." In *The Power of the Powerless*, edited by Jhon Keane. New York: Routledge, 1985. http://www.vaclavhavel.cz/showtrans.php?cat=eseje&val=2_aj_eseje.html&typ=HTML.

"High Level Consultation on the Ratification of the Maputo Protocol." African Union, 2020. https://au.int/en/newsevents/20180129/high-level-consultation-ratification-maputo-protocol#:~:text=To date%2C out of 55,have not ratified the Protocol.

Hoffmann, Lord. "The Universality of Human Rights." Judicial Studies Board Annual Lecture, 2009. https://www.judiciary.uk/wp-content/uploads/2014/12/Hoffmann_2009_JSB_Annual_Lecture_Universality_of_Human_Rights.pdf.

Hopgood, Stephen. "Human Rights: Past Their Sell-by Date." Open Democracy, 2013. https://www.opendemocracy.net/en/openglobalrights-openpage/human-rights-past-their-sell-by-date/.

———. "It Begins and Ends with Power." *Open Democracy*, 2013. https://www.opendemocracy.net/en/openglobalrights-openpage/it-begins-and-ends-with-power/.

Inglehart, R., C. Haerpfer, A. Moreno, C. Welzel, K. Kizilova, J. Diez-Medrano, M. Lagos, P. Norris, E. Ponarin, and B. Puranen. "World Values Survey: Round Six—Country-Pooled Datafile Version." World Values Survey, 2014. http://www.worldvaluessurvey.org/WVSDocumentationWV6.jsp.

Inglehart, Ronald, C. Haerpfer, and Alejandro Moreno. "World Values Survey: Round Seven—Country-Pooled Datafile Version." World Values Survey, 2020. http://www.worldvaluessurvey.org/WVSOnline.jsp.

Kaplan, Seth. "Religion: A Viewpoint Diversity Blind Spot?" *Heterodox Academy*, 2018. https://heterodoxacademy.org/blog/religion-a-viewpoint-diversity-blind-spot/.

Kelly, Caroline. "More States Are Expected to Pass Anti-Abortion Bills Challenging Roe v. Wade Ahead of Monumental Supreme Court Case." *CNN*, 2021. https://edition.cnn.com/2021/05/18/politics/mississippi-abortion-case-impact-supreme-court-abortion-bans-activists/index.html.

"Kenya: Activists to Stage Protests in Nairobi Monday Against ICPD25+." *All Africa*, 2019. https://allafrica.com/stories/201911110079.html.

"Kenya Hosts Top Reproductive Health Summit amid Storm over Abortion." *The Nation*, 2019. https://nation.africa/kenya/news/kenya-hosts-top-reproductive-health-summit-amid-storm-over-abortion-222542.

Kollontai, Alexandra. "The Labour of Women in the Evolution of the Economy," 1921. https://www.marxists.org/archive/kollonta/1921/evolution.htm.

Kristof, Nicholas. "A Confession of Liberal Intolerance." *The New York Times*. 2016. https://www.nytimes.com/2016/05/08/opinion/sunday/a-confession-of-liberal-intolerance.html.

———. "The Children of Pornhub." *The New York Times*, 2020. https://www.nytimes.com/2020/12/04/opinion/sunday/pornhub-rape-trafficking.html?action=click&module=Opinion&pgtype=Homepage.

———. "The Dangers of Echo Chambers on Campus." *The New York Times*, 2016. https://www.nytimes.com/2016/12/10/opinion/sunday/the-dangers-of-echo-chambers-on-campus.html.

Lipka, Michael. "Africans among the Most Morally Opposed to Contraception." Pew Research Center, 2014. https://www.pewresearch.org/fact-tank/2014/04/16/africans-among-the-most-morally-opposed-to-contraception/.

Magallanes, Adriana. "Durango Se Resiste a Garantizar Acceso Al Aborto Por Violación." *Milenio*, October 24, 2019. https://www.milenio.com/estados/durango-resiste-garantizar-acceso-aborto-violacion.

Magally, Silvia. "Esterilización Forzada: El Gobierno Admite El Exterminio." *Cimac Noticias*, 2002. https://cimacnoticias.com.mx/noticia/esterilizacion-forzada-el-gobierno-admite-el-exterminio/.

Makatia, Larissa. "Despenalización Del Aborto En Q Roo, Congelada." *La Izquierda Diario*, 2020. http://www.laizquierdadiario.mx/Despenalizacion-del-aborto-en-Q-Roo-congelada.

Mancera Espinosa, Miguel Ángel, Patricia Mercado Castro, José Ramón Amieva Gálvez, and Jacqueline L'Hoist Tapia. "Discriminación Laboral Hacia La Mujer En La Ciudad de México: Despido Por Embarazo," 2015. http://data.copred.cdmx.gob.mx/wp-content/uploads/2015/08/Informe-Discriminación-Laboral-hacia-la-Mujer-Despido-por-Embarazo.pdf.

Matias, Pedro. "El Aborto Es Ley En Oaxaca: 'la Maternidad Será Elegida o No Será'." *Proceso*, 2019. https://www.proceso.com.mx/nacional/estados/2019/9/25/el-aborto-es-ley-en-oaxaca-la-maternidad-sera-elegida-no-sera-231728.html.

Melton, Grace. "UN Nairobi Summit on Population and Development Shuts Out the Pro-Life Message." *The Heritage Foundation*, 2019. https://www.heritage.org/life/commentary/un-nairobi-summit-population-and-development-shuts-out-the-pro-life-message.

Méndez, Enrique, and Roberto Garduño. "Proyecto a Favor Del Aborto, Avanza En Comisiones." *La Jornada*. 2020. https://www.jornada.com.mx/2020/02/07/politica/008n1pol.

"Mexican Women Demanding Legalization of Abortion Clash with Police." *Reuters*, 2020. https://www.reuters.com/article/us-mexico-abortion-protest-idUSKBN26J35Q.

Montoya, Juan Ricardo. "Aprueba Hidalgo Aborto Legal Hasta Las 12 Semanas de Gestación." *La Jornada*, 2021. https://www.jornada.com.mx/notas/2021/06/30/estados/congreso-de-hidalgo-aprueba-la-interrupcion-legal-del-embarazo/.

"Morality of Abortion, 2018–2020 Demographic Tables." Gallup, 2020. https://news.gallup.com/poll/244625/morality-abortion-2018-demographic-tables.aspx.

Moreno, Alejandro. "Apoyo Mayoritario Al Aborto En CDMX y Baja California." *El Financiero*, 2019. https://www.elfinanciero.com.mx/nacional/apoyo-mayoritario-al-aborto-en-cdmx-y-bc.

———. "OMG! La Mayoría de Las Mujeres En México Están En Contra Del Aborto." *Nación 321*, 2019. https://www.nacion321.com/encuestas/omg-la-mayoria-de-las-mujeres-en-mexico-estan-en-contra-del-aborto.

Morrison, Sean. "Students at Boris Johnson's Former Oxford College Launch Petition to Have Him Banned from Campus." *Evening Standard*, 2019. https://www.standard.co.uk/news/politics/students-at-boris-johnsons-former-oxford-college-launch-petition-to-have-him-banned-from-campus-a4235566.html?utm_medium=Social&utm_source=Facebook&fbclid=IwAR05V9lEvAUlc2Chisg0LzH_ckMkGRGSO-RS8T5ATmRuuBQywhbnCNMQx.

"MP Seeks to Ban Demonstrations Outside Abortion Clinics." *BBC*, 2020. https://www.bbc.com/news/uk-politics-53150759.

Nares Feria, Yamil. "¿Qué Pensamos Los Mexicanos Sobre El Aborto?" *Animal Político*, 2013. https://www.animalpolitico.com/la-ventana-indiscreta/que-pensamos-los-mexicanos-sobre-el-aborto/.

"National Family Health Survey 1992–93," 1995. https://dhsprogram.com/publications/publication-FRIND1-DHS-Final-Reports.cfm.

Nzwili, Fredrick, and Elaine Ruth Fletcher. "US Rep At Nairobi Summit: No Support For Abortion In Family Planning." *Health Policy Watch*, 2019. https://healthpolicy-watch.news/us-rep-at-nairobi-summit-will-not-support-abortion-in-family-planning/.

"Oxford Professor given Protection Following Threats from Trans Activists." *BBC*, 2020. https://www.bbc.com/news/education-51248684.

Pontifical Council for Justice and Peace, Compendium of the Social Doctrine of the Church (2005)

"Presenta PRD Iniciativa Para Legalizar Aborto En Jalisco." *Proceso*, 2011. https://www.proceso.com.mx/265240/presenta-prd-iniciativa-para-legalizar-aborto-en-jalisco.

Pushter, Jacob, and Janell Fetterolf. "A Changing World: Global Views on Diversity, Gender Equality, Family Life and the Importance of Religion." Pew Research Center, 2019. https://www.pewresearch.org/global/2019/04/22/a-changing-world-global-views-on-diversity-gender-equality-family-life-and-the-importance-of-religion/.

"Q&A: Policy to Protect the Human Rights of Sex Workers." Amnesty International, n.d. https://www.amnesty.org/en/qa-policy-to-protect-the-human-rights-of-sex-workers/.

"Question Écrite N°40907 de Mme Bérengère Poletti." Assamblée Nationale, 2021. https://questions.assemblee-nationale.fr/q15/15-40907QE.htm.

Quinn, Ben. "Cambridge University Urged to Re-Invite Rightwing Academic Jordan Peterson." *The Guardian*, 2020. https://www.theguardian.com/education/2020/dec/10/cambridge-university-urged-to-re-invite-rightwing-academic-jordan-peterson.

"Religion." Atlas of European Values, 2008. http://www.atlasofeuropeanvalues.eu/new/ziewereld.php?year=2008.

"Report of the Commission on Unalienable Rights," 2020. https://www.state.gov/wp-content/uploads/2020/08/Report-of-the-Commission-on-Unalienable-Rights.pdf.

Roa, Wendy. "SCJN Discutirá Validez de Leyes Sobre Aborto Aprobadas Por Varios Estados." *Excelsior*, 2021. https://www.excelsior.com.mx/nacional/scjn-discutira-validez-de-leyes-sobre-aborto-aprobadas-por-varios-estados/1469928.

Rodríguez, Karla. "Morena Abre Proceso a Diputados Que Votaron Contra Despenalización Del Aborto En Hidalgo." *El Universal*, 2019. https://www.eluniversal.com.mx/nacion/politica/morena-abre-proceso-diputados-que-votaron-contra-despenalizacion-del-aborto-en.

Rose, David. "'I Was Tossed out of the Tribe': Climate Scientist Judith Curry Interviewed." *The Spectator*, 2015. https://www.spectator.co.uk/article/-i-was-tossed-out-of-the-tribe-climate-scientist-judith-curry-interviewed.

Roth, Kenneth. "Prepared Testimony to Commission on 'Unalienable' Rights." Human Rights Watch, 2020. https://www.hrw.org/news/2020/01/10/prepared-testimony-commission-unalienable-rights.

Salazar, Ariana, and Kelsey Jo Starr. "In the U.S. and Europe, Women Are about as Likely as Men to Favor Legal Abortion." Pew Research Center, 2018. https://www.pewresearch.org/fact-tank/2018/12/14/in-the-u-s-and-europe-women-are-about-as-likely-as-men-to-favor-legal-abortion/.

"Se Complica Reelección de Esmeralda Arosemena de Troitiño En La CIDH." *Press Reader*, 2019. https://www.pressreader.com/panama/critica/20190628/281560882336020.

Sen, Amartya. "Population: Delusion and Reality." *New York Review of Books* 41, no. 15 (1994). https://pdfs.semanticscholar.org/fa9e/62f54ea3b08e5aeeb6401598f7008a209f46.pdf.

Slack, James, and James Chapman. "I Will Defy Europe on Jail Votes, Says Cameron as He Sets on Collision Course with Judges in Strasbourg." *Daily Mail*, 2012. https://www.dailymail.co.uk/news/article-2149005/I-defy-Europe-jail-votes-says-Cameron-sets-collision-course-judges-Strasbourg.html.

"Society." Atlas of European Values, 2008. http://www.atlasofeuropeanvalues.eu/new/ziewereld.php?year=2008.

Tamir, Christine, Aidan Connaughton, and Ariana Slazar. "The Global God Divide." Pew Research Center, 2020. https://www.pewresearch.org/global/2020/07/20/the-global-god-divide/.

"The Age Gap in Religion Around the World." Pew Research Center, 2018. https://www.pewforum.org/2018/06/13/how-religious-commitment-varies-by-country-among-people-of-all-ages/.

"The Changing Global Religious Landscape." Pew Research Center, 2017. http://assets.pewresearch.org/wp-content/uploads/sites/11/2017/04/07092755/FULL-REPORT-WITH-APPENDIXES-A-AND-B-APRIL-3.pdf.

Theodorou, Angelina, and Aleksandra Sandstrom. "How Abortion Is Regulated around the World," 2015. https://www.pewresearch.org/fact-tank/2015/10/06/how-abortion-is-regulated-around-the-world/.

Topping, Alexandra. "Woman with Down's Syndrome Loses UK Abortion Law Case." *The Guardian*, 2021. https://www.theguardian.com/world/2021/sep/23/woman-with-downs-syndrome-loses-uk-abortion-law-case.

Westoff, Charles. "Desired Number of Children: 2000–2008," Demographic and Health Surveys 2010. https://www.dhsprogram.com/pubs/pdf/CR25/CR25.pdf.

Wike, Richard. "Europeans Hold More Liberal Views on Moral Issues." Pew Research Center, 2014. https://www.pewresearch.org/fact-tank/2014/04/16/europeans-hold-more-liberal-views-on-moral-issues/.

Zambrano, Pilar, and William Saunders, eds. *Unborn Human Life and Fundamental Rights: Leading Constitutional Cases under Scrutiny*. Peter Lang, 2020.

INDEX OF AUTHORITIES

www.ingramcontent.com/pod-product-compliance
Ingram Content Group UK Ltd.
Pitfield, Milton Keynes, MK11 3LW, UK
UKHW021852100926
8556IPUK00020B/1188

9 781636 673561